THE FAITHS OF OTHERS

THE FAITHS OF OTHERS

A History of Interreligious Dialogue

THOMAS ALBERT HOWARD

Yale
UNIVERSITY PRESS
New Haven and London

Published with assistance from the Mary Cady Tew Memorial Fund.

Yale University Press books may be purchased in quantity for educational, business, or promotional use. For information, please e-mail sales.press@yale.edu (U.S. office) or sales@yaleup.co.uk (U.K. office).

Set in Janson type by Integrated Publishing Solutions,
Grand Rapids, Michigan.
Printed in the United States of America.

Library of Congress Control Number: 2020951711
ISBN 978-0-300-24989-7 (hardcover : alk. paper)

A catalogue record for this book is available from the British Library.

This paper meets the requirements of ANSI/NISO Z39.48-1992 (Permanence of Paper).

10 9 8 7 6 5 4 3 2 1

To students of the Jerusalem and Athens Forum

But the question of the nature of the gods is the darkest and most difficult of all.

—CICERO

Is the desire for Others appetite or generosity?

—EMMANUEL LEVINAS

Contents

Acknowledgments

THIS PROJECT HAS TAKEN ME to Sufi shrines in New Delhi, to the killing fields of Bosnia and Herzegovina, to "scriptural reasoning" groups in Cairo, to the Parliament of the World's Religions in Toronto (2018), and to archives and libraries in London, Rome, Chicago, and elsewhere. All of it has been a labor of love. Unfortunately, my memory cannot do justice to the many individuals who have provided me with assistance and encouragement along the way.

But permit an effort. I am especially grateful to Marcus Braybrooke, a veteran of interreligious dialogue, who kindly invited me to his home in Oxford for a conversation when this project was in its early phases. I am also deeply thankful to Valparaiso University's library and interlibrary loan staff, especially Sara Shoppa, who has helped me procure countless books and articles, and who repeatedly showed grace and patience to an absentminded patron. Mark Biermann, Peter Kanelos, Susan Van Zanten, Mark Schwehn, Joseph Creech, and Joseph Goss have provided me with wonderful working conditions for the vocation of a scholar/teacher. My deep regards, too, to Richard and (the late) Phyllis Duesenberg for their support of education, scholarship, and Christian intellectual and moral traditions.

In addition, the following individuals deserve a special "shoutout" of my gratitude: Ossama Abdelgawwad, Mohammad Ali, Ahmet Alibasic, (Anglican) Bishop Mouneer Anis, Mark Bartusch, Amanda Bropst-Renaud, Gretchen Buggeln, Jonathan Bull, Father David Burrell (CSC), Kerry Buttram, Kevin Cawley, Ruth Connell, Catherine Cornille, John Dayal, Ghulam Rasoul Delvi, Nicholas Denysenko, Lisa Driver, Sharon Dybel, Ashleigh Elser, Victor Erwin (SJ), Alison Foley, Jason Gerhke, Ryan Groff, Hans Gustafson, Hany el Halawany, Father James L. Heft (SM), George Heider, Nathaniel Hermann, Susannah Heschel, Alison Hinderliter, Tommy Howard, Slavica Jakelic, Jeanie Johnson, Bozana Katava, Heather Keaney, Allison Kroft, Shane T. MacDonald, Ebrahim Moosa, Eboo Patel, Mel Piehl, Matthew Puffer, Matthew Reese, Ronald Rittgers, Linda Schmidt, Naji Umran, Tharwat Wahba, Patrice Weil, Stephanie Wong, and Mato Zovkic.

I thank my students in Christ College at Valparaiso University for their thoughtful classroom engagement with material in this book. Christ College's Katie Goldbranson, Claire Ehr, and Noelle Canty served as wonderfully helpful research and editorial assistants.

I am grateful to the *Journal of the American Academy of Religion* for allowing me to reprint here portions of my article "'A Remarkable Gathering': The Conference on Living Religions within the British Empire (1924) and Its Historical Significance," *Journal of the American Academy of Religion* 86 (March 2018): 126–57.

I recognize a debt to Chicago's Interfaith Youth Core for helping sustain this project by supporting my efforts to convert its contents (or portions thereof) into classroom use.

Jennifer Banks and her colleagues at Yale University Press—as well as outside readers procured by the press—guided this project into book form with delightful courtesy and professionalism.

And once again I would like to thank my cherished wife, Agnes R. Howard, and the rest of my family for sharing the joys, complexities, and burdens of life.

THE FAITHS OF OTHERS

Introduction

> Come now, let us reason together.
>
> —*Isaiah 1:18*

IN 1997 THE INTERFAITH CENTER of New York began operations for the purpose of "overcom[ing] prejudice, violence, and misunderstanding by activating the power of the city's grassroots religious and civic leaders and their communities." Since then, through a variety of programs and activities, the center has brought thousands of individuals and organizations together and aims to become "a nationally and internationally recognized model for mutual understanding and cooperation among faith traditions."[1]

In the same year, in the wake of the destructive wars following the collapse of Yugoslavia, the Interreligious Council of Bosnia and Herzegovina was launched to "raise awareness of the importance of inter-religious dialogue and cooperation through developing relationships between churches and religious communities throughout Bosnia and Herzegovina." Serbian Orthodox, Croatian Catholics, and Bosnian Muslims (and several Jews) have been involved in the work of the council, which is seated in the religiously mixed city of Sarajevo.[2]

In November 2012, the King Abdullah bin Abdulaziz International Centre for Interreligious and Intercultural Dialogue (KAICIID) opened its doors in Vienna. UN secretary-general Ban Ki-moon helped inaugurate it in the presence of dignitaries from across the globe. The center defines itself as an "intergovernmental organization whose mandate is to promote the use of dialogue globally, to prevent and resolve conflict, [and] to enhance understanding and cooperation. . . . Intercultural and interreligious dialogue helps build communities' resistance against prejudice, strengthens social cohesion, supports conflict prevention and transformation and can serve to preserve peace."[3]

These are but three organizations drawn from numerous comparable ones established in the late twentieth and early twenty-first centuries. Since 9/11 such entities have mushroomed: Israel's Interfaith Encounter Association (2001), the Interreligious Council of Uganda (2001), the Chicago-based Interfaith Youth Core (2002), the Jordanian Interfaith Coexistence Research Center (2003), New Delhi's Indialogue Foundation (2005), the Doha International Centre for Interfaith Dialogue (2007), and Rome's John Paul II Center for Interreligious Dialogue (2010), among many, many others.[4] In 2011 U.S. president Barack Obama established the Interfaith and Community Service Campus Challenge, inviting institutions of higher education to commit to interfaith programming and service. Numerous seminaries and universities offer instruction in interreligious dialogue and cooperation. Professorships in interreligious studies have sprung up. "Interfaith chapels" exist, and one can even train to become an "interfaith minister." The United Nations, the U.S. Institute of Peace, along with other governmental and nongovernmental agencies spanning the globe, have promoted interreligious dialogue in some form or fashion.[5] Countless books and articles have appeared on the subject.

In short, even as stories of ethnically and religiously motivated violence assail us from the daily news, we live in a booming heyday for interreligious dialogue. From a historical perspective, this phenomenon is truly remarkable, a noteworthy departure from the more isolationist and skeptical postures that faith traditions have generally exhibited toward one another in the past. Hardly a century ago, the words *interreligious* and *interfaith* would have been unintelligible to most people.[6] Today, the realities that they signify have gained "unprecedented prominence" and have been hailed as "a global interfaith movement."[7]

But from where did this phenomenon come? Where is it headed? And how does one evaluate its broader historical, social, and ethical significance? This book hazards answers to these questions. It does so through an inquiry into several major turning points in the history of interreligious dialogue, for even as many today extol, practice, theorize, and/or theologize about interreligious dialogue, few have attended carefully to its genesis and past. Bluntly put, the topic is heavily theologized but scantly historicized.

Our entry point is the premodern world, where we shall examine several harbingers of interreligious dialogue, albeit avant la lettre. Examples from the Mediterranean basin, the Islamic world, and the medieval West will be considered before profiling the captivating case of the sixteenth-century Islamic Mughal Empire in India, during which the emperor Akbar (1542–1605) organized and presided over conversations among representatives from the Indian subcontinent's vast patchwork of faith traditions. In his imperial city, Fatehpur Sikri, south of Delhi, Akbar built the Ibadat Khana (House of Worship). The evening before Friday prayers, he regularly gathered religious leaders there to discuss and compare views. Muslims of differing outlooks were his first interlocutors, but soon he included Hindus, Buddhists, Jains, Parsis, Jews, and Christians. The latter, Jesuit missionaries from their mission outpost in Goa, have left extensive records of their encounters at Akbar's court—and there are many other sources as well. Canvassing the premodern world for harbingers helps us to see that while contemporary interfaith dialogue is in some respects a novelty, it is nonetheless not altogether discontinuous with the past. Some knowledge of this past helps us better appraise its contemporary historical significance.

After Akbar's death, in both East and West, there is surprisingly scant evidence of other major, formal interreligious dialogues until the modern era, even if the Enlightenment—typified in G. E. Lessing's irenic *Nathan the Wise*—helped create intellectual conditions conducive for dialogue.[8] But the great Mughal's legacy quietly endured and received fresh attention in the nineteenth century during the ascendancy of political liberalism, European imperialism, and scholarly "Orientalism." Alfred Lord Tennyson immortalized Akbar in his poem "Akbar's Dream": "I cull from every faith . . . the best / and bravest soul for counselor and friend." The poem was published in 1892.[9]

The next year, coincidentally, witnessed Chicago's World's Parliament of Religions, which convened in the new American metropolis in conjunction with the Great Columbian Exposition of 1893.[10] This parliament, the next major turning point in this study, is widely considered as the launching point of the modern interfaith movement, even as it also encouraged the development of the new academic fields of "comparative religion" and "the history of religion."[11] Friedrich Max Müller, a founding father of these fields, sized up the significance of Chicago's 1893 parliament as follows: "Such a gathering of representatives of the principal religions of the world has never before taken place; it is unique, it is unprecedented; nay we may truly add, it could hardly have been conceived before our own time."[12] While Müller was aware of Akbar's earlier endeavor, he judged the Chicago affair different in aim and scope—a plausible contention that will be examined in this study. Praised by many, the parliament also met strong opposition and even condemnation from prominent evangelical leaders in America, the archbishop of Canterbury, and the Ottoman sultan—each worrying that such a mingling of faiths would result in a confused syncretism and/or relativism.

Inspired by Chicago's parliament, London's Conference on Some Living Religions within the Empire (1924) serves as the third turning point examined in this study. At once a spectacle of British imperial grandeur, an exhibition of Orientalist understanding, and a genuine effort to build cultural bridges, this little-remembered conference, which took place under the aegis of the British Imperial Exhibition of 1924, brought scholars, imams, pandits, priests, and other "holy men of the Empire" to London from 22 September to 3 October.[13] The keynote speaker was the larger-than-life explorer Sir Francis Younghusband (1863–1942), president of the Royal Geographical Society and an early, influential enthusiast for interfaith gatherings. Among the conference's goals, according to one of its chief architects, the Theosophist William Loftus Hare, were "to show men, in the most impressive way, what and how many important truths the various religions held and teach in common" and "to inquire what light each religion has afforded or may afford to the other religions of the world."[14] Through various twists and turns, this conference paved the way for the establishment in Britain of the World Congress of Faiths (1936), among the oldest continuously existing organizations in the world devoted to interreligious dialogue.[15]

As instances of interreligious dialogue multiplied in the twentieth century, the Catholic Church for the most part stood on the sidelines. Pope Leo XIII (r. 1878–1903), in fact, disparaged interreligious events as "promiscuous religious gatherings."[16] In the encyclical *Mortalium animos* (1928), Pope Pius XI (r. 1922–39) even warned against dialogue with other branches of Christianity.[17] But this stance changed abruptly and consequentially with the Second Vatican Council (1962–65). Accordingly, the fourth and final turning point concentrates on the council, and especially its groundbreaking document "Declaration on the Relation of the Church with Non-Christian Religions" (*Nostra aetate*) of 1965, which urged Catholics "to enter with prudence and charity into discussion with members of other religions."[18] Among other results, *Nostra aetate* helped make possible the historic interfaith-promoting papacy of Pope John Paul II and his convening of religious leaders from around the world for a day of solidarity and prayer in Assisi, Italy, in 1986—an unprecedented event for the Catholic Church and one that has received a diverse range of reactions from within and without the church.[19] In the wake of this event, Catholic interfaith projects and institutions have multiplied and stimulated others, including among non-Catholics.[20] Pope Francis has actively championed both *Nostra aetate* and what he has called the "spirit of Assisi."[21] (The pope's namesake, Francis of Assisi, will be considered in chapter 1 as a medieval precursor of interfaith engagement.)

These ventures into the past—Emperor Akbar's court, preceded by a glance at several premodern harbingers of dialogue; Chicago's parliament of 1893; London's Conference on Some Living Religions within the Empire in 1924; and Vatican II's *Nostra aetate* (1965), along with consideration of their legacies—will prepare the way to consider, in the conclusion, several contemporary instances of interreligious dialogue and to discuss some of the larger normative issues at stake in promoting dialogue as a force for peacemaking and intercultural understanding.

No attempt is made in what follows to catalogue the numerous examples of interreligious dialogue in the recent past. There are simply too many. However, the ones selected, not coincidentally, represent major "centers," not "peripheries," to borrow analytic terms from the great social theorist Edward Shils. Leaving the early modern Mughal capital Fatehpur Sikri aside, the modern centers treated include Chicago (symbol of the New World, and particularly of the United States, as a rising colossus), London (metropole of an empire "on which the sun never set"), and Rome (spiritual home to the world's largest Christian community). Historically viewed, as Shils argues, centers possess an outsized capacity to radiate authority in the "realm of values and beliefs" that "impinge[s] . . . in various ways on those who live within the ecological domain in which the society exists."[22] While centers do not inexorably dictate social trends for all others, what happens in their precincts rarely stays there but is influentially disseminated in the larger social field, modifying the possible and the plausible.[23]

Focus on turning-point moments in these locations, moreover, allows for narration and comparative analysis of key moments in the evolution of interreligious dialogue. By "turning point," borrowing language from the sociologist Andrew Abbot, I mean "a peculiarly essential juncture" in a social process that changes the dynamics of the possible and inaugurates or furthers "an extensive process of change."[24] Specifically, I am interested in how interreligious or interfaith dialogue goes from being virtually nonexistent, or rare and episodic at best, in the premodern and much of the modern era to gaining discursive status and becoming a widely embraced ideal and practice (or what some have even called a "civic virtue") in the twentieth century of how religious communities and individuals ought to comport themselves in relation to one another.

Permit me to recognize a distinction between interfaith dialogue and interfaith social action; my focus is primarily on the former, but the border between them is often porous, so the latter will sometimes make an appearance too. As shall become clear, *dialogue* has come to be recognized as an umbrella term for a wide range of peaceful exchanges, gatherings, interactions, and/or collaborations between two or more religious traditions.[25] More generally, it signifies an ethos, a *mentalité*, an attitude informing and encouraging irenic, purposeful engagement among religious others toward one another.[26] Throughout, I will use *interreligious* and *interfaith* more or less interchangeably, reserving *ecumenism* largely to refer to efforts of intra-Christian irenicism and action.

This work inevitably reflects my own training (and limitations) in modern European/Western intellectual and religious history; a scholar of the Indian subcontinent or the Middle East would likely give the topic a very different treatment. At the same time, it is widely recognized that interreligious dialogue, while far from being an exclusively Western phenomenon, has been theorized and advanced most extensively within the social and intellectual ambit of "Christendom" (very broadly understood), particularly within its modern-day, national successor polities. Precisely why this is the case would merit a separate inquiry; yet permit me to suggest that it owes much to the confluence of theological and political factors. Theologically, Christianity contains a powerful imperative to reach out to foreign cultures (the Great Commission, Paul's Areopagus speech) and an ethic—too often miserably realized—for peaceable engagement with others (the Sermon on the Mount, the Good Samaritan, and other parables). But theological reasons alone do not suffice, for other traditions have comparable imperatives and Christianity also possesses countervailing tendencies, such as, often, a trigger-happy employment of the categories of "idolatry" and "heresy." Turning to politics, therefore, Christian culture(s) became globally ascendant in an age of Western colonialism, when interfaith dialogue first fully came into its own. Power, wealth, status, and mobility created the conditions of possibility for a magnanimity toward (religious) others (even as, alas, they also allowed for colonial-era misdeeds and various forms of untoward paternalism), to which weaker and less wealthy members of the modern colonial system could not readily aspire, much less attain. In short, the historical arc of modern-day interfaith dialogue owes a debt both to the things that are not Caesar's and to the things that are.

Religio: Ruminations on a Fraught Term

Approaching the topic of interreligious dialogue historically presents several steep challenges. For starters, not only are the words *inter-*

religious and *interfaith* of modern provenance, so too is the word *religion*—or at least our contemporary understanding of the term.[27] What is more, the taxonomy presupposed behind the common phrases "world's great religions" or "major religions of the world" is also a fairly recent, largely Western construction. We do not need Ludwig Wittgenstein to remind us that terminology is important: the deployment of words and the (changing) meanings that we ascribe to them profoundly shape our perceptions of and responses to the social world around us.

Anyone intent on thinking well and wisely about "religion" owes an enduring debt to Wilfred Cantwell Smith's classic study, *The Meaning and End of Religion* (1962). Smith observes that from classical antiquity until the early modern era, *religio* did not define some general genus, of which there consisted various species ("isms"—Judaism, Hinduism, Buddhism, and so on). In earlier usage, the term was rather imprecise, although generally it referred to forms of worship, ritual observances, and piety.[28] There were *religiosae locae*, sacred places, and *viri religiosi*, reverent individuals, careful in fulfilling their duties to the gods and, later, to the Christian God. Most commonly in its Roman usage, *religio* denoted a series of standardized devotional practices or acts as well as the proper attitude one should have while performing them.[29] The Christian appropriation of the term added new dimensions to it, but it gained little in clarity. The notion of performing pious acts or duties continued, notably in the Vulgate, in which Jerome used *religio* to translate the Greek word *threskiea*, "pious observance."[30] And it also came to refer almost exclusively to the beliefs, worship, and organizational structure of the Christian Church. Augustine used it in this sense in his *De vera religione*, fittingly rendered in English as "On True Worship" or "On True Piety," suggesting what one properly owed to the God of Christianity, the Creator, and no longer to the Greco-Roman deities nor to mere things created by God.[31]

This usage persisted into the Middle Ages, even if the word was employed infrequently. The preferred term was *faith* (*fides*), the dynamic response through the sacraments, mediated by the church, whereby one entered into fellowship with the Triune God.[32] Those going above and beyond typical devotion, the monks, received the designation *religious*, while the parish priests, who mixed more in "the world," received that of *secular*—a distinction still maintained in Roman Catholicism. In his *Summa theologiae*, under the virtue of justice, Thomas Aquinas deploys *religio* in three different senses: the external expression of faith, the inner motivation to worship God correctly, and the worship itself. But again, the word was used uncommonly and mostly in reference to worship.[33] There was no sense of religion as genus; nor was it used to denote some transcultural, transhistorical human phenomenon, tucked away in the interior of each human being; nor was there a clear sense of a secular-religious divide in society at large. These are all modern and distinctly Western phenomena, transmitted outside the West by processes of colonization and globalization.[34]

The violent splintering of Western Christendom due to the Reformation and, roughly concurrently, Europe's accelerated contact with other civilizations and religious traditions resulting from voyages of exploration and discovery nudged the word *religio* toward its modern usage.[35] Both Zwingli and Calvin employed the term—respectively, in the former's *De vera et falsa religione commentarius* and in Calvin's landmark *Christianae religionis institutio*—to distinguish their understanding of correct belief from the false (Roman Catholic) variety.[36] In his *De veritate religionis Christianae*, the seventeenth-century Dutch legal scholar Hugo Grotius went a step further, associating the word with the correct teaching (*doctrina*) offered by Christianity in contrast to other known faiths, mainly Judaism and Islam—the latter long seen as a particularly reviled Christian heresy.[37] This *doctrinal* understanding of the term is also seen in the writings of the seventeenth-century English diplomat and historian Herbert of Cherbury, who painstakingly sought to devise a method for assessing whether a teaching was true or not.[38] Furthermore, it was during the early modern era, particularly in the writings of John Locke and Jean Bodin, that religion began to be conceived of as a distinct, privatized sphere of activity residing essentially in the mind, the excess zeal of which should not disrupt the (secular) nation-states coming into existence after the Peace of Westphalia (1648).[39] When this nonsecular sphere was assessed globally from a European standpoint, it was generally given a quadripartite structure: the Christian and Jewish faiths, Islam, and what was generally tagged as "paganism," "heathenism," or "idolatry," catchall terms for the vaguely known belief systems and practices of South Asia, Africa, and the New World.[40] Incrementally, this begins to change in the seventeenth century.

But only during the Enlightenment and the nineteenth century did the full etymological development take place, whereby *religion* came to be understood as a quasi-Platonic essence or master genus, transhistorical and transcultural in nature, the species of which—"world religions"—were scattered across the globe.[41] The classificatory urge of the Western Enlightenment, the Romantic and liberal Protestant preoccupation with the "experience" of religion, combined with greater knowledge of the world wrought by overseas colonialism, shattered the older fourfold model and other "religion*s*" were named in a new taxonomy of "world religions."[42] The entry on religions, plural, appears only with the ninth edition of the *Encyclopedia Britannica* (1875–89). "For the major living religions of the world," as Cantwell has written, "modernity has conferred names where they did not exist."[43] "Mahometanism" or "Muhammadism," only later Islam, emerged as a relatively stable category by the nineteenth century, while the suffix "ism" was first attached to define and name other profoundly heterogeneous, internally complex faith traditions: "Hindooism" (1787), "Boudhism" (1801), "Taouism" (1839), "Zoroasterianism" (1854), and "Confucianism" (1862).[44] During this same period, Christianity and Judaism, too, came into their own as umbrella nouns transcending the manifold differences (and feuds) among their adherents. These and a handful of others—such as "Shintoism" (1894)—were soon denominated together as *major world religions*.[45] With an assist from Jungian psychologizing theories about religion, the taxonomy became wildly popular in the twentieth century, especially through the best-selling writings of Huston Smith and in other publications, such as *Life* magazine's series on "the world's great religions" in the 1950s.[46]

Furthermore, the (essentially Lockean) liberal political project, gaining actuality through influences of the American and French Revolutions (1776, 1789), molded *religion* to denote a transhistorical, transcultural phenomenon, best separated from the "secular" realms of politics, science, law—the realms, in short, of "secular modernity."[47] The social theorist Talal Asad has gone so far as to call secularism religion's "Siamese twin"—the modern meaning of each

Cover of Life *magazine (7 February 1955), part of its series on "the world's great religions." (Photography by Leonard McCombe. Image courtesy of Getty Images.)*

has depended on the meaning of the other; each are products of particular historical developments and epistemological configurations within Western modernity—and yet, the secular-religion distinction, not to mention the notion of religion as genus or transhistorical essence, has been exported around the globe due to the culture-shaping force of Western colonialism and its more recent offspring, globalization.[48]

What does all of this mean for this study? Since interreligious dialogue, at least in recent history, has rested heavily on the assumption of religion understood as a genus differentiated into particular species, and since this, as we have seen, is largely a colonial-era construction, it follows that the practice of interreligious dialogue is perhaps not as straightforwardly therapeutic or neutral or universalistic in its assumptions and applicability as it has seemed to many of its (preponderantly Western or Western-influenced) advocates and practitioners. This is not to say that interreligious dialogue is altogether misguided nor, as some have proposed, that we should simply drop the word *religion*. It is meant, however, to call attention to a major instance in which, to refer to the work of Dipesh Chakrabarty, the parochial nature of some European ideas and concepts, through the power arrangements and knowledge-shaping force of colonialism, have been mistaken for the "normative horizons" of human thought.[49] To quote William T. Cavanaugh on this point: "*Religion* is originally a Western concept, and it only became a worldwide concept through—and [in] reaction to—Western influence." And Cavanaugh again: "The concept of religion was introduced outside the West in the context of European colonization, and the introduction of the concept often served the interest of the colonizers."[50] I do not intend to jettison the term, but I do think the interests of candor and insight are served by making clear at the outset of this study its complex, fraught genealogy.[51]

Pluralism and Cosmopolitanism

Interreligious dialogue depends on the relative proximity of those holding different religious views (pluralism), and it has traditionally sought to offer its participants a more capacious, sympathetic understanding of the world's civilizations and their various faith traditions. I hope this study, therefore, makes a contribution to ongoing discussions about the nature of religious pluralism and the ethical theory of cosmopolitanism—the latter associated in recent years especially with the writings of the philosopher Kwame Anthony Appiah, the former with many figures, although I owe a special debt to the work of the late sociologist Peter Berger and Harvard University's Diana Eck.

For Berger, the master narrative of modernity can no longer be regarded as one of "secularization." Under the influence of pioneering social theorists such as Auguste Comte, Émile Durkheim, and Max Weber, social scientists in the middle decades of the twentieth century latched on to this concept—usually tagged as "secularization theory" or the "secularization thesis"—as the dominant paradigm for explaining social and intellectual changes wrought by modernization. Simply put: as societies transitioned from the "traditional" (rural, hierarchical, communal) to the "modern," a process of secularization would reliably occur, incrementally draining the plausibility and influence of religion from institutions and the consciousness of individuals.[52] In the 1990s, Berger defected from the consensus of his guild, convinced that the global religious data simply did not support the secularization thesis as it had been handed down; he was also bothered by how the idea was often presented in quasi-teleological terms as a "law" of history. To be sure, Berger made some exceptions: Western Europe and Western-educated intellectuals, grouped primarily in urban and educational centers around the globe, appeared in aggregate more secular than others.[53] But these were the exceptions that confirmed the rule of enduringly religious societies throughout the world. In many areas, religiosity of various forms, especially Islam and Pentecostal Christianity, appeared to be on the rise.[54] This was true despite processes of modernization, which Berger succinctly defines as "the transformation in the human condition from fate to choice."[55] This transformation, in turn, owes its existence to prior enormous changes in transportation, communication, education, free trade, and the rise of democratic forms of government that have taken place over the last few centuries. Generally speaking, a child in twenty-first-century London has prodigiously more "life options" than a child, say, in thirteenth-century London.

And these options include religious options or "preferences." In this sense, modernization has not been without significant effect on religious traditions worldwide, but "secularization" is perhaps not the most apt descriptor of these changes. A better one is pluralism. People have more religious options and, yes, secular ones too. As Berger puts it: "Modernization unleashes all the forces that make for pluralism—urbanization, mass migration (including tourism), general literacy, and higher education for increasing numbers, and all the recent technologies of communication. In our globalized modernity, almost everyone talks with everyone else. . . . [Most people] are aware of the fact that there are different ways of life, different values, different worldviews."[56] What is more, modernity/pluralism does not look the same in every country and region. No standard-issue modernity exists, but rather what the Israeli sociologist Shmuel Eisenstadt has called "multiple modernities."[57] Modernity in Norway does not look exactly as it does in Indonesia; in India, it differs from that in Belgium. But in all cases, modernity has brought about a shift from relative cultural and religious homogeneity to relative cultural and religious heterogeneity—especially but not only in urban areas. To a significant degree, religious allegiance has become "de-territorialized."[58] People more often talk to, trade with, text, email, even marry the religious "Other"; things become more complicated, more fluid—if not downright confusing.

And thus pluralism happens. Alterity moves in next door. A sizable Sikh community now lives in Alabama.

The reality of pluralism helped give birth to the Pluralism Project at Harvard University in 1991, directed by Diana L. Eck. A scholar of Indian religious traditions and a collaborator on interreligious initiatives for the World Council of Churches and the World Conference on Religions for Peace, Eck realized that she no longer had to travel to India for research to robustly encounter the religious Other, for the Other was increasingly found in her native country, the United States. Spurred in particular by the Immigration and Nationality Act of 1965, the so-called new immigration has profoundly altered the ethnic and religious landscape of American society—with comparable changes, if not always for the same reasons, taking place in other Western (and non-Western) nations.[59] "The religious landscape of America," Eck wrote in 2001, "has changed radically in the past thirty years, but most of us have not yet begun to see the dimensions and scope of that change, so gradual has it been and yet so colossal." "The relationship and interdependence of religious communities," she elaborates, "is now enacted in both local and global sites—Hindus and Christians in India and Indianapolis, Muslims and Jews in the Midwest and the Middle East, Vietnamese Buddhists and their Christian neighbors in a rundown neighborhood of Roslindale [in Boston]."[60] Los Angeles, Eck plausibly claims, is the most religiously diverse city in the world. For the sake of a healthy democracy and peaceful coexistence, the Pluralism Project aims to bring scholarly inquiry and data on religious affiliation to bear on broader public debates and concerns.

The current study is inspired by a similar motivation. But its focus is not so much on religious actors per se (although certainly many appear in the book), but rather on the individuals, institutions, and events that have conceptualized and promoted (forgive the pedantic locution) *organized, formal interfaith discursive practices.* It does so, again, by investigating several key historical turning points (along with their geneses and legacies) that have in their own way contributed to an intellectual climate in which an initiative such as Harvard's Pluralism Project would seem like the right and proper thing to do. Such an initiative would likely not have occurred in ancient China, nor medieval Europe, nor in just about any other period in human history until the recent past. Why is this case? What are the antecedents for present-day interreligious dialogue? What are its more recent forms and trajectories?

Understanding historically the discursive terrain and trajectories of interreligious dialogue helps us to become better citizens of the world, cosmopolitans, living in conversation with a creed as old as the Stoics. Admittedly, the word *cosmopolitanism* can sound snobbish, and to some it implies the rejection of all local allegiances in the name of a bloodless abstraction: humanity. But I do not invoke the word in this sense nor do I see our more local attachments necessarily pitted against cosmopolitanism in a zero-sum struggle.[61] Rather, following Kwame Appiah, I employ it to designate both a challenge and a proposal. As indicated, modernity has drastically shrunk the globe, bringing people into greater proximity with one another, whether actually or virtually—a reality made dramatically clear by the coronavirus crisis. At least for the educated and the urban, we already live in a cosmopolitan cultural space, and this space is growing rapidly.[62] Getting along in this space is the challenge. And the solution is not to abjure it in the name of atavistic tribalisms, nationalisms, or fundamentalisms, although sadly these options appear compelling to many. Rather, this new reality should enjoin us to engage in conversation, learn from one another, deepen our capacities for cross-cultural literacy and for sincere seeking of truth and wisdom. "The world is getting more crowded," writes Appiah. "Depending on the circumstances, conversations across boundaries can be delightful, or just vexing: what they mainly are, though, is inevitable."[63] Interreligious dialogue is one vehicle in which these conversations have taken place.[64] What can we learn, positive and negative, from past conversations? And how might they contribute to a compelling cosmopolitan ethic today that does not unwarrantedly degrade more local attachments and identities?

Unfortunately, theorists of cosmopolitanism sometimes give religion short shrift. In a recent scholarly project, *The Cosmopolitanism Reader*, editors Garrett Wallace Brown and David Held failed to include a single contribution dealing substantively with religion.[65] If anything, religion is often associated with parochialism and the past, with xenophobia and untowardly narrow attachments—something proponents of cosmopolitanism should strive to get beyond. But ignoring faith commitments—and the role that they play, both constructively and destructively, in individual and communal identities—suggests blinkered incomprehension of a major agency in human affairs, past and present. Instead, advocates of a cosmopolitan ethic ought to learn not only *about* but *from* various faith traditions if they truly wish to accomplish their aims. In particular, moral teachings of human worth and practices of human solidarity, not to mention prescriptive advice on behavior, found in many faiths should be examined and employed in thinking about ethics on a global scale.[66] And practically speaking, as Rabbi Jonathan Sacks has argued, religious communities are often "better adapted to a world of global communication than are nation states and existing political institutions."[67] In short, inattention to or supercilious disdain for religion not only fails to serve a cosmopolitan ethic, it suggests a secularist myopia that actually vitiates it.[68]

Religion, Civilizations, and Violence

Proponents of interreligious dialogue often claim that dialogue among "world religions" is a sine qua non for global peace. The German theologian Hans Küng, for example, in advocating for a "global ethic," has coined the often-cited mantra: "There will be peace on earth when there is peace among the world religions. No world peace without peace among religions; no peace among religions without dialogue between religions."[69] To be sure, Küng captures something truthful here, and advocates of interreligious dialogue regularly regard world peace, or at least a more peaceful world, as a major goal of dialogue. Embedded in this view, however, is the telltale modern Western belief that "religion" is a phenomenon uniquely prone to violence, easily marked off from other aspects of culture, and standing in special need of containment from the "secular" state. But as William Cavanaugh has convincingly argued, this belief—or "myth," as he labels it—is the questionable product of particular political arrangements and intellectual circumstances in the post-Enlightenment West. For contemporary Western intellectuals, Cavanaugh argues,

> the conventional wisdom is that there is an essential difference between religions such as Christianity, Islam, Hinduism, and Judaism, on the one hand, and secular ideologies and institutions such as nationalism, Marxism, capitalism, and liberalism. . . . [This claim is] unsustainable and dangerous. It is unsustainable because ideologies and institutions labeled secular can be just as absolutist, divisive, and irrational as those labeled religious. It is dangerous because it helps marginalize, and even legitimate violence against, those forms of life that are labeled religious. . . . The myth of religious violence tries to establish as timeless, universal, and natural a very contingent set of categories—religious and secular—that in fact are constructions of the modern West. Those who do not accept these categories as timeless, universal, and natural are subject to coercion.[70]

Simply put, what the West sees as universal, "the rest" has often viewed as Western.

We need not embrace Cavanaugh's argument in toto to recognize that many global cultures outside the modern West simply have not possessed a fixed notion of a secular-religious divide, nor has it been universally held, as we have seen, that "religion" is understood as a transhistorical genus presiding over a variety of "ism" species.[71] Far too often in the past, proponents of interreligious dialogue have assumed otherwise and, even with the noblest of intentions, shoehorned different world cultures into the Western paradigm. (And as an ironic aside: it is arguably a Western-bred, secular political "solution" to religion, Marxism-Leninism, that, with its Maoist offspring, has actually proven to be the most pitiless angel of death in modern history.)[72]

In his much-discussed *Clash of Civilizations*, the political scientist Samuel P. Huntington offers a more compelling view of the relationship between religion and violence. Regrettably, it is more fashionable to dismiss this engaging book (often on assumptions about the meaning of the title) than it is to read it attentively. Huntington defines a civilization as "the highest cultural grouping of people and the broadest level of cultural identity people have short of that which distinguishes humans from other species." Or again: "Civilizations are the biggest 'we' within which we feel culturally at home as distinguished from all the other 'thems' out there."[73] Religion is a key ingredient of a civilization, according to Huntington, but it is not the only one. Other factors—language, geography, ethnicity—come into play along with, and crucially, shared historical experiences over long stretches of time—experiences that usually involve one powerful civilization's running conflict with another in addition to rival narratives about the nature of their shared history. The clash of Slavic-Orthodox civilization and Turkish-Muslim civilization in the Balkans offers one clear example. To be sure, religion has been a factor in this struggle, but the violence that has episodically erupted at this civilizational fault line involves many other factors—and not least the *political* incitement and manipulation of faith communities during times of crisis and uncertainty.[74] Put differently, it is not some abstract "Christianity" or "Orthodoxy"—understood as a "world religion"—that has encountered an equally abstract "Islam" in the Balkans, but rather a far more complex struggle between two longstanding *civilizational powers*, each harboring divergent *memories* about the significance of their struggle. Religion is not incidental to the struggle, to be sure, but it is also not a readily isolatable, single cause. Anyone seriously committed to interreligious dialogue must keep these messy historical and geographical factors in mind and not indulge in the fantasy that "Religion A" extracted from its historical particularities can either come into conflict or have a conversation with an equally extracted "Religion B." Too often in the past, however, practitioners of interreligious dialogue have made these assumptions.

Putatively religious conflicts, furthermore, are in fact sometimes actually products of modern political secularism.[75] This is the claim of Saba Mahmood's trenchantly argued *Religious Difference in a Sec-*

ular Age: A Minority Report. Using Egypt as a case study but one with implications for other polities, she argues that secularism is much more than a neutral umpire of religious difference, some supra-ideological leftover after the "modern state's retreat from religion"; it is rather "a historical product" with its own commitments and "with specific epistemological, political, and moral entailments." Far from being a neutral arbiter of religious difference and an above-the-fray custodian of religious freedom, moreover, secularism is always shaped by majoritarian pressures, ideological configurations, and historical memories within a given nation-state and will thus look different from country to country. Religious minorities—whether Copts in Egypt, Muslims in France and India, or Mormons in America—will therefore regularly have grievances with where majoritarian pressures have attempted to draw the secular/religious, public/private line. Consequently, Mahmood assays, "The question of how and where to draw the line between religion and politics, between what is deemed public and private, acquires a particular salience in liberal polities and is constantly subject to legal and political contestation." Ironically, then, in response to political pressures to (re)negotiate this line, the state is often dragged ever deeper into matters traditionally under the purview of religious communities: the definition of marriage, the display or wearing of religious symbols, the morality of circumcision, the education of the young, and a host of other issues come to mind. Because of this, Mahmood concludes, "the modern state and its putative political rationality have played a far more decisive role in transforming preexisting religious differences, producing new forms of communal polarization, and making religion more rather than less salient to minority and majority identities."[76]

For the present study, Mahmood's work should serve as a cautionary tale, reminding us of the complex, compound causes of what ostensibly might come across and be hurriedly labeled as "religious violence." Theorists and practitioners of interreligious dialogue such as Küng, moreover, too often harbor intemperate beliefs about its peace-making potential: if only religious virtuosi (representing or claiming they represent various religious communities) would sit down and empathize with one another, then, lo, peace would be at hand.[77] Interreligious dialogue is vitally important and instructive, no doubt. At the same time, it bears remembering that the violence ailing our world cannot be reduced to religious factors alone, with interreligious dialogue tendered as the expedient remedy. Far more thorny civilizational factors come into play, as Huntington and others have argued, that require the work of political prudence and diplomacy based on searching historical understanding at both a macro- and micrological level—with perhaps a healthy dose of Niebuhrian realism thrown in.[78] And as for secularism: as Mahmood indicates, it sometimes actually exacerbates religious differences, pitting religious majorities and minorities against one another in easily ignited squabbles over the very definition of secularism and its legal and political embodiments.[79]

Any serious student of religious conflict and interreligious dialogue ought to keep these considerations in mind.

"Orientalism" and Its Limits

Modern interreligious dialogue has often involved representatives from "the East" talking with those from "the West," with conversations frequently, if not always, planned, funded, and organized by the latter. The East here should be understood capaciously as the non-European, the non-Western, geographically stretching from North Africa to the Holy Land to the Indian subcontinent and the rest of South Asia. Because of European colonialism in the modern era, East and West have rarely met on a level playing field; the power dynamics are tilted heavily in favor of the latter. European scholars, writers, and clergy have enjoyed a "cultural hegemony" and a "positional superiority" vis-à-vis the East.

These coinages are those of the late Edward Said, whose 1978 book *Orientalism* sparked a debate about European (and American) attitudes toward and depictions of "the Orient" that continues unabated in the present. "Orientalism," as Said defined it, "can be discussed and analyzed as the corporate institution[s] [in the West] . . . dealing with the Orient—dealing with it by making statements about it, authorizing views of it, describing it, by teaching it, settling it, ruling over it; in short, Orientalism is a Western style for dominating, restructuring, and having authority over the Orient." In Said's view, since the eighteenth century, knowledge produced about the East by Western scholars, and even by Western-influenced Eastern ones, has been indelibly stamped with the colonialist mindset of North Atlantic states, especially Great Britain and France, and, since the twentieth century, the United States. This pervasive "political imperialism," in Said's severe judgment, has "govern[ed] an entire field of study, imagination, and scholarly institutions—in such a way as to make its avoidance an intellectual and historical impossibility."[80]

Said's epoch-making thesis has garnered copious praise and criticism. This is not the place to review this immense literature.[81] But in light of our topic and the fact that I sometimes employ the term *Orientalist*, several comments are in order. For starters, Said's general claim is hard to gainsay. Western attitudes toward and scholarship about the East often take for granted the "advanced" state of the West and the "primitive" state of the East. The material resources of the colonial powers, their capacity to project power through commercial strength, their technological know-how and military might, their institutions of education and research, their unflappable sense of being on "the right side of history" have, historically viewed, translated into a confident posture of superiority, a general sensibility, a persuasion—perhaps more often assumed than spoken—that in turn has contributed to fashioning a view of the "Orient" as backward, exotic, irrational, infantile, effeminate and, not least, as a cauldron of obscurantist religiosity.[82]

At the same time, the category of Orientalism can be profoundly reductionist. Employing it indiscriminately yields an overly politicized understanding of the West's relationship to the East. Western scholars—including Western promoters of interreligious dialogue—are turned into passive minions of colonialist ambition, unwitting scholarly pawns armed with notebooks and footnotes in a much broader geopolitical power struggle. Such a hermeneutic works against a more subtle, multifaceted understanding of how interreligious dialogue planners and practitioners have understood themselves. "The essential weakness of Edward Said," writes Irfan Habib, "lies in the failure to see that colonialism does not form the *only* major influence over oriental scholarship in the west or in the Orient."[83] In what follows, then, one should not expect to find Western knowledge of and engagement with the East reduced to colonialist motivations alone, although I do not deny such motives and will sometimes spotlight their prevalence. But other factors merit consideration: simple inquisitiveness, the formation of cross-cultural friendships, scholarly ambition, a desire in fact to critique "the West," and even altruism. Not infrequently, as shall be seen, promoters of interreligious dialogue were themselves critical of Western colonialism and saw conversation with religious Others in the colonies as a means of exposing colonialism's darker aspects.

Furthermore (and this criticism of his work is long-standing), Said pays scant attention to the religious, and specifically Christian-theological, motives for Western involvement in the East.[84] After all, the Middle East witnessed the origins of all three Abrahamic faiths and is the place of Christianity's holiest sites. Pious motivations, in other words, and not political-colonialist ones alone, drove scholars to the East in search of the roots of their own faith commitments and communities. Nineteenth-century German-speaking scholars (whom Said inexcusably failed to treat) in particular produced reams of knowledge about the origins of Christianity and those of other religions; and they did this despite the fact that "Germany" did not exist until 1871 and did not have overt colonial ambitions until the 1890s after the coming to power of Kaiser Wilhelm II.[85]

Finally, taking Said as the final word on Western engagement with the East contributes to what the literary critic Rita Felski has diagnosed as an overwrought posture of critique, a "hermeneutics of suspicion" (Paul Ricoeur's locution) insufficiently suspicious of itself, governing the contemporary academy today. Again, from Said's point of view, practically all forms of modern Western knowledge about the East are at some level infected by "Orientalism." One should therefore be hyper-vigilant, assuming reprehensible motivations when Western subjects engage Eastern topics—even if these motivations might be only dimly recognized by the subject.[86] Such a critical stance might yield important insights, to be sure, but over-applied, it also obstructs from view other motivations beyond the crypto-colonialist pursuit of power, control, superiority. Totalizing such a point of view as Said does, yields, to use Felski's words, "skepticism as dogma," an unwarrantedly confident tunnel vision incapacitated from recognizing more neutral, plural, or innocent motivations. "At a certain point," Felski writes, "critique does not get us any further. To ask what comes after the hermeneutics of suspicion is not to demolish it but to decenter it, to decline to see it as the be-all and end-all of interpretation."[87]

Sometimes a cigar is just a cigar, as Freud once said; perhaps sometimes, too, Western interest in the East is, well, simply Western interest in the East.[88]

Theologies of Other Religions

Insofar as this study possesses a broadly Western orientation, and since centuries-long accretions of Christian thought have profoundly colored Western perceptions of and responses to other religions, it merits briefly laying out here a typology of Christian-theological approaches to other religions. For theologians conversant in these matters, these categories will come as old news, but I would rather state the obvious than not mention terms of art crucial for understanding the outlooks of people encountered in this study. Briefly put, we may speak of three dominant ideal-typical approaches to "other religions" from the standpoint of Christian theology: *exclusivism*, *inclusivism*, and *pluralism*.[89] Each position has received commendation and each criticism.[90]

The exclusivist position possesses age-old sanction in the Christian intellectual tradition. It is pervasively Christological and Trinitarian in nature, stressing the unique soteriological message of Christianity. As such, it provides a strong rationale for Christian mission, stressing the universal relevance of the Gospel to all peoples. Its biblical and patristic support is copious, succinctly summed up in Acts 4:12: "And there is salvation in no one else [than Christ], for there is no other name under heaven given among men by which we must be saved" (RSV). In modern times, arguably the staunchest and most articulate representative of this position was the Dutch theologian Hendrik Kraemer (1888–1965), who, appropriating language from Karl Barth, made a sharp distinction between Christian revelation in Christ on the one hand, and the (misguided) project of "human religion" on the other.[91] Christian revelation, Kraemer wrote, "contradicts and upsets all human religious aspiration."[92] Or, as Barth had formulated the matter: "From the standpoint of revelation religion is clearly seen to be a human attempt to anticipate what God in his revelation wills to do and does do. It is the attempted replacement of the divine work by human manufacture."[93] From this starting point, Kraemer's and Barth's theological kindred spirit Dietrich Bonhoeffer posited the desirability of a seeming paradox: "religionless" Christianity.[94] Variations on this position, if less rigorously theologized, have been championed by many Christians at the more "conservative" end of the theological spectrum.[95]

Theologically understood, the strength of this outlook, again, resides in its strong support in both Scripture and Christian tradition. "Not even the most detached reader of the New Testament," Alan Race has written, "can fail to gain the impression that the overall picture of Christian faith which it presents is intended to be absolute or final."[96] But historically and sociologically viewed, the strength of this position has also been the source of weakness, for it has sometimes fostered triumphalism about one's certitude, which in turn has given birth to ham-fisted missionary enterprises and cultural chauvinism.[97] In addition, exclusivists have a hard time reckoning with biblical figures (Noah, Melchizedek, Job) who seem to stand in a right relationship with God apart from the Abrahamic Covenant and the Christian Gospel.[98] Beginning in the late nineteenth century, as shall be seen, liberal Protestants (often joining arms with Unitarians and Theosophists) saw themselves battling against hard versions of exclusivism in an attempt to offer a more open-armed theology of non-Christian religions and of "religion" more generally, and to justify the task of interreligious dialogue.[99]

A distinctly Catholic, more ecclesially oriented version of this position—*extra Ecclesiam nulla salus* (outside the church, no salvation)—generally prevailed until the Second Vatican Council, at which time the Catholic Church revisited its tradition (*ressourcement*) and developed a version of inclusivism.[100] (We shall recount this theological transformation in some depth in chapter 4.)

Inclusivism, then, might be defined as the belief that other religious traditions have much to offer, but they are only partial measures, seeking, if unwittingly, completion or "fulfillment" in Christianity. From this perspective, subscribed to by both Catholics and other Christians, other religious traditions are not so much misguided or pernicious, as some exclusivists might say, as they are incomplete, awaiting higher fulfillment in Christ and the church.[101]

If exclusivism offers a stark either-or between religion and revelation, inclusivism offers a both-and solution. In the language of Vatican II's *Nostra aetate:* "The Catholic Church rejects nothing that is true and holy in these [non-Christian] religions. She regards with sincere reverence those ways of conduct and of life, those precepts and teachings which, though differing in many aspects from the ones she holds and sets forth, nonetheless often reflect a ray of that Truth which enlightens all men. Indeed, she proclaims, and ever must proclaim Christ 'the way, the truth, and the life' (John 14:6), in whom men may find the fullness of religious life, in whom God has reconciled all things to Himself."[102] One finds here a more generous view of other faiths. But note that they possess only a "ray" of truth, while Catholic Christianity bears witness to the fuller Truth found in Christ alone. Developing ever-more nuanced versions of theological inclusivism became a major concern among Catholic (and many non-Catholic) theologians after the council. The Jesuit theologian Karl Rahner's notion that the morally upright and devout non-Christian might be considered an "anonymous Christian" served as a major catalyst for these postconciliar discussions.[103]

The strength of this position is that it confers value on other faiths, allowing for their admiration, while also upholding the exceptional status of Christianity. It also enjoys considerable support in the Christian tradition. Arguably, the Apostle Paul espoused a version of it in his speech on the Areopagus (Acts 17:22–31), where he favorably acknowledged the authenticity of the Athenians' devotion to an "unknown god" before identifying that god with Christ. Early Christian thinkers such as Justin Martyr and Clement of Alexandria also lend support to inclusivism; both held that goodness and truth exist abundantly in the created order, including in other faiths and philosophies, but in the providential scheme of things they are ultimately trussed to the eternal divine Logos, Christ.[104]

In the eyes of its critics, however, inclusivism also possesses serious weaknesses. Exclusivists have complained that it soft-pedals biblical passages proclaiming the unique nature of Christ and that it fails to provide sufficient impetus for Christian mission and apologetics. By contrast, pluralists have felt that it does not go far enough in recognizing God working in other religious traditions, and that it even fosters Christian condescension toward them.

Finally, then, there is the pluralist position, a viewpoint forcefully set forth by theologians John Hick and Paul Knitter, among others.[105] Arguably, it has been the most influential justifier of interreligious dialogue in recent decades. Paul Griffiths has called it "the underlying scholarly orthodoxy on the goals and functions of interreligious dialogue."[106] For adherents of this viewpoint, neither exclusivism nor inclusivism passes muster: the former is too narrow-minded, the latter too patronizing. While drawing from explicitly Christian moral notions (such as charity or humility), the pluralist unseats Christianity entirely as the final destination or arbiter of religious truth and salvation.[107] Rather, knowledge of God is partial in all faiths and all are, or should be, linked together in a common pursuit of understanding. Religions must therefore acknowledge their need for one another if the full truth is ever to be available to humankind. For some pluralists, the goal of dialogue among religions is the creation of a future religion or a "universal religion," one that incorporates the best insights from all faiths. For others, the goal is to peel away secondary and tertiary matters separating religions from one another and arrive at the already-existing "true essence" or "essential sameness" of religion.[108] Still others see dialogue simply as a vehicle for learning and achieving mutual appreciation and understanding.

The strength of this position is that it harmonizes well with modern notions of tolerance and equality, even as it often deploys the language of Christian virtues. The weakness is that it was virtually nonexistent before the modern period (Hick spoke of it, somewhat grandiosely, as effecting a "Copernican Revolution" in modern theology) and heavily rests (as the other positions do, in varying degrees) on the colonial-era redefinition of religion as genus manifesting itself in distinctive "ism" species. With respect to interreligious dialogue, moreover, this position begs the question of whether a Christian who disavows the manifold biblical and historic claims of Christian uniqueness can in good faith participate in dialogue *as a Christian*, for doing so would seem to deprive his or her interlocutor of the face-to-face experience of Christian alterity.[109] From another angle, pluralists tend to adopt a bird's-eye or meta-religious attitude to religions, a feat more difficult for those whose more tradition-embedded ways of life and patterns of thought have not been shaped by the Western Enlightenment and the "high-altitude" academic milieux of colonial power.

Exclusivism, inclusivism, and pluralism do not exhaust Christian stances vis-à-vis other religions, and it should be noted that more subtle distinctions and nuances exist *within* each position.[110] Moreover, some theologians have felt that one need not necessarily pick between them but, variously arranged, they can be held in creative tension with one another for the purposes of interreligious dialogue. But whatever the case, these categories provide a measure of heuristic assistance (whether or not they were explicitly invoked by historical personages) with respect to Western/Christian engagement with other religions, and some familiarity with them now will provide guidance for the path ahead. Finally, permit me to note that the theological divisions implied by these approaches suggest a recurring irony about interreligious dialogue: even though dialogue is often advocated as a means toward peace, debates over its permissibility and proper modality have not infrequently been a source of internal rifts within both Christianity and other faith traditions.

The Other in the Past, the Past in the Other

No shortage exists, among Christians and adherents of other faiths, of attempts to think theologically about interreligious dialogue. Providing a rationale for dialogue, proposing "models" for it, musing sensitively on what "the Other" has to teach us, suggesting topics and guidelines for dialogue, bringing various "sacred texts" into conversation with one another, and staging actual dialogues—all these things have been done aplenty. But my aim differs fundamentally. It is more genetic than theological in scope, more attentive to the messy stuff of historical specificity and accident. Through detailed attention to the aforementioned turning points occurring in influential "centers," I hope to provide broad historical perspective on the entire phenomenon of interreligious dialogue, beginning with its antecedents in the premodern world and coming close to our own present. My working assumption is that the topic is at once highly significant and poised to grow in the future, but suffering from a yawning deficit of historical perspicacity.

What then, finally, might history offer?

In medieval and Renaissance art, the virtue of prudence (or wisdom) was often depicted with three eyes, representing the past, present, and future. This was meant to suggest that the well-ordered individual or society must understand the past to promote the well-being of the present and the future. As a medieval proverb puts it, "From past experience the present acts prudently lest future action be vitiated." Sometimes, prudence was allegorized as a Janus-faced woman, one youthful face staring hopefully forward into the future and the other, an aged face, staring contemplatively backward into the past. But the implication is the same: knowledge of the past is necessary for human flourishing, individually and collectively.[111] As Charles Taylor writes, "Our past is sedimented in our present, and we are doomed to misidentify ourselves, as long as we can't do justice to where we come from."[112] Or, as Cicero laconically put it, history is the teacher of life, *historia magistra vitae.*

This book attempts to provide a retrospective gaze into a topic of first-order contemporary concern and interest: interaction and communication among religious traditions. It is neither casual antiquarianism nor an attempt to know the past merely for the sake of knowing the past. Instead, it concurrently strives to operate as historical *and* moral inquiry, motivated by a desire to understand *historical others* (themselves in the act of attempting to understand *religious others*) in their full complexity—in their strivings and defeats, insights and incomprehensions, high-mindedness and meanness, joys and sorrows. I stand with the great Swiss-German historian Jacob Burckhardt, who once mused that the truest subject of history "is that past which is clearly connected with the present and with the future. . . . Actually one ought to stress especially those historical realities from which threads run to our own period and culture."[113]

In the case of interreligious dialogue, the threads from "then" to "now" are thick and numerous. Unfortunately, history rarely offers simple or straightforward lessons. "Historical reality, because it is human," the French philosopher Raymond Aron once averred, "is ambiguous and inexhaustible."[114] Even so, as creatures of time without powers of clairvoyance, we have only the retrospective gaze to guide the path ahead and the path beneath our feet. Knowledge of it, therefore, is an indispensable prerequisite for living well, wisely, and in service to things that truly matter. In this respect I hope this book provides some illumination into those doughty souls, key moments, and significant events that have brought the world's diverse faith traditions into greater proximity to and conversation with one another. Beyond that, the book aims simply to provide food for thought for all people of goodwill living in our globalized, pluralistic, postcolonial, cosmopolitan, perduringly religious world and who seek to make deeper sense of it.

CHAPTER ONE

Harbingers

No religion is an island.

—ABRAHAM JOSHUA HESCHEL

WHILE CHICAGO'S PARLIAMENT OF RELIGIONS (1893) is justifiably seen as launching the modern interfaith movement, this major event did not take place without premodern historical antecedents. This chapter offers a *tour d'horizon* of some of these, concluding with a profile of the Mughal emperor Akbar (r. 1556–1605), who on the cusp of the modern age represents an especially arresting case in his efforts to bring multiple religious voices from the Indian subcontinent, together with European Jesuit missionaries, into conversation with one another. Even so, Akbar's example, too, is not without precedent.

But permit several caveats before proceeding. First, I make no pretense of providing an exhaustive list of harbingers of interreligious dialogue; I only seek to spotlight several salient examples. What is more, these examples reflect my own social and intellectual limitations; I draw preponderantly from Western and, to a lesser extent, Islamic civilizations after the advent of Christianity—with the partial exception of the Mongol court and Akbar, which take us farther east.[1] Second, let me remind the reader that not only do the terms *interreligious* and *interfaith* not exist in the premodern world, but the same is true for our present-day usage of *religion*—a fact that was elaborated on in the introduction. Third, I am not primarily interested in governmental policies of religious toleration, even if these are often a necessary precondition of dialogue; nor am I interested in mere "encounters" between different faiths; examples of these are well-nigh endless in the historical record.[2] To define my aim more precisely, I am above all interested in instances of and ideas about conversation/debate/dialogue among various religious groups or individuals that, whether intentionally or not, resulted in mutual understanding or at least bear witness to "religious others" interacting and intellectually taking stock of one another. To be sure, in the premodern world, these ideas and practices almost invariably came with a polemical, proselytizing, or apologetic element, or else they were put forth for largely Hobbesian political reasons to promote stability and trade within a state or territory. Still, one cannot rightly appraise the significance of the 1893 parliament and more recent efforts of interreligious dialogue without at least considering historical antecedents, however sketchy and remote in time and spirit they may seem. We will discover, in fact, that while modern efforts of interreligious dialogue represent significant discontinuity with the past, they also bear witness to continuities. This fact is sometimes lost on practitioners of interreligious dialogue today, as well as on diagnosticians of contemporary religious pluralism; both are given to touting the radical novelty of our contemporary situation. Yes, modernity has ushered in distinctive forms of pluralism and dialogue, as I argued in the introduction. But rarely in history is something entirely unprecedented. Assuming otherwise impoverishes historical explanation and burdens present-day interreligious endeavors with amnesia about its own past.

The Ancient Mediterranean World

From the moment of its inception in ancient Palestine, Christianity faced the presence and challenge of other faiths. It developed out of Judaism and gradually marked itself off from its parent; it took root and grew in the world of Hellenism and the Roman Empire with its great variety of philosophies, deities, myths, beliefs, and ritual practices, among which Christianity sought to find its own ground and make a stand for itself.[3] The speeches recorded in the Acts of the Apostles provide examples of what we might even consider proto-interreligious dialogue. Of particular significance is Paul's well-known speech at the Areopagus, where he addressed a "very religious" Athenian society that in his judgment already stood in unwitting contact with the Christian God at its altar dedicated to an "unknown god."[4]

Although early Christians developed a variety of views toward neighboring faiths, we might nonetheless speak of three dominant strategies, respectively directed at Judaism, pagan beliefs, and pagan philosophy. These strategies are important, because they set in motion habits of interpretation and interaction with other faiths that have had a long history, and they have analogues in the self-understanding of other religious traditions. Rejecting the views of Marcion, who sought to dispense with Christianity's Jewish roots altogether, early church fathers tended to see the two faiths as interconnected.[5] Yet the hidden message of the Hebrew Scriptures—the "Old Testament," in Christian parlance—was to be understood figuratively or allegorically through Christian theological lenses; it no longer spoke to the Jewish people alone, but to all people, for it bore witness of the promised Messiah, Jesus Christ, the bedrock of Christian revelation and the foundation of the church, the "New Israel" that had supplanted the old.[6] From this perspective, Judaism, paradoxically, could be at once valued and regarded as passé. It had played an indispensable role in preparing the way for Christian revelation, but now that this cosmically singular event had taken place, Jews were called to convert and blamed when they failed to do so. What is more, early church leaders—beginning with Paul's famous rebuke of Peter in the Letter to the Galatians—repeatedly warned their flocks against relapsing into "Judaized" understandings of the faith.[7] Treatises such as John Chrysostom's *Against the Jews* and others from the patristic era bear witness to this conflicted attitude toward Judaism—a measure of retrospective gratefulness on the one hand, but grave displeasure on the other, for Jews had failed to recognize the promised Messiah.[8] Yet irenicism was not always absent. Justin Martyr's *Dialogue with the Jew Trypho*, for instance, presents a dialogue between a

Christian and Jew remarkable for the cordial way in which the speakers address one another.

By the time of emperors Constantine (272–337) and Theodosius (306–95), the fact that Jews persisted in unbelief only hardened the Christian stance against them. "The victory of the Church [in the empire] signified the demise of Judaism," as Robert Wilken has written. Early Christian thinkers therefore "created a caricature to meet their expectations and refused to look at Judaism for what it really was. . . . It had not come to an end in Jesus, and it was still a force to be reckoned with in the Roman empire."[9] Regrettably, and despite numerous ground-level interactions among Christians and Jews, Christian thinkers' negative attitude toward Jews contributed to later currents of anti-Judaism and anti-Semitism.[10] From a Christian standpoint, any "dialogue" that took place between the two faiths usually began (and ended) with the premise that Jews had obstinately refused to accept God's universal dispensation for humanity. From their standpoint, Jews came to regard Christians as perpetrators of an immense apostasy, unwarrantedly appropriating their own Scripture in support of a mistaken belief.[11]

Early Christian thinkers tended to see Greco-Roman pagan beliefs as misguided and idolatrous, a corrupting influence on the faithful. In his *Preparation for the Gospel*, Eusebius of Caesarea singled out the Hebrew religion as a way station toward Christianity, contrasting it with Greek polytheism, which he saw as erroneous, absurd, even demonic, as were various other religious currents in the ancient world.[12] Gregory the Great adopted a similar line. In his well-known *Life of Saint Benedict*, he portrayed the famous monk fighting against Satan and his demons in his efforts to found the monastery of Monte Cassino on the site of a temple to Apollo.[13] In a famous letter to the abbot Mellitus, Gregory advised that pagan temples in England, although not to be destroyed if they were "well built," should be "converted from the worship of demons to the service of the true God."[14] In taking such a hard line against pagan deities, early Christians regularly saw themselves abiding by God's prohibition to the Israelites against worshipping false gods and idols: "For you shall worship no other god, because the Lord . . . is a jealous God" (Exodus 34:14). A comparable line of reasoning has informed various versions of Christian theological *exclusivism* up to the present.

If early Christians contemned pagan polytheism, they tended to hold pagan philosophy—or at least some of its dominant currents—in a more favorable light.[15] While some followed Tertullian in condemning Greek philosophy root and branch, many sought to take "the spoils of Egypt" (Greek philosophy) and put it to better (Christian) use, as Augustine famously proposed. Of particular importance was the Greek ideal of reason or wisdom (*logos*), which early Christians associated with the divine *Logos*, Christ, as mentioned in the Gospel of John. Justin Martyr saw in Greek philosophy, therefore, the "seminal Word" (*logos spermatikos*), Christ making his presence felt insofar as philosophy sought after truth and virtue; he even believed that the wisdom of pagan philosophers, somehow, had been earlier cribbed from the Hebrew prophets.[16] Perhaps most famously, Augustine in his *Confessions* recounted how he was providentially prepared for his conversion by reading Cicero and Neoplatonic philosophy.[17] For Clement of Alexandria, furthermore, "philosophy was a direct gift of God to the Greeks. . . . Philosophy was to the Greek world what the Law was to the Hebrews, a tutor escorting them to Christ."[18] Since Plato, Aristotle, and others had themselves been critical of pagan polytheism, early Christians did not even have to come up with their own indictment; they could appeal to the Greeks themselves.

The indictment of pagan polytheism, the belief that Judaism had been supplanted, and the (at least partial) embrace of classical philosophy shaped "interreligious" understanding among educated Christians in the period of late antiquity and long afterward. As processes of Christianization proceeded in the early Middle Ages, the worship of the classical gods declined and eventually ceased—even as in the north the showdown between Christ and the Germanic and Norse gods was just heating up.[19]

It merits mentioning that some church fathers and their medieval successors possessed knowledge of religious traditions further afield, of Buddhism and of "Brahman" holy men in India, and likely even of Jain monks, known in the West as gymnosophists (*gymnosophi*), "naked philosophers." This knowledge came largely through secondhand sources, going back to the time of Alexander the Great, who, according to Plutarch, engaged in religious conversation with gymnosophists.[20] Practitioners of these faraway faiths were judged in diverse ways, ranging from contemptible idol worshippers to examples of righteous gentiles. In the popular imagination, the distant East was the land of dog-headed men, strange races, unicorns and griffins, and other exotic phenomena.[21] Firsthand knowledge of South Asian religious traditions would not resume until the westward intrusions of the Mongols and their envoys and the travels of Marco Polo and a handful of other Europeans in the High Middle Ages.[22]

Additionally, it should be remembered that early Christianity itself presents no monolithic voice at this time—and nonclassical religious movements such as Manicheanism and Mithraism arose, spread, and exhibited considerable staying power.[23] Nonorthodox Christian movements such as Arianism, Docetism, Donatism, Pelagianism, and others proliferated during this period. And this is to say nothing of the cleft that opened between the orthodox churches and the so-called Oriental orthodox churches—Armenian, Syriac, Ethiopian, and Coptic—that had dissented from the formulation on Christ at the Council of Chalcedon in 451.[24] Early orthodox Christian apologetic literature attests to this wide scope of religious pluralism. In his "Address on Religious Instruction," for example, Gregory of Nyssa advises that "we must adapt religious instruction to the diversities of teaching. . . . A man of Jewish faith has certain presuppositions; a man reared in Hellenism, others. The Anomoean [a variant of Arianism], the Manichaean, the followers of Marcion . . . have their preconceptions."[25]

The Germanic invasions that eventually toppled the empire in the West brought in still other strains of religious complexity, even if conversion to Christianity—in both orthodox and nonorthodox forms—became widespread among Rome's invaders. With the decline of the empire in the West in the 400s and 500s, it fell to the Byzantine Empire in the East to buttress Christianity with political force.

Farther to the east, it should be noted, nonorthodox versions of Christianity, particularly "Nestorian" or Syriac forms of Christianity, thrived, often interacting with Zoroastrianism, pockets of rabbinic Judaism, pagan beliefs, and, still farther east, with Buddhism and various "shamanistic" beliefs of the central Asian steppe and the churning religious cauldron of the Indian subcontinent.[26] Indeed, the Persian Empire and the ancient Silk Road (ca. 300s to 600s) doubtlessly witnessed countless religious interactions, and likely some we might label "dialogues," most of which, however, are buried in the sands of time.[27]

Islam, Eastern Christianity, and Dialogue

Against this set of historical circumstances, the world witnessed a religious novum of profound consequence: the rise of Islam. As is well known, Islam spread rapidly after the Prophet's death in 632 CE. The Persian Sasanian and the Greek Byzantine Empires had exhausted themselves in a power struggle over territories in southwestern Asia.[28] This allowed Islam to occupy a power vacuum in the many areas where it spread, eventually taking form politically in the Umayyad Caliphate (661–750), with Damascus as its capital.[29] These events triggered Zoroastrianism's rather sudden dispersion and decline—an epochal development in the history of the ancient world.[30] Portentously, Christians and Muslims often met one another on the battlefield before any sustained intellectual exchange took place. In areas ruled by Muslims, Christians and Jews were routinely given "dhimmi" status as "people of the book" and paid a poll tax (*jizya*) for their protection. While many Christians interpreted Islam's spread in apocalyptic terms, some Eastern churches actually welcomed Muslim rule as a relief from the yoke of Byzantium. What is important for our purposes is that from this time up to the modern era, the principal religious actors in the greater Mediterranean and European worlds were threefold: Jews, Christians, and Muslims, the so-called Abrahamic faiths.[31] Nevertheless, older beliefs—Zoroastrianism, Manicheanism, pagan polytheism, and more—endured, contributing to a climate of considerable if ebbing diversity from the 600s to the 1000s. And this is to say nothing of splits within the Abrahamic faiths, not least the Sunni-Shia rupture and the split in Judaism opened up by the Kairite movement.[32]

The Qur'an and Sira and Hadith literatures presuppose a diverse religious environment filled with "inter-religious encounter and debate."[33] The phrase "people of the book" (*ahl al-kitab*) is used over fifty times in the Qur'an to describe Christians, Jews, and to some extent Zoroastrians.[34] In the Qur'an, Muhammad is instructed "[to] invite [others] to the way of your Lord with wisdom and good advice and dispute with them in a manner that is best" (Q 16:25). In accepting the message of the Prophet, Muslims were enjoined to forsake all other gods, join the community of true believers, and issue a summons or invitation (*da'wa*) to others to embrace Islam. Da'wa is a key concept for our purposes. Although in many contexts it entailed preaching Islam to unbelievers, it also provided justification for formal interreligious engagements and disputations (*munazara*) that took place in the Umayyad and Abbasid Caliphate (750–1258), sometimes involving Christians and Jews. Often highly anticipated public spectacles, these religious disputes took "the form of oral debates between proponents of competing positions."[35] According to Avril Powell, significant continuities exist between early Islamic munazara and Emperor Akbar's interreligious forum (Ibadat Khana), which we shall explore later.[36]

It would, of course, be a stretch to characterize early medieval interactions among the three Abrahamic faiths as dialogue in the modern sense, but various polemical exchanges bear witness to efforts to make sense of the alterity of rival faiths and to explain one's own position.[37] Among the first Christians to comment on Islam was the Syrian monk John of Damascus (676–749), learned in Greek and Arabic, perhaps active at the Mar Sabas monastery in Palestine but also a financial administrator for the Umayyad caliphs. In his opus *The Font of Knowledge*, under a section titled "Heresies," he treated Islam as "the superstition of the Ishmaelites which to this day prevails and keeps people in error."[38] He also wrote a short polemical work, *Disputation between a Saracen and a Christian*, in which the Christian interlocutor defends Christianity against Muslim criticism.

Ishmaelite or *Saracen*, not *Muslim*, were the terms of choice for Christian commentators. The former comes from the biblical story of Ishmael and Isaac; the latter, the more common term in the Middle Ages, is of obscure origin, already applied to Arabs before the rise of Islam, and generally thought to derive from the Greek *Sarakēnos*, which perhaps in turn came from the Arabic *šarķī*, meaning "eastern" or "sunrise." Medieval commentators, however, erroneously associated the term with the biblical Sarah.[39] *Hagarenes*, from the biblical Hagar, was another term of choice, used, for example, in a "disputation between John [the Miaphysite Patriarch of Antioch] and the Emir," preserved in an undated Syriac manuscript from the 700s.[40]

An early medieval exchange of considerable significance took place between the Byzantine emperor Leo II (r. 717–41) and the Umayyad caliph, Omar II (r. 717–20), according to the tenth-century Armenian chronicler Ghevond and the Byzantine chronicler Theophanes. Shortly after an unsuccessful attempt to besiege Constantinople, Omar sent a solemn appeal to Leo, asking him to explain the Christian faith. "Why do [Christians] worship three gods? . . . Why do they adore the bones of apostles and prophets, and also pictures and the cross?" the caliph asked. In his response, Leo, evincing considerable knowledge of the Bible and the Qur'an, asserted that Islam was the younger of the two faiths and replete with secondhand distortions.[41] But Leo also admitted that both communities sought to worship the same God and both faced similar problems, such as divisions within their ranks.[42]

The Arab-speaking "Melkite" bishop of Harran, Theodore Abu-Qurrah (ca. 750–ca. 820), represents another notable example of early medieval Christian engagement with Islam and other religious traditions.[43] In a number of treatises written in dialogue form, Abu-Qurrah, like his teacher John of Damascus, expressed a negative attitude toward Islam. But the arguments he deployed, as John Meyendorff notes, "are conceived in such a manner as to be understood by the opponents; they correspond to an attempt at real conversation." He tried, for instance, to explain the doctrine of the Trinity—ridiculed by Muslims as blasphemous tritheism—by arguing that the Qur'an remains one even if many copies of it exist. He sought to explain Christian teachings on the Eucharist by deploying medical imagery. He argued against polygamy by holding up the God-ordained monogamous bliss that Adam and Eve enjoyed in paradise, contrasting this against quarrels and scenes of jealousy in a harem.[44]

In one remarkable treatise, *God and the True Religion*, Abu-Qurrah likened the human condition to a sick son who had traveled far away from his father, a king. Knowing that his son was ill, the king sent a messenger to recommend the correct medicine. Unfortunately, the king had many enemies who sent false messengers with erroneous recommendations. Standing before the son, they all "began to declare . . . the others to be liars, while at the same time affirming themselves to be the true messengers. As for the [actual] true messenger, he was right there among them, declaring them to be a liar. He had [in the eyes of the son] become as one of them, with nothing to set him apart." The analogy should be clear: the messengers are various prophets, founders of religious movements, and the messages are their sacred books. To deliver the son from this dilemma of religious pluralism, Abu-Qurrah strikingly suggests that "we must lay the books to one side and inquire of the mind." In essence, he makes an argument from "nature"; once we figure out by the "mind" what human nature and its specific sickness are, we can more readily recognize the right messenger.[45] From this starting point, Abu-Qurrah goes on to defend Christianity as offering the most compelling interpretation of human nature while also supplying a remedy for its flaws. And while Islam was Abu-Qurrah's principal worry, he sought to defend Christianity against Judaism, Manicheanism, Marcionism, and various sects of Gnosticism as well.[46]

Abu-Qurrah took part in actual discussions with Muslims in the context of a *majlis* (literally, "place of sitting").[47] More broadly, the term refers to a salon-like session in a caliph or an emir's court in which scholars participated in debate (*jadal*) and disputation (*munazara*).[48] Often these included only Muslim scholars debating the finer points of Islamic theology and law, but beyond the example of Abu-Qurrah, ample evidence indicates that Christians and Jews sometimes took part as well, turning the majlis into "a forum in which different religions were discussed."[49] The early Abbasid Caliphate was an especially fertile time for such interactions. Its third caliph, al-Mahdī (r. 755–85), in fact took part himself in a two-day religious discussion with Timothy, patriarch of the Eastern church in Iraq, in which the usual topics, such as the nature of Christ and the Trinity, were discussed.[50]

Under Caliph Harun al-Rashid (r. 786–809) and his son Caliph Al-Ma'mun (r. 813–33), the fabled House of Wisdom (*bayt al-hikma*) in Baghdad was established and became a major intellectual center during what is often referred to as Islam's Golden Age.[51] Jews and Christians engaged in scholarship and works of translations there alongside Muslims, and sometimes they came into fruitful dialogue with one another.[52] The ethos of the Abbasid *majalis* and the House of Wisdom are well captured by words attributed to the caliph in one of Abu-Qurrah's works. When acrimony between Christian and Muslim interlocutors threatened to end conversation, the caliph intervened: "This is a court of justice and equity: none shall be wronged therein. So advance your arguments and answer without fear, for there is none here who do not speak well of you. . . . Let everyone speak who has the wisdom to demonstrate the truth of his religion."[53] A tenth-century visitor from the Maghreb was taken aback by what he discovered in Baghdad; not only were Muslims engaged in debate, but so were "unbelievers, magicians, materialists, atheists, Jews, and Christians, in short unbelievers of all kinds."[54] In the later Abbasid era, the redoubtable Jewish scholar Ibn Kammuna produced his *Examination of the Three Faiths*, an early instance, we might say, of the comparative study of religion based on extensive conversations among Jews, Christians, and Muslims.[55]

The ethos of the Abbasid Caliphate spilled over into the caliphates of Fatimid (909–1171) and Ayyubid (1171–1250) in Egypt, which witnessed various "interreligious" disputes and dialogues, as attested to by Muslim, Christian, and Jewish sources, even if the evidence is often scanty.[56] Francis of Assisi probably participated in one of these (as we shall shortly see) when he traveled to Egypt on a missionary errand during the Fifth Crusade (1217–21).

The intellectual ferment of the early Abbasid period witnessed the production of one "dialogue" in particular destined to have significant influence in both the Christian East and the West: the *Risalat al-Kindi*, or *Apology of al-Kindi* (ca. ninth century), a critique of Islam and an apology for Christianity. Written in the form of a dialogue between a Muslim and a Christian, who are referred to respectively as "Servant of Allah, son of Ishmael" and "Servant of the Messiah, son of Isaac," the work probably reflects the contents of actual discussions at the Abbasid court, although the Christian author/editor took considerable liberties with the material. The Muslim first invites the Christian to convert to Islam. The Christian declines and in turn invites the Muslim to convert. The Christian response then comprises some six-sevenths of the text. In it, the Christian disparages Muhammad's status as a prophet and criticizes several key Muslim teachings before mounting a defense of Christianity, focusing on the doctrine of the Trinity. While the work is highly polemical, the author displays extraordinary knowledge of the Qur'an, the life of Muhammad, and early Islamic history. Produced probably in the 800s, it was translated into Latin in the twelfth century and became a source of knowledge about Islam for learned Europeans. After circulating in manuscript form for several centuries, it was published in print for the first time in the sixteenth century with a preface by none other than Martin Luther.[57]

The *Risalat al-Kindi* was also known in the Byzantine Empire, which, due to its geography, witnessed considerable engagement with Islam in the early centuries of Islam's expansion, as we have already seen. From the ninth to thirteenth centuries, Byzantine scholars such as Samona Gazes, Euthemios Zigabenos, Niketas Choniates, and Bartholomew of Edessa cultivated knowledge of Islam and the Qur'an.[58] One figure that deserves notice is Nicetas Byzantius. After receiving a letter from the caliph summoning him to convert to Islam, Emperor Michael III (r. 842–67) turned to Byzantius to offer a rebuttal, which he dutifully did in two letters. During the mid-800s, moreover, he wrote a lengthy Christian treatment on the Qur'an, relying on a Greek translation of unknown provenance.[59] Not surprisingly, he begins with a long defense of the Trinity. Thereafter, he devotes thirty chapters to a refutation of the Qur'an. Regrettably, Byzantius passed down several canards that would long shape Christian engagement with Islam. To offer but one example, he ridiculed Muslims for believing that humankind came from a "leech," a mistranslation of an Arabic word (in sura 96) that actually means "particle of congealed blood."[60] Eastern Christian engagement with Islam in the next several centuries frequently looked back to Byzantius for guidance.

If I may skip ahead in time, the Ottoman threat of the fourteenth and fifteenth centuries gave rise to a new phase of Byzantine-Muslim engagement. The monk and archbishop of Thessaloniki, Gregory Palamas (d. 1359), for example, traveled in 1354 to Turkish-occupied Asia Minor on a political errand, during which he was detained by Turkish forces and forced to spend a year in captivity. During this time, he frequently came into dialogue with Muslims, and at least on one occasion with Jews too. In these, although stridently expressing Christian positions, he sought to make the case that genuine conversation must reflect reason (*logos*) and wisdom (*sophia*), since these were God's own traits. Failing to convert his captors, he extolled the virtues of "friendly coexistence."[61]

The emperor John Cantacuzens (d. 1383) composed several apologetic works directed against Islam. He claimed that Christians stood on higher ground for being more willing to enter into dialogue than their Muslim counterparts: "The Muslims hinder their own from engaging with the Christians. . . . The Christians . . . do not prevent anyone from engaging in dialogue, but with permission and authority, each one of them engages in dialogue with all those who are willing and desire to be engaged in dialogue."[62] Presumably, Muslims held a different view of themselves.

As Ottoman power waxed, the fifteenth century witnessed perhaps the most learned Byzantine commentator on Islam: Emperor Manuel II Palaiologos (d. 1425), who entered into direct conversations with Muslim scholars around 1391/92 in Ankara. Based on these conversations, but almost certainly mixing fact and fantasy, Manuel subsequently published *Dialogue Held with a Persian, the Worthy Mouterizes of Ankara of Galatia*. In it, he designates himself as "the Christian philosopher" conversing with a learned Muslim scholar (*müderris*). The debate is comprised of twenty-six exchanges over disputed theological matters, with Manuel at every juncture indicating who won and who lost. At the outset, Manuel insists that dialogue between the two faiths must be free from the threat of violence and based on reason (*logos*), for how could a righteous and good God, he asks his interlocutors, willfully contravene reason? Not surprisingly, Manuel wins the debate in its written form (whether or not he won the actual one) and portrays the müderris on the brink of conversion by the end of the dialogue.[63] This little-known exchange made the headlines in recent years when Pope Benedict XVI invoked Manuel's name at a lecture held in 2006 at Regensburg University in Germany, in which the pope appeared to imply that Christians were more willing than Muslims to base interreligious dialogue on reason.[64]

To be sure, much more could be said about Byzantium's centuries-long interactions with Islam. But permit me to quote Anastasios Yannoulatos, who has nicely captured the general shape of things: Byzantium's "meeting with Islam not only took the form of a polemical clash and confrontation, but also evolved into many centuries of silent coexistence, often articulated on the intellectual level with a concrete form of theological dialogue that sought to define the differences and the positions of the two religious forms and experiences."[65] Something similar, I should add, could be said about Byzantine interactions with Jews, even if patristic-era accusations against Judaism enduringly shaped the Eastern theological milieu, and the records of Jewish-Byzantine interactions are much scantier than Muslim-Byzantine ones.[66]

Western Europe and the Religions

While Byzantine civilization witnessed the earliest intellectual engagement with Islam—which continued under drastically altered circumstances after the loss of Constantinople in 1453—the Latin West had its own encounters and exchanges with Muslims—and Jews. Most of these could hardly be counted as genuine dialogue in the modern sense, but notable, suggestive exceptions exist.

The much-discussed *convivencia* ("coexistence") in Muslim Spain or Al-Andalus is one well-known example. A fertile if sometimes romanticized period of intellectual exchange among Christians, Jews, and Muslims, this convivencia lasted in some form or another from the time of the Umayyad conquest of the Iberian Peninsula in the eighth century until, in greatly diminished form, the expulsion of the Jews and the fall the Emirate of Granada in 1492. Like Baghdad in the East, the cities of Cordoba and Seville emerged as major centers of learning and interreligious interaction. Here, the recovery and translation of classical authors, notably Aristotle, left an enduring legacy on Western thought, especially through the mediation of figures such as Thomas Aquinas and his Scholastic peers.[67] Arabic translations of Christian Scripture and other sacred texts were also undertaken. And not least, the diverse intellectual environment of Al-Andalus helped give rise to the thought of the Jewish polymath Maimonides (ca. 1135–1204), a figure of enduring interest from an interreligious standpoint.[68]

The period of the Crusades, from the eleventh through the fifteenth century, constitutes another (mostly unhappy) chapter in the story of Christian and Muslim interactions. While Western scholars during this time were often far more interested in refuting than understanding "religious others," some notable examples of irenic engagement exist, even if polemical or proselytizing motives were usually present. In 1143, for example, at the request of Peter the Venerable, abbot of Cluny, the English scholar Robert of Ketton produced the first Latin translation of the Qur'an. Regrettably, many Latin word choices in the translation presented Islam in a poor light.[69] But from this time, Western scholars, at least in principle, had the ability to read the Qur'an for themselves. Peter himself wrote two works on Islam. In one, addressed to Muslims at large, he came close to sounding sorry about the Crusades: "[I] do not attack you, as some of us often do, by arms, but by words, not by force, but by reason, not in hatred, but in love."[70] Elsewhere, Peter deplored the Crusades, convinced that his co-religionists did not fully grasp the gravity of sending slain Muslims to eternal perdition.[71]

In 1218–19 a remarkable event took place. Francis of Assisi and a fellow friar persuaded the papal legate Cardinal Pelagio Galvani to allow them to accompany the armies of western Europe to Damietta, Egypt, during the Fifth Crusade. For years, Francis had yearned for an audience with the Ayyubid sultan of Egypt, al-Malik al-Kamil (r. 1218–38), renowned for his wisdom and curiosity. The two mendicants knew dangers awaited, but they persisted, even welcoming the prospects of martyrdom. At one point, Francis, as quixotically as unsuccessfully, tried to stop the crusaders from fighting at the battle of Damietta. During the conflict the two mendicants were arrested, roughed up by Arab soldiers, and eventually taken to the sultan, a nephew of the fabled warrior Saladin. After Francis and the sultan attempted and failed to convert one another, the two mendicants ended up staying in the sultan's learned court for several days, discussing prayer, theology, and the mystical life, among other topics. When Francis left, al-Kamil gave him an ivory trumpet, which is still preserved in the crypt of the Basilica in Assisi. Giotto rendered the remarkable encounter in a fresco cycle of Francis's life; Bonaventure mentions it his life of Francis, as does Dante in his *Paradiso*.[72] Although the sources lend themselves to different interpretations of what actually took place between Francis and the sultan, Paul Moses fairly concludes that the encounter nonetheless "endures as a memorable forerunner of peaceful dialogue between Christians and

Francis and the sultan of Egypt, depicted in Giotto's fresco cycle of St. Francis's life in the Upper Church of the Basilica of St. Francis in Assisi, Italy, ca. 1297. (Image courtesy of Wikimedia Commons.)

Muslims."[73] What is more, mission to Muslims became a fixed aspect of the Franciscan *vita apostolica.* As the earliest extant version of the Franciscan Rule (1221) puts it: "Any brother who, by divine inspiration, desires to go among the Saracens and other nonbelievers should go with the permission of his minister and servant. And the minister should give permission and not oppose them."[74] This led to no small number of Franciscans traveling to Muslim lands to bear witness of their faith.[75]

The Franciscan missionary impulse led the Flemish mendicant William of Rubruck (ca. 1220–ca. 1293) to journey beyond Muslim lands to the Mongol court at Karakorum in present-day Mongolia.[76] A long-standing threat to both Europe and the Muslim world, Mongol forces altered the course of history when they sacked Baghdad in 1258, effectively ending the Abbasid Caliphate. At Karakorum, at the request of the Mongol chief, Möngke Khan (r. 1251–59), the intrepid friar engaged in a remarkable "conference" (*collatio*) that included a Latin Christian (Rubruck), Nestorian or Syriac Christians, Muslims, and Buddhists, who were likely from Tibet.[77] (This is the first known formal dialogue between a European Christian and Buddhists in world history.) The Syriac Christians wanted to debate with the Muslims first, but Rubruck, making ad hoc common cause with the "Nestorians" (heretical from his perspective), argued that the two Christian parties should engage the Buddhists first. Worried about lack of education among the Syriac Christians, Rubruck even staged a mock debate with them before the formal session, playing the role of a Buddhist and peppering them with possible questions.[78] (What he actually knew of Buddhists' beliefs and practices is unclear and likely minimal.)

The actual debate lasted an entire day. At the outset, the great khan laid the ground rules through his secretaries, including the directive "that no man should be so bold as to make provocative or insulting remarks to his opponent, and that no one is to cause any commotion that might obstruct these proceedings, on pain of death."[79] A large audience had assembled, as Rubruck's account of his travels records: "A great many people were present, as each party had summoned the wiser men of the nation, and many others too had gathered."[80]

A Buddhist opened by requesting that they first discuss whether the world was created and what happened to people after death. To this, Rubruck replied: "Friend, this is not the proper beginning. All things come from God. He is the fount and head of all. Therefore, let us speak first about God, concerning whom you differ from us."[81] The khan's secretaries supported this suggestion and apparently the Buddhists consented too, so thus the conversation began on the question of God. Rubruck then set forth that "that there is only one God, and that He is one in a perfect unity. What do you believe?" "It is fools," one Buddhist responded, "who claim there is only one God. Wise men say that there are several. . . . There are different gods in different regions," adding: "There is one supreme god in Heaven, of whose origin we are still ignorant, with ten others under him and one of lowest rank beneath them; while on earth they are without number." Some wrangling over the merits of monotheism and the origins of evil ensued before Rubruck asked if their unknown supreme god was omnipotent. This question was met with silence until the khan's secretaries mandated a response. "Finally he [a Buddhist] gave the answer that no god is all-powerful, at which all the Saracens burst out in laughter." Rubruck's account of the debate's conclusion follows:

> At this point I made way for them [that is, for the Syriac Christians to speak]. But when they sought to argue with the Saracens, the latter replied: "We concede that your religious rule [*lex*] is true and that all in the Gospel is true; and therefore we have no wish to debate any issue with you." And they admitted that in all their prayers they beg God to grant that they may die a Christian death. There was present an old priest of the Iugur [Muslim] sect, which holds that there is one God but nevertheless makes idols; and they had a long discussion with him, relating everything down to the coming of Christ in judgement, and also using analogies to explain the Trinity to him and to the Saracens. Everybody listened without challenging a single word. But for all that no one said, "I believe, and wish to become a Christian." When it was all over, the Nestorians and Saracens alike sang in loud voices, while the *tuins* [Buddhists] remained silent; and after that everyone drank heavily.[82]

Unfortunately, Rubruck's account is the sole source of this remarkable event, so it is hard to know exactly what to believe and what to make of the abrupt, mirthful ending, in which Rubruck's position seems vindicated and the Muslims pray to die as Christians even as the Buddhists remain silent and fail to convert. This conclusion certainly raises many questions, even if the general contours of the discussion appear plausible. We do know from other sources that the khan's court—due to the Mongols' highly pragmatic, often syncretistic approach to different faiths—frequently witnessed discussions among religious groups.[83] Major Taoist-Buddhist debates, for instance, took place in Karakorum in 1255 and 1259.[84] Kwand Amir, a Persian observer at the court of Khublai Khan (r. 1260–94), successor of Möngke, recorded the following: "Khublai Khan used to . . . gather the *ulema* [religious scholars] of Islam, the learned of the Jews, Christian monks, and the wise men of China and hold deliberations, for he enjoyed listening to philosophical and religious debates."[85] Regrettably, detailed records of these discussions are for the most part lost, or were never recorded in the first place—although their legacy arguably lived on in the Mughal (a corruption of the word *Mongol*) emperor Akbar, a descendant of Tamerlane.[86]

The khan himself did not attend the debate in which Rubruck participated, but he met with the friar the next day. During the exchange, Möngke expounded his own creed, which might be seen as a blueprint of the Mongol's pluralist court policy toward different faiths: "[We Mongols] believe that there is but one God, through whom we live and through whom we die. . . . But just as God gave diverse fingers to the hand, so did he give diverse ways (*diversas vias*) [of belief] to men."[87]

Knowledge about the influence of Rubruck's written account of his mission is scant. Although the work circulated in several manuscripts in the thirteenth and fourteenth centuries, it appears not to have been widely read. One major exception, however, was the English philosopher and Franciscan friar Roger Bacon (ca. 1220–92), who read it enthusiastically and even met with Rubruck in Paris. By all accounts an idiosyncratic thinker, Bacon constructed a "science of religion" in which he sought to explain the diversity of faiths as a result of astrological influences and then to situate them in a Christian eschatological scheme of world history. He felt that the Crusades had largely failed and that rational argumentation, in the spirit of Rubruck, offered a more high-minded approach to converting infidels. "The rational soul [in all human beings] was born to know and to love. . . . Truth however can be perceived in a sect (*secta*) to the extent in which all sects contain knowledge of God in whatever way because all sects (*sectae*) refer to God."[88] What is more, Bacon argued that all faiths were in various stages of progressing toward God; Christianity just happened to be well ahead of the pack. Put differently, he conceived of other faiths not as idolatrous antitheses to Christianity, but as garbled, imperfect forms of it.[89] A variant of this line of reasoning, as we shall see later, resurfaced in the modern era among both liberal Protestants and Catholics as they sought to formulate an inclusivist theology of other faiths and justify interreligious dialogue.

If the medieval Franciscan strategy toward non-Christians tended toward missionary errands that often courted martyrdom, another leading strategy, one associated most closely if not exclusively with the Dominicans, sought to engage non-Christians in formal debates or "disputations" that centered on the question of which faith accorded most felicitously with human reason.[90] But reason had limits. In Dominican theology, Christianity was regarded as consistent with reason, but not provable by it. Otherwise, faith would be unnecessary. Even so, if deployed judiciously, reason could be harnessed to point out the irrationality of rival creeds. This construal of the relationship between faith and reason served as a general framework for dialogue with Jews and Muslims. One can find it articulated in Thomas Aquinas's well-known *Summa contra gentiles* (certainly written with Muslims and Jews in mind), but also in one of his shorter treatises, *Reasons for the Faith against Muslim Objections*. There, in a chapter entitled "How to Argue with Unbelievers" (*qualiter sit disputandum contra infideles*), Aquinas assayed:

> [I] wish to warn you that in the disputations with the unbelievers about articles of the faith, you should not try to prove the faith by necessary reason. This would belittle the sublime nature of faith, the truth of which exceeds not only human minds but also those of angels; we believe in them only because they are revealed by God. Yet whatever comes

> from the Supreme Truth cannot be false, and what is not false cannot be repudiated by any necessary reason. Just as our Faith cannot be proved by necessary reasons, because it exceeds the human mind, so because of its truth it cannot be refuted by any necessary reason. So any Christian disputing about the articles of Faith should not try to prove the faith, but defend the faith. Thus blessed Peter [1 Peter 3:15] did not say "Always have your proof," but "have your answer ready," so that reason can show that what the Catholic faith holds is not false.[91]

Reliant on such reasoning, Dominican friars, and others cribbing from them, sought to expose the irrationality of rival faiths while vindicating the compatibility—if not the absolute demonstrability—of Christianity with reason. What is more, in the 1200s Dominicans were at the forefront in setting up schools to promote knowledge of Arabic, Aramaic, and Hebrew as well as the study of Jewish and Islamic holy texts, so that Christian clergy could engage "infidels" on a more knowledgeable basis.[92] During this time, several debates took place between Dominicans and Muslims, especially in the recently re-Christianized parts of Spain. Two Muslims, 'Abid Allâh al-Asîr and Muhammad al-Qaysî, produced anti-Christian polemics purported to be based on actual debates that had taken place. Al-Qaysî left a partial record of one of these debates.[93] Roughly concurrently, Dominican missionaries such as Ramond de Penyafort, Ramond Martini, Alfonso Buenhombre, and Riccoldo da Montecroce deployed their skills in rational argumentation against Muslims in northern Africa and elsewhere. The Florentine Montecroce in particular became renowned for his knowledge of the Qur'an and skills in debating Muslim savants.[94]

Theological melees with Jews took place more commonly, especially in medieval Spain, even if the outcome was sinisterly and regrettably predetermined. Often elaborate affairs, these involved learned rabbis pitted against Christian clergy and theologians, and they were usually staged before a secular ruler.[95] Among the several that took place, two stand out in significance: the Paris Disputation of 1240 and the Barcelona Disputation of 1263. The former took place at the royal court of Louis IX in June 1240. With assurances of protection from the crown, four leading rabbis, led by Rabbi Yehiel ben Joseph of Paris, were asked to defend the Talmud against charges leveled against it by one Nicholas Donin.[96] A Christian convert from Judaism, Donin had sent a letter itemizing putatively anti-Christian blasphemies and other imbecilities (*stultitiae*) in the Talmud to Pope Gregory IX, who in turn sent letters of warning to all the monarchs of Christendom. The actual debate lasted several days, during which the rabbis presented a spirited defense against the charges. But their defeat was a foregone conclusion. Shortly after the disputation ended, a Christian commission, including the bishop of Paris, condemned the Talmud and other Jewish manuscripts to be burned on the streets of Paris. By making more widely known the gap between Christian and Jewish belief—and by reminding European Christians that Judaism was no "Old Testament" holdover but a living tradition in the midst of Christendom—this disputation played no small role in stoking currents of anti-Judaism that began to swell in Europe at this time, as seen in activities of the Inquisition.[97]

The Barcelona Disputation of 1263 excited even greater interest. By comparison, the Paris Disputation appears more of an interrogation than a debate, and thus Barcelona more fittingly claims our attention as a distant harbinger of modern-day interreligious dialogue.[98] What is more, we have more complete accounts of the 1263 debate, in Latin and Hebrew; the latter is even written in dialogue form. The debate lasted four days, 20–24 July 1263, and pitted the Dominican Pablo Christiani against Rabbi Moses Nahmanides, among the most learned Jewish scholars of the Middle Ages.[99] Organized by the aforementioned Ramond de Penyafort, the superior of Christiani and the confessor of King James I of Aragon, it took place in the royal court. The king took a personal interest in the affair, and Nahmanides, according to the rabbi's own account, had been given "permission to speak freely." At several points, however, Nahmanides sought to halt the discussion, worried about reprisals against the Jewish community. But the king insisted that the disputation continue.[100]

The debate turned on three topics: whether the prophesied Messiah had appeared, whether the Messiah is divine or a human being, and whether Jews or Christians held the true faith. Unlike the interrogative spirit of the Paris Disputation, the Barcelona event witnessed a more open exchange, with each discussant learnedly appealing to both Jewish and Christian sacred texts to make their points. In customary fashion, Christiani charged that Nahmanides held an irrational, superseded faith. He also felt that the Talmud and other classical rabbinical texts could even be enlisted to support Christianity. But Nahmanides proved hard to pin down, and the rabbi ably appealed to reason in his own cause. In an exchange about the Incarnation, for example, Nahmanides claimed that only folly could lead one to believe that "the Creator of Heaven and Earth resorted to the womb of a certain Jewish lady, grew there for nine months and was born as an infant, and afterwards grew up and was betrayed into the hand of his enemies who sentenced him to death." Priests, he told Christiani, had "filled your brain and the marrow of your bones with this doctrine" and only from long "accustomed habit," and not from "reason," do people believe such outlandish teachings.[101]

Although the Dominicans claimed victory at the debate's conclusion, Nahmanides had performed excellently, as both the Latin and Hebrew accounts attest—even if the former also contains much that is unflattering about the rabbi. Impressed, King James awarded Nahmanides three hundred gold coins and declared that never before had he heard "an unjust cause so nobly defended." Shortly after the debate, the king even attended the synagogue in Barcelona—something practically unheard of during the Middle Ages—to pay respect to his Jewish subjects.[102]

Even as their side officially prevailed, several Dominicans were displeased with Christiani's performance. Ramond Martini in fact decided to take up the pen and write *Pugio fidei* ("Dagger of the Faith"), a Dominican handbook for future debates with Jews. He organized the work with the debate of 1263 in mind, specifically trying to parry the arguments made by Nahmanides. The aggressive purpose of the *Pugio fidei* is clear: Dominicans were to seek out Jews, whether in Europe or as missionaries abroad, and force them into debate, attacking the heart of their teaching based on their own learned study of it.[103] In Europe, subsequent debates took place—notably at Tortosa, Bonn, Rome, and Hanover. But for intellectual firepower and political prominence, few could rival Barcelona, which has been described by one scholar as "the greatest confrontation between Christianity and Judaism of the Middle Ages."[104] (In 1986, a movie was made about the disputation, with Christopher Lee [Saruman in the *Lord of the Rings* films] playing Nahmanides.)

In addition to actual disputations, the Middle Ages witnessed the production of numerous "disputatio" or dialogues, a literary genre for those writing apologetically on interreligious topics. Examples include Peter Abelard's *Dialogue between a Philosopher, a Jew, and a Christian;* Rupert of Deutz's *Dialogue between a Christian and a Jew;* Gilbert Crispin's *Dialogue between a Jew and a Christian concerning the Christian Faith* and *Disputation of a Christian and a Heathen on the Faith of Christ;* and Peter Alphonsi's *Dialogue with the Jew Moses*, among several others.[105]

Although Christian theologians produced the majority of these, several Jews and Muslims wrote them as well. Judah Halevi's well-known apologetic work *Kuzari*, written between 1130 and 1140, provides a Jewish example. In it, the so-called king of the Khazars dreams that his thoughts are pleasing to God, but not his actions; and he is commanded in the dream to find out what truly pleases God. This leads him "to ponder over the different beliefs and faiths," and eventually to engage in a series of short dialogues in turns with a Hellenistic philosopher, a Christian scholar, and a Muslim imam before he is finally won over by the arguments of a Jewish sage.[106] A Muslim example of the genre is Ibn Taymiyya's *The Correct Answer to Those Who Changed the Religion* [din] *of Christ* (1317), in which the author appeals to "sound rational argumentation and correctly revealed knowledge" against people of faith who are too quick to rely on "extraordinary wonders" and bogus scriptural interpretations.[107] In all of these "dialogues," the faiths of the religious opposition and/or the outlook of a generic "pagan philosopher" are usually presented in an unflattering light while the faith of the author winds up robustly vindicated.[108] Thus understood, one could hardly describe these works as fair-minded, even as they seek to simulate (and to some degree reflect the existence of) real conversations about genuine religious differences.

Pioneers: Ramon Llull and Nicholas of Cusa

But two important examples deviate from the general template and merit a lingering glance: Ramon Llull's *Book of the Gentile and the*

Three Wise Men (ca. 1274–76) and, jumping ahead in time, Nicholas of Cusa's *On the Peace of Faith* (ca. 1453), written directly after the fall of Constantinople at the hand of the Ottoman Turks. The latter work, in fact, merits singling out as the truest Western medieval forerunner, even if only in literary form, of what today we would recognize as interfaith or interreligious dialogue.

But Ramon Llull (ca. 1232–ca. 1315) is no slight figure in the history of dialogue. Born in Palma on the island of Majorca (which had recently been wrested from Muslim rule by the kingdom of Aragon), Llull led a life at once conventional and dissolute, according to his biography, *Vita coaetanea*, compiled by admirers toward the end of his life. At this time, Majorca had emerged as a bustling crossroads of trade and culture, with roughly one-third of its inhabitants being Muslim slaves. In 1263, the same year as the Disputation of Barcelona, Llull experienced a vision in which Christ on the Cross, suspended in midair, appeared to him. The vision recurred six times, he later claimed, and resulted in him leaving friends and family to pursue a devout life, eventually becoming a Franciscan tertiary. The visions also led him to formulate three life goals: (1) to die in service to God while seeking to convert pagans and especially "Saracens," (2) to establish monastery schools that would teach foreign languages to enable missionary work, and (3) to write a book of apologetics. To prepare himself for these tasks, he lived a life of solitude for nine years, during which he learned Arabic and read deeply in Christian, Islamic, and Jewish theology as well as in science and classical philosophy.[109]

In 1274, while at a hermitage on Puig da Randa, Llull wrote the first of several works outlining his so-called art (*ars*). Esoteric and complex, if not downright baffling, Llull's "art" was a system using semi-mechanical techniques combined with symbolic notation and diagrams intended to serve as a basis for apologetics in addition to being applicable to other aspects of human inquiry.[110] While the details of this abstruse system need not detain us, what merits noting is that Llull, departing from the Dominican point of view, felt that faith was in fact demonstrable by reason if the right methods for apprehending truth were employed. Too long had disputants of different faiths appealed to sacred texts and authorities, Llull held; this had only produced interminable wrangling, with each side claiming victory. "There is no end to disputes based on authorities," as he succinctly put it.[111] Llull sought a better way, one based on general human reason, which could prove, first, the necessary truths of monotheism (which all Abrahamic faiths shared) and, second, the ultimate truths of Christianity. For much of his life, Llull purveyed his art before kings, abbots, bishops, and even popes—often disappointed that he never obtained the sympathetic hearing that he felt he deserved. He also feverishly expounded his views, writing no fewer than 265 works by the time of his death—most of them in some way connected to his art.[112]

Llull journeyed to Muslim lands on several occasions, according to his *Vita*. In 1291, he traveled to Tunis and announced that he was prepared to convert to the "sect of Mohammed" if the Muslims he encountered could prove Islam superior to Christianity. He also claimed that he could "clearly prove" the truth of Christianity "using arguments based on a certain Art divinely revealed, as it is believed, to a Christian hermit [himself] not long ago, if you [Muslims] would care to discuss these things calmly with me for a few days."[113] After entering into conversation with several Muslim scholars, the *Vita* recounts, he was expelled from Tunis because the authorities there feared he might undermine Islam. Not one to be easily dissuaded, Llull returned to Tunis on two separate occasions, in 1307 and 1314, but did not make much headway. Whether or not the *Vita* is historically accurate is hard to tell; but it does convey Llull's dogged sense of mission, to Muslims foremost, but also to Jews, whom he engaged on several occasions.[114]

And this brings us to his *Book of the Gentile and the Three Wise Men*, written in the mid-1270s, first published in Arabic and then Catalan, Llull's native tongue. A major inspiration for Nicholas of Cusa, as we shall see, the *Book of the Gentile* is a landmark work in the history of interreligious dialogue and one, as indicated, that does not conform to the harshly polemical pattern of the dialogue genre.[115]

The work is comprised of four books and includes a prologue and an epilogue. In the prologue, Llull introduces readers to "the Gentile" who, although learned in philosophy, is perplexed about religious matters. Fearful of death and the fate of his soul, the Gentile becomes pensive and anxious and decides to set out from his native country "to see if he could find a remedy for his sadness."[116]

Eventually he stumbles upon three wise men—a Jew, a Christian, and a Muslim—already in deep discussion with one another. Before the Gentile's arrival, the three wise men encounter "Lady Intelligence," who converses with them on the nature of virtue and vice (in relation to Llull's art). When she departs, one of the sages (Llull does not say which) laments religious discord and pleads for unity:

> "Ah! What a great fortune it would be if . . . every man on earth could be under . . . one belief, so that there would be no more rancor or ill will among men, who hate each other because of the contrariness of beliefs and of sects! . . .
>
> "Think gentlemen," the wise man said to his companions, "of the harm that comes from men not belonging to a single sect, and of the good that would come from everyone being beneath one faith. . . . This being the case, do you not think it would be a good idea for us to sit beneath these trees, beside this lovely fountain and discuss what we believe. . . . And since we cannot agree by means of authorities, let us try to come to some agreement by means of demonstrative and necessary reasons."[117]

At this point, the Gentile arrives, weeping, and conveys his plight to the wise men. In turn, they seek (in book 1) to comfort him, explaining that God created the world, that there is life after death, that both the good and evil will receive their just deserts, and a number of other beliefs upon which all three faiths agree. The Gentile's spirits begin to lift, but he becomes distraught anew when he learns that the three men do not profess the same faith. Nonplussed, he asks them why their faiths are not in concord. In response, each wise man agrees to make the case for his respective faith, but "none would contradict the other while he was presenting his arguments, since contradiction brings ill will to the human heart . . . [and] clouds the mind's ability to understand."[118]

Book 1 is then devoted to the Jewish response, in which Judaism is presented in eight essential doctrines. In book 2, the Christian makes his case in fourteen articles, followed by the Muslim in book 3, who summarizes Islam in twelve articles. The Gentile alternates between listening attentively and asking questions. While Llull, more implicitly than explicitly, portrays Christianity in a more favorable light than the other two, the work is surprisingly free from slander, caricature, and accusation. There are no broadsides against Muhammad or the Qur'an, no charges of Jewish deicide or of the blasphemy of the Talmud. "Scrupulous in his use of authentic Jewish and Muslim sources," Llull, according to John V. Tolan, "presents a remarkably fair and accurate portrayal of each of the three religions. Llull's tract stands out as an irenic island in a sea of tempestuous disputation and polemic."[119]

The ending, too, is noteworthy. Customarily in medieval written dialogues, a dramatic, often contrived, conversion takes place at the end of the work. In Llull's book, this does not happen. Instead, the Gentile simply thanks his three interlocutors for pointing him in the direction of true faith, for which he wants "to work for the rest of my life to honor and proclaim." As he prepares to depart, he asks the men if they want to know which of their faiths he has chosen. Remarkably, they indicate that they would rather not know. Then one continues: "And if, in front of us, you state which . . . it is that you prefer, we would not have such a good subject of discussion nor satisfaction in discovering the truth." Astonished, the Gentile departs as the three men "by force [of] reason and by means of [their] intellects" continue their previous conversation. Movingly, each also "asked forgiveness of the other for any disrespectful word that he might have spoken" during the conversation with the Gentile.[120]

Such irenicism was rare in Llull's time. Llull pushed "admiration and appreciation of the religious other to its limits," to quote Tolan again. Because of this and flummoxed by his abstruse philosophy, many contemporaries thought Llull was simply loony. Accordingly, and despite Llull's indefatigable efforts, neither his irenicism nor his art achieved much influence. Toward the end of his life, he grew despondent and, sadly, resorted to advocating more prevalent aggressive means of confronting Muslims and Jews. Figures such as Aquinas, Penyafort, and Martini exercised more actual influence on the church's engagement with non-Christians.[121] Among fifteenth-century humanists, however, Llull's ideas experienced a brief revival, influencing one figure of enduring significance: Nicholas of Cusa.

A redoubtable polymath, Nicholas of Cusa (1401–61), or Cusanus, is a fascinating figure in the Christian intellectual tradition. A native of Kues (Cusa) on the Mosel River in present-day Germany, he received his education at Heidelberg, Padua, and Cologne. Absorbing diverse intellectual influences, he owed a special debt to Neoplatonic thought and to theologians such as Augustine, Pseudo-Dionysus the Areopagite, Bonaventure, and Meister Eckhart. At Padua and Cologne, he became familiar with the writings of Llull and studied the Catalonian's corpus assiduously.[122] His personal library (preserved today in Kues) contains no fewer than sixty-eight writings by Llull. Ordained a priest in 1426, Cusa charted a meteoric career within the church, becoming a cardinal in 1448 and then bishop of Brixen in the Tyrolian Alps and a papal legate to German lands in 1450.[123]

The search for irenicism and unity pervades Cusa's thought. He worked tirelessly for the reconciliation to the church of the Hussites in Bohemia. In 1433, he published *De condorantia catholica*, a comprehensive reform program for the church and the Holy Roman Empire. In 1437 Pope Eugenius IV sent him to Constantinople to work for reunion with the Orthodox Church—which became a short-lived reality as a consequence of the Council of Ferrara-Florence (1438–45). While in Constantinople, Cusa drank from the wells of Eastern Orthodox theology and became acutely aware of the challenge posed by Ottoman forces, which had essentially encircled the city. Cusa also met several actual Muslims and viewed the Qur'an in its original Arabic. Earlier, his knowledge of Islam had been enriched while attending sessions of the Council of Basel (1431–45). There he met the Salamancan theologian Juan de Segovia (1393–1458), widely known for his knowledge of Islam, and had copied for himself Ketton's Latin translation of the Qur'an. That he pored over the Qur'an and other works on Islam, especially those of Riccoldo da Montecroce, is attested to by his copious marginalia preserved at the library in Kues.[124] To Segovia, he once wrote that the solution to religious conflict should not be settled on the battlefield but through some sort of "dialogue" (*colloquia*).[125]

Making sense of the diversity of human opinions, religious or otherwise, informed most of Cusa's later works, not least his famous *Learned Ignorance* (*De docta ignorantia*), completed in 1440. In it, he defended his two most celebrated principles, "docta ignorantia" and "conincidentia oppositorum." The former—an awareness of human beings' fundamental ignorance that, paradoxically, can only come from extensive learning—was the highest stage of wisdom accessible to the intellect, since truth is infinite and, for human minds, perpetually unknowable in its fullness. Greater knowledge only expands awareness of what one does not know. The road to truth therefore leads beyond reason and beyond Aristotle's principle of noncontradiction; only in intuition can one hope to glimpse God, in whom all contradictions meet.[126] With such ideas, Cusa hoped to chasten human vanity and foster intellectual humility among people with different outlooks.[127]

In the summer of 1453, Constantinople finally fell to armies of the Ottoman sultan, Mehmed II, "the Conqueror"—a stunning turn of events in world history that sent shockwaves through all of Christendom, East and West.[128] News of Ottoman troops desecrating and looting ancient Christian sites of worship exacerbated long-standing anti-Muslim sentiments. From this point on, "the Turk"—and not just "the Saracen"—became an especially reviled Other in the Christian imagination, inciting intellectual refutations, eschatological speculation, and successive martial actions to forestall further Ottoman advances.[129]

But for Cusa, the events of 1453 inspired a different kind of thinking. Vexed and saddened by religious divisions, in that year he wrote and published *De pace fidei* ("On the Peace of Faith"), based on a vision that he claimed to have experienced. In the vision, a number of angelic beings—whom he calls "intellectual powers"—gathered before the throne of God lamenting violence done in the name of different beliefs.[130] One figure, speaking for the others, addresses God:

> You [God] sent the different nations different prophets and teachers, some at one time and others at another. However, it is a characteristic of the earthly human condition that a longstanding custom which is taken as having become nature is defended as truth. Thus not insignificant dissensions occur when each community prefers its faith to [that of] another. Therefore, come to our aid. . . . For each one desires . . . only the good which you are; no one is seeking with all his intellectual inquiry for anything other than the truth. . . .

> Therefore, it is you, the giver of life and being, who seem to be sought in the different rites by different ways. . . . O Lord, be merciful and show your face. . . . If thus you would deign to do this, the sword and the bilious spite of hatred and all evil sufferings will cease; and all will know that there is only one religion in the variety of rites [*religio una in rituum varietate*].[131]

Moved by the angels' entreaty, the "Word" (the second person of the Trinity) responds that human beings have "free will" and therefore cannot be coerced into one faith. Nonetheless, "truth is one" and, ideally, "all religious diversity" (*omnis religionum diversitas*) "ought to be brought into one orthodox faith."[132]

It is then agreed to try to unite the world's different religious traditions. The plan entails bringing "the most eminent men of this world," as representatives of the world's religious traditions, into a cosmopolitan "assembly" (*coetu*) that would take place "most suitably" in Jerusalem. According to Cusa's vision, these representatives, "carried aloft as in a state of ecstasy," are summoned from various parts of the world to meet and seek out "a unique and propitious concordance, and through this to constitute a perpetual peace in religion."[133]

Reflecting the medieval dialogue genre, *On the Peace of Faith* then presents a discussion among these luminaries. In addition to the heavenly representatives, which include God, "the Word," an archangel, and the Apostles Peter and Paul, there are seventeen interlocutors representing different ethnicities, languages, and faiths. These include representatives from Europe (a Greek, Italian, Frenchman, Spaniard, Englander, German, and Bohemian), from the Middle East (an Arab, Chaldean, Jew, Sythian, Persian, Syrian, Turk, and Armenian), and from the Far East (an Indian and a Tatar). Cusa's knowledge of the distant East was scanty, derived in large part from reading Marco Polo, but that he included figures beyond the "Abrahamic" fold testifies to the breadth of his aim.[134]

In the conversation that follows, the "Word" (*Verbum*)—and to a lesser degree the Apostles Peter and Paul—functions similarly to Socrates in Plato's dialogues, questioning and coaxing others to admit to certain truths. As was the case with Llull, Cusa treats each speaker sympathetically, having them represent with considerable accuracy their respective faiths—at least insofar as Cusa understood them. He even draws approvingly from Islamic theology, although, unlike Llull, he did not read Arabic. In point of fact, Cusa treats non-Christian outlooks so sympathetically that commentators have been divided over whether Cusa is still operating in a Christian theological register at all or else had espoused an idealistic, pan-religious universalism.

The conversations that take place reflect the diverse influences on Cusa's thought. Neoplatonism shines forth practically on every page, as the Word enjoins all discussants to recognize that beyond the many, there is the One; beyond all plurality, an ultimate, higher unity. These sentiments are often connected to Trinitarian notions: the threefold Godhead is the perfect image of plurality reconciled into a higher unity. Echoing an argument from Cicero's *On the Nature of the Gods*, Cusa suggests that knowledge of a single God, the originator of all things, is deeply embedded in human nature; there is "an innate sense of the divine" (*religio connata*), even if this sense assumes a diversity of forms.[135] Strains of Orthodox and mystical theology make themselves felt in Cusa's repeated claims that God is ultimately beyond all means of knowledge, ineffable in his otherness; human language at best dimly approximates divine realities. Finally, and unusually, drawing from the Qur'an, of all sources—which he also knew through Ketton's translation—Cusa makes the case that God himself has ordained religious diversity. As the archangel puts it: "You [God] appointed for your people different kings and seers, who are called prophets. . . . You sent to the nations different prophets and teachers. . . . Therefore it is you, the giver of life and being, who seem to be sought in the different rites by different ways [and you] are named with different names."[136]

Of course, the problem with religious diversity among finite, fallible human beings was that it had led to animosity, persecution, and war, as the recent "savageries" in Constantinople had made clear. Nonetheless, slowly but surely, the interlocutors, prodded along by their heavenly betters, work their way, not toward constructing a newfangled super-religion, but toward recognizing together "the one and same faith that is presupposed everywhere."[137] For the monotheists, this recognition often comes easily. For polytheists and "idolaters" (that is, the "Indian" and possibly the "Tatar" in the dialogue), it requires more work, but they too, through the arguments made by members of the heavenly hosts, are enabled to see the one true religion. A favorite (Platonic) tactic of Cusa led him to point out that all instances of the color white, no matter how blemished, presume the existence of a primal "whiteness." Similarly, wisdom espoused by different philosophers, he insists, bears witness to a primal, higher Wisdom. Applying this logic to religious traditions: all instances of devotion to deities, and even to idolatry, presume at some level one true God and one true faith.

Perhaps not surprisingly, the one faith "presupposed everywhere" toward the end of the dialogue looks a lot like Christianity. The non-Christian voices, however, are not simply refuted or maligned in the dialogue; rather, they come to understand that, whether by confused intention or misguided piety, they all along had "implicitly" (*implicite*) been worshipping the one true and triune God.[138]

But as unity of belief comes into sight toward the end of the dialogue, the Tatar wonders if, despite people recognizing the same God, the diversity of rites exhibited in the world would nonetheless still incite them to hatred and violence against one another: "For diversity [of rites] leads to division and hatreds and war."[139] The Word asks Paul to address this concern. He does so in language that would have pleased Martin Luther and John Calvin! What finally is important, Paul says, is faith, not works, of which "rites" are a species. In his own words: "It is necessary that it be shown that salvation of the soul is not granted from works but from faith. For Abraham, the father of all believers, whether Christians or Arabs or Jews, believed in God, and this was credited to him as a righteousness: the soul of the just will inherit eternal life. When this is acknowledged these varieties of rites will not be a cause of disturbance."[140] Paul qualifies this by saying that faith must be informed by love, but in any case, the worship of one God as an act of common faith can allow for a diversity of rites. He even argues that diversity of rites might be a good thing, for it would goad people into a friendly competition of worship.[141]

With this final issue addressed, the interlocutors are given access to a hitherto unmentioned celestial library. As they read and discuss what they find, it becomes clear to them that "diversity is located more in rites than in the worship of God, whom all have always from the beginning presupposed and cherished in all worship." Cusa then brings the dialogue to a close: "And it was commanded by the King of Kings [God], that the wise men return and lead the nations to the unity of the true worship. . . . And finally endowed with full authority for all, they should gather in Jerusalem as the common center and in the name of all accept the one faith [*unam fidem*] and upon it establish perpetual peace [*perpetuam pacem*], so that the Creator of all may be praised in peace."[142]

De pace fide did not exhaust Cusa's concern with peace and other faiths. They remained lifelong preoccupations. In 1460 he published *Cibratio Alchoran* ("Sifting the Qur'an"), an attempt to interpret Muslim teachings with the irenic intention of reconciling them to Christianity. This work was written explicitly for Cusa's friend the humanist Pope Pius II (r. 1458–64), who in turn wrote a letter to Mehmed II, enjoining him to convert to Christianity and then rightfully assume the Byzantine throne. "Do this [convert]," the pope wrote the sultan, "and there is no prince in the world who will exceed you in glory, or equal you in power. We will call you the Emperor of the Greeks and of the East. The land which you now occupy by force you will then hold by right."[143] Presumably flattered, Mehmed declined.

Besides his influence on Pius II, Cusa left a short-term legacy that is difficult to gauge. He was read avidly by Giordano Bruno, who spoke frequently of "divine Cusanus." But because of Bruno's trial and execution for heresy, Cusa came to appear to many in the church as guilty by association. In the long term, however, his influence is patent, even if his legacy has been contested. As indicated earlier, many have been inclined to see him as a proto-modern thinker, discarding medieval Christian modes of thought in favor of a distinctly modern understanding of religious toleration and dialogue. But others have challenged this view, arguing that, while his thought was outfitted in novel, idiosyncratic dress, Cusa remained firmly within the bounds of established orthodoxy. Whatever the case, he left an extraordinary legacy, rivaled in the Christian Middle Ages only by Llull, for the task of interreligious dialogue.[144] His work, writes James E. Biechler, "set a new record of inclusiveness. It is probably the first Christian work that attempts to come to grips in

Nicholas of Cusa, detail of the altar in the chapel of the St. Nicholas Hospital, Kues, Germany, ca. 1480. (Image courtesy of Heritage Image Partnership Ltd / Alamy Stock Photo.)

a concrete way with the problem of world religion using an approach along lines other than conversion or mission."[145] Cusa himself seemed to recognize that his approach to other faiths might at first be met with skepticism; but he held out the hope, in the introduction to *De pace fidei*, that one day his heavenly vision "might come to the knowledge of those who [actually] resolve such important matters."[146] As we shall see in chapter 4, the German theologian Karl Rahner—arguably the most significant modern Catholic thinker on interreligious matters—and the Second Vatican Council, which Rahner influenced, adopted lines of inclusivist reasoning that strongly echo Cusa.[147]

Holy Men at Akbar's Court

Cusa died in 1464 as the Ottoman Empire ascended to the status of a world power. Shortly thereafter, a new, comparably powerful Islamic Empire arose in the East, destined to leave a lasting legacy of interreligious interactions. This, of course, is the Mughal Empire, and the figure of particular interest is Emperor Akbar (r. 1556–1605). To be sure, religious currents on the Indian subcontinent and greater South Asia had witnessed countless, often dimly known interactions, fusions, and conflicts over the centuries. For our purposes, particular mention should be made of the *Milinda Panha*, a Pali Buddhist text dating from circa 100 BCE–200 CE that purports to record a dialogue between the Buddhist sage Nagasene and the Indo-Greek king Menander I.[148] Menander ruled in Bactria, a successor state descended from the time of Alexander the Great, at a time when Buddhist influence permeated India due to the influence of Emperor Ashoka, a convert to Buddhism and a notable purveyor of religious irenicism.[149]

But as intriguing as the *Milinda Panha* and Ashoka's reign are, the later Mughal emperor Akbar represents something altogether different and more relevant, if our aim is to identify plausible precursors to modern-day interreligious dialogue. Akbar's religious curiosity and his fabled Ibadat Khana (House of Worship) are known to us through several sources. One of Akbar's chief and most influential courtiers, the Sufi-influenced Abu'l-Fazl (1551–1602), left behind a highly sympathetic treatment of Akbar's court in his three-volume

Akbarnama ("Book of Akbar") and in other works.[150] A more critical (secretly composed) assessment came from the staunchly Sunni Abdul al-Qadir Bada'uni (1540–1605) in his *Muntakhab al-Tawarikh* ("Selections of Chronicles").[151] The chronicler Nizamuddin Ahmad (1551–1621) left behind a monumental history of Muslim India, including aspects of Akbar's reign.[152] The great Persian work comparing different beliefs and traditions, *Dabistan-i Mazaheb*, or "School of Manners," although penned after Akbar's death, records religious conversations putatively held in the Ibadat Khana.[153] Finally, Jesuit missionaries from Goa, frequent guests at Akbar's court, recorded in letters, diaries, and memoirs their experience of the "Great Mughal" and religious discussions during his reign.[154]

The name Mughal is a variant of the word *Mongol* as the empire's founder, Babur (r. 1483–1530), was descended from Genghis Khan and Tamerlane. From the Central Asian steppe, Babur led military expeditions in the late 1400s and early 1500s that greatly enlarged his territory. In 1504 he captured Kabul, from which he then launched forays into the Indian subcontinent. In 1526 he defeated the ruler of the Delhi Sultanate (a Turkic Islamic power) and established his imperial seat at Agra—later to witness construction of the Taj Mahal.[155] Although a Sunni Muslim, Babur brought with him policies of religious pragmatism and toleration that, as we have seen, characterized Mongol rule. He did not harass the Hindus that he had conquered, but treated them with respect, allowing, for instance, the building of Hindu temples and even at times forbidding the slaughter of cows.[156]

Babur was succeeded by his son Humayun (d. 1556), who experienced a turbulent reign, which entailed periods of exile in Safavid Persia that had the consequence of significant Shia influence on the royal family.[157] Persian also became the official language of the Mughal court. In 1556 Akbar, Humayun's son, ascended to the "Peacock throne."[158] A man of considerable military prowess, Akbar pursued actions and policies that extended and consolidated the Mughal Empire in northern and central India. Some of this took place through warfare, but much occurred through matrimonial alliances; Akbar himself married several Rajput (Hindu) princesses, one of whom bore his successor, Jahangir (d. 1627).[159] Not infrequently, Akbar gave Hindus high-ranking positions in his government, and he permitted Hindu festivals to be celebrated at court.[160] Akbar's irenic stance toward Hindu customs and beliefs contributed decisively to the spread of his empire.

At its height in the late 1500s, the Mughal Empire teemed with religious diversity. Besides the Muslim ruling class and the large Hindu population, Parsis, Jains, Sikhs, Buddhists, Christians, and Jews contributed to a pluralistic society. Although Akbar's deep interest in religious matters appears to have been genuine, it bears keeping in mind that he had an abiding political interest in keeping a lid on religious strife. To this end, he pursued a policy of *sulh-i-kull*, often translated as "universal peace" or "toleration," although it literally means "lasting reconciliation." In 1564 he repealed the widely loathed poll tax that all non-Muslims were required to pay. Earlier, he had repealed fees that Hindus normally had to pay to go on pilgrimages. In the arts, he encouraged Muslims and Hindus to work together—a practice that led to some extraordinary fusions of culture.[161] He also promoted several translation projects aimed at reducing religious tensions. "Being aware of the . . . hatred between Hindus and Muslims," Abu'l-Fazl recorded, "and being convinced that this arose out of mutual ignorance, the enlightened ruler [Akbar] sought to dispel this ignorance by making the books of each other accessible to the other."[162]

As a young emperor, Akbar exhibited sincere religious devotion. He observed daily prayers, pored over the Qur'an, and was even known to sweep the floor of the palace mosque himself. Although he showed respect to the leading Sunni scholars of his day, he reserved his most reverent devotion to the deceased Moinuddin Chishti (1142–1236), a hallowed Sufi saint, who established the Chishti order of Sufism and whose tomb at Ajmer was an object of popular veneration, to which Akbar made several visits.[163] This dedication led to Akbar's interest in a living holy man who also shared this devotion: Salim Chishti (1478–1572), who resided at Fatehpur Sikri, south of Delhi. Chishti Sufism, then and now, emphasized love, openness, self-sacrifice, and the unity of being (*wahdat al-wujud*). As such, it aligned closely with the Vedanta school(s) of Hindu philosophy.[164] This outlook enduringly influenced Akbar.[165] So smitten was Akbar with Salim Chishti, in fact, that he built a new royal city at Fatehpur Sikri, dedicating it to the Sufi saint, for whom he also built a mausoleum in the royal courtyard.[166] Alongside other architectural projects, Akbar built there in 1575 the aforementioned Ibadat Khana as a place set aside for religious conversations—what we might see in continuity with the majlis (assembly) and munazara (disputation) of earlier Muslim tradition. Although the structure no longer stands, and disputes linger over its exact location, sources tell us that the house stood close to the royal palace, that it was shaped in a square with four alcoves, and that it was built around a central cell with a domed roof.[167] "My sole object, oh wise mullahs," Akbar was recorded as saying to an assembly in the Ibadat Khana, "is to ascertain truth [in this place], to find out and divine the principles of genuine religion, and [to] trace it to its divine source."[168]

Discussion in the Ibadat Khana usually took place on Thursday evenings, lasting sometimes until Friday before noonday worship. At first, they were strictly among Muslims, segregated into the four parts of the building: the sheiks and ascetics; Sayyids, or descendants of the Prophet Muhammad; nobles of the court; and the ulema, or jurists.[169] The intolerance of the Sunni orthodox party often produced bitter quarrels, jealousies, and reprisals. Bada'uni described their rude behavior, confusion in their ranks, and how "the veins of their necks swelled up" when matters became testy.[170] Eventually Akbar had enough of this wrangling, and in the late 1570s he decided to make some changes—radical changes.

Of particular importance, he arrogated authority to himself to serve as the final arbiter in disputed religious matters. On 26 June 1579, Akbar gave the *khutbah* (the Friday sermon) himself at the central mosque in Fatehpur Sikri, making clear the unity of spiritual and secular power in his person. Next, he issued a *mahzar*, or decree, on 2 September 1579, inveigling the ulema to endorse it, that made explicit that the "just ruler" (*sultan-i-adil*) is above the "interpreter of the law" (*mujtahid*).[171] Although members of the Sunni orthodox party chafed against the decree, it became the law of the land. From this point on, Akbar's imperial authority in religious matters provided the basis for greater openness to different religious voices. His key minister, Abu'l-Fazl, encouraged him in these actions.

The Ibadat Khana was quickly thrown open to a wider range of Muslim perspectives. Hitherto marginalized, Shia scholars and holy men were granted admittance, and with them came topics dear to their hearts—such as the neuralgic issue of rightful succession after the Prophet. Various sectarian movements also gained a hearing, many of which claimed loyalty to a particular Mahdi, the "Guided One," destined to appear at the end of time to rid the world of injustice, according to Muslim eschatology.[172] And not least, Sufi mystics and dervishes received greater latitude to expound their views. In short, the Ibadat Khana quickly become pan-Islamic: "All . . . scholars, dervishes, theologians, and courtiers interested in religious affairs would assemble in the Ibadat Khana and discuss religious subjects in the royal presence."[173] The orthodox Sunni ulema stood aghast at this state of affairs, but they had little choice but to persist in arguing their views before Akbar.

Soon the range of religious views expanded further, to non-Muslims, making the Ibadat Khana truly "a real parliament of religions."[174] At this time, as Abu'l-Fazl records, the Ibadat Khana "became the home of the enquirers of the seven climes, and the assemblage of every religion and sect."[175] Brahmin pandits and holy men began to participate and instruct Akbar in Hindu spiritual traditions, some of which he already knew from his Rajput wives and their courtiers. Akbar came to believe, for instance, in the transmigration of souls. As suggested earlier, the translation into Persian of many Sanskrit sacred works was undertaken. Numerous Hindu beliefs and practices were discussed and debated at the Ibadat Khana, even controversial ones, such as *sati*, the practice of burning Hindu wives upon their husband's death. (Akbar eventually forbade this practice.) Still, he sympathized with Hindu beliefs enough to make many suspect he had converted.[176]

Zoroastrianism gained a hearing. While besieging Surat in Gujarat in 1573, Akbar had encountered Parsis and become fascinated by the dualistic nature of their faith, with its reverence for fire and light. He became acquainted with the Dastur Meherji Rana, the spiritual leader of the Parsi community in India. In 1578 Akbar invited Rana to participate in discussions at the Ibadat Khana. Both Abu'l-Fazl and Bada'uni recorded that other Parsi holy men visited as well, taking part in conversations. And their influence was felt; Akbar established a sacred fire to be kept in the palace, entrusting Abu'l-Fazl to be its custodian.[177]

Jains, too, showed up at the Ibadat Khana. In 1582, a Jain delegation that included the renowned ascetic Hiravijaya Suri (1527–95) paid a visit at Akbar's request. Akbar, Abu'l-Fazl, and others conversed with Hiravijaya and his co-religionists at great length, and their influence was soon felt. Admiring if not fully subscribing to the Jain teaching of *ahimsa* (nonviolence to all that lives), Akbar placed restrictions on when hunting and fishing could take place. Later, he issued orders stopping the slaughter of animals for certain periods throughout the year. Akbar conferred on Hiravijaya the title *Jagat-Guru*, or world-teacher. After Hiravijaya's departure, Akbar detained several Jains to read and discuss their holy books with them.[178] In the *Dabistan-i Mazaheb*, the aforementioned Persian work of comparative religion, the author (likely a Parsi) records a noteworthy challenge offered, presumably by a Jain, to the other scholars present in the Ibadat Khana, illustrating the religious diversity assembled:

> A learned philosopher came into the hall, where Hindus also were present, and three other learned men; a Muslim, a Christian, and a Jew: these were summoned, and raged in opposition to the learned philosopher. The latter opened the discussion in this manner: The divine mission of your prophets has not been proven, for several reasons: the first is, that whatever the prophet says ought to conform to reason; the second is, that he ought to be free from crime, and not be hurtful to other beings [that is, *ahimsa*]. But Moses, according to the opinion of the Jews, was brought up by Pharaoh, and yet he [Moses] caused him [the Pharaoh] by a stratagem to be drowned in the waters of the Nile. . . . Jesus permitted the killing and ill-using of animals. And Muhammed himself attacked the forces and caravans of the Koreish; he shed blood [and] with his own hand put to death animated beings.[179]

Following Hiravijaya Suri's visit, additional Jain delegations spent time in Fatehpur Sikri.

Jews also had a presence in the Ibadat Khana, according to the *Dabistan* and other sources. Abu'l-Fazl mentions Jews explicitly: the Ibadat Khana "shone brightly with the light of holy minds—Sufis, doctors, preachers—Jains, Christians, and *Jews*."[180] The Jesuits at

Akbar's court also mentioned Jews with whom they conversed.[181] In the *Dabistan*, the author mentions that "a Jew was present and participated in the discussion with a Sunni and a Shii," and refers to another disputation at which "a Jew presented himself and Akbar placed the Christian in opposition to him for a religious discussion."[182]

While the presence of Sikhs and Buddhists at Fatehpur Sikri appears scantier than those of other traditions, evidence suggest that these two indigenous faiths of "Hindustan" played a role at Akbar's court as well. Abu'l-Fazl, in fact, recorded that Buddhists had come along with others into the Ibadat Khana. What is more, a painting from the era portrays what is likely a Buddhist monk taking part in discussions.[183] The Sikh movement was in its infancy during Akbar's reign, but we know that Akbar had several dealings with Sikhs concerning political matters; he also had numerous interactions with them once he moved his capital to Lahore in the late sixteenth century. Further, he gave them the land around Amritsar, where they established their famous Golden Temple. It is almost certain, therefore, that Sikhs, too, visited the Ibadat Khana or, at the very least, Sikh ideas were discussed there.[184]

Akbar's engagement with Catholicism, mediated largely through Jesuit missionaries, is a significant aspect of the emperor's legacy—and of East-West contact more generally during this period. Akbar first met some Portuguese in 1573 at the siege of Surat, when he received a deputation from one Anthony Cabral, who came "with instructions to make peace." Conversations with Cabral turned, among other things, on the state of European and Christian civilization. Akbar subsequently became intrigued by the Jesuits when he heard news that two of their members, Anthony Vaz and Peter Dias, who arrived in Bengal in 1576, had rebuked Portuguese merchants for defrauding the Mughal state treasury by not paying taxes. Akbar was impressed by a faith that insisted on such honesty.[185] But ensuing interactions with the Portuguese could not satisfy Akbar's curiosity, so in 1578 he appealed directly to the Jesuit mission in Goa to send "two of your learned men . . . [for] I honestly and sincerely desire to acquire a full understanding [of Christianity]."[186] Taken aback at first by the warm invitation, the Jesuits of Goa eventually responded positively and sent a delegation to Fatehpur Sikri. Arriving in early 1580, the delegation consisted of the Italian Rudolf

Acquaviva, the Spaniard Antony Monserrate and, as a translator, a Persian convert to Catholicism who had taken the name of Francis Henriquez. They received a friendly welcome from Akbar, who thanked them for the polyglot Bible they had brought as a gift. Akbar immediately ordered parts of it to be translated into Persian and he built for them a small chapel in the palace where they could celebrate Mass.[187]

The Jesuits' letters attest to their participation in discussions at the Ibadat Khana, as do several miniature paintings from the time that display the black-robed fathers sitting next to Akbar and other religious interlocutors. "After arriving we held several discussions with mullahs," Acquaviva wrote his provincial, "about some aspects of their mushaf [Qur'an] and prophet, and of our holy faith concerning the judgment and the resurrection of the dead . . . and other similar matters."[188] And again from Acquaviva's pen: "At present we have very frequent discussions on the divine law so that we have them at least once a week, till midnight and at times beyond that. I think that they are not without significant fruit, as least for the King [Akbar], as I know from him." As suggested by these lines, the Jesuits ardently tried to convert the Great Mughal, but their hopes were routinely dashed, and they frequently mistook his interest in Catholicism as a sign of imminent conversion. On several occasions, Akbar reprimanded the fathers for disparaging Islam, although he also apologized to them for the offensive behavior of the mullahs.[189]

Christian teachings on the Trinity and monogamy especially troubled Akbar—he had a sizeable harem! More generally, he took offense at the exclusive nature of the Jesuits' theological claims, even as these also nudged his thinking toward what we might call the comparative study of religion. As Monserrate recorded Akbar as saying: "I perceive that there are varying customs and beliefs. . . . But the followers of each regard the institution of their own piety [*suae religionis*] as better than those of any other. Not only this, but they strive to convert the rest to their own way of belief. If these refused to be converted, they not only despise them, but also regard them for this very reason as their enemies. And this caused me to feel many doubts and scruples. Therefore, I desire that on appointed days the books of all [religious] laws [*libri omnium legum*] be brought forward and the doctors meet together and hold discussions, so that

I may hear them, and that each one may determine which is the truest and mightiest way."[190]

Akbar showed keen interest in the political and religious conditions of Europe, about which the Jesuits freely conversed. After learning of the expulsion of Jews and Muslims from the Iberian Peninsula in 1492, Akbar grew angry and wrote to King Philip II of Spain, calling for him to imitate his own example. "Most men," Akbar wrote, "are fettered by bonds of tradition, and by imitating ways followed by their fathers. . . . Everyone continues, without investigating their arguments and reasons, to follow the religion in which he was born and educated, thus excluding himself from the possibility of ascertaining the truth, which is the noblest aim of the human intellect. Therefore we [in India] associate at convenient seasons with learned men of all faiths, thus deriving profit from their exquisite discourses and exalted aspirations."[191] The letter likely never reached Spain. It was slated to be delivered in conjunction with setting up an embassy there, but for various reasons these plans collapsed, and no evidence suggests that the letter was independently sent; and even if it was, a response from Philip II is not known to exist.[192]

The first Jesuit mission to Akbar's court ended in 1583. A second began in 1591 after a Greek Orthodox traveler had visited Akbar in Lahore and reported that the emperor appeared to have altogether forsaken Islam and was perhaps ready for conversion. Once this news reached Goa, plans for a new mission soon got under way. Two Jesuit fathers, Edward Leioton and Christopher di Vega, along with a lay brother, Estavas Rillerio, were given the task. They arrived at court in November 1591. Unfortunately, warfare then preoccupied Akbar and he had scant time for religious discussions. Little evidence exists of what this mission accomplished, and it appears that the missionaries became impatient or lost heart; they returned to Goa after several months.[193]

A third Jesuit mission commenced in 1595; it brought to Akbar's court Emmanuel Pinherio, Benedict of Goes, and Jerome Xavier, the nephew of the well-known Jesuit missionary Francis Xavier.[194] The three were treated with much goodwill from Akbar and made some notable inroads. According to their communiqués, Akbar stood far from Islam—he had by this time formulated his own religious

Mughal miniature of the Ibadat Khana (House of Worship) in Fatehpur Sikri, showing the presence of two Jesuit fathers, Rudolf Acquaviva and Francis Henriquez. Illustration in the Akbarnama, *painted by Nar Singh, ca. 1605. (Image courtesy of Wikimedia Commons.)*

system, the Din-i-Ilahi (more about it momentarily). The emperor showed the priests respect and honor, allowing them to open a Christian school and even to baptize those who desired to convert. But little evidence suggests that religious debate took place as avidly as it had earlier in the Ibadat Khana. This mission petered out in the early 1600s.[195]

In the end, no Jesuit father succeeded in converting Akbar to Christianity. A leading reason, perhaps, was that in the 1580s and 1590s Akbar and Abu'l-Fazl had in fact quietly been formulating their own novel religious outlook, known later as the Din-i-Ilahi, or "the religion of God," but at first as Tawhid-i-Ilahi, "divine monotheism." Exactly what this "religion" (*din*) was has been the subject of much debate. But it is generally accepted that it was the fruit of Akbar's long-standing attachment to the universalizing tendencies of Chishti Sufism and a concomitant desire to aggregate the best from different religious outlooks in his kingdom. Muslim, Christian, Jain, Hindu, and Zoroastrian influences can be detected in the Din-i-Ilahi. Piety, prudence, abstinence, and kindness were among its key virtues. Lust, sensuality, slander, and pride constituted its leading vices. It respected celibacy but did not require it, and it forbade the wanton slaughter of animals. At its core, it sought to elevate the pursuit of reason (*aql*) over reliance on tradition (*taqlid*) as the royal road for arriving at religious truth (*din*).[196] Initiation into the Din-i-Ilahi was always by invitation only, and it never possessed more than a handful of adherents, drawn from Akbar's close circle of confidants—Abu'l-Fazl being among its leading architects and proponents. Hence it was extremely elitist, mirroring in many respects the character of Sufi brotherhoods. It persisted briefly after Akbar's death, was presented in the *Dabistan*, but declined in the early 1600s amid a barrage of criticism from orthodox Muslim clerics.

In the theologian James Laine's insightful summary, Akbar's Din-i-Ilahi represents something between a "Sufi cult for elite courtiers" and a "meta-religion designed to adjudicate between the various religious communities of his [Akbar's] vast and diverse realm." It effectively replaced Islam among its few adherents, Laine continues, "with something that does not explicitly deny the truths of Islam, but appeals in abstract and universalist language to something that supersedes all religions (including Islam) both in the name of reason and in the name of Akbar's authority as a radiant authority ruling a divinely sanctified state."[197]

For our purposes, the Din-i-Ilahi testifies to the influence of discussions held in the Ibadat Khana and to Akbar's curious, broad-minded outlook, for it was certainly the product of both. As such, it adumbrates at least one possible response to interreligious dialogue typically associated with pluralism: the view that all religious outlooks reflect some unitary, deeper reality. Again, one could find support for such a view in South Asian Sufi and Vedantic thought prior to Akbar. Looking forward, it was given forceful expression at Chicago's World's Parliament of Religions by the charismatic Indian swami Vivekananda, who will be discussed in the next chapter, although he was more indebted to Vedanta than Sufism.

Permit a final summary description of the Ibadat Khana in session—or what one observer called "feasts of truth." In the Ibadat Khana, according to Sheikh Nur al-Haq, "learned men from Khorasan and Iraq and Transoxiania, and India, both doctors and theologians, Shia and Sunnis, Christians, philosophers and Brahmins assembled together. . . . Here they discussed the rational and traditional manners of discourse, travel and histories of each other's prophecies. They widened the circle of debate and each attempted to prove his own claim and desired the propagation of his school."[198]

The activities of the Ibadat Khana, Akbar's Din-i-Ilahi, and his policy of *sulh-i-kull* (universal peace) have occupied important and often-invoked places in Indian history. To a significant degree, their legacies continued during the reign of Akbar's son Jahangir.[199] In more recent times, they have been frequently cited as precursors of the tolerant, multicultural secularism sought for in India's 1947 constitution. And to some, they anticipated the mindset of India's best-known twentieth-century figure, Gandhi, who devoted his life to a religious truth "above the teachings of particular religions," even if this same truth must be derived from cultivating knowledge of various faith traditions.[200]

For our purposes, Akbar and the Ibadat Khana, hands down, are among the clearest harbingers of interreligious dialogue in the premodern world, whether in the East or West. Because of his interactions with Jesuits, Akbar became widely known in Europe, although this knowledge faded after his death.[201] The rise of (internecine Christian) religious wars as a consequence of the Reformation, alongside the emergence of Protestant colonialism as a rival to its older Catholic variety, meant that most non-Western faiths in the seventeenth and early eighteenth centuries were met by Europeans in a spirit of competitive proselytism and/or refutation—not engagement and dialogue. India in particular came to be regarded by many Westerners as a bastion of mysterious heathenism and idolatry.[202]

But this image began to mutate in the late eighteenth and nineteenth centuries—as some Enlightenment-influenced voices (Montesquieu and Voltaire come to mind) began to idealize the East (often as a foil to criticize Europe)—during the heyday of European "Orientalism."[203] The growing dominance of the British Empire in India, moreover, coincided with a revival of genuine interest in the history of the declining Mughal Empire—which formally did not expire until the beginning of the Raj in 1858. Beforehand and after, the British had sought to assume the mantle of the Mughal Empire and appropriate its legacy and aspirations as their own.[204] At the great imperial Durbar in Delhi in 1877, the British viceroy Lord Lytton, for instance, went so far as to proclaim Queen Victoria as "plac[ing] her authority upon the ancient throne of the Moguls."[205] During this time, historically minded British officials and intellectuals alighted on Akbar's religious sensibilities as a model for Britain's own policy of religious neutrality. Present-day scholars Paul Stevens and Rahul Sapra argue for the existence of a phenomenon they label "reverse transculturation"; that is, the British did not blindly impose their cultural sensibilities on India, but rather found inspiration and legitimation for their policies in India's own past; they admired, even to the point of clumsy imitation, a figure such as Akbar and instrumentalized the memory of his religious policies in an effort to moderate unruly sectarian conflicts—an acute concern after the Indian Revolt of 1857.[206]

The apotheosis of this rose-colored (Western) gaze into the (Eastern) past arguably came in Alfred Lord Tennyson's poem "Akbar's Dream," published, coincidentally, in 1892—one year before the opening of the World's Parliament of Religions in Chicago. Permit a generous quotation from this admiring, if achingly Orientalist, poem, one that gives some evidence of the process of "reverse transculturation":

> I [Akbar] seem no longer like a lonely man
> in the king's garden, gathering here and there
> from each fair plant the blossom choicest-grown

to wreathe a crown not only for the king
but in due time for every Mussulman,
Brahmin, and Buddhist, Christian, and Parsee,
thro' all the warring world of Hindustan. . . .

I hate the rancor of their castes and creeds,
I let men worship as they will. . . .
I cull from every faith and race the best
and bravest soul for counselor and friend.
I loathe the very name of infidel. . . .

[Follow only] that All-in-all,
and over all, the never-changing One
and ever-changing Many, in praise of Whom
the Christian bell, the cry from off the mosque,
and vaguer voices of Polytheism
make but one music. . . .

But while I groan'd [about the intolerance of Akbar's successors],
from out the sunset pour'd an alien race [the British],
who fitted stone to stone again, and Truth,
Peace, Love and Justice came and dwelt therein . . .
by whatever hands
My mission be accomplish'd![207]

Tennyson has Akbar groaning in the last stanza because the Mughal emperors who came after his son Jahangir largely abandoned Akbar's religious interests and policies. Akbar's grandson, Emperor Aurangzeb (r. 1658–1707) promoted a strict interpretation of Sunni Islam at the expense of other faiths and, at least in religious matters, sought to erase the memory of his grandfather.[208]

But Akbar's Ibadat Khana was never fully forgotten.

CHAPTER TWO

Chicago

> Emperor Akbar no doubt did all he could to become acquainted with other religions, but he certainly was not half so successful as was . . . [the] religious congress in assembling [at Chicago in 1893].
>
> —FRIEDRICH MAX MÜLLER

> The Parliament was a genial transmutation of religious animosities into social friendships, but was neither Pentecost nor Babel, although it had resemblances to both.
>
> —M. M. TRUMBULL

SPEAKING AT CHICAGO'S WORLD'S PARLIAMENT of Religions in 1893, the Boston minister E. L. Rexford proclaimed that "Emperor Akbar, in overreaching the special limits of his chosen sect, that he might pay a fitting tribute to the Spirit of Religion, in its several forms, displayed a noble catholicity; but . . . his generosity [of spirit] was largely personal and resulted in no representative movement [after him]."[1] Although he did not attend in 1893, and later regretted it, the great scholar of comparative religion Friedrich Max Müller offered a similar sentiment, connecting Akbar's precedent to the gathering in Chicago.[2]

The implication, of course, was that in this erstwhile frontier, New World metropolis, Akbar's idea, an enduring movement of and forum for interreligious dialogue, appeared finally to have become a reality—or at least a possibility. In his history of the parliament, John Henry Barrows quoted lines from Tennyson's "Akbar's Dream":

> I dreamed
> That stone by stone I reared a sacred fane,
> A temple; neither Pagod, Mosque, or Church,
> But loftier, simpler, always opened-doored
> To Every breath from Heaven.[3]

Much has been written about the World's Parliament of Religions, which took place in the context of Chicago's landmark Columbian Exposition of 1893. Lately scholars have offered sharp critiques, claiming that the parliament, despite its vaunted fanfare about human solidarity and religious unity, exhibited telltale Western vices: paternalistic condescension toward non-Christian guests, unwarranted utopianism, colonialist self-righteousness, smug Orientalism, and more.[4] These criticisms are not beside the point, as shall become clear. But in an overweening desire to indict the parliament, many contemporary scholars commit the anachronistic fallacy: cavalierly applying present-day moral categories and judgments to the past and finding it, not surprisingly, wanting. This chapter aspires to something less grand. It seeks to understand the parliament from the standpoint of those who organized it and participated in it. Such an empathetic approach means neither forfeiting an inquiry into the parliament's broader context nor dispensing with normative evaluation altogether, although it might temper the latter.

In what follows, then, we shall first examine some of the forces and developments in the nineteenth century, and even earlier, that helped to set the stage for such a parliament. We shall then examine the planning and course of the parliament, which met from 11 to 27 September 1893. Only then shall we turn to evaluative judgments, pondering interpretations of the parliament and its legacy in the twentieth century and beyond.

Preparing the Way

One might understandably wonder whether Akbar's pursuit of interreligious conversation in the late sixteenth century was really the last significant precedent prior to Chicago's 1893 parliament. Must we really go back that far in history? The answer is both yes and no. With respect to formal, organized multilateral interreligious dialogues, one can answer affirmatively. Nothing quite like Akbar's Ibadat Khana can be found in the annals of modern history until Chicago's parliament—a point often made at the parliament.[5] At the same time, many intermediary historical forces and developments from Akbar's time until the late nineteenth century helped to prepare the way. In fact, these are too numerous to note exhaustively, so what follows should be understood as a selective inquiry.

The congeries of ideas and movements that we call the Enlightenment played an indispensable role in preparing the Western intellectual landscape for the inception of interreligious dialogue as a major event in 1893 and as an ongoing movement in the twentieth century. To be sure, significant strands of the Enlightenment evinced hostility to religion *tout court*, especially to institutional Catholicism.[6] But other strands championed religious toleration, moderation, and understanding, even if modern Europe produced no institutional equivalent to Akbar's Ibadat Khana.[7] G. W. Lessing's *Nathan the Wise* epitomizes this aspect of the Enlightenment. The well-known play about tolerance was published in 1779 and first performed in 1783. Set during the Third Crusade, and drawing on medieval traditions of the "ring parable," the play shows how the wise Jewish merchant Nathan, the fabled Muslim warrior Saladin, and a Christian Knight Templar bridged their differences while extolling a vision of universal humanity shorn of religious parochialism and polemics.[8]

At the risk of the stating the obvious, the parliament of 1893 would have been unthinkable without the emergence of religious liberty as a political ideal and legal norm (if not always a practiced reality). Recounting the origins of modern religious freedom far transcends our scope, but the parliament of 1893 no doubt owed a distant debt to the influence of John Locke, William Penn, Roger Williams, James Madison, Thomas Jefferson, and others.[9] The American and French revolutionary traditions, although certainly contested throughout the nineteenth century, powerfully shaped the general climate of Western public opinion. The U.S. Constitution's guarantee of religious freedom, freedom of expression, and freedom of assembly served as the legal infrastructure that made the parliament possible. More than a few participants at Chicago, upon mounting the stage to speak, paid homage to this reality.[10]

If the Enlightenment represents one crucial factor in explaining the conditions of possibility for the parliament, reactions against the Enlightenment, paradoxically, represent another. As mentioned, criticisms of religion (often tagged "superstition") and a spirit of anticlericalism characterized significant aspects of the Enlightenment. While not without influence, these criticisms generated a powerful counter-reaction in movements that we generally associate with the terms *Romanticism* and *Idealism* and with figures such as Friedrich Schleiermacher, G. W. F. Hegel, Friedrich Schelling, François-René de Chateaubriand, William Wordsworth, and Samuel Taylor Coleridge, among others. Even if they often did not champion traditionally orthodox beliefs and extant institutional manifestations of Christianity, they shared a general appreciation of "religion," understood as a vital aspect of humanity's development and ongoing flourishing.[11] Friedrich Schleiermacher's *On Religion: Speeches to Its Cultured Despisers* (1799), an epoch-making work of Romantic thought and early liberal Protestantism, signifies a broader pivot from advocating Christianity for its specific creedal truth to appreciating it as the noblest species of "religion" and, as such, for expressing humanity's complex interiority and deepest longings.[12] Schleiermacher's impassioned words in this book expressed and molded a mood in theology and in the philosophy of religion that, in the words of Sydney Ahlstrom, "was to remain a prominent aspect of the whole long [nineteenth] century."[13] "I would show you," Schleiermacher wrote, "from what human tendency religion proceeds and how it belongs to what is for you highest and dearest. To the roofs of the temple I would lead you, that you might survey the whole sanctuary and discover its innermost secrets."[14] What Schleiermacher and his followers accomplished yielded a novel attitude toward religion, neither confessional nor enlightened, but one that concentrated on humanity's affective relations to the mystery and majesty of "the Absolute" (to use a term popularized by the philosopher

Schelling). Although for the most part Schleiermacher and his Romantic contemporaries did not conduct original scholarly research on non-Western faiths, they helped foster an intellectual climate that, to quote Ahlstrom again, "awakened people to the depths of religion, to see it expressing the profoundest potentialities of human nature, and thus providing new reasons for investigating and understanding all religions and a new spirit in which to approach them."[15] Such a view certainly attracted critics—especially among revivalist evangelicals, ultramontane Catholics, and contrarian thinkers such as Søren Kierkegaard; still, noting its century-long ascendancy, especially in elite circles, is important because the parliament witnessed its profession in spades.[16]

It is particularly relevant to note that the actual study of non-Christian religions—what came to be called alternately comparative religion, the history of religion, or the science of religion (*Religionswissenschaft* in German)—is largely a product of the late eighteenth and nineteenth centuries and, as such, forms another crucial element of context for understanding the shape of the parliament in 1893.[17] In this discourse, the transition from religion understood as piety to religion understood as a genus with globally dispersed species is clearly seen. This discourse owes its genesis to still earlier Western overseas colonialism in the early modern period when the global diversity of religious beliefs and practices became better known to literate Europeans.[18]

Writings taking stock of this diversity, to be sure, often tell us more about Western attitudes toward "religious others" than about the religious traditions described. Nonetheless, the emergence of this literature indicates the beginning of a major shift in European consciousness. Permit a few examples. In 1614 the English writer Edward Brerewood published *Enquiries Touching the Diversity of Languages and Religions through the Chief Parts of the World.* Alexander Ross's *Pansebia, or a View of All Religions of the World* appeared in 1653.[19] These and a handful of other such works paved the way for subsequent sweeping surveys, such as Daniel Defoe's *Dictionary of All Religions* (1704) and, not least, Bernard Picart and Jean Frederic Bernard's multivolume *Ceremonies et coutumes religieuses de tous les peuples du monde* (1723–37), a work recently touted as offering the "first global vision of religion."[20] In 1755, David Hume sought to find the "natural" origins of religious belief in his influential *Natural History of Religion*, while Charles Brosses's *Du cultes des dieux fétiches* (1760) explored various "primitive" beliefs, coining the term *fetish* in the process.[21] These works preceded still others, such as Nicholas-Sylvestre Bergier's *L'origine des dieux de paganisme* (1767); C. F. Dupuis's *Origins de tours les cultes* (1795); Joseph Priestley's *A Comparison of the Institutes of Moses with Those of the Hindoos and Other Ancient Nations* (1799); Christoph Meiners's *Allgemeine kritische Geschichte der Religionen* (1806–7); Hannah Adams's *A Dictionary of All Religions and Religious Denominations* (1817); Josiah Condor's *An Analytic and Comparative View of All Religions Now Extant among Mankind: With Their Internal Diversities of Creed and Profession* (1838); and Charles A. Goodrich's *A Pictorial and Descriptive Account of All Religions* (1851). And this is a truncated list.

Eighteenth- and nineteenth-century European colonialism, especially that of the British in India, opened further vistas for comparative religious inquiry. The extraordinary linguist and "father of British Orientalism" Sir William Jones (1746–94) published in 1788 his seminal essay, "On the Gods of Greece, Italy, and India."[22] He also translated several "Brahmin" legal and holy texts from Sanskrit to English, not to mention famously advancing the now-accepted theory that Sanskrit and European languages shared a common "Indo-European" root.[23] Jones's work heralded an avalanche of "Orientalist" scholarship on the languages, cultures, and religious beliefs and practices of South Asia. The Frenchman Eugène Burnouf—to offer another example—published in 1844 *An Introduction to the History of Buddhism in India*, a path-breaking work of modern Buddhist studies, while Samuel Johnson's multivolume *Oriental Religions and Their Relation to Universal Religions* appeared in the 1870s.[24]

Such studies sometimes had an empirical mien, but others possessed a speculative, philosophical character, especially among Romantic, Idealist, and (in North America) Unitarian and Transcendentalist authors.[25] Friedrich Schlegel epitomized this outlook in 1808 with the publication of *On the Language and Wisdom of the Indians*, which effusively praised the "spiritual" nature of Eastern thought as an antidote to Western rationalism and materialism—a commonplace distinction in later literature.[26] American thinkers such as Ralph Waldo Emerson, Andrews Norton, Amos Alcott, Henry David Thoreau, and James Freeman Clarke also turned to the East for spiritual succor and intellectual excitement, theorizing, in the words of Michael Altman, about "an essentially spiritual and mystical India, which provided needed balance to Western materialism and Protestant practicality."[27] In 1857, Emerson's "Brahma" appeared in the *Atlantic Monthly* to great fanfare. In 1871 Clarke published *Ten Great Religions: An Essay in Comparative Theology*, a work that passed through no fewer than thirty editions before 1893.[28] "Due in no small part to the romantic's fascination for strange and remote phenomena, the whole field of religion in the Near East, India, and the Far East gradually became [throughout the nineteenth century] the object of intensified labor," according to Ahlstrom.[29]

Scholarly enthusiasm for "the East," typified by William Jones in the late eighteenth century, arguably reached its apogee in the work of the German expatriate Oxford scholar Friedrich Max Müller (1823–1900), widely considered the founder of comparative religion as an academic discipline. At the Royal Society in London in 1870, Müller delivered a series of lectures, later published as an *Introduction to the Science of Religion*, that gave definition and shape to the emerging field.[30] At Paris in 1873, he met with like-minded scholars at the first of many international congresses of Orientalists that took place in the late nineteenth century.[31] Beginning in 1879, Müller spearheaded a monumental fifty-volume editing project—"the Sacred Books of the East" (1879–1910)—which set as its goal to translate and edit major texts of Asian religions into English, most for the first time.[32] The project sought nothing less, Müller averred in the preface to the first volume, than "to comprehend the height and depth of the human mind in its searchings after the Infinite."[33] For all these reasons, it should come as no surprise that speakers at Chicago in 1893 frequently invoked the name of Müller, who did not attend himself but sent a paper to be read aloud. Shortly after the parliament, he forecast that the gathering would go down as "one of the most memorable events in the history of the world."[34]

Müller did not work in isolation. Several scholars and institutions on both sides of the Atlantic helped to expand and define the field of comparative religion. They too paved the way for Chicago. One could point to Cornelis Petrus Tiele (1830–1902), P. D. Chantepie de la Saussaye (1848–1920), E. B. Tylor (1837–1917), Otto

Pfleiderer (1839–1908), Morris Jastrow (1861–1921), and Albert Réville (1826–1920), among others.[35] In 1873 the University of Geneva established lectures in comparative religion, followed shortly by similar chairs at other Swiss universities. In 1876–77, the Dutch Universities Act led to chairs in the "science of religion" at the universities of Amsterdam, Gröningen, Leiden, and Utrecht. Other universities soon followed suit, including the Collège de France (1880), Brussels (1884), Oxford (1886), and Cornell (1891).[36] On the eve of the Columbian Exposition, books by occupants of these chairs included titles such as *Prolègomènes de l'histoire des religions* and *Historie des religions* (both by Réville), *Lehrbuch der Religionsgeschichte* (Chantepie), and *The Religious Systems of the World* (Tiele). In 1880, the journal *La revue de l'historie des religions* began publication in France—the first journal of its kind.[37] In sum, the scientific study of religion or comparative religion—in contradistinction to Christian theology—was coming into its own as the parliament in Chicago was planned and launched. As we shall see, many speakers conversant with this new academic field spoke at the parliament, which is widely credited with aiding the field's expansion and popularization in the early twentieth century.[38]

But specifically Christian *theological* interests were emphatically not incidental to the parliament. Most planners and boosters of the parliament had been powerfully shaped by the Protestant experience of the nineteenth century. Over and beyond Schleiermacher's influence on elite opinion, this meant, principally, three things. First, it meant acquaintance with the manifold efforts of Protestant missionaries across the globe. As is well established, Protestant missionary work went from a trickle in the late eighteenth century to a roaring stream by the eve of the parliament.[39] Data, stories, and artifacts from missionaries made available a hitherto unknown wealth of ethnographic information on non-Western cultures, languages, and religions.[40] In an effort to understand the mission field in which they operated, Protestant missionaries, often going beyond comparable efforts by their Catholic counterparts, went to great lengths to make sense of alien religious beliefs and the various sacred texts and traditions behind them.[41] The Protestant emphasis on *sola scriptura*, moreover, provided a powerful boost to linguistic and textual work. Alongside the aforementioned scholars of religions, missionaries (sometimes serious scholars in their own right) contributed to a massive upsurge in general knowledge about global religiosity. "It was by and large in the nineteenth century," Mitch Numark has written on the influence of missionaries, "that the religions labeled Hinduism, Zoroastrianism, Buddhism, Jainism and their associated texts were more substantially explicated, studied, and compared, translated into English [and other Western languages], and situated on a world religions map that remains essentially unchanged to this day."[42]

Second, more detailed knowledge of non-Western religious beliefs affected the taxonomy that Western Christians deployed to make sense of other religions. Prior to the modern era, European and North American Christians tended to lump religious beliefs, globally viewed, into a quadripartite scheme: Christian, Jewish, Muslim, and what was alternately labeled paganism, heathenism, polytheism, or idolatry.[43] More detailed knowledge of other religious traditions, especially those of South Asia, brought an end to this taxonomy and the beginnings of another system, namely, a list of roughly ten or a dozen "world religions"—often designated in the twentieth century as "major world religions" or "great world religions." This new system, according to Tomoko Masuzawa, "has since turned into a convention, which is still regnant today." The latter half of the nineteenth century saw this new scheme gaining widespread recognition; it was a transitional period, an extended time of "taxonomic disturbance" between the old system and the new.[44]

Finally, this taxonomic fluidity and greater knowledge of other religious beliefs affected Christian theology itself. Prior to the modern era, and admitting some exceptions, most Christian theologians, whether Protestant or Catholic, held a highly exclusivist understanding of Christianity: Christianity was the correct faith and others were simply false, if not positively diabolical. The changes outlined above attenuated this view, but did not necessarily demote Christianity from its superlative status. Rather, at least among liberal Protestants, other faiths came to be viewed as not so much wrong as incomplete, inchoate forms of what Christianity expressed with greater fullness. This view heralded the "inclusivist" view of other faiths. In its day, it was often tagged as the "fulfillment view," whereby Christianity does not simply negate and replace other beliefs but rather enriches and completes them.

Frederick Denison Maurice's *Religions of the World and Their Relations to Christianity* (1847) typifies this outlook; the book, based on lectures he had given, was wildly popular in the late nineteenth century, reprinted multiple times before the parliament. For Maurice, all religions—each having its origin in the "spiritual nature and faculties of man"—yearn for what is truly transcendent and universal. But only Christianity can satisfy this ultimate desire, and hence all religions, if they ascertain what is best and truest in them, should aspire to merge with Christianity, submitting their more particular truths to its higher truth. As Maurice expressed it in the 1881 edition of his book: "Do not all [religions] demand another ground than the human one? Is not Christianity the consistent asserter of that higher ground? Does it not distinctly and consistently refer every human feeling and consciousness to that ground? Is it not for this reason able to interpret and reconcile the other religions of the earth? Does it not in this way provide itself to be not a human system, but the Revelation, which [all] human beings require?"[45] In themselves, each religion at some level expressed the goodness of God's creation, since humankind, Christians and Jews had long held, had been created in the image of God. They thus deserved a measure of respect and admiration. But ultimately this did not suffice, according to Maurice, until each religion found "fulfillment" in the higher unity offered by Christianity. This global reconciliation of all religious traditions into the magnanimous bosom of Christianity constituted for Maurice nothing less than what Scripture called "the Kingdom of God."[46]

On the eve of the 1893 parliament, a veritable industry of books expressing similar theological views had emerged—mostly by and for Protestants of a liberal bent. Adherents of newer movements, such as Swedenborgianism and Theosophy, also sympathized to varying degrees, as did Unitarians.[47] On the one hand, the opinions expressed in these books could be read to justify Protestant missionary endeavors which, again, had been extensive throughout the nineteenth century. On the other hand, they provided grounds not for contesting and attempting to confute other beliefs, as much past missionary activity had done, but rather for entering into conversation with them and attempting to find connecting points between their (more limited) outlooks and the higher truths of Christianity. Drawing

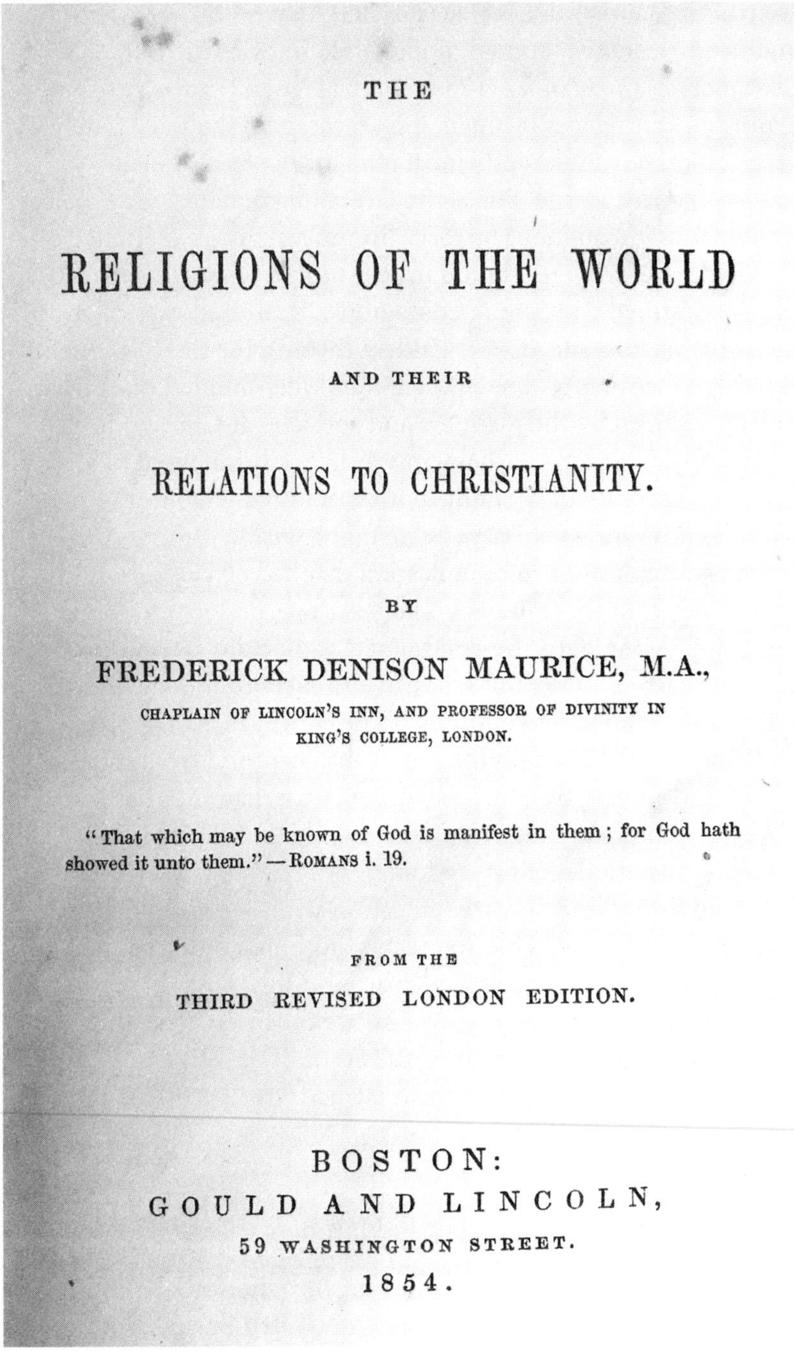

THE

RELIGIONS OF THE WORLD

AND THEIR

RELATIONS TO CHRISTIANITY.

BY

FREDERICK DENISON MAURICE, M.A.,

CHAPLAIN OF LINCOLN'S INN, AND PROFESSOR OF DIVINITY IN KING'S COLLEGE, LONDON.

"That which may be known of God is manifest in them; for God hath showed it unto them."—ROMANS i. 19.

FROM THE

THIRD REVISED LONDON EDITION.

BOSTON:

GOULD AND LINCOLN,

59 WASHINGTON STREET.

1854.

Title page of Frederick Denison Maurice's Religions of the World and Their Relations to Christianity. *(Author's collection.)*

from both Maurice and Schleiermacher, Alexander V. G. Allen (1841–1908), for instance, argued along these lines in his influential *The Continuity of Christianity* (1884). In his view, all faiths at some level expressed "the deeper instincts and yearnings of the soul, as they were seen not merely in the individual man, or the local transitory phases of some particular age, but as they were illustrated in the experience of humanity throughout history." In the religious experience of humanity, therefore, one should expect to find what Allen called, in a phrase destined to become contagious, "scattered rays of truth"—gems of wisdom and partial truths yearning for the fulfillment offered in Christianity.[48] Such a view and like-minded ones were repeatedly voiced by the planners and speakers at Chicago in 1893.

Finally, Chicago's parliament was not only indebted to ideas and religious currents of thought, but to developments in the material world. The event would have been unimaginable without revolutions in transportation and communication that had taken place during the nineteenth century. The technologies of steam locomotion and the telegraph, along with the emergence of globally aware newspapers and journals, allowed for types of cross-civilizational interactions impossible in previous centuries. "The conveyance of people, goods, and news was released [in the nineteenth century] from the shackles of the bio-motor system," as Jürgen Osterhammel has written.[49] "We have entered upon a new era," as J. N. Farquhar expressed it in the early twentieth century, adding: "All parts of the world have at last been brought into communication with one another. . . . From now on it will be possible to talk of full human intercourse: in the past all has been but racial and partial. Only now do we begin to hear the music of humanity."[50] This moonstruck sense of progress, of modernity, while influencing the ethos of the larger exposition at Chicago, also reflected realities that had made possible the ambitions behind the parliament.

A Plan Is Hatched

A booming, gritty industrial and transportation hub conjured into being from the economic needs of the United States' westward expansion, the city of Chicago made a bold bid to host the world's fair to mark the four hundredth anniversary of Columbus's voyage to the New World in 1492. The competition was stiff. New York, Washington, DC, and St. Louis also contended for the honor. But Chicago won out, in part, according to the fair's official history, because "the growth of Chicago from a frontier camp to an active city of more than a million inhabitants with corresponding advances in commercial, industrial, and intellectual activities best typifies the giant young nation that occupies the fairest portion of the New World whose discovery the projected fair is to commemorate."[51]

Known alternately as the World's Columbian Exposition, Chicago's World's Fair, or the Columbiad, the fair did not open to the public until 1 May 1893, a year behind schedule, due to construction delays. Although taking its cue from previous world fairs, such as London's famous Crystal Palace Exhibition in 1851 or the Paris Exposition of 1889, Chicago's fair outdid them all in scale and grandeur; it was a Gilded Age confection, a blunt statement of the nineteenth century's preening sense of progress stamped with American exceptionalism.[52] U.S. president Benjamin Harrison had invited "all the nations of the earth to take part in the commemoration of an event that is pre-eminent in human history."[53] A congressional committee report of May 1892, a year prior to opening, read: "In its scope and magnificence, the [Chicago] Exposition stands alone. There is nothing like it in history. It easily surpasses all kindred enterprises."[54] Covering hundreds of acres in what is today Jackson Park on Chicago's South Side and featuring two hundred new buildings, the fair welcomed around 27 million guests from all over the world before closing on 30 October 1893. Total costs came to over $35 million—a huge sum by the standards of the day.[55] Facades of buildings were made not of stone but of a mixture of plaster and cement and painted white; hence, the fairgrounds came to be known as "the White City." Thirty-six nations and forty-six American states and territories built exhibits to display their contribution to civilization's forward march. Technological, scientific, and industrial emphases predominated, but visitors could ponder a magnificent jumble of so much else. One could ride in the world's first Ferris wheel, for instance, stroll down the Midway Plaisance, walk down a simulated "Street in Cairo" (replete with belly dancers), visit life-size reproductions of Columbus's three ships or, just off the fairgrounds, attend Buffalo Bill's Wild West Show. Frequently mesmerized and overwhelmed, visitors walked and gawked, attempting to comprehend the modernity and diversity of it all.[56] "Chicago asked in 1893 for the first time the question," Henry Adams wrote after visiting the fair, "whether the American people [as a nation] knew where they were driving."[57] (Adams doubted that they did.)

To say the least, this was a peculiar environment to host an extended discussion among representatives of the world's religious traditions. That it happened is in large part due to the ruminations and ambitions of Charles Carroll Bonney (1831–1903), a Chicago lawyer and Swedenborgian, who in his youth had become fascinated by "the Science of Comparative Religion," as he later recorded.[58] Once Chicago had been selected as the host city (by an act of Congress) and planning began, Bonney and a handful of confidants began to wonder if the "material" emphases of the impending fair should be balanced with something more "spiritual" in nature. "The crowning glory of the World's Fair," he opined in the *Statesman* on 20 September 1889, "should not be the . . . material triumphs, industrial achievements, and mechanical victories of man, however magnificent that display might be. *Something higher and nobler is demanded by the enlightened and progressive spirit of the age.*"[59]

Planners of the fair heard his voice and invited him to submit an idea for what he had in mind. He proposed the formation of an auxiliary commission to plan for several congresses on cultural, religious, and humanitarian topics to coincide with the fair. The proposal passed muster. Accordingly, on 30 October 1890, "the World's Congress Auxiliary of the World's Columbian Exhibition of 1893" came into existence, with Bonney as its appointed president. Its motto captured its aim: "Not things but men, not matter but mind."[60] This body in turn formed "the General Committee of the World's Congress Auxiliary on Religious Congresses" for the planning and preparation of denominational congresses, but also, crucially, to set in motion planning for a general event involving representatives of the world's major religions.[61] Bonney invited the Reverend John Henry Barrows (1847–1902), pastor of Chicago's First Presbyterian Church, to chair this body, which consisted of sixteen members altogether.[62] Protestants of a liberal bent dominated the committee, but it also included Unitarians; Swedenborgians; a Catholic, Patrick A. Feehan, archbishop of Chicago; and a Jewish rabbi, Emil Hirsch of Sinai

Temple in Chicago.[63] The Unitarian minister and editor of the liberal religious weekly *Unity*, Jenkin Lloyd Jones (1843–1918), became the committee's secretary and proved to be an especially active member.[64] From the work of this committee, and from ongoing interactions between Bonney and Barrows, the idea for the World's Parliament of Religions gradually took shape. As one scholar has put it: "It was Bonney's inspiration . . . but it was Barrows' energy and single-minded determination that made the idea a reality."[65] Or, as Barrows himself later wrote about the committee's aim in a communiqué to potential advisors for the project: "The plan of holding a Parliament of Religions, at which the representatives of the great historic faiths shall sit together in frank and friendly conference over the great things of our common spiritual and moral life, is no longer a dream."[66]

Before convening the Committee for Religious Congresses for the first time, Bonney prepared a "Preliminary Publication" to define the committee's general aim. In their work, he stated, members should strive "to unite all religion against all irreligion; to make the Golden Rule the basis of this union; to present to the world in the Religious Congresses, to be held in connection with the Columbian Exposition of 1893, the substantial unity of many religions and the good deeds of the Religious Life; to provide for a World's Parliament of Religions, in which their common aims and common grounds of union may be set forth, and the marvelous Religious Progress of the Nineteenth Century be reviewed; and to facilitate separate and Independent Congresses of different Religious Denominations and Organizations, under their own officers, in which their business may be transacted, their achievements presented, and their work for the future considered."[67] Bonney gave the committee several additional charges, asking its members to examine the social influence of religion, note its influence on art and literature, provide contemporary global religious statistics, and explore harmonies between religion and science. In short, the committee's mandate proved rather immense, suffused with the unrestrained ambition and optimism of the fair at large.[68]

Barrows received the mandate eagerly and with a sense of high purpose. He began to court businessmen to obtain funding. Working with the committee, he discussed precedents for the endeavor, singling out "Akbar, the greatest of the Mogul Emperors."[69] He prepared a "preliminary address" to serve as the basis of an invitation to the parliament, which he sent out to thousands of the "most eminent" religious leaders across the globe.[70] "Believing that God is and that he has not left himself without witness," the address began, and

> believing that the influence of Religion tends to advance the general welfare, and is the most vital force in the social order of every people, and convinced that of a truth God is no respecter of persons, but that in every nation he that feareth him and worketh righteousness is accepted of him, we affectionately invite the representatives of all faiths to aid us in presenting to the world, at the Exposition of 1893, the religious harmonies and unities of humanity, and also in showing forth the moral and spiritual agencies which are at the root of human progress. It is proposed to consider the foundations of religious Faith, to review the triumphs of Religion in all ages, to set forth the present state of Religion among the nations and its influence over Literature, Art, Commerce, Government and the Family Life, to indicate its power in promoting Temperance and Social Purity and its harmony with true Science, to show its dominance in the higher institutions of learning, to make prominent the value of the weekly rest-day on religious and other grounds, and to contribute to those forces which shall bring about the unity of the race in the worship of God and the service of man.[71]

In addition, Barrows and the committee formulated several guidelines and ten goals to serve as a general basis for the parliament. With respect to the former, Barrows communicated to prospective speakers that they should speak in English (or arrange for translation), articulate their views with "frankness" but not voice "unfriendly criticisms" of others' faiths, abide by the spirit of the preliminary address sent to them, and not submit any resolutions for a vote.[72] "By far, the most important of all these rules," Bonney later recorded, "was that which excluded controversy and prohibited strife. . . . The rigorous exclusion of this spirit [of controversy] from the Parliament of Religions made its success possible."[73]

As was also true of the invitation, the parliament's ten goals were strongly inflected with liberal Protestant sensibilities. Six of them were formulated as follows:

> 1. To bring together in conference, for the first time in history, the leading representatives of the great Historic Religions of the world.
> 2. To show to men, in the most impressive way, what and how many important truths the various religions held and teach in common.
> 3. To promote and deepen the spirit of human brotherhood among religious men of diverse faiths, through friendly conference and mutual good understanding, while not seeking to foster the temper of indifferentism, and not striving to achieve any formal and outward unity.
> 7. To inquire what light each religion has afforded, or may afford, to the other religions of the world.
> 9. To discover, from competent men, what light religion has to throw on the great problems of the present age, especially the important questions connected with temperance, labor, education, wealth and poverty.
> 10. To bring the nations of the earth into a more friendly fellowship, in the hope of securing permanent international peace.[74]

Despite the heavy Christian flavor of many of these goals and the fact that scant recompense was offered for participation, the response to the invitation, nationally and globally, proved extensive—even if American Protestants ultimately came to dominate the parliament's lineup.

Numerous luminaries accepted the invitation and/or voiced approbation of the project as a whole, including the highly regarded Cardinal James Gibbons, archbishop of Baltimore and leading American Catholic prelate; Isaac Mayer Wise, guiding light of American Reform Judaism; the well-known Congregationalist minister Lyman Abbot; the leader of Christian Science, Mary Baker Eddy; advocate of Theosophy Annie Besant; Philip Schaff, renowned church historian and ecumenist; and Daniel Offord, spokesman for the Shakers.[75]

REV JOHN HENRY BARROWS, D.D., CHICAGO.

John Henry Barrows. (From John Henry Barrows, ed., The World's Parliament of Religions, *vol. 1 [Chicago: Parliament Publishing, 1893]. Author's collection.)*

Other notables included Bishop John J. Keane, rector of the Catholic University of America; historian and Unitarian minister Edward Everett Hale; Washington Gladden, champion of the Social Gospel; social activists and suffragists Elizabeth Cady Stanton and Frances Willard; and Sephardic rabbi H. Pereira Mendes.[76] The former prime minister of Britain, William Gladstone, also warmly blessed the project, as did the acclaimed poets John Greenleaf Whittier and Alfred Lord Tennyson.[77] Bishop Keane spoke for many when he sized up the parliament as an opportunity for the "friendly and brotherly comparison of convictions," adding: "Such an assemblage of intelligent and conscientious men . . . will be an honorable event in the history of Religion, and cannot fail to accomplish much good."[78]

Countries and regions represented among those accepting the invitation included Britain, Sweden, Switzerland, France, Germany, Russia, Turkey, Greece, Egypt, Syria, India, Japan, China, Ceylon (Sri Lanka), New Zealand, Brazil, and Canada. The general program indicated that religious outlooks to be considered included "theism in general," Judaism, Islam, Hinduism, Buddhism, Taoism, Confucianism, Shinto, Zoroastrianism, Catholicism, Eastern Orthodoxy and, not least, Protestantism (in many forms)—in short, practically every "major world religion" and some minor ones as well.[79] Leading representatives of Eastern faiths included, inter alia, Syoen Shaku (Buddhism in Japan), Pung Kwang Yu (Confucianism), Anagarika Dharmapala (Buddhism in Ceylon [Sri Lanka]), Virchand Gandhi (Jainism), Pratap Chandra Mojumdar (Reform Hinduism or Brahmo Samaj), and Swami Vivekananda (Vedanta Hinduism). Vivekananda cut an especially striking figure at the parliament, as we shall see. Regrettably, the only Muslim speaker was Mohammed Alexander Russell Webb, an Anglo-American convert to Islam.[80] In the final analysis, even if Protestants and Americans preponderated at the parliament, the diversity among those who accepted the invitation still made for an unprecedented historical event. Barrows was very pleased by the response.[81]

But all was not smooth sailing. Latter-day Saints (Mormons), for instance, felt jilted because they were intentionally excluded.[82] There was only negligible recognition of Native American or African American religious views—although Frederick Douglass showed up one day, offering impromptu remarks on racial injustice and the importance of human unity.[83] What is more, the parliament received censure from some influential quarters. While some American Catholic leaders had embraced the parliament, the hierarchy in Rome expressed skepticism, and Pope Leo XIII (r. 1878–1903), as we shall see, would later condemn all such "promiscuous" religious gatherings.[84] The archbishop of Canterbury, Edward White Benson, surprised many when he came out against the parliament, claiming that "the Christian religion is the *one* religion" and its appearance alongside others could not take place "without [it] assuming the equality of the other intended members and the parity of its position and claims."[85] The Ottoman sultan Abdul Hamid II also strongly dissented and discouraged Muslim participation—a fact that helps explain the lack of Muslims present. At home, popular Protestant evangelists, such as D. L. Moody, criticized the parliament for giving "heathen" views a national platform. Several Baptist groups demurred on Sabbatarian grounds once they got wind of lectures scheduled to take place on Sundays. Finally, the Presbyterian General Assembly—to which Barrows's own church belonged—officially denounced the parliament, although this act received widespread censure from others within the denomination and in fact many Presbyterians participated.[86]

As the opening of the parliament drew near, a buzz of anticipation was in the air.[87] "The Parliament of Religions to be held in Chicago from September 11 to 27," the daily *Outlook* wrote in late August of 1893, "will the first tangible effort toward uniting the different religions of the world in common cause for a greater humanity. Many successful Congresses have been held thus far, but not one of them has challenged the attention of thinking people in so marked a degree as will this unique Parliament of Religions."[88] Similarly, the *Chicago Tribune* informed its readers of the "unique assembly" happening in their midst; "it will be the most novel and at the same time the most interesting exhibit that a World's Exposition could make."[89]

Earlier, Barrows had stoked excitement in an address given at Madison Square Garden in New York to the National Convention of the Societies of Christian Behavior. His words reflected his understanding of the coming parliament as an educational opportunity on the one hand, but also as a chance to render the Christian Gospel compelling in a hitherto unprecedented public way. "The Exposition will not only furnish an unparalleled spectacle to the eye, it will also provide for the mind an unequaled feast," he told the crowd. "At the Parliament of Religions the nobler and grander facts of our Christian civilization will be presented to the candid judgement of the world." Lest anyone worry that other faiths would outshine Christianity, Barrows asserted that "no one [should] fear that the solar orb of Christianity is to be eclipsed by the lanterns and rushlights of other faiths." Even so, the smaller lights of other faiths would have the opportunity in Chicago to criticize actions of the

United States and those of other Western nations, particularly with respect to imperialism. And Barrows welcomed this: "The time has come when Christendom [will] repent in dust and ashes," he said before cataloguing Western misdeeds such as the rum trade on Africa's west coast and the opium trade across South Asia.[90] To those who felt that the very idea of the parliament contravened the Gospel's missionary aspect, Barrows replied that "any wise missionary in Bombay or Madras would be glad to gather beneath the shelter of his roof the scholarly and sincere representatives of the Hindu religion, so Christian America invites to the shelter of her hospitable roof, at her grand Festival of Peace, the spiritual leaders of mankind, for friendly conference over the deepest problems of human existence."[91] In essence, Barrows's broadly inclusivist vision sought to preserve the superlative status of Christianity, yet justify dialogue with other faiths, while welcoming foreign criticism of Western misdeeds abroad. An ambitious goal, it would seem, but not a scarce outlook at the parliament.

The Parliament Opens

On the morning of 11 September 1893, a facsimile of the Liberty Bell tolled ten times in the White City, paying homage to "the ten great religions of the world"—Confucianism, Taoism, Shinto, Hinduism, Buddhism, Jainism, Sikhism, Judaism, Christianity, and Islam. Concurrently, seven miles away in the newly built Memorial Art Palace (today Chicago's Art Institute), more than sixty religious leaders processed in and huddled together on a single platform in the Hall of Columbus to begin the parliament's first day.[92] Thousands crammed into the hall to witness the spectacle. The Christian aegis of the gathering became clear when those assembled were led in reciting the 100th Psalm and the Trinitarian Doxology before Cardinal Gibbons led them in the Lord's Prayer.[93] Still, the diversity of the scene was remarkable. There were "men [and women] from all the nations of the earth, representing all the religions of the earth," the *Chicago Tribune* reported the following day; "strangers from the farther points of the world with their picturesque garbs [sat] in front."[94] Another eyewitness spoke of "the most picturesque and impressive spectacle."[95]

The newly built Memorial Art Palace (later the Chicago Art Institute), location of the World's Parliament of Religions in 1893. (From B. C. Cigrand, The Rise, Fall, and Revival of Dental Prosthesis *[Chicago, 1893]. Image courtesy of Wikimedia Commons.)*

After the Lord's Prayer, Bonney and Barrows delivered opening speeches. Both waxed grandiloquent. "The importance of this event, its influence on the future relations of the various races of men," Bonney told the crowd, "cannot be too highly esteemed. If this Congress shall faithfully execute the duties with which it has been charged, it will become the joy of the whole earth, and stand in human history like a new Mount Zion, crowned with glory and marking the actual beginning of a new epoch of brotherhood and peace." Thereafter, Bonney recounted the work that had made the parliament possible and attended to logistical matters before uttering his conviction that "no attempt is here made to treat all religions of equal merit. . . . In this Congress each system of Religion stands by itself in its own perfect integrity, uncompromised, in any degree, by its relation to any other." He then enjoined everyone to eschew controversy and seek together "a better knowledge of the religious condition of all mankind, with an earnest desire to be useful to each other and to all others who love truth and righteousness."[96]

Barrows followed Bonney at the lectern. Greeting the crowd and also recounting aspects of the "colossal undertaking" that had brought them all together, he made clear his view that their assembly in this "young capital of western civilization" constituted "an event of race-wide and perpetual significance." More so than Bonney, however, Barrows saw their work as infused with Christianity refracted through the American experience. Referring to the United States as a "Christian nation," he remarked that "in America they [church and state] are separated, and in this land the widest intellectual and spiritual freedom is realized." This reality empowered the planners to act, Barrows believed. Their primary tasks, he opined, was to expose how little Americans knew about other traditions while demonstrating that religious belief in general (despite what its cultured despisers might say) constituted an able contributor to human flourishing and progress. In his own words: "It is our desire and hope to broaden and purify the mental and spiritual vision of men. Believing that nations and faiths are separated by ignorance and prejudice, why shall not this Parliament help to remove one and soften the other? . . . We are met here together . . . [as] children of God, sharers with all men in weakness and guilt and need, sharers with devout souls everywhere in aspiration and hope and longing. We are met as religious men, believing even here in this capital of material wonders . . . that there is a spiritual root to all human progress."[97] After Barrows sat down, others gave shorter speeches, beginning with Archbishop Feehan of Chicago, regarded essentially as a co-host of the event. In turn came Cardinal Gibbons of Baltimore; Universalist minister and women's rights activist Augusta Jane Chapin (the first of several women to speak); H. N. Higinbotham, president of the Columbian Exposition; and Boston's Congregationalist pastor Alexander McKenzie.

Thereafter, several religious notables from around the world offered brief opening remarks. None made a more lasting impression than the much-anticipated, charismatic Swami Vivekananda of India: when he addressed the audience as "'sisters and brothers of America,' peals of applause followed that lasted for several minutes."[98]

Most thanked their hosts, and many marveled at the wonders of modern travel and communication that had made such a gathering possible. Bishop Benjamin W. Arnett of the African Methodist Episcopal Church, who had been asked to speak "to give color" to the parliament, spoke last, representing both Africans *and* African Americans! When he finished, it was nearly 5 p.m.—the whole day was taken up with opening remarks. "For the most part the hearers remained to the end," recorded the *Chicago Tribune*, "and many lingered to obtain closer views of the strangers from far away countries."[99] Another eyewitness recorded the scene of the first day as "most remarkable. There were strange robes, turbans and tunics, crosses and crescents, flowing hair and tonsured monks."[100] Yet another reporter crowed about "a spectacle that has never been equaled in the history of the world. . . . Here in the invigorating atmosphere of this young continent the learned men of these old Eastern nations came to exchange confidences with the leaders of thought from Europe and shake the hand and feel the heart-throb of the versatile and practical American at home." In the evening, a reception was held at the elegant home of one A. C. Bartlett on Prairie Avenue.[101]

Sixteen days of lectures followed, over two hundred in all, each averaging about thirty minutes.[102] Barrows had attempted to corral speakers to address one of sixteen themes, one for each day. In one report, he listed these as "God, Man, Religion Essentially Characteristic of Humanity, Systems of Religion, Sacred Books of the World, Religion and the Family, the Religious Leaders of Mankind, Religion in its Relation to the Natural Sciences and to Arts and Letters, Religions in its Relation to Morals, Religion and Social Problems, Religion and Civil Society, Religion and the Love of Mankind, the Present Religious Condition of Christendom, Religious Reunion of Christendom, the Religious Reunion of the Whole Human Family and Elements of Perfect Religion." Many of these, to be sure, expressed specifically Christian concerns. One speaker from India, Manilal Dwivedi, said as much: the topics seemed "intended to cover points of principal interest to the Western mind."[103]

While many of the proposed topics received coverage, coordinating them all proved cumbersome, as many speakers arrived with their own agenda and not infrequently followed a train of thought inspired by the moment. Hence the structure of the whole possessed a higgledy-piggledy character, to which several guests attested. The schedule was further complicated by the fact that concurrent with the parliament's lectures those of individual "denominational congresses" and those of various "scientific" sessions took place; these too had been planned by Barrows's Committee for Religious Congresses. Hence, guests went back and forth from the Hall of Columbus, where most of the parliament's lectures took place, to other rooms in the Memorial Art Palace. To appease overflow crowds, sessions were sometimes even staged twice.[104]

To illustrate the cornucopia of offerings, a single day, 15 September, merits profiling. On this day, attendees could listen to the lectures "What the Dead Religions Have Bequeathed to the Living," "Points of Contact between Christianity and Mohammedanism," "Study of Comparative Theology," "Real Religion of To-day," "Confucianism," "Comparative Study of the World's Religions," "Importance of the Serious Study of Religions," "Social Office of Religious Feeling," and "Buddhism of Siam [Thailand]." Down the hallway in the "scientific" section, moreover, one could take in "Practical Service of the Science of Religion to the Cause of Religious Unity and the Missionary Enterprise," "Japanese Buddhism," "Influence of Egyptian Religion on Other Religions," and "Genesis and Development of Confucianism" as well as a panel discussion of a paper entitled "Religio Scientia" submitted by Canadian geologist Sir William Dawson.[105]

Outside the official program, conversations took place and friendships were made, and this, Barrows recorded, was a key legacy of the event: "Very much of the best life of this first great convention of the world's religious leaders was lived outside the daily meetings in the Hall of Columbus. The friendships which were formed, and the social intercourse enjoyed will be a part of the Parliament's [legacy]." In addition to hallway encounters, several individual denominations and organizations held "devotional meetings" to which other guests were invited. Evening receptions also took place, at which speakers and distinguished guests mingled. Referring to one of these, Barrows recorded: "Probably no such company, representing so large a diversity of nations and faiths, ever gathered before in an American residence."[106] In all, over one hundred thousand guests attended the parliament over its seventeen days, making it one of the best-attended and most-discussed events of the larger exposition.[107]

The makeup of the speakers is instructive. There were 196 speakers altogether, the vast majority of them American Protestants with most, but not all, inclined toward the liberal side of the theological spectrum, and who thus conceived of the parliament in broadly inclusivist terms. In addition, there were twelve Catholics, eight Eastern Orthodox, eleven Jews, and one Muslim. From Asia came twelve Buddhists, eight Hindus, and two representing Shintoism, two Zoroastrianism, two Confucianism, one Jainism, and one Taoism. Finally, a smattering of individuals represented smaller, newer movements, such as the Hindu Reform movement Brahmo Samaj and Baha'i, which made its American debut at the parliament and has retained a strong presence in Chicago to the present day.[108]

The parliament's last day, 27 September, was positively "pentecostal" in character, as several attendees described it. The halls of the Memorial Art Palace were filled to overflowing. A long line had formed simply to gain entrance and a black market had arisen to procure tickets. Inside, Chicago's Apollo Choir sang Mendelssohn's "Judge Me, O God," Handel's "Lift Up Your Heads, O Ye Gates," and the "Hallelujah Chorus" from the *Messiah*, among other numbers. Speaker after speaker arose and thanked Bonney and Barrows for their vision and hospitality. The city of Chicago was praised "as the first city in America, the first city in the world" and enjoined "with trumpet tones . . . [to] tell it [news of the parliament] to all the world." "The very atmosphere," as one guest later opined, seemed "pregnant with an indefinite, inexpressible something."[109] "Never since the confusion of tongues at Babel," another guest reflected, "have so many religions, so many creeds, stood side by side, hand in hand, and almost heart to heart, as in the great amphitheater last night. . . . The great Hall of Columbus . . . was [filled] by the greatest crowd that ever sat within its walls. On the stage . . . [the] somber raiment of the West only intensified the radiantly contrasted garbs of the Oriental priests."[110]

Jenkin Lloyd Jones, secretary of the congress, caught up in the moment, conveyed to the crowd that he had had a "vision" that future parliaments would take place—and he even proposed the Indian holy city of Benares as the next site.[111] An English clergyman,

Alfred Williams Momerie, similarly rapt, opined that the parliament was an "impossibility" that had nonetheless happened and now should be regarded as "the greatest event so far in the history of the world. . . . The Parliament is a new thing in the world."[112]

When their turns came, moderation restrained neither Barrows nor Bonney. "Our hopes have been more than realized," Barrows told the crowd. "We have learned that truth is large and there are more ways than one in God's providence by which men emerge out of darkness into the heavenly light." "If any honor is due for this magnificent achievement," he continued in a theologically inclusivist register," let it be given to the spirit of Christ, which is the spirit of love, in the hearts of those of many lands and faiths who have toiled for the high ends of this great meeting." After Barrows sat down, Bonney went even further: "What many deemed impossible God has finally wrought. The religions of the world have actually met in a great and imposing assembly; they have conferred together on the vital questions of life. . . . The influence which this Congress of Religions of the World will exert on the peace and prosperity of the world is beyond the power of human language to describe." At the close of Bonney's address, Rabbi Emil Hirsch led the crowd in a prayer and Bishop Keane offered a benediction before Bonney, in a fit of patriotism, led all in singing "America."[113]

And thus Chicago's World's Parliament of Religions came to an end. Akbar's legacy had been given new life.

Themes, Delegations, Performances

The rough details of the parliament are straightforward enough. Assessing the content of the speeches, however, not to mention the broader significance and legacy of the parliament, is a different matter entirely. These require analysis and interpretation. In light of the large-scale nature of the parliament, moreover, one should expect multiple layers of interpretation and many trajectories of influence. In what follows, I restrict myself to spotlighting several major themes of the speeches and notable performances by individuals and delegations that are relevant to the study of religion in general and the shaping of interfaith dialogue in particular. Thereafter, we shall look at dominant interpretations of the parliament offered directly after its closing before, finally, touching on the parliament's long-term legacy.

Given the striking modernity on display at the exposition, it should not surprise that many speakers, Western and Eastern, sought to rebut the notion that religion was a regressive or declining force in history. Instead, "Religion" (often capitalized in the proceedings) was widely depicted as a civilizing and progressive agent, at one level compatible with modernity but at another supplying modernity with an affective, spiritual dimension that it sorely lacked. We have already seen how Bonney and Barrows articulated such a view. But they were not alone. "Out of the heart of our materialistic civilization has come the cry of the spirit hungering for its food," as the Jewish writer Josephine Lazarus put it. "This cry had been heard by the religions of the world, which now had the opportunity, working together, [to] re-fashion it [modern civilization] upon a nobler plan, and consecrate it anew to a higher purpose and ideals." In a similar vein, the Unitarian Edward Everett Hale predicted that the twentieth century, nourished by "spiritual truths" derived from the world's religions, would build a new and enduring civilization dedicated to universal education, global healthcare, and the permanent avoidance of war by peaceful means.[114] Without the ennobling and humanitarian impulses of religion, speaker after speaker (Western and Eastern) warned, the modern world risked becoming a barren place, oppressed by technology, commerce, and the raw interests of power.

While a liberal Protestant inclusivist interpretation of Christianity constituted the dominant outlook among Western delegates at the parliament, some speakers went farther and advocated for, or at least alluded to, a "new religion" in the future, sometimes referred to as a "universal religion," one that humanity ought to strive for and whose time had perhaps arrived. Speakers presented different versions of such a religion, but two dominant views prevailed: (1) a least-common-denominator religion, organized around a single or several basic unifying principles that all faiths presumably shared, or else (2) an amalgamation of the best things found in each separate religion. In an address entitled "Elements of a Universal Religion," the liberal Chicago rabbi Emil Hirsch, for instance, proclaimed that "the universal religion has as yet not evolved," but it was only a matter of time. This religion would bring all of humankind into a higher unity. Knowing boundaries neither of race nor nationality, this religion would "embrace in one covenant all the children of man." Adolph Brodbeck of Germany also called for a new religion on the basis of a sweeping idealism, understood as the perfection of the individual and human society. "The new religion is something new. Its name is Idealism. . . . Its chief aim is . . . the perfection in everything for the ideal of mankind."[115] In a similar key, the renowned French scholar of religion Albert Réville, although not in attendance, sent a paper read by a proxy entitled "Conditions and Outlook for a Universal Religion." Like Hirsch, Réville felt that "at present it would be vain to seek doctrinal accord among the great religions." Nonetheless, "this parliament marks the first step in the sacred path that shall one day bring man to *the* truly humanitarian and universal religion."[116]

In stark counterpoint, advocates of religious exclusivism also made their voices heard at the parliament. In a talk entitled "The Invincible Gospel," the evangelical pastor George Frederick Pentecost argued that Christianity "is not intolerant . . . but will in no case compromise with error, or enter into fellowship with a religious system that is not built on the Rock of Ages." Similarly, in "The Attitude of Christianity to Other Religions," William C. Wilkinson contended that, biblically understood, other faiths amounted to "idolatry." "According to Christianity," therefore, "they hinder, they do not help. Their adherents' hold on them is like the blind grasping of drowning men on roots or rocks that only tend to keep them to the bottom of the river."[117] Such pointedly exclusivist views were articulated by only a handful of speakers, but they too constitute part of the parliament's historical record.

Troubled by disunity on the mission field, many Protestant leaders on the eve of the parliament had made striving for Christian unity—what today we would call ecumenism—a priority in their thinking.[118] Not surprisingly, this topic often made its presence felt at the parliament. The dean of American church historians, the Swiss-German émigré theologian Philip Schaff, was especially grieved by Christian disunity and regarded the parliament as an ideal platform to offer his blueprint for the "reunion of Christendom."[119] An octogenarian, Schaff proved too feeble to lecture himself, but he sat winsomely on the stage while his paper was read by a proxy. Trying to separate the wheat from the chaff in major Protestant denominations, and speaking quite positively of Roman Catholicism (a relative rarity for a Protestant divine), Schaff made his case for "the reunion of the entire Catholic Church, Greek and Roman, with all Protestant Churches." The job of scholars like himself, he felt, was to "show the way to harmony, in a broader, higher, and deeper consciousness of God's truth and God's love." This could never be a coerced unity, however. A zealous convert to the American voluntary principle in religious matters, Schaff argued that any progress toward reunion that ran roughshod over the conscience of the individual or the will of a particular denomination vitiated the cause that it sought to serve. What is more, unity did not mean uniformity; Schaff envisioned a future harmony in quasi-Hegelian terms in which distinctions that had developed due to church divisions were preserved and yet somehow reconciled into a higher unity: "The world will never become wholly Greek, not wholly Roman, nor wholly Protestant, but it will become wholly Christian, and will include every type and every aspect, every virtue and every grace of Christianity—an endless variety in harmonious unity, Christ being all in all."[120] (Exactly where non-Christians fit in this scheme was a topic Schaff did not take up.)

If Protestant voices were the most voluble at the parliament, Catholics and Jews also made themselves heard. In a sense, the parliament represents an early transition in American life from unquestioned Protestant hegemony—often underwritten by currents of nativism—to what the scholar Will Herberg in the 1950s defined as the American trifecta of Protestant-Catholic-Jew captured in the twentieth-century neologism "Judeo-Christian."[121] Besides the quasi-hosting role played by Archbishop Patrick Feehan of Chicago, Cardinal Gibbons of Baltimore (the titular leader of American bishops) and Bishop John Keane, rector of the Catholic University, occupied notable positions.[122] Along with a prominent layman, William J. Onahan, Keane was largely responsible for securing Catholic participation in the first place despite considerable skepticism from other Catholics. In November 1892, he had written to the board of American archbishops arguing that the parliament was "an exceptionally good opportunity" and that the church's very presence would be "the best refutation of the error that one religion is as good as another."[123]

Cardinal Gibbons approved, later christening Chicago "Thaumatopolis," "the city of wonders, the city of miracles." He advised fellow Catholic participants to be charitable to all, recalling the famous words of St. Vincent Lerins: "In essentials, unity; in doubtful things, liberty; in all things, love."[124] In Gibbons's talk, "The Needs of Humanity Supplied by the Catholic Religion," the eminent cardinal focused largely on the social services and ministries offered by the Catholic Church. By far the most liberal Catholic address was given by Merwin-Marie Snell, who expressed sympathy with participants in search of a "universal religion." Among the last speakers, Keane struck a more conservative note, worrying about a syncretistic impulse lurking in the parliament's ethos and making clear his loyalty to Roman Catholicism: "We understand why the world [is] craving for unity [but this] can never be satisfied by mere aggregations and confederations of separate bodies for such a man-made union can never realize the oneness prayed for and predicted by the Son of God. Jesus Christ is the ultimate center of religion. He has declared that his one organic church is equally ultimate."[125] "Catholic participation at Chicago became a highly symbolic event of lasting importance," writes the contemporary scholar Dennis B. Downey; it helped "secure the wider acceptance of the Church and her tradition in American culture."[126] From afar, however, Rome remained skeptical and later said so.

The Jewish delegation was made up entirely of American Jews, who, theologically, leaned in a moderate or progressive direction, although more conservative and even incipiently Zionist voices were also present.[127] At the time of the parliament, Judaism's relation to modernity remained a contested topic, the relatively stable Orthodox, Conservative, and Reform branches having not yet been fully consolidated.[128] Papers by Jews included "Human Brotherhood as Taught by the Religions Based on the Bible" (Kaufmann Kohler), "The Theology of Judaism" (Isaac Mayer Wise), "Popular Errors about the Jews" (Joseph Silverman), "The Voice of the Mother of Religions on Social Questions" (Henry Berkowitz), the aforementioned "Elements of a Universal Religion" (Emil Hirsch), and "The Outlook of Judaism" (Josephine Lazarus). Kohler made a plea for mutual toleration, appealing to Lessing's *Nathan the Wise*. An outspoken liberal, Chicago's Emil Hirsch offered a stirring vision, as we have seen, of a future universal religion. Lazarus claimed Jews to be the "God-intoxicated race" and warned against a rising tide of anti-Semitism in Europe and "even in our own free-breathing America." "Mankind at large may not be ready for a universal religion," she averred, contravening Hirsch, "but let the Jews, with their prophetic instinct, their deep, spiritual insight, set the example and give the ideal."[129] But others urged caution, insisting that separatism must be an enduring characteristic of Judaism even if this did not preclude cooperation with members of other faiths. As was the case with Catholics, Jews effectively sought and gained through the parliament a more prominent and accepted, if still constrained, place in American national life and culture.[130]

Islam was underrepresented at the parliament. This certainly owes much to the fact that the Ottoman sultan Abdul Hamid II had criticized the whole endeavor. Two Indian Muslims, Amir Ali and Seid Ali Bigrami, were slated to give lectures, but neither showed up; nor did they send in papers. The only "cradle Muslim" to gain a (brief) hearing at the parliament was the Paris-based J. Sanna Abu, who sent a short letter that was read aloud in which he made the case for Islam's compatibility with the modern world. Several Protestant missionaries presented on aspects of Islam; mostly negative in tone, they interpreted Islam strictly through Christian theological lenses. Perhaps the most fair-minded view came from George Washburn, president of Robert College in Istanbul, who made a point-by-point comparison/contrast between Christian and Muslim beliefs. But even he concluded on a note of disapprobation. In contrast to Christianity's loving, redeeming God, he told the audience, "the God of Islam is apart from the world, an absolute monarch, who is wise and merciful but infinitely removed from man."[131]

The only actual Muslim, albeit an American convert, present at the parliament was Mohammed [Alexander Russell] Webb, dubbed "the Yankee Mohammadean" by the *Daily Inter Ocean*, or the "Koranized American" according to the *Methodist Review*.[132] To full, curious audiences, Webb delivered two addresses: "The Spirit of Islam" and "The Influence of Islam on Social Conditions." In them, he lambasted English sources on Islam and Muhammad as "inaccurate, untruthful, and full of prejudice." In an effort to rebut these prejudices, he emphasized Islam's egalitarian aspects ("caste lines are broken down entirely") and its rich intellectual heritage ("there was no civilization in the world as high as Moslem Spain"). But these efforts were overshadowed by his clumsy references to practices of polygamy, which precipitated a ruckus in the audience, with some hissing at him and yelling, "Shame!" Webb's presentation on Islam, Barrows later recorded, "was an exceptional event in the proceedings of the Parliament, for the fact that it was attended with strong and even violent impatient expressions of disapproval."[133] The *Chicago Tribune* ran a cartoon showing Webb prostrate on the ground with an irate (presumably Christian) woman on his back whacking him with her umbrella.[134] His appearance was "odd," according to the *Tribune*, with his head "surmounted by a red fez and his bushy brown beard."[135]

Religious traditions from South Asia fared better. In fact, their colorfully robed representatives and the content of their speeches—some of which pluckily contested the prevailing Western/Christian "fulfillment" ethos—emerged as a dominant story line of the parliament as a whole. At the time, even educated Americans' knowledge of Asian faiths was scanty, to say the least, with most viewing them hardly as living traditions but as so many "mysterious form[s] of mysticism, exotic and hoary with antiquity."[136] But the erudition and urbanity of speakers from Asia made clear, at least to some, that these guests could not simply be dismissed as "Oriental pagans" or "ignorant heathen"—they needed to be understood and engaged in a more intellectually sophisticated way than had been the case in the past.

Buddhism and Hinduism were well represented at the parliament, with twelve and eight speakers, respectively. Most other Asian faith traditions boasted just one or two representatives. Altogether, 43, or 22 percent, of the 196 delegates hailed from Asia, and twenty-nine speeches were given by non-Christian Asians. Sometimes a speech was delivered in English by its author, but because of the language barrier speeches were not infrequently read by a proxy with the author sitting nearby, as Philip Schaff had done. In addition to speeches by actual practitioners of a particular religion (what the planners had most hoped for), Western scholars or missionaries delivered several lectures *about* various Eastern faiths. In the course of the parliament, audiences heard about Taoism, Confucianism, Shinto, Hinduism, Buddhism, Jainism, and Zoroastrianism. A couple of papers, moreover, dealt with Brahmo Samaj, a much-discussed Hindu reform movement in nineteenth-century India.[137] It was widely accepted among participants, whether Western or Eastern and despite low levels of actual knowledge of the East among Westerners, that the "the East" in some regard was the primal seedbed of human religiosity.[138] Barrows frequently referred to India in particular as "the mother of religions."

The papers on Asian faiths fell roughly into three categories. The first was a no-frills description of a particular faith, laying out its main tenets, sacred texts, and so forth. The second was more a scholarly disquisition on some aspect of a particular tradition, often comparing it to Christianity or to another faith. The third—and the most noteworthy type—might have elements of the first two, but its author used the occasion as a platform to address the whole world and/or to offer analyses of the parliament itself and the East/West encounter that it had brought about. Speakers in this category, to quote Richard H. Seager, often "managed to combine traditional religious convictions with an understanding of the ideas and ideals of Western civilization and a personal charisma that was appealing to an American audience."[139] Several speakers fit this bill, but four stood out: Syoen Shaku of Japan, Anagarika Dharmapala of Ceylon (Sri Lanka), and Protap Chunder Mojumdar and Swami Vivekananda, both from India.[140] In different ways, each contested the dominant Western ethos of the parliament and together they played an extraordinary role in introducing Asian religious ideas and practices to the United States and to the West more generally. Some of these—yoga, for example—proved to have remarkable staying power.[141]

The Rinzai Zen priest and monk Soyen Shaku's appearances at the parliament combined an apologia for Buddhism with an impassioned call for world peace based on belief in human equality.[142] Proclaiming the Buddha to be "the first discoverer" of the moral laws of the universe, Shaku challenged the audience to regard him as equivalent to other major religious figures: "Who shall utter a word against him . . . who has saved and will save by his noble teaching . . . millions and millions of falling human beings? Indeed, too much approbation could not be uttered to honor his sacred name!"[143] But regardless of one's religious persuasion, the challenges of the moment, Shaku proclaimed, should compel all faiths to come together in the name of helping the needy and promoting human solidarity:

"Let [all faiths] . . . unite ourselves for the sake of helping the helpless and living glorious lives of brotherhood under the control of truth." To this plea, the Buddhist monk added, on a more practical note, a call to strengthen "international law" so that "arbitration instead of war" could decide conflicts between nations. International law, he pointedly added, presupposed that one people or one faith could not be regarded as higher than others: "We must not make a distinction between race and race, between civilization and civilization, between creed and creed."[144]

Soyen Shaku's contribution proved pivotal for introducing Buddhism to America.[145] During his stay, he was hosted in LaSalle, Illinois, by Paul Carus, an accomplished scholar of Eastern thought, also a speaker at the parliament, and a major publisher of Asian religious literature in America. Upon returning to Japan, Shaku was a hailed as a *bukkyo no chapionra*, a defender of Buddhism. Press coverage in his native country portrayed him as having "triumphed in Chicago," unleashing a Buddhist revolution that would soon sweep the world. Shaku made two return trips to the United States, lecturing on Buddhism and Eastern thought more generally.

Equally important, Shaku helped introduce to America his younger co-religionists: Sokei-an Sasaki, Nyogen Sensaki, and Daisetsu Teitaro Suzuki. Suzuki came to live with Paul Carus shortly after the parliament. There he translated several key Asian texts into English before embarking on extensive speaking tours—performing in masterful English—that familiarized thousands of Americans and Europeans with Buddhist teachings. In 1936 he spoke at London's World Congress of Faiths (more about this later). Toward the end of his life, Suzuki took a teaching position at Columbia University where, among many other accomplishments, he participated in a dialogue between Zen practitioners and enthusiasts of Freudian psychoanalysis and influenced the Beat-Hip generation in the late 1950s and 1960s in their explorations of Asian religions.[146] In 1936 he was nominated for the Nobel Peace Prize.

While perhaps not as influential as Suzuki, Sasaki and Sensaki also left their mark after the parliament. The former helped found the first Buddhist Society of America (1931) in New York City, later renamed the First Zen Institute. The latter was instrumental in spreading Buddhist ideas on the West Coast, where he taught Zen meditation practices and Japanese culture. Sadly, although he was a critic of Japanese nationalism, the still-active Sensaki was placed in an internment camp in Heart Mountain, Wyoming, after the attack on Pearl Harbor.[147]

At the parliament, Dharmapala of Ceylon also spoke on and for Buddhism, albeit in its South Asian Theravada form. A critic of Western colonialism and an advocate of Sinhalese language and culture, Dharmapala had founded the Maha Bodhi Society in Colombo, which worked to restore India's sacred Buddhist city of Bodh Gaya as the site for a Buddhist monastery and school. Presenting in Chicago a paper entitled "The World's Debt to Buddha" in excellent English with a small statute of the Buddha next to him, Dharmapala emphasized the universal message of Buddhism and its genesis "six centuries before Jesus of Nazareth." The religion of Buddha, he preached, offers "a comprehensive system of ethics and a transcendental metaphysic embracing a sublime psychology." Demonstrating extensive knowledge of Western scholarship on Buddhism, he claimed Buddhism was more fully compatible with modern science than other religions; unlike Christianity, Buddhism does not have a specific doctrine of Creation and could thus sidestep debates about human origins and Darwinian theory then taking place in the West. This implicit criticism of Christianity became manifest when he took on Western missionaries. In blunt language, he argued that "the [Western] missionary is intolerant; he is selfish. Why do not the natives mix with him? Because he has not the tolerance and unselfishness he should have. Who are his converts? They are all men of a low type. Seeing the selfishness and intolerance of the missionary not an intelligent man will accept Christianity. Buddhism had its missionaries before Christianity was preached. It conquered all of Asia and made the Mongolians mild. But the influence of western civilization is undoing their work."[148] Like Shaku, Dharmapala had an enduring influence after the parliament. Several days after it ended, he traveled to California, where he gave numerous lectures, organized mainly by Unitarians and Theosophists. In Santa Cruz, he met with Philangi Dasa, a self-described Swedenborgian-Buddhist and Theosophist, who edited the *Buddhist Ray*, the first Buddhist journal in America. Later Dharmapala made two other trips to America, the longest in 1896–97 at the invitation of Paul Carus. En route to the United States, he stopped in Britain to meet with the acclaimed scholar of Asian thought, Thomas Rhys Davids, and Friedrich Max Müller. He also returned to Chicago and reconnected with many involved in the parliament, including Bonney.

An indefatigable advocate of Buddhist rights, Dharmapala also spent time in India, preaching Buddhism and pursuing his aim to restore Bodh Gaya to Buddhist oversight. He died in 1933, desiring to be reincarnated as a Brahman in Benares so he could exercise influence in releasing Bodh Gaya from Hindu control. An obituary in the journal of the Maha Bodh Society hailed him as "the greatest Buddhist missionary after Asoka the Great" and a modern-day *Bodhisattva*.[149]

A leader of Brahmo Samaj and the only Asian at the parliament to have previously traveled to America, Protap Chunder Mojumdar (1840–1905) gave a spirited defense of Eastern thought in "The World's Religious Debt to Asia." Due to the open and absorptive nature of Brahmo Samaj, Mojumdar possessed extensive knowledge of many religious systems and even regarded himself as a Hindu follower of Christ. In 1883 he had published *The Oriental Christ*, comparing and contrasting Christianity and Hinduism and arguing for their extensive compatibility.[150] Toward the end of his life, this publication brought him into correspondence with Friedrich Max Müller and made his name familiar to many other Western scholars and divines.[151]

In his lecture, Mojumdar cast a broad net, speaking generally about "the Oriental mind," which in his interpretation stretched practically from Palestine to Japan. This mind, he declared, was responsible for the original impulses behind Judaism, Christianity, and Islam. He contrasted these impulses and comparable ones in other Asian religious traditions with what he regarded as problematic characteristics of modern Western civilization: "In the West you wrest from nature her secrets, you conquer her, she makes you wealthy and prosperous, you look upon her as your slave, and sometimes fail to realize her sacredness. In the East nature is our eternal sanctuary, the soul is our everlasting temple, and the sacredness of God's creation is only next to the sacredness of God himself."[152] The East had much to teach the West concerning work, worship, and leisure: "In the West you work incessantly, and your work is your worship. In the East we meditate and worship for long hours, and worship is our work." Mojumdar also harshly criticized Western missionary activity and Western colonialism in general—criticisms that, according to one commentator, fell upon his listeners "like biting flames."[153] Even so, the East stood to benefit from the West in some respects, and Mojumdar concluded his talk by calling for a higher unity between East and West.[154]

Mojumdar lingered in the United States after the parliament, giving lectures, mostly on the East Coast. He was especially sought out by liberal Protestants and Unitarians, who felt that the Brahmo Samaj movement represented a Hindu liberalizing religious spirit comparable to those animating their own faiths. Many, included Friedrich Max Müller, tried to convince Mojumdar to go one step farther and convert to Christianity. None of these efforts succeeded. He died a Hindu devotee of Christ in Calcutta (Kolkata) in 1905.[155]

If anyone could be singled out as possessing the most charismatic appeal and exercising the most enduring influence at the parliament, it would be another speaker from India: Swami Vivekananda, a major figure in modern Indian intellectual history. "Beyond question," as one observer noted, "he was the most popular and influential man at the Parliament."[156] Born Narendranath Datta in Calcutta, then the British capital of India, the portly, cherubic Bengali absorbed diverse spiritual and intellectual influences in his youth. A devoted reader of ancient Hindu spiritual texts and a student of classical Indian music, he encountered Western learning and religion during his studies at the General Assembly Institution (later the Scottish Church College) in Calcutta. Christianity, Unitarianism, Transcendentalism, Hegelianism, Herbert Spencer's evolutionism, and other strands of Western thought figured in his education, as did the Hindu reform movement Brahmo Samaj.[157] However, the all-important turning point in his early life came in the 1880s when he met the yogi and mystic Ramakrishna Paramahamsa (1836–86), whose intense search for God through meditation and advocacy of service to others left a lasting impression on the young Vivekananda. After Ramakrishna's death in 1886, Vivekananda and a handful of other devotees of Ramakrishna took formal monastic vows and gave themselves entirely to the spiritual life. Only then did he take the name Vivekananda—literally, "the bliss of discerning wisdom." Between

1888 and 1893, the young monk toured India as a spiritual vagabond, living on alms, seeking out holy men from various traditions, and gaining a deeper and disconcerting knowledge about the workings of the British Raj.[158] The plight of the poor and the colonial subjugation of Indians especially vexed him, and he began to associate his own sense of vocation with the stirrings of anticolonial Hindu nationalism.[159]

Delighted by the prospects of the coming parliament, Vivekananda arrived early in Chicago in the summer of 1893 after travels in China, Japan, and Canada. At first prevented from participating because he was not attached to a recognized institution, he gained entry after the intervention of Harvard professor John Henry Wright, who had heard of him and invited him to speak in Cambridge, Massachusetts, prior to the parliament's opening.[160] Once back in Chicago, Vivekananda's fluent English, bright saffron monastic garb, and yellow turban bedazzled the audience.[161]

In several speeches, Vivekananda articulated what has been characterized as a Neo-Vedanta philosophy, based on the *Upanishads:* an all-embracing, modernizing view of India's faith traditions, which envisioned Hindu spirituality, not Christianity, as the magnanimous custodian of other beliefs and the unmatched promoter of human dignity and global spiritual fraternity. In essence, Vivekananda, a close observer of missionaries in India, snatched inclusivist language and "fulfillment" theology away from American Protestants and applied it adroitly to his understanding of "Hinduism," embracing the Western term. His brief speech on the opening day, deftly blending Indian spiritual pride and a searching universalism, set the tone for his general message: "I thank you in the name of the mother of all religions. . . . I am proud to belong to a religion which has taught the world both tolerance and universal acceptance. We believe not only in universal toleration, but we accept all religions to be true. . . . I am proud to belong to a nation which has sheltered the persecuted and the refugees of all religions and all nations of the earth." In subsequent speeches, he emphasized Hinduism's capacious inclusivity, arguing that religious differences in the final analysis were more apparent than real, more a result of circumstance than an intention of divinity. "God is the inspirer of [all religions]. . . . Why, then, are there so many contradictions? They are only apparent, says the

Hindu. The contradictions come from the same truth adapting itself to the different circumstances of different natures."[162] From these different circumstances, humanity, he felt, was now, in 1893, called to a higher unity.

Religious exclusivism, especially as practiced by Christian missionaries, worked against this unity, Vivekananda held, and he therefore pointedly rebutted what he regarded as common Western misconceptions of Hinduism. Hinduism emphatically should not be associated with "polytheism" or "idolatry," as missionaries proclaimed. These terms might seem to capture popular religious practices in India, he admitted, but they instead should be interpreted only as the first rung on a ladder toward greater spiritual refinement: "Idolatry in India does not mean a horror. It is not the mother of harlots [as missionaries suppose]. On the other hand, it is the attempt of undeveloped minds to grasp high spiritual truths." Images, pictures, and other tangible objects might not be needed by the more spiritually advanced, he elaborated, but these advanced devotees should not look contemptuously on the unlearned who might need them.[163]

Vivekananda's Chicago audiences showed particular approval for his denunciation of religiously motivated strife and violence. As he put it on opening day: "Sectarianism, bigotry and its horrible descendent, fanaticism, have possessed long this beautiful earth. It has filled the earth with violence. . . . But its time has come, and I fervently hope that the bell that tolled this morning [at the parliament's opening] . . . may be the death knell to all fanaticism." At the same time, the message of his language—different faiths traveling toward the "same goal"—carried pluralist or universalist implications that many Christians in Chicago, whether more exclusivist or inclusivist, found unacceptable. In his concluding speech, Vivekananda directly spelled out these implications: "If anyone here hopes that this [religious] unity would come by the triumph of any one of these religions and the destruction of the others, to him I say 'Brother, yours, is an impossible hope.' Do I wish that the Christian would become Hindu? God forbid. Do I wish that the Buddhist would become a Christian? God forbid. . . . The Christian is not to become a Hindu or a Buddhist, nor a Hindu or a Buddhist to become a Christian. But each must assimilate the others and yet preserve its individuality and grow according to its own law of growth." "Swami Vivekananda was always heard with interest by the Parliament," Barrows later commented on this speech, "but very little approval was shown to some of the sentiments expressed in his closing address."[164]

Even so, Vivekananda was a much-sought-out conversation partner at the many receptions and a favorite among newspaper reporters. What is more, he lavishly praised the parliament itself, investing it with world-historical significance, thereby flattering the city and the country that hosted it. "The present Convention, which is one of the most august assemblies ever held," he gushed, "is in itself a vindication to the world of the wonderful doctrine preached in the [Bhagavad] Gita. 'Whoever comes to me, through whatsoever form I reach him, they are all struggling through paths that in the end always end in me.'" On the closing day, he pronounced that the parliament had entered the annals of history as an "accomplished fact" that had shown the world "that every [religious] system had produced men and women of the most exalted character."[165]

Vivekananda's performance at the parliament served as a prelude to a flurry of activities afterward, both in the West and back in India.[166] He remained in Chicago as a guest of prominent people for several months before contracting with a lecture bureau that launched him on speaking tours in the United States and Europe. He inspired the founding of various Vedanta societies and retreat centers, and taught classes on Hindu devotion and the practice of yoga.[167] In 1896 he published lectures that he had given in New York under the title *Raja Yoga*, a key text for introducing yoga and transcendental meditation to the West. His assertive lecturing style, praising Vedanta while often criticizing Christian missionaries, assured him copious attention in the press, and more than once he found himself in public arguments with pastors and priests, including once with the Catholic bishop of Detroit.[168] But others offered their friendship, including William James, who mentions Vivekananda in his seminal *Varieties of Religious Experience* (1902).[169]

Once back in India, Vivekananda was received as a hero, arousing and stoking powerful currents of anticolonial sentiment, spiritual fervor, and Hindu pride.[170] In 1897 he founded the Ramakrishna Mission Association with the goal of spreading Vedanta. Shortly after completing another lengthy visit to the West, he died on 4 July 1902, and his body was cremated under a sacred vilna tree in Calcutta. A

Swami Vivekananda at the World's Parliament of Religions, 1893. (Photography by Thomas Harrison. Image courtesy of Wikimedia Commons.)

temple was built to mark the spot, with his remains placed in a receptacle on the altar of his guru Ramakrishna. Vivekananda's sojourns abroad, as Narasingha P. Sil has nicely summarized, offered "an audacious challenge from a colonial native to the metropolitan West—a powerful response to the West's *mission civilisatrice* for the non-European world. . . . The scientifically progressive and materially prosperous West had yet to learn [in Vivekananda's eyes] the secrets of authentic spirituality from the colonized Orient."[171] Vivekananda's role in 1893, moreover, suggests the limits of understanding the parliament as strictly as an "Orientalist" phenomenon, for in Vivekananda it had given an eloquent "Oriental" a platform to make a case for the East largely on his own terms.

Vivekananda and other speakers called attention to the need for the comparative study of religion. As mentioned earlier, the emergence of comparative religion as a field of study had preceded the conference, but several speeches enthusiastically promoted it. Prominent European scholars such as Friedrich Max Müller, J. Eslin Carpenter, Albert Réville, and C. P. Tiele all sent papers that were read aloud. "Now the science of religion," Tiele wrote, "has no other purpose than to lead to the knowledge of religion in its nature and origin." Characterizing this science as still in its "infancy," Tiele recruited potential scholars to "select a field" of their own and attempt to "probe [it] to the bottom" and thereby make a "fresh" contribution to the edifice of this new science. C. D. D'Haerlez echoed this theme in a lecture entitled "Comparative Study of the World's Religions," as did Eliza P. Sunderland in "Serious Study of All Religions."[172]

Other causes besides comparative religion received a boost from the parliament. The increasing role of women in faith communities was also accentuated. The nineteenth century had witnessed a growing body of thought on and conversations about the place of women in society. The parliament brought that discussion powerfully and publicly to the religious sphere. No fewer than twenty-three women gave speeches at the parliament, even if only one was a non-Christian, the Zoroastrian Jeanne Sorabji.[173] The American reformer Julia Ward Howe spoke for many when, in a tirade against Islam but with broader implications for other religious traditions, she proclaimed: "I think nothing is religion which puts one individual absolutely above others, and surely nothing is religion which puts one sex above another. . . . Any religion which sacrifices women to the brutality of men is no religion." Some other titles furthering women's interests included "The Influence of Religion on Women," by Annis F. F. Eastman, "A New Testament Woman," by Marion Murdock, and "The Divine Basis of the Cooperation between Men and Women," by Lydia Fuller Dickinson.[174] Concurrent with the parliament, it should be noted, a separate Congress of Women met under the auspices of the Department of Woman's Progress. Nearly two hundred women addressed this congress, with many touching on religious matters.[175]

Finally, given the New World context and the particular com-

Group picture at the World's Parliament of Religions in Chicago, 1893. (From John Henry Barrows, ed., The World's Parliament of Religions, *vol. 1 [Chicago: Parliament Publishing, 1893]. Image courtesy of Wikimedia Commons.)*

memorative occasion of the parliament, it should not surprise that the significance of the United States for religious belief surfaced frequently as a topic. Many speakers referenced the United States' constitutional assurance of religious liberty. But some went further, attributing grand significance to the *novum ordo seculorum* in the larger drama of humanity's unfolding religious story. Despite his criticisms of Western missionary activity and colonialism, Vivekananda heaped praise on America for helping realize the Vedantist universal religion. Mentioning Akbar, he nonetheless dismissed the Mughal emperor's religious discussions as "only a parlor meeting," for it "was reserved for America to call, to proclaim to all quarters of the globe that the Lord is in every religion. . . . Hail Columbia, mother-land of liberty! . . . It has been given to thee to march at the vanguard of civilization with the flag of harmony." In a different key, in "The World's Religious Debt to America," Celia P. Woolley, advocate of women's concerns and Unitarian preacher, proclaimed that America "is defined in one word: Opportunity. The liberty men had known only as a distant ideal [has] . . . now reached the stage of practical experiment." After recounting aspects of American history, she concluded in rousing language: "If the world's religious debt to America lies in this thought of opportunity or religion applied, it is a debt the future will disclose more than the past has disclosed it. If ours is the opportunity, ours is still more the obligation. Privilege does not go without responsibility; where much is bestowed much is required."[176]

Interpretations and Legacies

When the parliament ended on 27 September, those who had spoken, those who had listened, and those who had followed the proceedings in the press knew that something extraordinary and perhaps unique had taken place. Defining exactly what that "something" was, however, elicited a range of responses, as numerous interpretations spilled onto the pages of both secular and religious periodicals, books, and newspapers in the weeks, months, and years following the parliament. "When the Parliament was past," George S. Goodspeed nicely summed up, "it really only then began to live. Its members scattered . . . and carried with them the spirit and influence of that gathering."[177]

A spate of post-parliament publications provided fodder for those hazarding interpretation. All along, Barrows and his committee had planned to publish a "permanent record" of the parliament based on stenographic notes taken of the lectures. The result was the two-volume, fifteen-hundred-page *The World's Parliament of Religions: An Illustrated History and Popular Story of the World's First Parliament of Religions, Held in Chicago in Connection with the Columbian Exposition of 1893* (Chicago, 1893). The work, ornamented with photographs of religious scenes from around the world, provides a brief history of the parliament and printed versions of (most) talks given. A second noteworthy collection appeared in the same year: *Neely's History of the Parliament of Religions and Religious Congresses at the World's Columbian Exposition (Compiled from the Original Manuscripts and Stenographic Reports)*, edited by historian Walter R. Houghton and published by F. T. Neely. In addition, two less exhaustive (and less reliable) volumes came out shortly after the parliament: J. W. Hanson's *The World's Congress of Religions: The Addresses and Papers Delivered before the Parliament* (Chicago, 1893) and Jenkin Lloyd Jones's *A Chorus of Faiths as Heard in the Parliament of Religions* (Chicago, 1893).[178] Again, whether drawn from direct memory, press reports, and/or these volumes, opinions about the parliament were fashioned and disseminated in the 1890s and beyond. Among the welter of viewpoints, several dominant tendencies stand out.

Perhaps not surprisingly, those directly involved in planning the parliament emphasized its epochal nature and positive qualities. It signified "a new era of religious fraternity," according to Barrows himself, who felt that its true significance would be grasped only in the future: "It has summoned mankind to a friendly conference over those themes which divide the race. If many years shall need to roll away before the leading idea of the Parliament shall be actualized, let us not forget that [the] greatest things have at first been a dream, an inspiration, a hope."[179] "The Parliament of Religions will live," echoed Bonney. "Its influence will endure, and will extend throughout the world . . . [and] will multiply a myriadfold in all the continents."[180]

Similarly, Jenkin Lloyd Jones, a zealous booster of the parliament from the outset, felt that the meeting of minds in Chicago amounted to a promissory note for the future religious life of humankind: "I look for no revolution in religious thought and institutions; but there will come a more rapid evolution of both. . . . People will demand a church that will be as inclusive in its spirit as the Parliament. The Parliament will teach people that there is a Universal Religion." A Unitarian minister, Jones repeated this latter point in multiple venues, insisting that the parliament above all taught "that the message of the great teachers of religion is essentially the same. Jesus, Buddha, Confucius, Moses, Zoroaster, Sokrates, and Mohammed taught, not so many different ways to God, but the same way, the only way, the way of service, . . . of truth-seeking, . . . of loving and helping."[181] Jones dedicated the remainder of his life to this message, with considerable effect, at least in Unitarian and liberal Protestant circles. Like others, Jones regarded the meeting in Chicago as giving birth to a "movement."[182]

A kindred spirit in many respects, George Candlin, a Protestant missionary to China and a participant in 1893, exulted in the publication of Barrows's book. He felt that it extended the reach of the parliament by allowing readers to enter into the mindset of practitioners of different faiths: "To sympathetically understand [another's] religion, we must, at least, temporarily see it from his point of view. This book, alone of books, enables us to see all the great religions of the world in this manner."[183] In Candlin's judgment, the parliament held implications for how Christian missions should be conducted, even while betokening an epoch-making, if still inchoate, meaning for the future of religion in general. Writing Bonney from the steamship returning him to China from Chicago, Candlin opined that "the world cannot be converted until we are all ready to own the truth and goodness and heavenward aspiration we find all over the world as to impart our own. . . . If anyone cares to call this a compromise of creeds, I am not disturbed." The parliament, he averred in the same letter, was the "greatest religious meeting of the modern world [and] is prophetic of the twentieth century, and will dominate and guide the religious thought of the future. . . . It was a *prelude* not a *finale*, a promise not a boast, a prospect not a recollection. Like Christianity itself it was a rapt gaze into the [coming] millennium."[184]

Although he did not attend, Friedrich Max Müller closely followed the parliament's proceedings; among cognoscenti his opinion especially mattered. And he did not fail to deliver. "There are few things I so truly regret having missed as the Parliament of Religions held in Chicago," he wrote in 1894. "Instead of a show," he continued, "it developed into a reality, which, if I am not greatly mistaken, will be remembered . . . when everything else of the mighty Columbian Exhibition has long been swept away from the memory of man." With no small dose of professional opportunism, Müller assayed that the parliament should be viewed alongside his own publishing project, the Sacred Books of the East; both projects had provided a major stimulus to the comparative study of religion as well as to pan-religious human solidarity. Of particular significance, he held, was the decision to invite "living witnesses" of various religions, especially those from the East. While his own project surveyed humanity's religious past, these witnesses from East and West meeting in Chicago "were making the history of the future."[185]

The editor of the *Monist*, Paul Carus, similarly felt that the East-West encounter stood out as the parliament's chief legacy. Commending somewhat uncritically "the tolerant principles of our Oriental guests," he judged the parliament an "extraordinary success." "The Parliament of Religions," he gushed, "is undoubtedly the most noteworthy event of modern times. . . . It is evident from its date we shall have to begin a new era in the evolution of man's religious life."[186] Claiming "a grand unity of East and West" after the parliament, Carus went on to write fifteen books on Asian thought, while his Open Court Press published another thirty-eight between 1893 and 1915 in an effort to familiarize Western audiences with "Oriental" truths and to promote general religious literacy and unity.[187]

Significantly, and working with others, including Charles Bonney, Carus attempted to capture the spirit of the parliament in an enduring organizational form by launching "the World's Religious Parliament Extension" in 1895. Its lofty goals were "to establish friendly relations among all religions for a better mutual understanding, to awaken all over the world a lively interest in religious problems, and above all to facilitate the final and universal attainment of religious truth."[188] The group held its inaugural meeting in Chicago. But as things turned out, it did not receive the international support that Carus had hoped for, nor did its key supporters always agree on what direction it should take.[189] Accordingly, it quietly fizzled out, even if the idea for such an ongoing institution emphatically did not.[190]

Across Asia, the parliament's commingling of East and West and its pleas for unity and cooperation had struck a chord. This took the form of high praise, such as the Hindu scholar M. N. D'Vivedi's pronouncement in the *Times of India* that the parliament represented "a success unique in the history of mankind." Its aftereffects also called into question traditional Western missionary practices, as an article in the *Calcutta Statesman* made clear: "The old stock methods of missionary enterprises are [now] useless, if not positively harmful. What is wanted now is an exposition made in a friendly, conciliatory way, as by one seeker after the truth to another in the fraternal spirit which pervaded the Parliament of Religions."[191] As spelled out earlier, in India, the parliament transformed Swami Vivekananda into a South Asian celebrity and a symbol of Hindu cultural pride, even as it abetted the popularization of the Ramakrishna missions that he established.

Japan also felt the parliament's impact. "It seems to me from what I observed in Japan," J. T. Yokoi wrote to Barrows, "that the effects of the Parliament have been exceedingly good. . . . I cannot help thinking that the mental horizon of a great many has since been greatly widened."[192] Japanese newspapers and journals had followed the parliament with considerable interest and praised the Japanese delegation for its "victorious" performance in Chicago.[193] Two small-scale, imitative religious congresses took place in Japan in 1896 and 1897, involving representatives of Buddhism, Shinto, and Christianity.[194]

As knowledge of the parliament spread globally, it attracted critics at home. Skepticism about its prospects in fact had begun much earlier. "There were those," L. W. Bacon remembered in 1897, "who stood aloof and prophesied that nothing could come of such an assemblage but a hopeless jangle of discordant opinions."[195] America's leading evangelist, the Chicago-based Dwight L. Moody, was one such naysayer. In an effort to counter the influence of the parliament and reach out to visitors of the Columbian Exposition, he launched a major evangelistic crusade in Chicago in the summer of 1893, preaching the absolute sufficiency of Christianity over and against the "idolatry" of other religions on display at the parliament.[196] Herrick Johnson of Presbyterian McCormick Seminary dismissed the parliament as a "monstrous absurdity," while the baseball-player-turned-popular-preacher Billy Sunday pronounced the parliament a "curse" on American national life.[197]

Arguably, the most relentless evangelical critic of the parliament, however, proved to be the premillennialist preacher and missionary Arthur T. Pierson. From the pulpit and in print, Pierson lashed out at the very idea of the parliament. Editor of the *Missionary Review*, he lambasted the event in an article appearing in December 1894 as "the attempted amalgamation of the one and only true faith and saving Gospel with the imperfect, iniquitous, idolatrous systems of so-called 'religion.'" In his view, the parliament misrepresented Christianity and misled the crowds that attended it, establishing a worrisome precedent for the future, and provided "false faiths" with a national platform: "it gave both occasion and encouragement for the propagation of false systems not only in heathen territory, but in Christian lands [that is, the United States]." But the parliament's truly unpardonable sin in Pierson's eyes was that it undercut the work of foreign missions: "The crowning mistake of the Parliament of Religions was the fatal blunder of at least implying that *salvation is not in Christ alone*. And in so far, the Parliament was and still is the foe of Christian missions, and has already done measureless harm."[198]

The views of Moody, Johnson, Sunday, and Pierson, among others, exercised considerable influence within conservative American Protestantism. Anticipating the modernist-fundamentalist conflicts of the twentieth century, the parliament "created a split" within American Protestantism along "conservative" and "liberal" lines, as Dana L. Robert has argued.[199] Or, as Sydney Ahlstrom observed in 1962: "The Parliament . . . [set the stage] for a genuine confrontation of attitudes. So fundamental . . . [were] the issues involved in the confrontation, moreover, that it clarifies the most important (and tragic) rift in American Protestantism, a rift that still remains unbridged."[200] Put differently: it was not only different views of Darwinism and historical criticism of the Bible that divided American Protestants from one another beginning around this time, but also their different approaches to non-Christian faiths. From 1893 forward, if I might be permitted a rough generalization, liberal Protestants moved in the direction of an inclusivist and eventually even a pluralist stance toward other faiths, while conservatives tended to double down on theological exclusivism, even if we might distinguish between hard and soft versions of it.[201] This reality illustrates the irony of how interreligious dialogue, its potential of peacemaking notwithstanding, has often sewn divisions within faith traditions, not least within Christianity.

Indeed, the parliament not only divided and unsettled Protestants; it similarly affected Catholics. As we have seen, under the guidance of Archbishop Gibbons, Archbishop Feehan, and Rector John Keane, the American Catholic hierarchy decided to make the most of the parliament, seeing it as an opportunity, in an age of nativist anti-Catholicism, to make further inroads into American society while commending their faith to others.[202] After the parliament, they and kindred spirits made efforts to moderate extreme interpretations of the parliament.[203] Cardinal Gibbons even proclaimed that "permanent blessings" would result from it.[204] But the hierarchy in Rome, and ultramontane and more traditionalist Catholics in Europe and America, felt differently. Criticism was sotto voce at first but became more vociferous after the parliament.

Catholic skeptics of the parliament voiced two main complaints. First, they took issue with the grand schemes of pan-Christian unity voiced by Protestant divines such as Philip Schaff. While Schaff was more favorably disposed to Catholicism than many of his co-religionists, he felt that the Church of Rome, especially since the recently proclaimed dogma of papal infallibility, presented a major obstacle to Christian concord. At the parliament, he had even humorously suggested that an infallible pope could by his own power infallibly declare himself to be fallible once again. This attitude raised the ire of the Paulist priest A. F. Hewit who, writing in spring 1894 in the *Catholic World*, responded that Schaff's view of unity was insufficient, based as it was on "compromise." True unity "in Christendom," he averred, "has never existed except in the form of a great circle or sphere having its centre in the Roman See of St. Peter. . . . All who have become separated from the Church should return to her bosom."[205]

A second critique focused on Catholic participation in the parliament in the first place. Ultramontane Catholics in Europe and America had for some time voiced worries about liberal, democratic forms of government, such as that found in the United States, and modern teachings on freedom of conscience and the separation of church and state.[206] In such societies, all people, including Catholics, were prone to succumb to "indifferentism," an apathy about orthodoxy and the eternal fate of others seemingly promoted by liberal society. In the eyes of such critics, the parliament appeared as a colossal manifestation of this indifferent spirit, a prime example of American liberalism. By participating, Catholics had unwittingly relativized their own faith, making it appear as just another religious option.

In August 1894, a German American delegation to a Catholic conference in Cologne condemned the liberal tendencies in the United States, citing as a clear example the "unholy memory" of the recent parliament.[207] In France, conservative Catholics began to worry when their more liberal co-religionists wondered if a similar parliament could take place in Paris.[208] Such attitudes were also present in the Eternal City, and in September 1895, Rome acted.[209] In a letter from Leo XIII to Archbishop Francis Satolli, the apostolic delegate to the United States, the pope expressed his mind: "We know that from time to time there are held in the United States of America assemblies to which both Catholic and those who dissent from the Church come promiscuously to discuss together religion and morals. In this we recognize the interest of religion. . . . But although these common gatherings have been tolerated hitherto, it would seem more advisable for Catholics to have their meetings by themselves."[210] To drive home the point, Keane, the leading advocate for Catholic participation in the parliament and someone far too "Americanized," in Rome's judgment, was dismissed from his position as rector of Catholic University.[211] Additionally, the parliament figured significantly in the Vatican's condemnation in 1899 of "Americanism," a vaguely defined quasi-heresy understood as impermissible accommodation to liberal principles and ideas.[212]

Until the Second Vatican Council, a negative attitude toward interreligious dialogue prevailed in official Catholic teaching. As various interreligious and ecumenical meetings took place in the early twentieth century, Pope Pius XI (r. 1922–30) felt the need, in the encyclical *Mortalium animos* (1928), to double down on his predecessor's rebuke. Recognizing that in an effort to achieve "religious unity," many "conventions, meetings, and addresses are frequently arranged . . . at which a large number of listeners are present, and at which all without distinction are invited to join in the discussion, both infidel of every kind, and Christians, even those who have unhappily fallen away from Christ. . . . Certainly such attempts cannot be approved by Catholics, founded as they are on that false opinion which considers all religions to be more or less good and praiseworthy. . . . It clearly follows that one who supports those who hold these theories and attempt to realize them, is altogether abandoning the divinely revealed religion."[213] Not only did the pope forbid interreligious gatherings, but Christian ecumenical ones as well: "It is clear that the Apostolic See cannot on any terms take part in their [Protestant] assemblies, nor is it any way lawful for Catholics either to support or to work for such enterprises; for if they do so they will be giving countenance to a false Christianity, quite alien to the one Church of Christ."[214]

As we shall see, the Second Vatican Council radically amended these sentiments.

Anyone looking for "Orientalist" mentalities and Western paternalism at the 1893 parliament will not come away empty-handed. But criticism of the parliament in this vein has been made with enough frequency, and stridency, as to render it hackneyed. The more enduring significance of the parliament lies in its far-flung influence, in its ability to inspire "copycat" versions of itself as well as to encourage new departures in religious inquiry and dialogue. Often these operated under a broadly Christian aegis, but sometimes they did not. The parliament of 1893, Richard Seager has written, marks "the beginning of the modern interreligious dialogue movement." Indeed, many organizations devoted to cultivating understanding among religions or fostering peaceful coexistence regularly trace their inspiration back to the parliament.[215] The parliament also spurred the comparative study of religion in universities as a promising academic field and as an enterprise linked to that of interreligious dialogue. As early as his classic 1905 *Comparative Religion*, Louis Henry Jordon commented on "the wide and permanent usefulness of the Chicago Parliament of Religion" for the study of the world's religious traditions.[216]

With respect to the comparative study of religion, the parliament's effects came immediately—and in Chicago, no less. A woman of considerable wealth, Caroline Haskell had attended the parliament and was deeply moved by its "fraternal spirit" and by the irenicism displayed by the speakers. In May 1894, she wrote the president of the newly established University of Chicago, William Rainey Harper, praising the "energy, tolerance, and catholicity of spirit" that Barrows had brought to the parliament.[217] Shortly thereafter she donated $40,000 to the university to established two lectureships: the Haskell Lectureship on the comparative study of religion, to be given in Chicago, and another, suitably entitled the Barrows Lectureship, to be held in India, where "the great questions of the truths of Christianity, its harmonies with truths of other religions, its rightful claims, and the best methods of setting them forth" were to be presented to "the scholarly and thoughtful people of India." Barrows himself agreed to travel to India in 1896 to inaugurate the lectureship, spreading the word about the parliament wherever he went.[218] An additional gift from Haskell of $100,000 helped establish the University of Chicago's "Oriental museum." An inscription on the cornerstone of this building, which now houses the Department of Anthropology, proclaims one of Haskell's most cherished ideals: *Lux ex orient*, "light from the East."

Coming directly on the heels of the parliament, Haskell's endowments set an influential precedent. Soon other universities and educational institutions scrambled to get into the act. "Comparative religion" and the "science of religion" became buzzwords in the early twentieth century, suggesting a more neutral approach to religion than "theology" at a time when many universities aspiring to world-class status sought to distance themselves from their "sectarian" origins. President Harper, although a devout Baptist, led the charge, not only warmly embracing these lectureships but serving as the driving force behind the establishment in 1903 of the explicitly nonsectarian, nontheological Religious Education Association (REA).[219] This organization remains in existence today, seeking "to create opportunities for exploring and advancing the interconnected practices of scholarship, research, teaching, and leadership in faith communities, academic institutions, and the wider world community."[220]

Internationally viewed, the parliament in Chicago served as a catalyst for scholarly congresses on comparative religion. In 1897, making explicit reference to Chicago, a Congress of the Science of Religion took place in Stockholm in connection with King Oscar II's Silver Jubilee. While this congress turned out to be mostly a Protestant affair, it served as a stepping-stone to Paris's 1900 Congrès international d'historie des religions, dubbed by Eric J. Sharpe as the first "genuinely scientific congress of comparative religion."[221] These congresses paved the way for similar ones held at St. Louis and Basel (both 1904), Oxford (1905), Leiden (1912), Paris (1923), Lund (1929), Brussels (1935), and Amsterdam (1950). The Amsterdam congress witnessed the establishment of the International Association of the History of Religions (IAHR), which has been sponsoring congresses and collaborations ever since.[222]

With respect to institutions and organizations dedicated to interreligious dialogue, Chicago's legacy is equally far-reaching. As we have seen, the parliament extension, conceptualized and briefly realized under the influence of Paul Carus, proved a harbinger of things to come even if it never fully got off the ground. As we shall see in the next chapter, the parliament played a significant role in inspiring London's Conference on Some Living Religions within the Empire in 1924.

But leaving this initiative aside (for now), the parliament of 1893 encouraged a long lineage of international interfaith meetings and organizations, not to mention Christian ecumenical ones.[223] In 1900, for instance, the International Association of Religious Freedom was formed in Boston under largely Unitarian and liberal Protestant influence. While interreligious dialogue was not at first its major aim, it became one as this organization evolved, as did discussing issues pertaining to freedom of conscience. Several of its founding members had been at Chicago in 1893 and were moved to act by what they had beheld there.[224] Follow-up meetings after the one at Boston took place in London (1901), Amsterdam (1903), Geneva (1905), Boston again (1907), and Berlin (1910). The International Association of Religious Freedom remains in existence today.[225]

The parliament of 1893 stimulated Christian-Jewish cooperation. American Reform Judaism in particular drew strength from the gathering, and in the following decades sought to strengthen its ties and connections to Christian churches and other non-Jewish religious organizations. In 1927–28, the National Conference of Christians and Jews was founded to realize aspects of the parliament's legacy. During the moral darkness of the Holocaust, it launched in 1944 an annual Brotherhood Week endorsed by Franklin Delano Roosevelt as an opportunity to recognize that "men [can] . . . live together as members of one family rather than as masters and slaves. . . . It is our promise to extend such brotherhood earthwide which gives hope to all the world."[226]

With respect to Christian ecumenical initiatives, Philip Schaff's pan-Christian vision in 1893 became realized, if only partially, at the famous Edinburgh Missionary Conference of 1910, itself the progenitor of additional ecumenical and interfaith endeavors.[227] From this conference's legacy, the twentieth-century World Council of Churches (WCC) emerged; it became a hotbed for discussions about the relationship between Christian mission and dialogue with the world's religious traditions, as shall be touched upon later.[228] Mirroring the experience of other ecclesial bodies, the WCC came to regard the tasks of ecumenism and interreligious dialogue as distinct but related phenomena: one seeking intramural unity, the other extramural friendship.

In 1933, in conjunction with Chicago hosting another world's fair, the idea arose to stage a second parliament of religions. As things turned out, nothing as epochal as the 1893 parliament occurred. Even so, a "Fellowship of Faiths," which had come into existence prior to 1933, became better known through the parliament and played a significant role in the emergence of Britain's World Congress of Faiths in 1936.[229]

The parliament's impact was felt beyond North America and Europe. A cauldron of religious diversity, India became a site of several interreligious gatherings in the early and mid-twentieth century, notably ones in Bombay (Mumbai) in 1936 and another in Calcutta (Kolkata) in 1937. Vivekananda's legacy bears significant responsibility for these, given his influence in India after the parliament. The Second World War and the postwar partition of India in 1947 put a damper on these types of events. But soon afterward, several interfaith initiatives resumed. In April 1953, the sixtieth anniversary of the Chicago parliament was marked in India by a major conference in Sivanansdanagar, Rishikesh, organized under the leadership of Sri Swami Sivananda, an influential promoter of Vedanta and an admirer of Vivekananda.[230] Shortly thereafter, in Delhi in 1957, the (India-based) World Fellowship of Religions was launched; this organization has staged subsequent conferences at several global locations.[231]

Oddly, the United States, arguably the cradle of the modern interfaith movement, witnessed only a handful of interfaith conferences in the middle decades of the twentieth century.[232] The Depression and World War II partially explain this. The situation changed dramatically after the watershed of the Second Vatican Council, which ushered in a heyday of interfaith exchanges and activities. Further, the coming of the hundredth anniversary of Chicago's parliament in 1993 provided a major impetus for interreligious activities, in the United States and globally. In the late 1980s, scholars and activists came together, particularly members of Chicago's Vedanta Society, to form an organization called, not surprisingly, the Parliament of the World's Religions, to prepare for a major centenary conference in 1993.[233]

While Chicago's parliament of 1893 elicited diverse responses, gave birth to different interpretations, and spawned various trajectories of influence, few would deny that its legacy has influentially hovered over many interfaith events in the twentieth and twenty-first centuries. In the decades after it took place, as Robert S. Ellwood has nicely summed up, the parliament became "a milestone in the history of interreligious dialogue, the study of world religions, and the impact of the Eastern religious traditions on American [and Western] culture."[234]

CHAPTER THREE

London

> In the world of spirit the more enterprising must build their Himalaya and attract the lesser upward to the heights.
>
> —SIR FRANCIS YOUNGHUSBAND

CHICAGO'S 1893 WORLD'S PARLIAMENT of Religions and the 1910 Edinburgh Missionary Conference heralded major religious trends of the twentieth century: respectively, the growth of interreligious dialogue and Christian ecumenism. In the minds of many Christians the two were interrelated phenomena, and both were tied to the question of Christianity's relationship to the rest of the world in the heyday of Western colonialism. Of course, the Great War of 1914–18 administered a massive jolt to the global order; after it, neither Europe nor its colonies were the same, even if processes of decolonization took off fully only after the Second World War. As is well known, the Great War felled the long-standing empires of Russia, Germany, and Austro-Hungary. The Ottoman Empire went the same way in the early 1920s amid a bloody conflict with Greece that evoked deep-seated religious passions and historical memories. With the Ottoman collapse, the Middle East began to lurch from one crisis to the next; and in many respects diplomats and politicians might still be regarded today as grappling with the evacuation of Ottoman power from the region.[1]

But postwar Great Britain presents a different picture entirely. Because of territorial acquisitions after the war, the empire "upon which the sun never set" managed to grow larger still, extending its imperial reach unbroken from the Suez Canal to Singapore, from Cairo to the Cape of Good Hope. Yet even as Britain sought to consolidate its global supremacy, London faced growing opposition from a range of anticolonial movements destined to seethe and grow in the 1920s and 1930s. Several of these movements were shot through with religious passions, particularly Muslim and Hindu, targeted against the hypocrisy and smug superiority of their war-weary colonial masters.[2] India in particular amounted to a powder keg of religio-political tensions and anti-British sentiment. In short, the high noon of the British Empire after 1918 might also be considered the beginning of its end.

But we know this only from hindsight. From the standpoint of the 1920s, no one, with perhaps the exception a few prescient souls, grasped the severity of the situation or foresaw the complete collapse of empire in the second half of the twentieth century. In fact, pride in the empire continued apace and was even strengthened in some quarters among the British in the postwar period.[3] This pride coexisted with a novel vision of global peace embodied in the League of Nations.[4] Among the most vivid expressions of the postwar mood was Sigismund Goetze's grandiose allegorical mural *Britannia Pacifatrix* (1921), commissioned by and for London's Foreign Office; it depicts a triumphant Britain and her allies presiding over the vanquished and lesser peoples of the world under the Latin inscription "Gloria in excelsis Deo et in terra pax hominibus bonae voluntatis."[5] This same spirit led the British government, in 1924, to stage in London the British Empire Exhibition, a world fair of sorts, but one designed exclusively to display, both to Britons and visitors from abroad, the economic and cultural marvels of the British Empire.

This chapter spotlights a major interreligious event that took place during this exhibition: the Conference on Some Living Religions within the Empire (22 September–3 October 1924). Sponsored by London's School of Oriental Studies and the British Sociological Society, the conference was held at the Imperial Institute in London's South Kensington district.[6] An unprecedented event in British history, it brought representatives from major religious traditions of the British Empire—excluding Christianity and Judaism because of their presumed familiarity—to London to expound before a general British audience the chief tenets and practices of their faiths. For many attendees, it was their first time to hear directly from a Muslim, a Hindu, a Buddhist, and a Parsi, among other religious voices. Those who did not attend could read about the curious event in the copious newspaper coverage it received.

In addition to offering a historical account of this conference, we shall discuss its legacy—the main one being the creation of the World Congress of Faiths (1936), the oldest continuously existing organization devoted to interreligious dialogue. We shall also pay especially close attention to Sir Francis Younghusband (1863–1942), the keynote speaker at the 1924 conference and the driving force behind the establishment of the congress in 1936.

Four principal arguments accompany this chapter. First, the 1924 conference makes a fascinating case study for the emergent subfield of "religion and empire," which has focused attention on how metropole elites throughout history have understood and managed religious groups differing in outlook and often far away from metropole "centers" such as London, and, conversely, on how religious groups at the margins have understood and dealt with the "center."[7] Second, this conference, as was true for Chicago's parliament, partly confirms and partly contests Edward Said's Orientalism thesis: that colonizers' knowledge of the colonized regularly served as an instrument of control and domination. In this case, while the British organizers of the conference certainly possessed "positional superiority" vis-à-vis those invited to speak, it is also true that they took steps to understand the other qua other and not strictly through the lenses of preconceived notions about religious and racial hierarchies.[8] This is seen most clearly in the decision taken to invite figures who could speak not only *about* but *from* a particular religious standpoint. It is also apparent in the organizers' decision—following Chicago's example in 1893, which the planners self-consciously imitated—to avoid religious controversy by dispensing with discussion after each presentation, so that the presenters themselves might have the final word. Third, despite some organizers' and participants' wishes that "religion" (idealistically and generally understood) might foster imperial cohesion, the conference in fact heralded the decline of the British Empire; the heterogeneous religious forces and cultural sensibilities represented at the conference pointed to the inherent difficulty of managing what had become after World War I "a huge and extremely variegated Empire."[9] On a related note, the conference anticipated the multicultural Britain that arose after decolonization had run its course.[10] Finally, and more generally, this conference and its legacy, while scantly remembered today, have played an important role in shaping assumptions about and practices of interreligious dialogue in the twentieth century and beyond. Therefore, the event deserves recognition alongside Chicago's better-known parliament of 1893.

The British Empire Exhibition, 1924–25

On 23 April 1924 (the feast day of St. George), King George V opened the British Empire Exhibition with a speech to a crowd of around one hundred thousand at Wembley Stadium on the northern outskirts of London. Later that evening, the BBC broadcast the speech to the entire country—an unprecedented event, the first time many Britons had heard their monarch's voice.[11] In the speech, the king made clear his hope that the exhibition would contribute to British citizens' knowledge of their empire, and that it would make all parts of the empire feel knit together as a "family of nations."[12] A month later, as the exhibition got under way, an "Empire Thanksgiving Service" took place, during which the bishop of London offered "thanksgiving for the Empire Builders of the past" and enjoined "the Empire Builders of the Present and of the Future . . . [to] work together to further God's peace on earth."[13]

The exhibition of 1924–25 was the latest in a series of world's fairs and international exhibitions that harkened back to London's Great Exhibition of 1851. Subsequent fairs had taken place in Paris, Vienna, Amsterdam, St. Louis, and, of course, Chicago. But if similar in some respects to these, the exhibition of 1924 had its own distinctive features. It was international, to be sure, but only by virtue of showcasing the British Empire; British colonies alone were invited to participate, not other nations, as had been the case in 1851.[14] Seen in this light, the exhibition might be interpreted both as an effort to project imperial grandeur and as a plea for imperial cohesion in an age when European empires had witnessed the rise of anticolonial opposition, both in the colonies themselves and among domestic critics of empire.[15]

The Wembley Exhibition, as it came to be called, also stood out for its sheer grandiosity. Covering over two hundred acres, the exhibition represented a massive and costly undertaking. It featured commercial, technological, medicinal, and environmental displays; pavilions showcasing colonial territories; a huge stadium (Empire Stadium) built at Wembley for the occasion; "palaces" of industry and engineering; numerous restaurants and cafés; an artificial lake; and even an amusement park filled with "thrilling and laughter-raising contrivances."[16] In late July and August 1924, organizers staged an epic "Pageant of Empire," which took three days for a visitor to take in in its entirety. It had a cast of 15,000 people, 300 horses, 500 donkeys, 730 camels, 72 monkeys, 1,000 doves, 7 elephants, 3 bears, and a macaw.[17] The pageant amounted to a sweeping, rose-colored tour of the empire's history, including scenes such as "The Days of Queen Elizabeth, 1588" and "Missionary Enterprises, Livingstone and Stanley, 1871," as well as musical scores such as Sir Edward Elgar's "The Crown of India."[18]

An estimated 27 million people attended the exhibition. *The British Empire Exhibition, 1924, Official Guide* claimed that visitors would learn more about the empire in a few days than they might in months of travel in the colonies themselves. Stressing the educational benefits for the young and workers, exhibition organizers had sent promotional material to employers, trade unions, municipalities, teachers, and school boards. "An adequate knowledge of the Empire is for the modern boy or girl an essential part of citizenship," as one government circular put it.[19] Many schools, along with churches and civic groups, avidly participated. A ten-month international tour, begun in 1922 and led by Major Ernst Belcher, accompanied by the mystery writer Agatha Christie, sought to awaken global interest in the exhibition.[20]

The idea for an exhibition had first been proposed in the early

1900s by the British Empire League. In 1913, Donald Smith, Lord Strathcona, Scottish-born former Canadian high commissioner, revived the idea and sought to secure allies and funding.[21] The outbreak of war in 1914 delayed implementation, but after the war, plans resumed, boosted by a postwar imperative to restore national pride and promote knowledge of the expanded empire.[22] In 1919 the Prince of Wales, the future Edward VIII, became president of the committee, and the government of Prime Minister David Lloyd George secured official recognition and financial support, enjoining the Colonial Office to invite all parts of the empire to participate.[23] Of the fifty-eight territories making up the empire, fifty-six participated, some more extensively than others. According to the *Official Guide*, the aim of the exhibition was "to stimulate trade, to strengthen the bonds that bind the Mother Country to her Sister States and Daughter Nations, to bring all into closer touch the one with the other, to enable all who owe allegiance to the British flag to meet on common ground, and to learn to know each other. It is a Family Party, to which every part of the Empire is invited, and at which every part of the Empire is represented.[24] For such a grand occasion, the Imperial Studies Committee of the Royal Colonial Institute produced a massive twelve-volume work, *The British Empire: A Survey*.[25]

For both native Britons and guests, the exhibition offered much food for thought. A character in P. G. Wodehouse's short story "The Rummy Affair of Old Biffy," which has the exhibition as a setting, summarized the moonstruck experience of many visitors, describing it as "the most supremely absorbing and educational collection of objects, both animate and inanimate, gathered from the four corners of the Empire that has ever been assembled in England's history."[26] At the same time, the exhibition attracted critics who saw it as little more than a spectacle of imperial propaganda and bread-and-circuses entertainment for the masses.[27]

While the initial impetus behind the exhibition was to showcase industrial and agricultural production and promote trade among the colonies, familiarizing visitors with the cultural diversity of the empire emerged as another goal. This emphasis took many forms, such as an exhibition of Indian art, a model of Solomon's Temple and the Tabernacle in the pavilion of Palestine, and a large-scale replica of a Buddhist monastery in the pavilion of Burma (Myanmar).[28] Conferences and lectures were to be another means of transmitting knowledge about colonies' cultures. Toward this end, a planning memorandum expressed the "hope to arrange, in connection with the Exhibition, a series of inter-imperial conferences for the consideration of problems of mutual interest as well as lectures of a more popular character."[29] As knowledge about the exhibition's aims became known in the early 1920s, various individuals and institutions stepped forward with suggestions and ideas. And one of these took the form of the Conference on Some Living Religions within the Empire.

Planning and Preparation

The idea for the conference was first hatched in a letter from Theosophist, socialist, and Quaker sympathizer William Loftus Hare (1868–1943) to Sir Denison Ross (1871–1940), the globe-trotting, highly accomplished director of the recently founded School of Oriental Studies in London.[30] Coincidentally, the school had recently formed a committee "to deal with the question of making the School better known by means of the Empire Exhibition."[31] Ross therefore responded positively to Hare, suggesting that such a conference could succeed if religious controversy was avoided and if "the spokesman of each religion should be one who professed such religion."[32] Also keen to procure what he called "native expositors" of various faiths, Hare concurred and thereafter contacted the Empire Exhibition's organizers to set things in motion.[33] Ross and Hare also established a twelve-person Executive Committee to proceed with planning and to issue invitations.[34] They were assisted in this capacity by Mabel M. Sharples, who along with Hare served as conference secretary. Key members of the Executive Committee included Victor Branford, founder of the Sociological Society, which co-sponsored the conference; Caroline Rhys Davids, an expert on Buddhism and the Pali language; Sir Thomas Arnold, a leading authority on Islam; and Sir Francis Younghusband, a British army officer, traveler, and spiritual writer who later served as president of the Royal Geographical Society. Younghusband's involvement before, during, and after the conference, as we shall see, proved especially significant.[35]

The first of twelve committee meetings took place on 12 October 1923 at the School of Oriental Studies.[36] During these meetings, several significant points were voiced and decisions made. First, planners saw their conference in continuity with the 1893 World's Parliament of Religions in Chicago, which also had taken place in the context of a major world exhibition, as we have seen. Second, they recognized that the impetus for such a conference owed a significant debt to the comparative study of religion, or the "science of religion," which had emerged as a field of study in the late nineteenth century.[37] Third, at the same time, they did not see their conference as primarily academic in nature; it was meant to be more generally informative to the British people with, again, a focus on hearing from "native expositors." As Hare later expressed their aim: "Our duty was to be informative to the British people who are mostly professing Christians as to the nature and influence of the living sister religions of the Empire."[38] For this reason, they decided to exclude both Christianity and Judaism from the conference, since presumably most attendees would have more familiarity with these two faiths; internecine rancor and divisions among Protestant denominations also recommended to them the exclusion of Christianity. Fourth, they decided not only to treat time-tested religious traditions but also "modern movements" that had developed within them. Fifth, they created some space after all for a more academic or "scientific" component to the conference, but these presentations were to come only after representatives of the various religions had spoken. Hence the schedule of the conference came to have two parts: (1) presentations "on the Oriental Religions of the Empire and various Modern Movements arising out of them," and (2) presentations "on the Psychology and Sociology of Religion."[39] Sixth, they decided to hold their conference not on the Wembley Exhibition grounds but in central London. Toward this end, they secured the large "Upper West Room" at the Imperial Institute in South Kensington.[40] Finally, the committee recognized, quite accurately, the historic nature of the undertaking: never before on British soil had such an interreligious event taken place; and as such, its organizers felt it would supply a "spiritual" counterweight to the overtly economic and industrial emphases that had been the hallmark of imperial exhibitions past and present.

Soon communiqués and invitations were sent out to figures of notable religious stature throughout the empire—to Hong Kong, Singapore, Iraq, Palestine, South Africa, Kenya, Nigeria, Ceylon (Sri Lanka) and, not least, India, from where many key invitees hailed. Speakers sought out included representatives of various Hindu traditions, Jainism, Sikhism, Zoroastrianism, Islam, and Buddhism. In some cases, the committee members were not able to secure the speaker they desired, but quite often they did.[41] They were especially gratified by the acceptance of Mirza Basheer-ud-Din Mahmood Ahmad (1889–1965), the spiritual leader of the Ahmadiyya movement within Islam in northern India (more about this later).[42] That invitations were sent to "modern movements" within older religious traditions proved gratifying to a number of invitees. After receiving an invitation, for example, Shoghi Effendi, the leader of the young Baha'i movement, which had its origins in Persia, wrote from its headquarters in Haifa, Palestine, to his co-religionists in the United States: "I feel that the opportunities now offered to the Bahá'i world should not be missed, as this chance, if properly utilized, might arouse and stimulate interest among the enlightened public." Accordingly, someone "qualified" should be tapped "to produce a befitting statement on the unique history of the movement as well as its lofty principles."[43] In the end, two "qualified" figures presented on Baha'i: Mountford Mills of Canada and Ruhi Afnan, Effendi's cousin, who traveled to London from Palestine.[44] Besides Baha'i and the Ahmadiyya, Brahmo Samaj and Arya Samaj—both reform movements within Hinduism—rounded out the "modern movements" represented at the conference.[45]

Course of the Conference

By the late summer of 1924, the scene was set for the conference to open on 22 September. As news of the conference trickled out, it became one of the most widely anticipated events of the exhibition.[46] Prior to opening day, newspapers waxed enthusiastic about its significance, calling the conference an "unusual event," a "unique gathering," and even "one of the most spectacular gatherings ever held in London."[47] To quote more fully, and more typically, from the *Yorkshire Observer* (30 August 1924):

> One of the most curious conferences of recent years will be held at the Imperial Institute next month. It will be a conference on living religions within the Empire, but curiously enough neither Christianity nor Judaism will be included. The promoters say they wish to concentrate on the lesser-known religions: Moslems, Buddhists, Parsees, Tavists [*sic*], Hindoos, and Brahmins will be present, as well as representatives of such little-known religious movements as Bahaism, which spread rapidly in Persia about a century ago. The three great branches of the Islamic faith—the Sunnis, Shiahs and the Ahmadia—will have representatives, and so will the Sufist sect. . . . Sr. Francis Younghusband, the well-known traveler, who has a probably unique knowledge of the affairs of the East, will open the conference.[48]

Following a press release by the conference's organizing committee, several newspapers printed the full schedule of the event.[49]

Many journalists assayed to comment more specifically on the conference's significance. Under the headline "Queer Religions of Empire," the *Evening News*, for example, connected the conference with the economic thrust of the Empire Exhibition as a whole: "If we are to get into touch with the producers of crops, minerals, and manufactures of the distant parts of the British Empire, it is necessary for us at home to know something of their hopes, fears, and religions. These form, in fact, the spring of thought and conduct of these citizens of the Empire."[50] The *Daily Mirror* emphasized the educational value of the conference: "Such an opportunity to learn about the religions of the East has never before been given to theological students in this country."[51] The *Inquirer* seconded this, noting that British citizens tended to have "abysmal ignorance . . . about the world religions."[52] Several newspapers claimed that such a conference could not be possible were it not for the Crown's policy of religious neutrality toward the colonies: "Under the tolerant flag of the British Empire," the *Glasgow Herald* opined, "there are not persecuted sects, and it is not surprising, therefore, that there should gather at the hospitable heart of the Empire [London] representatives of [the world's religions]."[53]

As the "holy men of the Empire" arrived in London, news coverage intensified. No figure aroused more curiosity than Mirza Basheer-ud-Din, caliph of the Ahmadiyya Muslim community and the second successor of Mirza Ghulam Ahmad (1835–1908), who in the late nineteenth century claimed to be the Mahdi, the messianic renewer of Islam in the end times, according to some Islamic traditions—a claim, then and now, widely disputed by other Muslims.[54] From its starting point in Qadian, Punjab (northern India), the Ahmadiyya movement had spread rapidly, claiming roughly five hundred thousand followers by 1924. The fascination for the British public was at least twofold: the movement's leaders expressed intense loyalty to the Raj, and in the person of Mirza Basheer-ud-Din one had the opportunity to witness in the flesh someone claiming quasi-divine status.

Reporters followed Mirza Basheer-ud-Din's every move. After a long journey from India, he arrived in London with twelve companions on 21 August 1924 and was greeted by Sir Francis Younghusband, among others. As the *Evening News* reported: "Travelers at Victoria Station got a surprise when a party of green-turbaned foreigners headed by an imposing figure stepped straight from the Continental express and opened prayer on the platform. The long-drawn tenor cry of 'Allah-o-Akbur!' (Great is Allah) followed and they moved off."[55] The company visited London's Ludgate Circus, where its members offered a prayer in fulfillment of a prophecy that they should pray at "Bab-ul-lud"—an Arabic name remarkably similar to the London Gate of Lud. Prior to the conference, the company also traveled to Brighton to pay respects at the memorial to Britain's fallen comrades in arms from India during World War I. Furthermore, their charismatic leader laid the foundation stone for London's first mosque, Fazl Mosque, in Southfields, which an Ahmadiyya community has occupied until the present.[56] During many meetings with London's dignitaries, Mirza Basheer-ud-Din rarely failed to remind his interlocutors that Muslims formed one of the largest groups of any religious body in the empire, and he made scant effort to hide his proselytizing mission.[57] "I intend to observe conditions," he told one reporter, "[to] see how we can best set about converting Western people to Islam. . . . It is our belief that if the Christian . . . was to concentrate all his mind upon trying to discover the true religion, just as we do from our birth, he would be gradually led to our creeds by his own reasoning."[58]

For just such reasons, presumably, Ross and others had sought to eliminate "religious controversy" from the conference—a point that Ross reiterated in an article for the *Morning Post* that appeared on the conference's opening day, 22 September 1924. Ross underscored several distinctive features of the conference. First, he made clear that the event "is purely an Empire gathering" and that he and others had sought to align its goals with those of the Empire Exhibition as a whole, which concretely meant "familiaris[ing] people in this country with less well-known religions [of the empire]." Second, he emphasized the limitation of understanding religions from a "purely academic standpoint"; instead, "the only way to arrive at a true appreciation of any religion is to hear it personally expounded by one who believes in it." At the same time, he conveyed that the planning committee had sought speakers with a "dual capacity": those who "not only believe in their religion, but who have made an intimate study of it." Third, he stated that, while the history and teachings of a religion might be sketched by speakers, the focus of the conference would be on "applications of various religions to every day life." Fourth, he reminded the public that in addition to lectures on the major religions of the empire, minor ones and modern movements, such as the Ahmadiyya or Baha'i, would be treated as well. Fifth, he explained that the conference would conclude with several lectures on the "psychology and sociology" of religion but this more academic part would come only after hearing "from the lips of those who profess" a particular religion. "The Conference," he concluded in an optimistic register, "should do something to spread the knowledge of the religions of the Empire. I hope that it will do more. I hope that it will serve to illustrate that many widely held ideas and beliefs are a common possession."[59]

Preceded by a brief orchestral concert, the conference officially opened at 2:30 p.m. on the afternoon of 22 September.[60] Given the high-profile nature of the event, Ross, who chaired the opening lecture, had felt it appropriate to arrange for a telegraphed greeting by King George V, who bestowed a royal blessing on the event. Prime Minister Ramsay MacDonald also agreed to send a brief communiqué, which was read aloud. "I am glad to have this opportunity," he began, "to send a word of greeting to [this conference]. . . . Many religions and many creeds live in amity within our Empire, each by their different way leading our peoples toward some ultimate light. I welcome cordially the objects of this Conference and the knowledge which it spreads amongst us that our peoples, in the aspirations of the Spirit, 'walk not back to back but with a unity of track.' "[61] A reporter for the *Daily Mail* vividly captured the lecture hall's atmosphere on opening day by focusing on the women in the audience: "Many women were present—English and Indian. The latter wore flowing *saris* of purple and gold or of crimson and deep sea blue. Diamonds flashed from their hair and pearls gleamed in the bangles on their arms."[62] As Hare described the opening gathering: "The fez, the turban, the kaftan, the golden coat from India and the quiet robe from Arabia were symbols of variety" in the hall.[63]

Sir Francis Younghusband gave the opening speech. A well-known, larger-than-life figure, Younghusband has been aptly described as "the last great imperial adventurer."[64] As president of the Royal Geographical Society, he had chaired the Mount Everest Committee that supported George Mallory's fatal effort to ascend the fabled mountain. Born in India and educated in Britain, Younghusband had quickly risen in the ranks of the British army and traveled extensively in Asia, where he became a master of "the Great Game"—Britain and Russia's tense rivalry for influence in Central Asia—and came into close personal contact with representatives of Asia's various religious traditions.[65] All the while, he devoted himself to the assiduous reading of spiritual and philosophical works, absorbing a diverse range of influences from figures such as Ralph Waldo Emerson, Ernst Renan, William James, Friedrich Schiller, and G. F. W. Hegel. The thought of Leo Tolstoy particularly captured his imagination after he read the Russian author's *The Kingdom of God Is within You*. The book, Younghusband once recorded, "reached me in Chitral [today in Pakistan] on the far Northern Frontier and [it] determined the main trend of my life. So profoundly, indeed, was I affected . . . that I decided to make religion my main interest in life." Weary of the traditional Christianity of his youth, Younghusband at one point expressed a desire to found a "new religion" on the basis of Tolstoy's sweeping universalism and humanitarianism.[66] "I had visions," he later recorded, "of a far greater religion yet to be, and of a God as much greater than our English God as a Himalayan giant is greater than an English hill."[67]

In the early 1900s, the viceroy to India, Lord Curzon, tapped Younghusband to lead Britain's controversial expedition into Tibet, a place shrouded in numinous mystery to the European imagination, where he encountered the Dalai Lama.[68] This expedition provided the West with some of the first photographs of the region. In Tibet in 1904, Younghusband experienced some sort of mystical epiphany. While gazing at the Himalayas on a cloudless day, as he later recounted, he found himself overcome by "untellable joy. The whole world was ablaze with the same ineffable bliss that was burning within me." Extrapolating from the experience, he became convinced "of the essential goodness of the world. I was convinced past all refutation that men were good at heart, that all the evil in them was superficial . . . in short, that men at heart are divine."[69] Extrapolating still further, he arrived at the view that all belief systems were humankind's inchoate attempts to express the divinity that permeated all things, human consciousness in particular. As such, all religions should be esteemed, even venerated, and they should come into closer conversation with one another. In theological terms, Younghusband expressed an ardent pluralism, convinced that all religious paths, although differently routed, ultimately led to the same transcendent vistas and taught the same mystical unity. They also had a similar moral message, he felt—one that promoted altruism and human brotherhood. His beliefs took on a new urgency several years later after a cycling accident in Belgium almost took his life.[70] In his later years, Younghusband expressed his beliefs—often in fevered, rambling prose—in a number of general-audience books with titles such as *Within, the Living Universe* and *Vital Religion: A Brotherhood of Faith*. All the while, however, he never lost confidence in the British Empire and its necessary tutelary role to other civilizations.

In his opening address at the conference in 1924, Younghusband articulated his developing views, tying them to the particular aims of the conference and the larger objectives of the Empire Exhibition. Of all the addresses at the conference, his is the most significant in defining the purpose of interreligious dialogue. Several aspects of it, therefore, merit highlighting. Although he praised "the material development of the British Empire" on display at Wembley and the neutrality of the Crown toward the empire's various religions, he indicated that these things in themselves were insufficient, for far greater attention ought to be paid to the empire's "spiritual development." In fact, he startled many by claiming that "the ultimate basis upon which the British Empire should stand must be religion: not political constitutions nor economic agreements. These are only the bones and anatomy, not the spirit which makes and is the man, and which should make and be the Empire." Anticipating critics who might wonder if religion sowed more seeds of discord than concord, Younghusband replied "that an instrument, which, if carelessly used is exceedingly dangerous, may, if properly used [for the purposes of peace], be superlatively effective."[71] He maintained this conviction for the remainder of his life, and it strongly informed the founding of the World Congress of Faiths in 1936, as we shall see.

Eager to make clear that he was no bookish pedant, Younghusband insisted that his convictions did not rest on "abstruse study in the library," but were the result of "years of work in the field—work among Hindus, Muhammadans, and Buddhists, as well as among my own countrymen." Even patriotism could not bind the empire together, he claimed, aware of the many tensions and conflicts throughout the colonies. Rather, religion, rightly understood—that is, a mutual recognition by colonies and Mother Country alike "of the realness of the spiritual world"—should help the empire "hold firmly together." This would also promote greater friendship among the different religious groups within the empire as represented before him at the conference.

But rightly understanding religion required a revolution in thinking about it. In Younghusband's estimation, patience should not be granted to those convinced that they alone were "wholly and exclusively right" in religious matters. One must rather hold the conviction that all religions in some capacity and in their own distinctive manner pointed ultimately to a higher harmony. This view he enjoined the conference attendees, and the empire as a whole, to adopt. As he more fully expressed it: "[The] exclusive attitude is not the attitude we would wish to see adopted at this conference. We may each of us hold that our own religion is more completely perfect than any other. But even then we may recognize that God reveals himself in many ways, and that to the followers of other religions than our own may have been revealed much that may be of value to us." Religious differences will perhaps always be present, he conceded, "but we need never lose our faith that all the time there may be an underlying unity and overarching harmony which may reconcile them all, if only we could reach it."[72]

Since Younghusband would later play the leading role in 1936 in establishing the World Congress of Faiths, it is noteworthy that already in 1924 he envisioned the religions conference as the first step toward future ones, ones in which his views might find more expansive development. "This conference," he concluded his speech, "will vivify interest in religion and declare its value. But later conferences may perhaps go further," leading those gathered into a "deeper truth" in which interlocutors would discuss together "the great ultimate problems of life—the nature of the world we live in, our relation to it, the aims we ought to have in view and the way to reach our aims." He admitted that these were also questions for philosophy and science, but "primarily and elementally" they were "religious" in nature, and he therefore praised those gathered for advancing the "sacred cause of religion."[73]

Younghusband's claims dominated news coverage of the conference's first day. The *Times of India* summed up his aim as suggesting that "the ultimate basis of the British Empire must be religion which used in the right way, might work for good, not dreamt of."[74] Hailing the conference as "the first of its kind in this country," the *Manchester Guardian* appeared impressed at Younghusband's "reverent wonder" for religion. A unity based on such reverence might in fact be a necessity rather than a luxury, the *Guardian* continued, summarizing a point frequently made by the conference's organizers, for "in the British Empire there are more Mohammedans than Christians, and at least twice as many Hindus as Mohammedans. That there are also many Buddhists, and very many millions of adherents of primitive religions." Only time would bear out Younghusband's aspirations, the *Guardian* averred, since at present "men of different faiths were still unaccustomed to discussing among themselves one another's religious beliefs. As they became accustomed to do that, might not future conferences frankly discuss religious truth itself?"[75]

Once Younghusband ceded the lectern, a host of the promised

News clipping, "Conference of Religions of the Empire." (From Sheffield Daily Telegraph, *[24 September 1924]. Image courtesy of the University of Southampton Library.)*

native expositors followed. Because of its numerical preponderance in the empire, Hinduism was heard from first in a lecture by Pandit Shyam Shanker of the Indian holy city of Benares (Varanasi), whose talk was "Orthodox Hinduism or Sanâtana Dharma." Arguing that India possessed ancient traditions of religious pluralism and accommodation, Shanker warmly embraced the aims of the conference: "The age of religious disputes or controversies is happily drawing to its close in the civilized world, and I am sure the spirit engendered by this Conference will stimulate friendly religious discussions and hasten the end of religious . . . bigotry and fanaticism."[76]

Islam followed Hinduism. In fact, the entire second day of the conference was devoted to Islam. Guests heard "The Basic Principles of Islam," by Al-Haj Khwaja Kamal-ud-Din, imam of the mosque in Woking, Surrey; "The Spirit of Islam," by Mustafa Khan of Lahore; "The Shi'ah Branch of Islam," by Sheikh Kadhim el Dojaily of Baghdad; "The Ahmadiyya Movement," by Hazrat Mirza Bashir-ud-Din of Qadian, India; and "Sufism," by Hafiz Raushan Ali of Ranmal, Punjab.[77] Before the lectures began, the mufti of the Woking mosque (Britain's first, built in 1889) chanted passages from the Qur'an, leaving a strong impression on those gathered. Conspicuously, a number of Hindu guests, present on the conference's opening day, did not attend the lectures on Islam—a fact that led one newspaper to editorialize skeptically: "It would appear from this that we are not all quite so ready as Sir Francis Younghusband supposes to hear one another's creeds exploited [*sic*] as parallel ways of approach to a common object."[78]

In subsequent days, guests heard presentations on Buddhism, Zoroastrianism, Jainism, Sikhism, and Taoism, bearing such titles as "The Status and Influence of Buddhism in Ceylon" (Dr. W. A. de Silva of Colombo), "The Influence of Buddhism on Education in Ceylon" (G. P. Malaasekera of Colombo), "Mahâyâna Buddhism" (Shoson Miyamoto of Tokyo), "Zoroastrianism: The Religion of the Parsis" (Shams-ul-ulema Dastur Kaikobad Adarbad Noshirvan of Poona [Pune]), "Jainism" (Rai Bahadur Jagmander Lal Jaini of Indore), "Sikh Religion" (Sardar Kahan Singh of Nabha), and "Taoism" (Hsü T-Shan of Peking [Beijing]).[79]

Presentations on traditional Asian faiths were followed by ones on modern movements within them as well as by ones on various so-called primitive religions found in the empire. For the latter, suitable native expositors were often lacking, so Western scholars were sought for guidance if they came from geographical locations where a particular religion was practiced and had long experience of observing it. On these topics, eight lectures were given in all, including two on Baha'i, a relative newcomer to the religious scene, and ones on the Hindu reform movements of Brahmo Samaj (N. E. Sen) and Arya Samaj (S. N. Pherwani of Shikarpur). Lectures on "primitive religions" included "Some Account of the Maori Beliefs" (Archdeacon Williams of New Zealand) and "Beliefs of Some East African Tribes" (Richard St. Narbe Baker of "Kenya Colony"), among others.[80]

The conference concluded with several lectures on "the psychology and sociology of religions"—described later by Hares as "the scientific section of the conference."[81] For the most part, native British scholars gave these presentations. Younghusband approached the lectern again to deliver "Man and Nature," which in fact was not scientific but rather a rhapsodic meditation on his view that intimations of divinity suffused the natural world. His talk was followed by "The Naturalist's Approach to Religion" (J. Arthur Thomson), "Primitive Occupations: Their Ideals and Temptations" (Victor Branford), "Holy Ways and Holy Places" (H. J. Fleure), "The Idea of the Sacred City" (Rachel Annand Taylor, the only woman to speak), and several others.

While the conference was in session, three official receptions were held: one at the Imperial Institute arranged by Lady Aaron Ron, a second at the Ritz Hotel hosted by Mirza Basheer-ud-Din, and yet another at the Claridge Hotel, arranged by Sara Louisa (Lady) Bloomfield, an early British follower of Baha'i.[82] London had never witnessed a social scene like this before.

Although the scientific presentations are not without interest, the lectures by native expositors more insistently merit attention. To be sure, in many cases these were quite predictable, offering straightforward overviews or introductions to various traditions. But here and there they provide fascinating glimpses into the postwar imperial milieu. What is more, several speakers used the platform to offer apologias for their beliefs or to rebut Western criticisms, while others, echoing Younghusband, sought to wax eloquent about the general significance of religion in imperial and human affairs. Still others used the opportunity to take swipes at the colonial system as a whole.

The fragile years after World War I had witnessed worldwide discussions about the promotion of peace and avoidance of war in the future—a discussion that took short-lived institutional embodiment in the League of Nations.[83] Not surprisingly therefore, several speakers addressed the topic of peace, proposing resources from their respective traditions for its promotion. Speaking of Baha'i, for example, Ruhi Afnan criticized the "spirit of nationalism" that had led to the "great world war" before extolling "the spirit of international brotherhood" that Baha'i sought to encourage. Afnan's coreligionist, the Canadian Mountford Mills, pointed out that 'Abdu'l-Bahá (the successor of Bahá'u'lláh, Baha'i's founder) had already in the late nineteenth century advocated for a "world federation" and "international tribunal" that resembled the League of Nations. Similarly, Lahore's Mustafa Khan emphasized in his lecture "The Spirit of Islam" that Allah was "the Sustainer, not of a particular nation or community, but of all humanity." "The cosmopolitan conception of God as the universal Father of humanity," he elaborated, "is a potent factor to cement the brotherly relation of different nations of the world, and thus to bring these apparently heterogeneous elements of humanity into a harmonious whole." Wilmot Arthur de Silva, furthermore, speaking on Buddhism in Ceylon, extolled the strife-reducing potential of Buddhism, which as a cultural force, he felt, served as an antidote to "civilizations that [have] exalted wealth, power and dominion."[84] He did not mention Europe, but the implication was clear enough.

While several speakers expressed a measure of gratitude for the British Empire, others voiced criticism—some subtly, some not so subtly. After lamenting the influence of the Portuguese and Dutch empires in Ceylon, de Silva, who contributed significantly to the Sri Lankan independence movement, deplored the work of Christian missionaries under the British flag; those who had converted he called "government Christians" before declaring such missionary efforts a "marked failure" in light of the resilience and spiritual riches of Buddhism.[85] The linguist Gunapala Piyasena Malalasekera, also speaking about Buddhism in Ceylon, offered a blistering critique of education there under British rule: "In the high schools, where English forms the sole medium of instruction, the system has been slavishly based on the high schools of England. . . . Our boys are taught of the Black Prince and Henry VIII and his six wives without a word being told them about the exploits of their own kings and heroes; they are told about Luther and Wolsey, and not one word about their own scholars and reformers. . . . They are made familiar with glowing descriptions of a robin's breast, but they are not told a thing about their own song-bird, the *kokila*." Few other criticisms were quite this blunt, but sporadically among the lectures others cropped up, as in the Taoist Hsü Ti-Shan's claim that empire always implies "authority, force and pressure" while the goal of the Taoist was to escape from such things and "submit one's self to nature."[86]

Of all the faiths represented, Islam elicited the greatest skepticism from the British populace—this was similarly the case at Chicago in 1893, as we have seen—due to its long confrontation with the West at Europe's borders and because of its status as a rival "missionary religion" to Christianity.[87] Those speaking on Islam seemed aware of the challenge and sought to controvert Western criticism. Rebutting frequent charges of Islam's intellectual backwardness, for example, Khwaja Kamal-ud-Din called attention to past Islamic achievements in science, proclaiming Muslims "the forerunners of the workers in modern sciences," anticipators of "modern civilization." In a similarly defensive register, Mirza Basheer-ud-Din sought to put the best possible glosses on polygamy and jihad—two frequent targets of Western disapprobation. The former corresponded better to "the demands of nature," he claimed, even if it should also be understood as a "heavy burden which a man is sometimes compelled to carry out and is not a device for indulgence." Jihad, he opined, does not give Muslims a license for violence, but only allows them to defend their faith against those intent on destroying it. He also defended Islam's looser strictures on divorce, arguing that critics "fail to realize that the temperaments of the husband and wife may, in some cases, chance to be so entirely incompatible that to compel them to live together would amount to an attempt to reconcile fire and water, which is bound to result in the destruction of both."[88]

After parrying such criticisms of Islam, Mirza Basheer-ud-Din pivoted sharply into an apologetic register: "Such and all similar criticisms . . . [of] the teachings of Islam are the result of ignorance or a lack of understanding, for the teachings of Islam are, more than those of any other religion, based on considerations of mercy and of wisdom, and offer a complete and perfect solution of the needs and problems of every age."[89]

In apologetics he was not alone; other speakers campaigned for the correctness of their outlook. Zoroastrianism, according to its sole expositor Shams-ul-ulema Dastur Kaikobad Adarbad Noshirvan, shone "more brightly" than other faiths and it deserved to be considered the "Universal Religion." Praising the fastidious nature of Jainist ethics, Rai Bahadur Jagmander Lal Jaini asserted that "it may be said that Jainist morality begins at a point where in most other religions it may seem to end." He also emphasized Jainism's durability and resilience as a religion: "The greatest proof of my position is this, that whereas most of the ancient religions born in India have been extinguished, assimilated or expelled by the other religions,

Jainism has survived all shocks and attacks, political or otherwise, since at least from 1000 BC." Representing the Hindu reform movement Brahmo Samaj, N. C. Sen argued that the movement's founder, Ram Mohan Roy, sought only "to promote the universal worship of the One Supreme Creator, the Common Father of Mankind" and gather all other religions into its capacious bosom. "This catholic idea, while it led him to embrace all creeds and sects in his comprehensive scheme of faith and worship, precluded the possibility of being classified with any particular religious denomination."[90] Similarly, both speakers on Baha'i implicitly argued for the superiority of their faith over others because, as Mountford Mills claimed, it constituted what was "fundamental and true in all religions alike" and therefore responded best "to the new and greater religious possibilities of this age."[91]

Although speakers frequently and proudly called attention to the antiquity of their faiths, none wanted to come across as passé or ill adapted to the present. The striking modernity on display at the exhibition at large, moreover, prompted speakers to defend the abiding relevance of their perspective in the contemporary world. According to Khwaja Kamal-ud-Din, for instance, Islamic theology had anticipated both modern democracy and socialism. The latter was seen in Islam's injunction of universal almsgiving to the needy, while the former was apparent in Islam's view that all were created equal before God. In his own words: Islam "demolishes all man-made barriers such as descent, race, colour and wealth. . . . Thus Islam brought to man for the first time the best form of democracy in all its ramifications." Similarly, Rai Bahadur Jagmander Lal Jain made the case for the compatibility of Jainism and "modern civilization." "In trade and commerce," he claimed, Jains "almost top the list [among religions of India]. There is not a district or town in which Jains . . . do not take a leading position as landed proprietors, bankers, merchants, lawyers. . . . Their community takes an interest in all modern movements, and they are very enterprising."[92]

As reform movements within Hinduism, both Brahmo Samaj and Arya Samaj, according to their respective expositors, had successfully begun to bring Hinduism into fruitful dialogue with the modern world. Comparing Ram Mohan Roy (the Bengali founder of Brahmo Samaj) to the Protestant reformer Martin Luther, N. C. Sen explained that the Brahmo Samaj sought to sweep away accumulated falsehoods from the past and present to humanity a purified new religious dispensation. He drew an analogy from modern chemistry: Brahmo Samaj "is the wonderful solvent which fuses all dispensations into a new chemical compound. It is the mighty absorbent which absorbs all that is true and good and beautiful in the objective world." Not to be outdone, S. N. Pherwani compared Arya Samaj's founder, Dayanand Saraswati, to Luther; not unlike the Saxon reformer, Dayanand Saraswati sought to return Hinduism to its sacred Scriptures (the Vedas) and thereby "to strengthen [it] . . . from within, by ridding it of some of its superstitious and degenerate elements, as well as the tyranny of priestcraft and a caste system by birth instead of by worth and works." Thus purified, Arya Samaj, he claimed, sought open dialogue with modernity: "Arya Samaj welcomes rationalism, fosters . . . the spirit of open discussion, and only limits it by the authority of revealed scriptures. It thus fits in with the present revolutionary epoch of the age of reason and free inquiry."[93]

Finally, many speakers remarked on the historic nature of their undertaking, seizing on this fact to extol the virtues of "East and West" coming together and the desirability of greater interreligious conversation and cooperation in the future. For instance, N. C. Sen, quoting his father Keshab Chandra Sen (1838–84), expressed deep satisfaction with the conference, asserting that "the true Kingdom of God will not be realized—indeed, can never be realized—unless the East and the West are joined together."[94] Mirza Basheer-ud-Din, likewise, expressed his delight at the gathering, exclaiming on the final day that "Kipling is mistaken. The East is East, and the West is West, but the twain have met today."[95] In a similar vein, Mountford Mills saw the conference as the practical realization of Baha'i's own aims: "For this conference, both in character and method, expressed that ideal of religious unity so indelibly impressed upon all members of the Baha'i Cause, and its [the conference's] very existence, under these conditions of impressive dignity and far-reaching influence, appears to us as the fulfilment of a glorious and long-cherished hope."[96] "Whatever the final intellectual residuum left in the minds of the members of the conference," as the conference secretary William Loftus Hare later noted, "There can be no doubt that on its personal and emotional side it was a very great success."[97]

The conference officially ended on 3 October 1924. Two papers rounded out the roster of speakers—one given by sociologist Victor Branford, the other by Unitarian minister J. Tyssul Davis. In stirring and superlative language, both expressed the view that something epochal had taken place. Branford thanked all the speakers before offering a brief analysis of their joint efforts. In his view, the "crippling defect of contemporary civilization" was a cleft between the world of intellect and science on the one hand, and the world of emotion and feeling on the other. By bringing both native expositors (feeling) and scholars (intellect) together, the conference, in his interpretation, had sought to bridge this divide and thereby bring a measure of "unity" and "vision" to modern life. Religion needed science and science needed religion, in short, and this he summed up as the "synthetic approach to religion."[98] Branford expanded on these sentiments in a book published shortly after the conference, *Living Religions: A Plea for the Larger Modernism.*[99]

"In ten days the whole field of religions has been roughly traversed." Thus J. Tyssul Davis began his remarks before launching into highly idealistic language—reminiscent of Younghusband's opening lecture—about the ultimate direction and congruity of all religions. Passing over the countless divergences of opinion expressed at the conference, Davis opined: "Every student of comparative religion knows that the same truths are taught in the great religions, that the fundamental principles are the same. This conference has again brought that out." In his final words, he took further flight: "The great prophets and founders of religion are not rivals. In all things of the spirit they speak the same language, they strike the same note. All the Christs, Buddhas, the Muhammads, the Gurus, the Rishis, the Avatars belong to the human family, and are the common possession of humanity. . . . To some of us it seems that the hour has struck when [all] religious devotees . . . shall work together in concord and harmony, in speech and act, in mind and heart, to win the world for Righteousness, Peace, for Fellowship and Brotherly Love—to win the world for God."[100] Davis elaborated on these thoughts in a short booklet, *A League of Religions* (1926), written shortly after the conference.[101] The book is noteworthy because it anticipates many of the aspirations of the World Congress of Faiths, as we shall shortly see.

Press coverage after the conclusion of the conference almost invariably noted the historic nature of what had taken place, even if reactions widely varied. In an approving tone, a reporter for the *Inquirer* asked, "What good will this conference achieve? It will make the exclusiveness of the Western faiths a mockery and a derision. . . . Beneath darker skin, and through uncouth tongues, the same passion for the living God flames eagerly."[102] In more descriptive language, the *Morning Post* editorialized that "those present had had an opportunity of hearing what men of other faiths believed from their own lips, and the Conference seemed to bear witness to a spirit of broad-mindedness and tolerance which had made it possible for men professing the most divergent creeds to give each other a hearing."[103]

But some Christian outlets voiced disappointment, because of the omission of Christian points of view during the conference, the lack of discussion following individual lectures, and/or because they perceived behind the endeavor an ideology that seemed to relativize all religious points of view. Writing for the *Catholic Times,* one observer charged that Younghusband in particular yearned for a "new religion" made up of "vague Christianity and educated paganism." "This kind of talk [at the conference]," the writer continued, "is practically a denial that Christianity is God's revealed religion, and that Christ Our Lord was God bringing God's truth to mankind."[104] Writing in the *Christian,* another observer noted that, whatever the intention of the planners, the conference in fact had helped Christians engaged in missions realize the "magnitude of the task" before them, since only one-sixth of the people of the empire were Christians. "The hope was expressed that the conference would 'serve to illustrate that many widely-held ideas and beliefs are a common possession,'" this observer continued, before offering a rebuttal: "We, on the other hand, are confident that thousands who have followed the proceedings will be more satisfied of the unique and triumphant power of the Gospel of Christ and, therefore, be emboldened to carry out the [missionary] work of the Master's Commission."[105] As had been true in Chicago, the sought-after irenicism of the conference had as one ironic result divided Christians from one another.

Spurred to action by the various reactions to the conference,

Younghusband in the pages of the *Guardian* offered his own gloss on what had taken place. "The main impression one got from listening to paper after paper," he assayed, "was that, if there was an extraordinary variety of religious belief in the British Empire, there was also a tremendous earnestness in seeking after God. And there was in each paper an absolute conviction that governing the world was a Great Spiritual Power for which different names were given, but Who ruled the world for good, and expected men to be their best. Religion is evidently a vital force in the Empire."[106] And if "the conference does no other good," he concluded, "it at least gave intense spiritual satisfaction to those who took part in it. . . . And possibly it also disposed each to show a kindlier consideration for the beliefs of others."[107] The experience of the conference, coupled with his previous religious reveries in Asia, led Younghusband to become Britain's most passionate champion of interfaith endeavors, as we shall shortly see. Picking up where the conference left off, in fact, Younghusband soon wanted to start what he began calling an "inter-religious movement."[108]

Since 1924, the phenomenon of interreligious or interfaith dialogue has expanded dramatically in the West and across the globe.[109] The Living Religions within the Empire Conference, like Chicago's parliament before it, represented both a harbinger of things to come and a catalyst to help achieve that future. The parliament is well known; the London conference, regrettably, is not. With the benefit of hindsight, what, then, are we finally to make of this gathering in London in the twilight decades of the British Empire? What inheritance and influence did it leave for future generations?

To begin with, it is not difficult to read the 1924 conference as an Orientalist undertaking cut from the same cloth as the works of scholarship analyzed by Edward Said and his many disciples. As might be inferred, many telltale binaries of Orientalist discourse were present in the assumptions behind the conference as well as its very structures: "the West" (or at least Great Britain) was seen as enlightened, progressive, and modern, outfitted intellectually and materially to understand and maintain power over "the East," which often came across as exotic, irrational, and backward.[110] But there are limits to this approach. By giving imperial subjects such a visible platform to express their beliefs, and in the British metropole no less, conference organizers, wittingly or unwittingly, punctured some Orientalist assumptions, as the invitees gave learned accounts of their views, sought to demonstrate their compatibility with the modern world, and in some cases even indicted Western colonialism. That many speakers spoke eloquently from their traditions about the importance of peace in the shadow of Europe's Great War, moreover, implicitly cast doubts on Europe's ongoing ability to justify its colonial positions vis-à-vis the rest of the world. In the final analysis, therefore, Orientalism, while illuminating in some respects, cannot serve as the exclusive hermeneutic for understanding the conference. This much was true of Chicago in 1893 as well.

Historical retrospection also suggests a troubling irony about the 1924 conference. As we have seen, it was the hope of some conference organizers, particularly Younghusband, that a vague, idealistic notion of "religion" might serve as a kind of glue for the empire. To quote Younghusband again: "Religion should be the centre of all interests—the essential element in the Empire's life."[111] But as any student of world history during the 1920s knows, anticolonial nationalist movements heavily imbued with ethnic and religious interests were coming to life and gaining momentum at this time, not least in northern India, whence many of the conference's participants hailed.[112] The furies of violence that would eventually lead to the bloody partition of India and Gandhi's assassination suggest then the limitation, if not the obtuseness, of Younghusband's hopes of pan-imperial fellowship through "religion." Put differently, far from serving as a glue for empire, religious forces, once *politicized*, proved to be significant agents of its undoing.[113] The divergence of views at the conference, appeals to peace notwithstanding, suggest then the difficulty, if not the futility, of holding together an empire as extensive as postwar Britain's on the basis of something as protean and subject to political manipulation as "religion."

Yet, although it did not save the empire, the conference did serve as an important catalyst for the establishment of organizations devoted to the study of religions and dialogue among religions. This aspect of its legacy—mainly a story of the late 1920s and 1930s—will serve as the guiding thread for the remainder of this chapter.

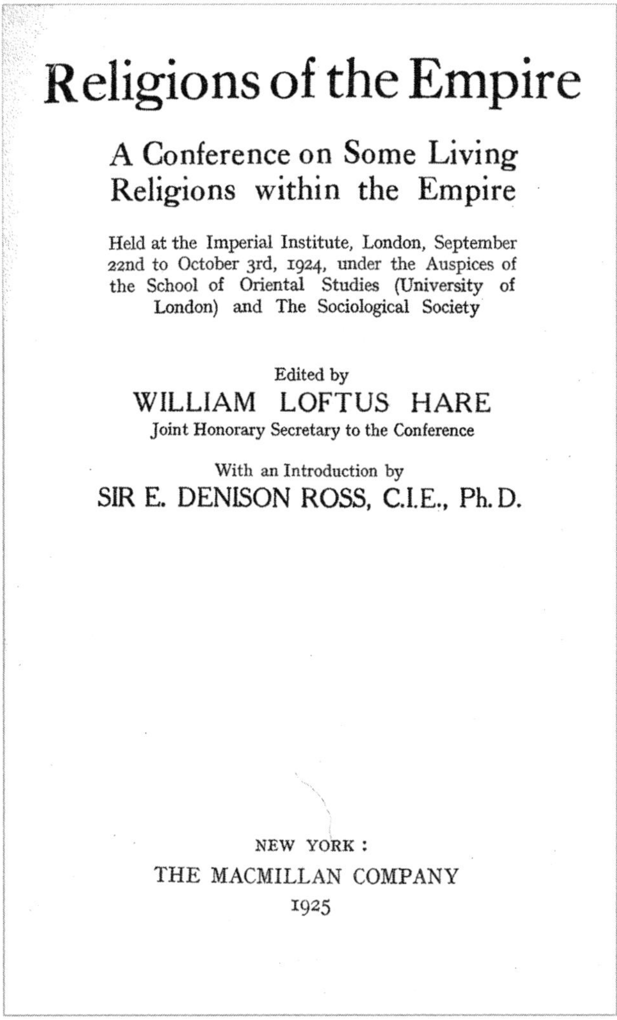

Religions of the Empire

A Conference on Some Living Religions within the Empire

Held at the Imperial Institute, London, September 22nd to October 3rd, 1924, under the Auspices of the School of Oriental Studies (University of London) and The Sociological Society

Edited by
WILLIAM LOFTUS HARE
Joint Honorary Secretary to the Conference

With an Introduction by
SIR E. DENISON ROSS, C.I.E., Ph. D.

NEW YORK:
THE MACMILLAN COMPANY
1925

Title page of William Loftus Hare's Religions of the Empire. *(Author's collection.)*

Institution Building

Already in the late 1920s, Sir Denison Ross and others lamented the fact that the 1924 conference constituted but a single event and had not resulted in an ongoing institution. More specifically, he regretted that hardly any organization existed in Britain for the study of religion per se apart from confessional standpoints. He and others—including conference participants Thomas Arnold, William Loftus Hare, Caroline Rhys Davids, J. Tyssul Davis, and, not least, Younghusband—therefore collaborated to establish in 1930 the Society for Promoting the Study of Religions. Ross explained the rationale for the society to a reporter in February of that year: "Many who wish to know more of the attitude of mind of men of other faiths do not know to whom to turn or what to turn to, for information, and the proposed society . . . should meet a real need."[114] From offices located at 17 Bedford Square, London, the society soon began publishing a journal—*Religions: Journal of Transactions of the Society for Promoting the Study of Religions*—that ran from 1931 to 1953.[115] Both the society and the journal owed their being to the 1924 conference; they were, as Ross put it in the inaugural issue of the journal, "the direct outcome of that notable Conference, for it was found in almost all countries that had contributed adherents that there were people who were intensely interested in the study of Religions, and [had] sympathetic appreciation of other people's faiths."[116]

But some society members began to ask themselves in the 1930s if scholarship *about* religion could substitute for the kind of in-the-flesh interreligious conversation that had taken place in 1924. Soon plans were in the works for something grander. And Francis Younghusband—who had long seen 1924 as "but one step"—stood at the center of this effort.[117]

As things turned out, the desire to revive the spirit of the 1924 conference in Britain coincided with a new world's fair taking place in Chicago in 1933—under the theme of a "century of progress"—and the concurrent effort to hold another parliament of religions there in imitation of the first one in 1893.[118] This idea was the brainchild of American social worker Charles Frederick Weller (1895–1957) and the Indian Kedarnath Das Gupta (1878–1942), who together in the late 1920s established on American soil the short-lived World Fellowship of Faiths.[119] As things unfolded, nothing quite like the event of 1893 materialized in Chicago in 1933. On the fairground, one could find a long, L-shaped Hall of Religion, but it mainly showcased Christian Scriptures and artifacts.[120] At the nearby Hotel Morrison in downtown Chicago, however, the World Fellowship of Faiths met. Several hundred delegates had accepted invitations from Weller and Das Gupta, including his Highness the Gaekwar of Baroda (Sayajirao Gaekward III), a wealthy, flamboyant Hindu maharaja from India who later became involved in Younghusband's World Congress of Faiths.[121] Bishop Francis J. McConnell of the U.S. Methodist Episcopal Church served as national chairman of the organization and gave various speeches over the course of several days of meetings.[122] In them, he declared that the goal of the organization was to overcome "rivalry, competition, mutual distrust and misunderstanding" among different faiths; instead, "it is *fellowship* that this movement promotes." The fellowship did not seek to establish a "synthetic" religion but encouraged fellowship among religions "as they are and as they aspire to be, in the common attempt to solve man's deepest problems."[123]

The World Fellowship maintained offices in New York, where preliminary and follow-up meetings were held. In the late 1920s and early 1930s, it had established contact with religious leaders and other organizations both in the United States and abroad. Gandhi and several other notables sent greetings to the meeting in 1933. For a period, the influential social worker and peace activist Jane Addams served as honorary president of the American National Committee of the fellowship. Based on its various meetings and solicitations of words of support, a publication emerged in 1935: *World Fellowship: Addresses and Messages by Leading Spokesmen of All Faiths, Races and Countries*, edited by Charles Weller. According to this volume, the fellowship saw itself as a "movement not a machine; a sense of expanding activities, rather than an established institution, an inspiration more than an achievement. . . . It believes that the desired and necessary human realization of the all-embracing spiritual Oneness of the Good Life Universal must be accompanied by appreciation (brotherly love) for all the individualities, all the differentiations of function, by which true unity is enriched." Animated by such lofty rhetoric, the actual gathering in Chicago in 1933 focused, more so than in 1893, on how faith traditions and other movements attendant to spiritual realities might contribute to the pressing practical needs of the world. The book, for example, has, in addition to explicitly religious parts, sections entitled "Economic Projects," "Woman," "Negroes," and the odd catchall "Machines, Fear, Security, Adult Education, Prohibition, Motion Pictures."[124]

Because of his growing "interfaith" profile in Britain, Francis Younghusband had been invited to attend in Chicago in 1933, but was unable to do so.[125] Nonetheless, a correspondence developed between him and Weller and Das Gupta, and he traveled to the United States in 1934 to meet with them personally.[126] In this year he spoke at several extension meetings of the World Fellowship that met in New York, Boston, Philadelphia, Washington, Pittsburgh, Cleveland, and again at Chicago.[127] During his visit, Weller and Das Gupta asked Younghusband to consider hosting the World Fellowship in London. Younghusband happily entertained the idea, reasoning, as he recorded later in a memoir, that "London is the capital city of an Empire which includes about 260 million Hindus, 77 million Muslims, about 12 million Buddhists, besides Jews and Christians. . . . Prominent adherents of all these religions are to be found in London . . . [and thus] the task of organizing a Congress should be much easier than the task of the organizers of the Chicago Congress."[128]

When he returned to Britain, Younghusband enthusiastically set about this task, seeking out those, including Sir Denison Ross, who had been involved in the 1924 conference. He only wanted the "best men," as he later recorded, because such a project "must be controlled and guided by men [and women too, as it turned out] who are in closest contact with the essential Spirit of the Universe and act in conformity with what we can find out of the fundamental universal laws. . . . It was not an easy task."[129] Some among those whom he sought out showed interest, and others did not; the latter included Ross, who simply had too many commitments at the School of Oriental Studies. But soon Younghusband assembled a willing supporting cast, including Sir Evelyn Wrench, founder of the Overseas League and the English Speaking Union; Sir Atul Catterji, who had been first high commissioner for India in London; Sir Shadi Lal, who served on the Judicial Committee of the Privy Council; Caroline Rhys Davids, an expert on Buddhism who had been active in the 1924 conference; Israel Mattuck, rabbi of the liberal Jewish synagogue in London; and Sir Regional Johnstone, once private tutor to the last Chinese emperor. The maharajah Gaekwar of Baroda, who came to bear the moniker "International President of the World Fellowship of Faiths," provided substantial funding and general encouragement.[130] And this list is only partial. In all, some fifty willing participants signed on to help realize what was clearly Younghusband's project.

Many difficulties lay ahead for Younghusband but, as an adventurer at heart, he seemed to relish the challenge: "Make the creation of a world fellowship a great adventure, a most difficult and heroic task requiring all the manliness, courage, skill, equanimity of any great military or exploring adventure," he once jotted in his private notebook.[131] Meanwhile, Younghusband had received additional inspiration from the well-known German theologian Rudolf Otto who, after traveling to India, had been inspired to propose the necessity of a global "inter-religious league" as a parallel organization to the League of Nations.[132]

The first planning meeting took place in London at 9 Arlington Street on 12 November 1934. "I explained to [those gathered]," Younghusband later reflected, "the main idea of holding a Congress, and reminded the meeting of what had been done in the London Congress in 1924 and the Chicago Congress of 1933." Further, Younghusband waxed eloquent about his spiritual ideals and the importance of such an initiative. The main goal of another conference was to establish from different religious perspectives what he called "world-consciousness" or a "world-soul." "But such a world-soul," he qualified, "would never be allowed to stifle the soul of the individual. Rather would we wish the soul of each different part in the one great whole preserved and developed." The "deepening and widening" of fellowship among members of different faith traditions would be another, related goal: "We would have human fellowship intensified to a degree not short of divine." In another venue, he expressed his aim as follows: "I have found that subtler and deeper meanings emerge as I study the idea [of fellowship] more closely. It is not exactly friendship, or companionship, or neighborliness, or co-operation, though these may develop from it. And the sentiment from which it springs is something more than compassion. . . . Even sympathy is associated rather with suffering than with enjoyment. At its intensest and highest fellowship seems to be a communion of spirit greater, deeper, higher, wider, more universal, more fundamental than any of these—than even love."[133] One could not accuse Younghusband of aiming too low.

In a meeting on 5 February 1935, Younghusband presented three

Sir Francis Younghusband, ca. 1937. (Image courtesy of the University of Southampton Library.)

related goals: (1) working toward a world fellowship of faiths, (2) welcoming differences among those in fellowship with one another, and (3) inspiring and uniting faiths to work together on "man's present problems." In the same meeting, he catalogued to those gathered hindrances to realizing these goals and aids toward their achievement. Under hindrances, he listed fear, mutual suspicion, nationalism, racial antagonism, poverty, and ignorance. Under aids, he included education, prayer, meditation, sharing spiritual experiences, the arts, and a common pursuit of truth and beauty.[134]

Additional meetings witnessed the sharpening of a vision for a conference, slated for 1936, and the formation of an ongoing society—what came to be the World Congress of Faiths, but initially was called the British National Council of the World Fellowship of Religion.[135] At first, Younghusband intended to operate under the auspices of the American World Fellowship established by Weller and Das Gupta. But gradually the World Congress became its own thing and eventually the successor of the World Fellowship, which soon petered out in the 1930s.[136] Not surprisingly, Younghusband was nominated and agreed to serve as chairman of the congress; the Gaekwar of Baroda served as its president. Eventually, in addition to a general council, an executive committee was formed, serving as the real seat of decision making—even if in the final analysis Younghusband usually got his way.

By the end of 1934 Younghusband had secured an office in Bedford Square in London, an assistant (Beatrix Holmes), and an "organizing secretary," Arthur Jackman, who had close ties to Britain's Theosophical Society. Mable Sharples, who served in the 1924 conference, also provided administrative assistance. Meanwhile, Younghusband continued efforts to recruit support from notable Britons, including H. G. Wells, Rudyard Kipling, G. K. Chesterton, Charles Williams, Gilbert Murray, Herbert Samuel, Aldous Huxley, J. S. Haldane, and George Bernard Shaw. Some smiled upon his endeavor; but many did not. Younghusband complained that he had to deal with many "blows" in realizing the congress.[137]

Shaw was among the naysayers. His response to Younghusband was characteristically forthright and expressed the skepticism that quite a few felt about the endeavor. Shaw doubted that men of "burning faith" could cooperate because they were usually "extraordinarily quarrelsome." "Get them around a table to agree on a basic manifesto or spend half a crown of public money, and most of them will make frantic scenes and dash out of the room after hurling their resignations at you."[138] Shaw's remark was not incorrect, as several internecine squabbles did hobble the congress's early efforts. But none proved insurmountable.

Soon concrete steps were taken to realize a major meeting in London in 1936. In many respects, Younghusband and other planners followed scripts that had been laid down in 1893, 1924, and 1933. But in other areas, the planning process charted a distinctive course. In addition to the general goal of promoting fellowship, it was decided that another theme—the "Supreme Ideal"—should be the topic of several public lectures; each invited speaker, drawing from his or her respective religious traditions, would be asked to define what for that individual was "the highest perfection of goodness" or "the universal, unsurpassable ideal"—a topic that proved baffling for some speakers.[139] Besides the public lectures, twenty smaller sessions made up of invitees only were to take place. In these, breaking sharply with precedent, discussion would be introduced, allowing representatives of different faiths to talk freely with one another. Younghusband recognized this as an innovation and one for which he needed to make a persuasive case. He did so in language that subsequently has been echoed at many interreligious endeavors. Permit, therefore, a lengthy quote from Younghusband's *Venture of Faith*, his memoir about the congress's founding:

> Discussion would be a new feature at such a Congress of men of different faiths. And I said that, having regard to the explosive nature of religion, and to the heat engendered when men of different faiths met in discussion. But I argued that in this case it would not be on the merits or defects of the different faiths: only on how the principles and inspiration of these faiths could be brought to bear upon the solution of a definite present-day problem. Those who took part in it might be persuaded, for the sake of the great end of fellowship, so to school themselves as to preserve their equanimity even under provocation. Such meetings should be a magnificent school in the great art of fellowship. And if participants in the discussion could thus discipline themselves, much good might accrue. For opposition was bracing: it arrested degeneration, and it stimulated effort to reach a higher ground upon which opposer and opposed might agree. Con-

> ducted under such conditions, discussion would be vitalizing, adding zest and interest to the whole proceedings, and keeping in touch with the everyday life of the world.[140]

Planning and preparations for the congress continued in 1935 and into the early months of 1936. Invitations went out to prospective speakers. During this time, the leaders and heads of several churches, however, expressed displeasure at the congress. The archbishop of Canterbury, Cosmo Gordon Lang, refused to take part, to Younghusband's great consternation—although the canon of St. Paul's in London, William Inge, signed on. One conservative Anglican journal described the congress as "perverse."[141] The Catholic Church was generally wary of the whole affair. An article from the Catholic *Tablet* found the coming congress "ominous," shot through with the "marshes and mists of subjectivism," and warned the faithful that they would "do well to treat this movement with nothing warmer than a benevolent neutrality."[142] Again, we see the irony of internecine Christian divisions over the permissibility of interreligious activity.

The attitude of Britain's royal house to the project was curious. Two letters from Buckingham Palace to Lambeth Palace (the London residence of the archbishop) exist, asking the archbishop how King Edward VIII should reply to Younghusband's apparent request that the king preside at the opening of the congress. The archbishop replied that he personally had declined because his participation "might be taken to imply that I thought Christianity was only one of many religions in spite of being . . . based on Divine Revelation." "I am disposed to think," he continued, that "His Royal Highness might well decline the invitation" too. In the end, while Younghusband did not gain the king's presence, he did secure an agreement that a royal greeting would be sent to participants via telegram on the first day of the congress and that allowance would be made for an official reception at Lancaster House in London's West End.[143]

For the congress itself, the Great Hall and the Queen's Hall at University College, London, were secured. At one point, a desire was expressed to hold a few sessions at Oxford University, but suitable venues had already been booked, so all events took place in London.[144]

In the months, weeks, and days preceding the congress, a considerable public relations agenda was set in motion. Mailings went out and leaflets were distributed. On 26 May, a luncheon was held for the London press, at which Younghusband described the congress's goal as nothing less than "laying the foundation for a new world order."[145] On 26 June, the BBC permitted Younghusband to speak about the conference on the radio just prior to the event's opening.[146] Posters were put up in underground stations, small advertisements appeared in newspapers, and, just before the event, men wearing sandwich boards were employed to walk the streets of London advertising the event.[147] Finally, several magazines and journals agreed to run lengthy pieces on the congress. The esteemed scientific journal *Nature*, for instance, ran an article, appearing just as the congress opened, entitled "Religion—A Changing Force?" The author wondered if those involved in the congress "are feeling their way towards a further and higher stage in the development of religious belief, in which the theological differences which antagonize will be forgotten in the pursuit of a common and universal ethical purpose."[148]

The actual congress lasted from 3 July to 18 July 1936. Six public lectures were held as well as twenty addresses (followed by discussion) given in more intimate settings. Several receptions took place in the evenings, including the one at Lancaster House, hosted by Lord Zetland, secretary of state for India, in addition to two others, one hosted by the Royal Geographical Society and the other by Lady Nunburnholm, president of the National Council of Women.[149] On the congress's first day, King Edward VIII's greeting was read aloud by the Gaekwar of Baroda. "I am much gratified," the king said, "to receive the message which Your Highness has sent me on behalf of those attending the World Congress of Faiths. Please express to them my sincere thanks. I earnestly hope that the deliberations of the Congress may help to strengthen the spirit of peace and goodwill on which the well-being of mankind depends."[150]

The congress's distinguished speakers included Yusuf Ali, a noted Muslim scholar and translator of the Qur'an from Lahore; the expatriate Russian Orthodox scholar Nicholas Berdyaev; Surendranath Das Gupta, author of several tomes on Indian philosophy; Sarvepalli Radhakrishnan, vice chancellor of Andhra University in India, holder of the Spalding Chair in Eastern Religion and Ethics at Oxford, and later president of India from 1962 to 1967; and Diasetz Teitaro Suzuki and G. P. Malalasekara, both notable Buddhist scholars, respectively from Japan and Ceylon (Sri Lanka).[151] The great French Catholic scholar of Islam, Louis Massignon, was not present personally, but he sent lecture notes that were read aloud. (He merits mentioning because he played an important role in the Catholic Church's turn to interreligious dialogue at the Second Vatican Council.) Shoghi Effendi, the worldwide leader of the Baha'i movement, and Sheikh Al Maraghi, rector of the Al-Azhar University in Cairo, also sent written speeches that were read aloud.[152]

While varied in form and emphasis, the addresses shared a common concern to promote human fellowship on the basis of spiritual resources drawn from the world's major religious traditions. Breaking with the example of Chicago's 1893 parliament, irreligious voices were also acknowledged, specifically in a paper entitled "The Humanist Point of View," given by the French writer Jean Schlumberger.[153] Other specific topics touched upon during the congress are too numerous to itemize, but a partial, illustrative list would include modern means of communication and transportation, the causes of ignorance, modern science and its limits, religious fanaticism and intolerance, East-West relations, atheism, love and charity, the nature of religion, prayer, nationalism, mystical experience, and pacifism. Threading the talks and discussions was the heartfelt conviction that those involved served as a high-minded avant-garde preparing humanity for a higher spiritual development. As Radharkhrisnan put it: "Those who believe in humanity and the power of the spirit to realise ideals must prepare the minds of men for the new world order."[154] Or, as Younghusband later wrote (connecting his geographical and spiritual interests): "In the world of spirit the more enterprising must build their Himalaya and attract the lesser upward to the heights."[155]

During their days together, speakers and discussants frequently took stock of the grave world situation in which they found themselves in the 1930s. Topics broached about the situation included the bitter legacy of the Great War; the emergence and shortcomings of the League of Nations; the rise of Stalin, Hitler, and Mussolini; and anti-imperial movements throughout the world.[156] Numerous speakers made reference to the League of Nations, and several saw their own meeting as supplying what the league lacked: a religious or spiritual dimension, an idealist basis for peace that aimed higher than simply the absence of conflict based on compromise and negotiation. As the prominent pacifist Lord Allen of Hurtwood put it: "This Congress meets at a most important moment in the history of the world. In Geneva [where the league met], there is assembled a Congress of Doubt. Here in London there is assembled a Congress of Faith."[157] Or, as Yusuf Ali noted on the congress's third day: "Many of us, who, after the Great War, hailed the foundation of the League of Nations as heralding a new era of peace and goodwill among men, have had shocks, disappointments, and disillusions." Ali then catalogued the problems and "human weaknesses" that assailed the league before concluding that these "can never be eradicated by political institutions, however wise and efficient they may be. Ultimately the whole brunt of the fight against these moral evils must be borne by Religion."[158] Expressing his views shortly after the passage of the Nuremberg Laws in Germany, a Jewish contributor, Rabbi Judah Leon Magnes of the newly founded Hebrew University in Jerusalem, noted with disturbing prescience: "Did not the Great War implant these evils [of national conflict] deep within us, and are we not already breeding inevitably the Greater War, Gog and Magog[?]" Finally, the Protestant theologian Adolf Keller of Switzerland worried, too, about ominous trends of the present before arguing that the world needed a deliberative body made up of idealists from different faith traditions to promote "the furtherance of peace and goodwill among men of different races, peoples, and religions." "In this common will to further peace and promote international relations," he added, "we extend our hands to each other."[159] Although nothing as internationally visible as the League of Nations came into existence as a result of the congress, it is important to note that many present beyond Keller saw the congress's mission as similar to that of the league. And today, regarding global peace as a major purpose of interfaith dialogue is practically axiomatic.

In addition to active discussion among participants, the congress introduced several other novelties to interreligious dialogue. For starters, the congress actually used the word *inter-religious* (usually hyphenated) more frequently than had been the case in the past, although it first appeared in English in the 1890s. Second, every morning before participants met, a "Devotional Meeting . . . at which all could be present" took place—"conducted respectively by a Christian, a Hindu, a Buddhist, a Jew, a Muslim, [and] a Confucian." This development makes the congress among the first organizations to promote what today is called interfaith worship—then and now often a subject of controversy.[160] Related, all participants visited Anglican services together: twice, in fact—once at an evensong at St. Paul's Cathedral in London and once traveling together to a Sunday service at Canterbury Cathedral.[161] At the former, upon entrance, the motley group had to endure protestors—some of whom likened Younghusband to Satan because they felt that a desecration of a Christian holy site was taking place. Finally, the World Congress of Faith operated much more in a pluralist mode than one of Christian inclusivism, the dominant tenor at the Chicago gathering in 1893. Accordingly, one finds in the congress's proceedings a sharp rebuke to Christian missionary zeal—as, for instance, in the paper by J. S. Haldane: "Many Christians entertain the ideal of converting non-Christian peoples to Christianity. I think that a much higher ideal is to understand and enter into sympathy with the religions which exist . . . and to use this understanding and sympathy as a basis for a higher religion."[162] To be sure, this was not an altogether new train of thought—one sees it in a minor key in 1893—but it became more insistent in 1936 and has since informed the assumptions behind many interfaith meetings.

While not as novel as the 1924 Conference on Some Living Religions within the Empire, the 1936 congress also captured Londoners' attention and received considerable press coverage in Britain and abroad. After several days of meetings, the *Inquirer* described the aim of the gathering as "the creation of a spirit of fellowship between East and West and the union of the inspiration of all Faiths upon the solution of man's present problems."[163] Near the end of the congress, on 17 July, the *Guardian* commented that visitors to the public events were "impressed with its [the congress's] sincerity and significance" as it had made seemingly exotic religious outlooks "more real to them."[164] On the same day, the *Evening Standard* summed up the congress's aim as seeking among different faiths "underlying unities" that could "contribute toward a solution of world problems—the problem of war and of social and economic difficulties."[165] "It is hoped," Montreal's *Gazette* opined shortly after the congress concluded, "that these meetings of representatives of the different faiths from many countries will make a deep impress on world opinion, stir into a more fervent activity that sense of community which usually lies dormant in mankind and so tauten the bond which binds them together."[166]

How, finally, ought one assess the legacy of the 1936 World Congress of Faiths, which itself is the legacy of prior conferences in 1893, 1924, and 1933? Some aspects of the legacy have been alluded to already, but now permit five final points that will also touch upon interpretation.

First, unlike prior meetings, the congress eventuated in an enduring society for the promotion of interreligious dialogue—one still in existence today, even if it never lived up to Younghusband's grandiose ambitions. Although functionally begun prior to and for the congress (and at first as a British extension of the American World Fellowship of Faiths), the World Congress of Faiths became officially established in its own right after the congress.[167] Younghusband sent a letter to Weller and Das Gupta of the Fellowship of Faith recognizing the congress's "debt to them" but explaining that the congress now needed to be "perfectly free to pursue . . . its subsequent work in our own way and in accordance with British practice."[168] The congress existed, its statement of purpose from 1936 explained, as the organizational seat of

> an inter-religious movement concerned with the awakening and strengthening of spiritual values and [it] provides a meeting place where all men and women of faith may, in fellowship, learn to understand one another's religion, where the seeker of Truth may find guidance and where all may strive to realise the fundamental principles common to all great spiritual teaching, transcending outward forms.
>
> The World Congress of Faiths aims to break down the barriers of exclusivism and to build bridges between the faiths. It in no way attempts to exalt one faith at the expense of another. . . . Its members are asked to be true to their own faiths and at the same time to work for tolerance, understand-

> ing and the wider conception. They dedicate themselves to the great task of awakening everywhere and revitalising all that is highest in man's spiritual nature.[169]

Presumably inspired by such an ambitious mandate, Younghusband and others were soon planning successor conferences, which were held in Oxford (1937), Cambridge (1939), and Paris (1939).[170] Planning for another in 1940 in The Hague had begun when war once again consumed Europe.

Second, the congress's founding and governing ethos is inseparable from the spiritual experience and determination of Francis Younghusband. Historians frequently debate whether individuals or impersonal forces drive human affairs. The congress strongly suggests, at least in this instance, the former. Pulling off such a gathering, as his biographer later put it, called for "the leadership of an idealist who has himself lived largely, strenuously and dangerously in the realm of both thought and of action." And again: Younghusband was "a man inspired by an indomitable passion to scale heights, whether of the Himalayas or of spiritual experience."[171] One might correct for some hyperbole in such statements, but not before recognizing what occasioned it in the first place. In 1938, the BBC again gave Younghusband a national platform to broadcast his message of fellowship through religion to all of Britain.[172]

Third, despite their accomplishments, Younghusband and his peers invite our criticism. In both 1924 and 1936, Younghusband made the appeal that all religions teach and learn from one another, and thereby draw closer into a greater, higher harmony. This idealistic, pluralist vision of interreligious dialogue was the animating impulse behind the congress (and that of other institutions) since its inception. On the surface, this seems harmless enough: who could possibly object to the peaceful coexistence of religions seeking a higher harmony? At the same time, given the historical context of the concept's articulation, one should not lose sight of the underlying imperialist habits of thought and possible motivations at hand. Younghusband remained a firm booster of the empire until his death. An empire replete with peaceful religions—together in search of some vague, higher harmonic essence—is one where imperial control and subordination can be more readily administered. Such a vision—a kind of soft Hobbesianism of pan-religious solidarity—might at some level be necessary to motivate and orchestrate interreligious dialogue in the first place. At the same time, one cannot help but wonder if it also encouraged some religious voices to soft-pedal their convictions and alterity from one another in an effort dutifully to follow the script of their imperial directors. British imperial realities in the 1920s and 1930s, at the very least, help explain at once both the successes of the 1924 and 1936 gatherings as well as their limitations.

Fourth, since the congress never took off, as some had hoped, to serve as a spiritual counterpart to the League of Nations, the 1936 meeting calls attention to an abiding problem of interfaith dialogue planned and orchestrated by elite religious figures: do they exert any actual influence among the rank and file of various faiths, or are they instead simply the idle "vapourings of amiable idealists," as the politician Sir Herbert Samuel dismissively said of the 1936 gathering?[173] Moreover, one reporter wondered critically in 1936, as others have since, "whether any practical outcome is to be anticipated from this attempt to secure cooperation among the more liberal spirits of the various religious beliefs to the solution of world problems."[174] The jury is still out, I would hazard, on this question.[175]

Finally, as was the case with Chicago in 1893, both the 1924 conference and the 1936 congress call attention to the ironic reality that efforts to achieve interreligious unity often result in internecine divisions among Christians over the aims and even legitimacy of interfaith dialogue. As we have seen, the archbishop of Canterbury in 1936, like his predecessor in 1893, refused to participate and voiced concerns. He was joined in his opposition by many others, especially among Nonconformist Protestants and Roman Catholics, who regarded the congress, despite its planners' protests to the contrary, as fostering religious relativism and syncretism. Rome especially kept its distance from what had taken place in London. Since Pope Leo XIII's rebuke of the American hierarchy's participation in Chicago's parliament, the official line of the Catholic Church toward interreligious meetings remained one of skepticism.[176]

But this was to change, and quite radically, in the second half of the twentieth century, even if the basis of the Catholic Church's pursuit of interreligious dialogue would differ considerably from that offered by Younghusband and the World Congress of Faiths.

CHAPTER FOUR

Rome

The difficulties met by the text on the Jews [what became *Nostra aetate*] . . . obliged the Church, in a positive way, to open herself to extremely new horizons.

—RENÉ LAURENTIN

The words from the Declaration *Nostra aetate* represent a turning point.

—JOHN PAUL II

ON 1 SEPTEMBER 1939, Germany invaded Poland, igniting the Second World War. The work of the World Congress of Faiths was significantly curtailed during the war years; its driving force, Francis Younghusband, passed away in 1942.[1]

The war and its aftermath had profound and enduring implications for interreligious dialogue. Roughly 6 million Jews perished in the Holocaust, the United Nations was founded (1945), and the state of Israel came into existence (1948)—at the tragic expense of displacing hundreds of thousands of Palestinian Muslims and Christians. The World Council of Churches was founded in 1948 to help rebuild society and promote Christian ecumenism, later turning to interreligious dialogue.[2] Furthermore, the war accelerated processes of decolonization, beginning with India's independence in 1947 and soon spreading to other countries in South Asia and Africa. In an age of mass media, the image of the nonviolent, religiously eclectic Gandhi had already soared into global consciousness, as did, slightly later, that of the young pastor Martin Luther King.[3] The plight of Tibet's Dalai Lama in the 1950s brought unprecedented global attention to Buddhism.

Often suppressed under colonialism, many indigenous ethnic and religious identities asserted themselves with new, politicized vigor—and sometimes with violence, as seen in the bloody partition of India. By the 1960s, the world stood on the cusp of the postcolonial age; Western countries entered into a new, uncertain relationship with regions and countries, the populations of which professed a variety of faith traditions.[4] Pan-Arab nationalism as promoted by Egypt's Gamal Abdel Nasser also bore witness to the changing global landscape. What is more, emigration from the "Rest" to the "West" began to rise significantly at this time, scrambling long-standing demographic realities and bringing hitherto religious strangers face-to-face in cities such as Paris, London, Amsterdam, and elsewhere.[5] And in all of this I have failed to mention the global spread of Marxist ideology and the specter of civilizational annihilation wrought by the Cold War.

Postwar intellectual and theological influences were diverse, to be sure. But in light of the trends and events of mid-century—and the pleas for mutual coexistence that they elicited—it should not surprise that the work of the Jewish theologian Martin Buber (1878–1965) gained a wide readership: particularly his essays *I and Thou* (1923) and *Dialogue* (1932), both translated into multiple languages in the 1950s and 1960s.[6] "A time of genuine religious conversation is beginning," he had presciently written in the latter, "not those so-called fictitious conversations where none regard and address his partner in reality, but genuine dialogues . . . from one openhearted person to another."[7] Other influential strands of European thought, often reckoning with colonialism, became preoccupied with "the Other."[8]

Postwar realities affected Roman Catholicism. Pope throughout the war, Pius XII passed away in 1958. After lengthy deliberations, the College of Cardinals settled on Angelo Giuseppe Roncalli, age seventy-six, to replace him as John XXIII (r. 1958–63). No one expected a remarkable pontificate from this rotund son of peasants. That changed dramatically on 25 January 1959, when he announced on the final day of the "Octave of Prayer for Christian Unity" at St. Paul's Basilica Outside the Walls in Rome his intention to summon a general church council. Claiming direct inspiration from the Holy Spirit, he defined the council's task as renewing the spiritual life of the church; bringing up to date (*aggiornamento*) its teaching, discipline, and organization; and fostering unity among Christians and goodwill toward all people. The announcement stunned the world. A council had not met since 1869–70, when the controversial doctrine of papal infallibility was defined. Most past councils, moreover, had met to condemn heresy, but this one was intended, more broadly, to engage the modern age and be "pastoral" in character.[9]

Although at first it did not register as a major concern among the bishops who gathered in Rome, the question of the church's relationship with the Jews soon became part of the council's agenda. The memory of the Holocaust weighed heavily on Europe; many connected it to past Christian anti-Semitism, and some had criticized Pius XII for not acting more proactively on behalf of Jews during the war.[10] But the declaration eventually approved by the council—*Nostra aetate*, "Our Age," or the "Declaration on the Relation of the Church to Non-Christian Religions"—included remarks not only about Jews but about other "non-Christians" as well. No one anticipated this at the start of the council, but it happened. "Few [conciliar] documents," John O'Malley has written, "bumped along on such a rough road as *Nostra aetate*."[11] For the first time in conciliar history, the church exhorted its members to enter into "dialogue and collaboration" with members of other religious traditions; "great world religions"—Judaism, Islam, Buddhism, and Hinduism—were mentioned explicitly in the text. Furthermore, other conciliar documents—*Sacrosanctum concilium* ("Constitution of the Sacred Liturgy"), *Lumen gentium* ("Dogmatic Constitution on the Church"), *Ad gentes* ("Decree on the Church's Missionary Activity"), and *Gaudum et spes* ("Pastoral Constitution on the Church in the Modern World")—and papal encyclicals appearing during the council expressed esteem for other faiths, even suggesting that their adherents might obtain salvation apart from explicit Christian commitment. The expression of such sentiments was unprecedented; they both amazed and disquieted the Catholic faithful, and paved the way after the council for Catholic interreligious engagements of various sorts, including the extraordinary World Day of Prayer for Peace that took place in Assisi in 1986 during the historic pontificate of John Paul II (r. 1978–2005).

How did these stunning changes come about? What assumptions, intentions, and figures of influence lay behind them? And how did they affect the church and the wider world in the postconciliar (and postcolonial) era?

Before the Council

Before the council, the stance of the Catholic Church toward other religious traditions had become Janus-faced. On one hand, the attitude of Roman officialdom stood implacably against interreligious dialogue—and ecumenism, for that matter. Nonetheless, a softening of the rigid teaching of *extra Ecclesiam nulla salus* (outside the church, no salvation) had been incubating for some time. This softening—coinciding with other events, experiences, and personalities—created by the early 1960s conditions of possibility for the unexpected direction taken at the council.

In the 1890s, Pope Leo XIII and the Roman Curia had not been pleased by the American Catholic hierarchy's participation in Chicago's 1893 World's Parliament of Religions.[12] Waiting until September 1895, the pope expressed his displeasure to the American hierarchy in a letter to Archbishop Francis Satolli, the first apostolic delegate to the United States. As we have already seen in chapter 2, the pope chided the American episcopate, recommending that they "have their meetings by themselves"—even if, he added, they might occasionally consider inviting non-Catholics as passive observers.[13] The rebuke was clear. Rome's attitude became more pointed still when several Catholic participants in the 1893 parliament were caught up in Leo XIII's 1899 encyclical against "Americanism."[14]

Leo XIII's successors followed in his footsteps for the most part, casting a skeptical eye at both interreligious engagement and Christian ecumenism. The two were in fact frequently seen as sides of the same worrisome coin and associated with liberal Protestantism. In *Mortalium animos* (1928), Pius XI condemned the modern ecumenical movement, noting that "the Apostolic See cannot on any terms take part in their [non-Catholic] assemblies, nor is it anyway lawful for Catholics either to support or to work for such enterprises."[15] In *Ecclesia catholica* (1949), Pius XII warned that ecumenism as promoted by Protestants came laced with "besetting particular dangers"—a sentiment he emphasized in *Humani generis* (1950), warning the faithful against an untenable irenicism promoted by non-Catholics. This "danger" was particularly wily, he held, because it came "concealed beneath the mask of virtue."[16]

Nonetheless, prior to the Second Vatican Council, the age-old teaching of *extra Ecclesiam nulla salus* had ceased to have an altogether intransigent character.[17] Already at the Council of Trent (1545–63), the notion of "implicit faith" was put forward as a possible means of attributing grace to those who had never heard the Christian Gospel. These formulations drew on Thomas Aquinas's distinction between those who lacked baptism in reality (*in re*) and those who lacked it in desire (*in voto*).[18] The Angelic Doctor held out considerable hope for the former. The Jesuit theologians Robert Bellarmine and Francisco Suarez developed this line of thinking—"baptism of desire," Aquinas had called it—in the Tridentine era, and still others followed their lead.[19]

Later, in the heyday of colonialism, the question of the eternal fate of "virtuous pagans"—those who had not heard the Christian message but devoutly followed their own faiths and lived morally upright lives—became an acute issue brought up by Catholic missionaries as they dispersed to faraway global destinations. Another Jesuit theologian, Giovanni Perone (1794–1876), was among the first to state that *extra Ecclesiam nulla salus* applied only to those who had heard and then rejected the church—*not* to those who had never heard the Gospel message in the first place. In *Quanto confiiciamur moerore* (1863), Pius IX called for Catholic missions but indicated that God in his inscrutable providence might have beneficent designs for those who, through "invincible ignorance," had never heard the message.[20] He also called on Catholics to befriend non-Catholics and work hard for their welfare, spiritually and physically. Another

Jesuit, Johann Baptist Franzlein (1816–86), went a step farther, arguing that there were in fact two means by which one could be saved: through explicitly "hearing the Christian message" (*fides ex auditu*) or, less conventionally but still a possibility, through "interior illumination" (*interna illuminata*), a grace that God in his limitless power could theoretically bestow on anyone.[21]

In the twentieth century, Pius XII's *Mystici corporis Christi* (1943) acknowledged the problem posed by non-Catholics who had never heard the church's message and urged the faithful "to reach out with burning charity to those who have not yet received the light from the truth of the Gospel." Whether they knew it or not, they, too, "by a certain unconscious desire and wish . . . may be related to the Mystical Body of the Redeemer."[22] Additionally, Pius XII sent a noteworthy rebuke to the archdiocese of Boston after an American Jesuit priest, Leonard Feeney, insisted that only through actual, visible membership in the Catholic Church could one be saved. In the letter, the pope invoked the Council of Trent's notion of "implicit desire": "It is not always necessary that this desire be explicit, as it is with catechumens. When one is invincibly ignorant, God accepts an implicit desire, so called because it is contained in the good disposition of soul by which a person wants his or her will to be conformed to God's will."[23] Furthermore, the letter implied, only God knows the actual disposition of any human soul; Catholics should accept this with due humility.

In the decade before the council, two influential theologians had taken up the question of the salvation of non-Christians: Karl Rahner (1904–84) and Jean Daniélou (1905–74). Destined to have considerable impact on the council, Rahner called attention to the globalizing world: now "everybody is the next-door neighbor and spiritual neighbor of everyone else in the world." Christians and non-Christians live "in one and the same situation and face each other in dialogue."[24] Even so, the "Gospel age," he argued, did not necessarily begin at the same time for all people. The present age, which brought with it the obligation to convert, came much later for non-Western peoples—and for some, arguably, it had not yet come.[25] Meanwhile, upright non-Christians, he argued, should be regarded not as unsaved pagans but as "anonymous Christians"—a phrase that received copious attention in the postconciliar period.[26] For his part,

Daniélou recognized the theological problem posed by the "holy pagans" of the Old Testament, such as Melchizedek and Job, who seemed to stand in a right relationship with God apart from the Abrahamic Covenant and the Christian Gospel.[27] Daniélou also argued that all people stood under God's "cosmic covenant," even if they did not (yet) stand under the "historic covenant," mediated through Christ. Rahner's and Daniélou's musings were echoed by other, minor theologians. And thus by the eve of the council, the question of the salvation of "others" and the church's relation to them were not negligible theological concerns, even if they were not front and center on the council's early agenda.[28]

But theological developments alone cannot explain the origins of *Nostra aetate.* The preconciliar experiences of Angelo Giuseppe Roncalli (Pope John XXIII) are also of critical importance. In 1925, the avuncular future pope was appointed titular archbishop of Areopolis and papal nuncio in Bulgaria. In 1925, he was transferred to the titular see of Mesembria and became nuncio for Turkey and Greece. Few Catholics lived in these places. Roncalli, therefore, had numerous interactions with Orthodox Christians, Muslims, and Jews. During the war years, he worked diligently in Greece to provide relief supplies for the largely Orthodox population. He also labored to arrange for false baptismal certificates and/or immigration cards for eastern European Jews, saving thousands from the death camps. These trying experiences highlighted for him the delicate question of the church's relations with non-Catholics, and particularly with Jews.[29] "When the war was over," as Thomas L. McDonald has written, "Bishop Roncalli was a changed man with a new understanding of the sufferings of the Jewish people."[30]

Near the end of the war, Roncalli was appointed papal nuncio to Paris; this was among the Vatican's top diplomatic posts. There he had to deal with a church whose various leaders, including bishops, had colluded with the German occupation forces and the Vichy regime. In this role, he was forced to make some tough decisions, reprimanding key prelates on the one hand, but working to prevent a witch hunt against the entire French clergy on the other. In this difficult position, he could not help but confront the church's own anti-Jewish prejudices.[31]

Coincidentally, before and after the war, France found itself in the vanguard of innovative thinking on Christian-Jewish relations that would later have an impact on the council.[32] I emphasize these relations here because, as we shall see, it was rethinking relations with the Jews that led to a more generous engagement with other faith traditions. In France, the influential anticlerical-turned-Catholic novelist Léon Bloy, for example, had publicly denounced Christian anti-Semitism after the Dreyfus affair (1894), highlighting the problem of right-wing attitudes toward the Jews.[33] Bloy was friend and mentor to Jacques and Raïssa Maritain (a Jewish convert to Catholicism), who cultivated a high-brow philo-Semitic circle in Paris in the interwar years. Later, as the reality of the Holocaust became clear, the couple (who had fled to the United States for safety) and their friends and allies condemned anti-Semitism and anti-Judaism, within and outside the church, in the strongest possible terms. As French ambassador to the Vatican after the war, Jacques Maritain brought his philo-Semitic message to Rome with some success—although Pius XII's caginess often frustrated him.[34] French philo-Semitism had another major champion in Henri de Lubac, author of *Israel et la foi chrétienne* (1942). A key voice of "la nouvelle theologie," Lubac served in the French resistance against Nazism and repeatedly condemned the "Aryan" project of purging Christianity of its Judaic roots—what he saw as the revival of the Marcionite heresy.[35] During the war, Lubac was part of an underground community in Lyons that focused on improving Jewish-Christian relations.[36] Admired by John XXIII for his words and deeds, Lubac became a significant theological consultor during the council.

However influential, the philo-Semitic legacies of Catholics such as Bloy, the Maritains, and Lubac must cede priority of significance to another (non-Catholic) Frenchman: the assimilated Jewish scholar Jules Isaac (1877–1963).[37] Having lost his wife, daughter, and son-in-law at Auschwitz, Isaac felt compelled after the war to try to understand the roots of anti-Jewish sentiment and work against it. In 1947 he founded the organization *Les amitiés Judeo-Chrétiennes* and helped draft the so-called Ten Points of Seelisberg, a notable interfaith statement (originating from a Jewish-Christian conference in Seelisberg, Switzerland) that reminded the world of Christianity's Jewish origins and sought to end anti-Judaic biblical exegesis and habits of thought.[38] In 1948, Isaac published a six-hundred-page tome, *Jesus and Israel*.[39] The results of his research for this project surprised him. Expecting to find clear roots of anti-Semitism in the Christian New Testament, he concluded that they simply were not there; Christian Scriptures could even be read as an antidote to Christian defamation of Judaism, which came into its own only later, Isaac held, in the patristic and medieval periods. Anti-Semitism, in other words, was an illicit tradition that a more authentic Christianity ought to excise. In particular, Isaac countered the charge that the Jews' dispersion after 70 CE was punishment for rejecting Jesus; that Judaism was a legalistic, dead religion; and that the charge of "deicide" could be applied collectively to all Jews. Setting New Testament principles against these accretions of tradition, as he regarded them, Isaac argued that Christianity had the resources and power "to break at last with evil habits of mind and tongue, contracted over a period of nearly two thousand years as a result of what I have called the teaching of contempt [*mépris*]—itself the child of bitter polemics now obsolete."[40] Throughout the 1950s, Isaac disseminated this message at home and abroad, penning an abridged version of his inquiries under the title *The Teaching of Contempt: Christian Roots of Anti-Semitism*.[41]

Meanwhile, shortly after the council had been called, Roncalli, now John XXIII, began to take concrete measures of his own to improve the church's relations with the Jews. In 1959, he summarily removed the word *perfidious* (*perfidis*) as a description of Jews from the Good Friday Mass.[42] In 1960, he met with thirteen hundred American Jews associated with the philanthropic organization United Jewish Appeal. To their delight, he greeted them humbly with words from Scripture: "I am your brother Joseph." On another occasion, he stopped his car when he saw Jews exiting the synagogue in Rome and publicly blessed them—a first in Catholic-Jewish relations. The Jews surrounded him and applauded enthusiastically.[43]

On 5 June 1960, John created the Secretariat for Christian Unity—a clear sign of the irenic and pastoral direction that he sought from the council. At first, it was given a rather vague mandate of helping non-Catholic Christians understand and follow the council.[44] But the significance and influence of this secretariat grew quickly, becoming a counterpoint to the voices of more traditionalist prelates averse to ecumenical outreach. Shortly after the council opened, the secretariat was elevated to function as a commission of the council on par with ten others that had been established—all presided over by the Central Preparatory Commission (later renamed the Coordinating Commission).[45] The pope had appointed Cardinal Augustin Bea, SJ, as the secretariat's president and Monsignor Johannes Willebrands as its secretary. Respectively from Germany and the Netherlands, both men were known for their ecumenical sensitivities and biblical scholarship.[46] John XXIII also appointed two other staff members, the American Paulist Father Thomas Stransky and the Corsican Jean-François Arrighi, along with fifteen bishops and twenty consultors, including Johannes Oesterreicher, an Austrian Jew converted to Christianity who had made a career in the United States.[47] In 1953 at Seton Hall University in New Jersey, Oesterreicher had established the Institute for Judeo-Christian Studies, among the first institutions of its kind.[48] The secretariat played an extraordinary role at the council, particularly with respect to the "Decree on Ecumenism" (*Unitatis redintegratio*), the "Declaration on Religious Freedom" (*Dignitatis humanae*) and, not least, *Nostra aetate*.[49] It did so often in tension with other commissions and with traditionalist stalwarts in the Curia.

On 13 June 1960, Jules Isaac gained an audience with the pope, arranged by the president of France with the support of the archbishop of Aix-en-Provence, where Isaac lived. Although the meeting lasted less than an hour, its impact on John XXIII appears to have been considerable.[50] In preparation, Isaac had written a memorandum for the pope in which he suggested that the "teaching of contempt" for the Jews was in essence un-Christian and should be purified by a more solidly biblical understanding of Judaism.[51] This argument, combined with Isaac's tragic personal story, moved the pope to action: he arranged for Isaac to be introduced to Bea. Several months after this meeting took place, on 18 September, Bea conferred with the pope and recommended that the Secretariat for Christian Unity be given the task of taking up the "Jewish Question" (*questione ebraica*) during preparations for the council alongside its prior task of fostering unity with other Christians.[52] This development is particularly striking because when the pope had previously polled bishops about what topics the council should address, hardly a single suggestion came forth to reconsider Catholic-Jewish relations.[53]

The pope granted Bea's request, directing him to handle the matter with discretion (*sub secreto*). In 1961, the trial of Adolf Eichmann in Jerusalem and the publication of Raul Hilberg's consciousness-raising *The Destruction of the European Jews* seemed to confirm the appropriateness of John's decision.[54] And thus the chain of events that led to *Nostra aetate* was set in motion. Neither the pope nor Isaac lived to see the completion of the council, and Bea was already in his eighties when its first session met in 1962.

A revolution of young Turks this was not.

Vatican II and Other Faiths

Nostra aetate had a turbulent history before it was finally promulgated on 28 October 1965 at the fourth and final session of the council. For the first time in the modern history of Roman Catholicism, other religions were positively engaged and dialogue with them was encouraged. Yet the document should not be read apart from other conciliar documents that also mention non-Christian faith traditions or have implications for understanding them. Of particular importance, again, are *Sacrosanctum concilium*, *Lumen gentium*, *Ad gentes*, and *Gaudium et spes*. These documents, along with John XXIII's encyclical *Pacem in terris* (11 April 1963) and Paul VI's first encyclical *Ecclesiam suam* (6 August 1964), provide crucial context for appraising the significance of *Nostra aetate*. We shall first explore the latter's complicated journey at the council, then its actual contents, before spotlighting relevant aspects of these other documents.

As the Secretariat for Christian Unity (SCU) began its work, Cardinal Bea appointed a subcommission to work on the Jewish question. It included the Benedictine abbot Leo Rudloff; the aforementioned convert from Judaism, John Oesterreicher; and another convert from Judaism, the theologian Gregory Baum.[55] Hardly had this commission begun its task when two difficulties occurred. First, once Arab governments got wind of a possible positive statement on the Jews, they fiercely protested, concerned that this would serve as a prelude to the Vatican officially recognizing the state of Israel.[56] Cardinal Bea responded to these protests, noting in a memorandum that the schema on the Jews dealt with religious matters only, not political ones, and thus "in no way will [it] acknowledge the State of

Israel by the Holy See."[57] Second, the council's Theological Commission, led by the arch-conservative cardinal Alfredo Ottaviani, voiced concerns that the secretariat was overstepping its boundaries and trespassing into its own territory.[58] But John XXIII countered that his original mandate to the secretariat remained in effect and that it should continue working on "the Jewish question."[59]

After several plenary meetings and multiple discussions, the first draft—*Decretum de Iudeais*—was worked out during an assembly held by the SCU in Ariccia near Rome from 27 November to 2 December 1961. At the time, Bea was in regular touch with several Jewish organizations, such as the American Jewish Committee, and theologians, notably Abraham Joshua Heschel.[60] In the draft, particular attention was paid to Paul's Letter to the Romans (chapters 9–11), in which the Apostle to the Gentiles discusses the "mystery" and the "salvation" of Israel in the divine scheme of things. The recent memory of the Holocaust of course also figured significantly in these discussions.[61] Permit a lengthy quotation from this pupal form of *Nostra aetate:*

> The Church, the Bride of Christ, acknowledges with a heart full of gratitude that, according to God's mysterious saving decree, the beginnings of faith and election are already found in the Israel of the patriarchs and prophets. . . .
>
> The Church in fact believes that Christ, who "is our peace," embraces Jews and Gentiles with one and the same love and that he made two one. . . . Even though the greater part of the Jewish people remains separated from Christ, it would nevertheless be an injustice to call this people accursed, for they are beloved. . . .
>
> As the Church, like a mother, condemns most severely injustices committed against innocent people everywhere, so she raises her voice in loud protest against everything done to the Jews, whether in the past or in our time. Whoever despises or persecutes this people does injury to the Catholic Church.[62]

The message was clear enough. The church was preparing an unprecedentedly generous statement on the Jews and a recognition of their historical plight. In the parlance of our own time, a far-reaching theological "reboot" was in the making.

But here things became more complicated. Intrigued by the Vatican's action, in June 1962, the World Jewish Congress dispatched Chaim Wardi, a senior official of Israel's Ministry of Religious Affairs, to Rome to take stock of what was going on. This triggered concerns not only from Arab states but also from Arab Christian communities, which believed that such a declaration concerning the Jews would unleash persecution against them. In short, because of the document, the church found itself unwittingly embroiled in the politics of the Middle East.[63] To calm matters, the council's Central Preparatory Commission removed the draft decree from the council's agenda.[64] But only briefly. After the end of the council's first session in December 1962, Cardinal Bea made his case directly to the pope again that there simply must be a statement on the Jews: after the death of 6 million Jews, Bea pled, the church "requires a purification of spirit and conscience." He argued that, sidestepping politics, the matter could be dealt with "strictly as a religious question" (*una questione puramente religiosa*).[65] Still, tensions among the bishops were high, and newspapers the world over had latched onto the political implications of the schema. In an effort to find a way forward, Bea indicated that the decree should not stand alone but be incorporated into the general schema on ecumenism. This became a reality in the second draft, "The Attitude of Catholics to Non-Christians, Especially the Jews," in which three introductory lines referencing other religions were diplomatically added.[66] A comparably controversial statement on religious freedom—what later became *Dignitatis humanae*—was also included in the schema. John XXIII remained supportive. "We have carefully read this report of Cardinal Bea," he wrote on 23 December 1962, "and we agree with him completely on the importance of this matter and on the responsibility which we have to give it due consideration."[67]

The secretariat approved the second draft in early March 1963, but it made it to the floor of the council only on 18 November, roughly two months after the second session of the council opened.[68] In the meantime, Rolf Hochhuth's play *Der Stellvertreter* ("The Deputy") had opened in Berlin; it was a rambling, accusatory dramatization of Pius XII's alleged "silence" during the Holocaust. The play created a sensation and was quickly translated into many languages.[69] Its message deeply troubled the Vatican and the new pope, Paul VI, who had been elected following the death of John XXIII on 3 June 1963. When the second draft of the declaration was discussed, some bishops wondered why the Jews were treated in a schema devoted to Christian unity, while many traditionalists questioned why Jews were being treated at all. Further, leaders of the Eastern churches, galvanized by Arab disgruntlement, linked arms in opposition. Cardinals Tappouni (Syrian), Maximos IV (Melkite), and Stephen I (Coptic Rite) demanded that it be withdrawn. They were joined by the Latin patriarch of Jerusalem, Alberto Gori, and the Armenian patriarch of Cilicia, Peter XVI, who maintained that the declaration should discuss other faith traditions, especially Islam, or none at all.[70] And in fact this was the direction in which the document was headed.[71] If this were not enough, crude anti-Semitic propaganda in the form of pamphlets and books began to be distributed on the periphery of the council, accusing the Jews of being a "deicide people," forever "accursed and harmful" to the Christian faithful. Such propaganda fueled sensational press reporting. Egypt's Gamal Abdel Nasser warned that a "world Zionist plot [was afoot] to capitalize on the Vatican Council to further the oppression of the Palestinian people."[72] All of this weighed heavily on the pope, Cardinal Bea, and many council fathers. The text was again temporarily withdrawn.[73]

Following the close of the second session, Paul VI did something that stunned the world: he embarked on a pilgrimage to the Holy Land in early January 1964, visiting both Jordan and Israel.[74] Although billed as an act of simple piety, it also had a favorable impact on the declaration and on the work of the secretariat in general. This was the first time since the early nineteenth century that a pope had left Italy. The highlight of the trip was the pope's meeting on 5 January with the ecumenical patriarch of Constantinople, Athenagoras I—a meeting that set up a future summit during which the two would formally "consign to oblivion" the excommunications of 1054. Many Jews were heartened by the trip—even if the pope emphatically neither recognized the Israeli state nor referred to it as "Israel." Some Arab commentary proved harsh, using the occasion to castigate the Jews as a uniquely immoral people and the Vatican as an abettor of Zionist crimes. The international press followed the pope's every step, parsed his every utterance. Untangling politics from piety proved practically impossible. Still, images of the pope abroad in Palestine signaled to the world that something momentous was afoot.[75] The question of the church's relations with Islam also rose in significance as a result of the trip.

But more challenges came before progress. In the spring of 1964, it was decided that the declaration on the Jews (generally tagged as *De Judaeis*) be relegated to an appendix of the schema on ecumenism, but then it was removed altogether, leaving its future in limbo.[76] The council's Coordinating Committee felt that the declaration and the statement on religious liberty should not be dealt with in a text on Christian unity. But its supporters clamored for action and the document managed to survive.[77] It had become clear, however, that its future depended on treating other faiths, especially Islam, to take into account Middle Eastern concerns. The pope appeared none too subtly to nudge the document in this direction in an Easter message given on 29 March 1964. "Every religion," he stated in an inclusivist theological idiom, "contains a ray of the light which we must neither discount nor extinguish, even when it is not sufficient to give people the clarity they need, or to realize the miracle of the Christian light in which truth and life are wedded. But every religion raises us toward the transcendent Being, the sole Ground of all existence and all thought, and all responsible action and all authentic hope."[78] What is more, bishops from South Asia had begun to argue that if Judaism and Islam were treated, why not Asian traditions such as Hinduism and Buddhism? Some African bishops in turn clamored for mention of animistic traditions from their continent. And thus a document originally intended as a theological statement on the Jews and a condemnation of anti-Semitism survived but underwent a metamorphosis to include many "major world religions."[79] Consequently, Bea began to reach out to scholars in Rome, such as Joseph Cuoq, PB, and Georges Anawati, OP, who knew something about Islam and Asian faiths, to serve as consultors.[80]

On 25 September 1964, in the third session of the council, Cardinal Bea introduced an updated draft under the title "Declaration on the Jews and Non-Christians" (*Declaratio de Judaeis et de non-Christianis*). In an unusual public show of support, those who stood by the indefatigable octogenarian cheered when he reached the podium. In anticipation, the German bishops, haunted by their country's tragic past, had published a statement supporting the schema.[81] American bishops also vocally approved. But the document had its critics.[82] Some objected to its pointed use of the term *deicide*, for example, suggesting that more moderate language be used; others wondered if the church had sufficient competence to say anything about the religious traditions of South Asia.

Jews had their own misgivings. Jewish organizations and leaders had been following the council closely since it began, making important contributions in articles and memoranda, and in behind-the-scenes conversations and correspondence with council participants.[83] When the updated version of the declaration was leaked to the press in early September, it ignited a new controversy. Since the text emphasized the eschatological hope for the reunion of Israel and the church, some Jews felt that the document would only encourage Christians' efforts to proselytize Jews. Theologian Abraham Joshua Heschel, working closely with the American Jewish Committee, garnered international attention when he protested that "faced with the choice of conversion or death in the gas chambers of Auschwitz, he would choose the latter."[84] Heschel, who had been in contact with Bea since 1961, met personally with the pope on 14 September 1964 (on the eve of Yom Kippur) and discussed his concerns, resulting in changes of language that muted the question of proselytization.[85] On 26 September, the archbishop of Westminster and member of the secretariat John Carmel Heenan gave a press conference in which he eschewed all "political" motivations and said that the rationale behind the document was purely religious because Jews have a "unique relationship with Christianity."[86] On 28 and 29 September, bishops at the Vatican gave speeches in favor or critical of the document; in all, thirty-five speeches were delivered and twenty-seven written memoranda were submitted.[87] Meanwhile, not only Jewish but Arab voices, too, lobbied the Vatican in an effort to shape the outcome.[88] In this heated atmosphere, progress toward a final outcome proved tricky and difficult. Rabbi Marc H. Tannenbaum, a student of Heschel's, memorably described these days as offering history's "greatest seminar in Catholic-Jewish relations."[89]

On 9 October, the secretary-general of the council, Archbishop

Rabbi Abraham Joshua Heschel and Cardinal Augustin Bea at a meeting in New York City at the headquarters of the American Jewish Committee, 31 March 1963. (Image courtesy of the American Jewish Committee Archives.)

Pericle Felici, had had enough and told Bea that it would be best to break apart the different components of the declaration and make personnel shifts, mixing various commissions, to handle the changes. The section on Jews would be reduced to a paragraph inserted at the end of the schema on the church (what became *Lumen gentium*); the sections on religious liberty and on other non-Christians would go elsewhere or be treated separately.[90] Cardinal Bea and his allies felt spurned by this intervention, which appeared to threaten all the work that the secretariat had accomplished. In an effort to safeguard their efforts, Bea appealed directly to the pope, who, along with other bishops—notably vocal was Cardinal Franz König, archbishop of Vienna and a scholar of world religions—sided with Bea, telling him that the declaration on the Jews would be "neither amputated nor diminished," but should become the heart of an independent declaration of the church's relationship to non-Christian religions.[91] As König put it to a group of theologians: "There seems to be only one way to save the text: if it is placed in a universal context, in which we treat not only the Church's relationship to the Jews but its relationship to all non-Christian religions."[92]

Paul VI agreed. With the pope's intervention, then, the course toward the final version was set. On 20 October, a working group of the secretariat began meeting, drafting some new material and reordering the old to shape a text with five parts: (1) on difficult questions about existence that confront all human beings, (2) on the responses of Hinduism and Buddhism to these questions, (3) on Islam, (4) on the Jews (the longest section), and, finally, (5) on the necessity of religious toleration and nondiscrimination.[93] Subsequent meetings, discussions, and solicitations of expert advice led to a document that began with the phrase "In our time": *Nostra aetate*.[94]

It was sent out to bishops in early November.[95] On 20 November, Bea presented it to the council, stressing the significance of what lay before them: "No Council in the history of the Church, unless I am mistaken, has ever set out so solemnly the principles concerning [relations to non-Christian religions]."[96] Voices inside and outside the council continued to jockey for influence. Internally, although most bishops supported the declaration, a tenacious minority continued to voice reservations. Externally, as John Oesterreicher noted, "it seems that the entire Middle East was drawn into the whirlpool of these hostilities, governments and people, Muslims and Christians, Orthodox and Catholic, laymen, priests and bishops."[97] Indeed, like no other issue at the council, the declaration became "the focus of intense media attention and public scrutiny."[98] In late November, for example, Radio Cairo, through the Constituent Council of the Islamic World, warned of trouble and bloodshed if the new schema was accepted.[99] "Many bishops from Arab countries," reported the *Guardian*, feared that "a statement filled with presumably comforting words for Jews would have political repercussions back home."[100]

But the document moved forward by means of a preliminary round of voting, in accordance with the council's regulations. Three votes were taken: first, on sections 1–3 (the introduction, on religious questions in general, and on Hinduism and Buddhism); then, on sections 4–5 (which dealt with the Jews and nondiscrimination); and finally, on the entire text. The first two votes were to be a straight-up "yes" or "no." The third vote could be "yes," "no," or "yes with reservations." Nearly 2,000 council fathers weighed in, with only 136 voting "no" on sections 1–3, and 185 on sections 4–5. On the whole declaration, out of a total of 1,996 votes cast, 1,651 were "yes," 99 were "no," and 243 were "yes with reservations." This revealed that, barring unexpected developments, *Nostra aetate* would likely survive a final passage and be promulgated at the council's final session the following year.[101] Paul VI had hoped that fewer than 400 would dissent, so he was pleased. A Vatican news release noted: "The importance and extreme value of this Declaration is in the fruit to be hoped for. For the first time in Conciliar history, principles dealing with non-Christians are set forth in solemn form."[102]

Bea was jubilant. Still, he worried about the political implications of the text, so he dashed off an article for the Vatican's newspaper, *L'osservatore romano*, to clarify what the document did not say. Stressing the strong majority support among the bishops, he argued that just as the sections on Hinduism, Buddhism, and Islam "have nothing to do with politics," so also "does the section on the Jews exclude political interpretation." It dealt strictly with religion, he underscored, and was "in complete accord with the Gospel . . . inspired by truth, justice, and Christian charity."[103]

Nevertheless, as 1964 became 1965, a final wave of opposition arose, accompanied by ongoing rumormongering and sensational reportage. Resistance came principally from two sources: (1) an outspoken group of reactionary bishops (led by France's Archbishop Marcel Lefebvre and Cardinal Ernesto Ruffini, bishop of Palermo) who collectively came to be known as the International Group of Fathers (Coetus internationalis patrum), many of whom would go into schism after the council, and (2) practically all of the bishops of the Middle East, who continued to insist, not without good reason, that religion and politics simply could not be so easily disentangled in their corner of the world.[104] It merits noting here that the Arabic word *din*, only problematically translated as "religion," does not carry the connotation that it can be readily isolated from other domains of human experience, and what in the final analysis might have been at issue were incommensurate understandings of what constituted a "religious" matter.

The pope and Bea were mainly concerned about the Middle Eastern bishops, who lived in proximity to Jews and Muslims and feared that their perduring dissent would tarnish the reception of the declaration. To minimize this possibility, Bea dispatched the secretariat's secretary, Cardinal Willebrands, and another member of his staff, Pierre Duprey, a member of the Missionaries of Africa (a so-called White Father), to the Middle East in an attempt to win over the bishops and their constituents. Their trip—to Syria, Lebanon, Egypt, and Israel—took place in March 1965. Some progress was made on the journey, but acute worries persisted.[105]

Meanwhile, members and consultors of the secretariat met to discuss matters and go over the wording of the document before it came to a final vote.[106] Numerous emendations (*modi*) had been suggested.[107] For his part, the pope had requested two changes: that the word *deicide* be dropped—even if the idea that it expressed remained, in different language—and that the verb *accursed* or *damns* (*damnat*), applied to those guilty of discrimination against Jews, be changed. Both of these changes were made, with *damnat* becoming *deplorat*, "deplores."[108] Thereafter, a final round of Middle East shuttle diplomacy was undertaken by the aged Bea himself. Following letters sent in advance by the pope to bishops of the Middle East, Bea traveled in July 1965 to Lebanon, Israel, and Egypt. While the bishops restated their past concerns, some relented and agreed to accept the text.[109]

The outcome was decided in October 1965 during the final session of the council. After eleventh-hour discussions and votes on parts of the declaration, a path opened up for a final vote on the whole. The document, Bea told the bishops, was of "the greatest importance for the church and for the world today."[110] When the votes were tallied, 2,221 bishops were in favor, with only 88 against it. Thus, "Declaration on the Relation of the Church to Non-Christian Religions," or *Nostra aetate*, was officially promulgated on 28 October 1965.[111] Remembering this day, Oesterreicher later reflected: "Whoever had witnessed all the crises and vicissitudes of the declaration . . . could only regard the triumph of that day as a miracle."[112]

SACROSANCTUM OECUMENICUM CONCILIUM
VATICANUM SECUNDUM

DECLARATIO
DE ECCLESIAE
HABITUDINE
AD RELIGIONES
NON-CHRISTIANAS

Nostra aetate *("Declaration on the Relation of the Church to Non-Christian Religions," 1965). (Author's collection.)*

Paul VI characterized the moment as an "astonishing phenomenon."[113] Newspapers the world over offered analyses similar to what the *Guardian* published on 29 October: "The long hard road this declaration has followed, since it was born as a suggestion made by Pope John to Cardinal Bea, has come to an end. . . . This marks the first time in Church history that the Vatican has gone out of its way to speak of its kinship with other non-Christian religions and to say that some truths can be found in those religions."[114] "This was the beginning of the Church seeing itself within a pluralist world," as the theological consultor Joseph Neuner later sized up the outcome.[115]

Just 1,140 words in its final form, *Nostra aetate* is the shortest of the council's sixteen documents. Comprised of five brief articles, it has fifteen footnotes, predominantly referring to passages in the New Testament, with particular emphasis on Paul's Letter to the Romans, the document's theological center of gravity. Additionally, one note refers to another conciliar document, *Lumen gentium;* four to passages in the Old Testament or Apocryphal writings; and one, oddly enough, to a letter that Pope Gregory VII (r. 1073–85) wrote to the Muslim king Anzir (Nacir), king of Mauritania, suggesting that Christians and Muslims "confess one God, although in different ways."[116]

But what did the final text of *Nostra aetate* actually say? What follows is a summary and brief analysis in six points.[117] First, the "Jewish question"—what had occasioned the document in the first place—remained in some respects center stage; it was distilled into a single, long article (4). Permit a generous quotation:

> The Church . . . [cannot] forget that she draws sustenance from the root of that well-cultivated olive tree [Israel] onto which have been grafted the wild shoots, the Gentiles. . . .
>
> Since the spiritual patrimony common to Christians and Jews is thus so great, this sacred synod wants to foster and recommend that mutual understanding and respect which is the fruit, above all, of biblical and theological studies as well as of fraternal dialogues [*fraternis colloquiis*].
>
> True, the Jewish authorities and those who followed their lead pressed for the death of Christ; still, what happened in His passion cannot be charged against all the Jews, without distinction, then alive, nor against the Jews of today.

> Although the Church is the new people of God, the Jews should not be presented as rejected or accursed. . . .
>
> Furthermore, in her rejection of every persecution against any man, the Church, mindful of the patrimony she shares with the Jews and moved not by political reasons but by the Gospel's spiritual love, decries hatred, persecutions, displays of anti-Semitism, directed against Jews at any time and by anyone.[118]

As mentioned, the church rejects here the "deicide" charge, even if the word was removed from the final draft. It also affirms with the Apostle Paul that God did not renege on his covenant with the Jews.[119] Jews and Christians are joined at the hip, as it were, the former owing the latter substantial parts of their own spiritual, theological, and liturgical heritage. Hostility to Jews is roundly condemned, and a deliberate effort is made to distance the statement from "political" causes—that is, Zionism. Finally, "fraternal dialogues" are encouraged; the Latin word used here is *colloquium*, which could also be readily translated as "conversation."[120]

Second, *Nostra aetate* recognized in its opening article that various globalizing forces had brought people with different outlooks "closer together" than had been the case in the past. This heightened awareness of a common humanity brought fresh salience to age-old religious questions: "the riddles about the human condition." The declaration articulated several: "What is man? What is the meaning, the aim of our life? What is moral good, what is sin? Whence suffering and what purpose does it serve? Which is the road to true happiness? What are death, judgment and retribution after death? What, finally, is that ultimate inexpressible mystery which encompasses our existence: from where do we come and where are we going?"[121] This "eloquent exposé of the deep questions that haunt human beings," according to Gerald O'Collins, "has no precedent in the teaching of earlier ecumenical councils."[122] The remainder of the declaration ought to be read in light of these questions, which echo venerable motifs in Catholic philosophy and theology—particularly the desire and ability of human reason, although beset by sin and even apart from an explicit embrace of Christian revelation, to pursue the truth, listen to one's conscience, and ponder perennial moral and religious matters.[123] Put differently, engagement with other faith traditions is enjoined not on the basis of dialogue as an end in itself, but on the basis of shared human questions about the purpose of human existence.

Third, *Nostra aetate* acknowledges faith traditions of South Asia and seeks to embrace whatever is "true and holy" in these—and other (unnamed) religions. Or, more fully:

> In Hinduism, men contemplate the divine mystery and express it through an inexhaustible abundance of myths and through searching philosophical inquiry. They seek freedom from the anguish of our human condition either through ascetical practices or profound meditation or a flight to God with love and trust. . . . Buddhism, in its various forms, realizes the radical insufficiency of this changeable world; it teaches a way by which men, in a devout and confident spirit, may be able either to acquire the state of perfect liberation, or attain, by their own efforts or through higher help, supreme illumination. Likewise, other religions found everywhere try to counter the restlessness of the human heart, each in its own manner, by proposing "ways," comprising teachings, rules of life, and sacred rites. The Catholic Church rejects nothing that is true and holy in these religions.[124]

To be sure, some Eastern traditions (Taoism, Sikhism, Jainism) are not mentioned explicitly—something widely remarked on at the time of writing. Even so, the document breaks new ground in the history of conciliar utterances—and not just for having positive things to say about Hinduism and Buddhism, but for mentioning them at all. While missionaries and the hierarchy in Asia had encountered these traditions for centuries, these words in an official conciliar document paved the way for engagement and conversation with Eastern thought in a manner that had not taken place in the past. This truly was an "extremely new horizon" for the church, to quote the French theologian René Laurentin, and one that resulted in numerous interfaith initiatives with Eastern faiths in the postconciliar period.[125]

Fourth, and certainly bespeaking a response to Arab reproaches of *Nostra aetate*, the declaration devotes an entire article (3) to Islam. This article also bears witness to Catholic scholars who had sought improved relations with Islam, foremost the French scholar Louis Massignon. The article reads: "The Church regards with esteem also the Muslims. They adore the one God, living and subsisting in Himself; merciful and all-powerful, the Creator of heaven and earth, who has spoken to men; they take pains to submit wholeheartedly to even His inscrutable decrees, just as Abraham, with whom the faith of Islam takes pleasure in linking itself, submitted to God. Though they do not acknowledge Jesus as God, they revere Him as a prophet. They also honor Mary, His virgin Mother; at times they even call on her with devotion. In addition, they await the day of judgment when God will render their deserts to all those who have been raised up from the dead. Finally, they value the moral life and worship God especially through prayer, almsgiving and fasting."[126] This article goes on candidly to acknowledge the many "quarrels and hostilities" that had arisen between Christianity and Islam over the centuries. These were not to be dwelt upon; instead the council urged all to "forget the past" and labor for mutual understanding to "promote together for the benefit of all mankind social justice and moral welfare, as well as peace and freedom."[127] Whether the past could (or should) be so readily forgotten, especially in light of Middle Eastern realities at the time of the council, was a point much commented on and criticized. Many wondered, moreover, why neither Muhammad nor the Qur'an were mentioned, while some traditionalist bishops regarded the elision of sensitive ethical issues, such as polygamy, reproachable. It merits noting, incidentally, that mention of Muslims in previous conciliar documents includes that in the constitutions of the Council of Lyons (1274), in which they appear as "enemies of the Christian name, the blasphemous and faithless Saracens."[128] Catholic-Muslim relations in the postconciliar era have been at once among the most promising and the most challenging.[129]

Fifth, even as *Nostra aetate* placed an unprecedented value on non-Christian faiths, it asserted, in strong continuity with previous tradition, the primacy of Christ over the human religious sphere: "Indeed, she [the church] proclaims, and ever must proclaim Christ 'the way, the truth, and the life' (John 14:6), in whom men may find the fullness of religious life, in whom God has reconciled all things to Himself." And further: "It is the duty of the Church to . . . proclaim the cross of Christ as the sign of God's universal love and the source of all grace."[130] Yet such lines should not be read in light of the older exclusivist notion of *extra Ecclesiam nulla salus*, but in light of the council's newly theologized inclusivist vision, outlined in particular in *Lumen gentium*.[131] They also adumbrate a major postconciliar quandary: figuring out the relationship between "mission" and "dialogue."

Finally, the declaration enjoined the church to recognize the "dignity" and "rights" of all people, to eschew discrimination and violence, and to labor instead for peace: "The Church reproves, as foreign to the mind of Christ, any discrimination against men or harassment of them because of their race, color, condition of life, or religion. On the contrary, following in the footsteps of the holy Apostles Peter and Paul, this sacred synod ardently implores the Christian faithful to 'maintain good fellowship among the nations' (1 Peter 2:12), and, if possible, to live for their part in peace with all men."[132] As we shall see, this powerfully echoes John XXIII's encyclical *Pacem in terris* (1963) and the conciliar constitution *Gaudium et spes* (1965), the "Pastoral Constitution on the Church in the Modern World"—not to mention the United Nations' Universal Declaration of Human Rights (1948). Ever present too, as we have seen in the document's genesis, was the memory of the Holocaust and the desire to address this singular tragedy of the twentieth century. Some have even called *Nostra aetate* the Catholic Church's official response to the Holocaust.[133]

Given the buzz *Nostra aetate* generated during its development, it should not surprise that its promulgation in October 1965 garnered international attention.[134] At the council in Rome, as the *Chicago Tribune* summed up, the church "insist[s] the entire Jewish people cannot be charged with Christ's crucifixion or depicted as accursed by God, pay[s] respect to Islam and other non-Christian religions, and reject[s] any kind of discrimination."[135] Newspapers throughout the world offered similar reportage and commentary, and this commentary has continued in many different venues—journalistic, academic, and political—especially on occasions of the document's major anniversaries. *Nostra aetate*'s fortieth anniversary in 2005, for example, even witnessed a U.S. congressional resolution recognizing the document for "fostering interreligious dialogue and mutual respect, including, in particular, new relationships of collaboration and dialogue between Jews and Catholics."[136]

The sixteen documents of the council were not meant to be interpreted in isolation from one another, but rather in a bundle as well as in the context of the broader tradition of the church, the magisterium, and the biblical witness. Both those who emphasize the continuity of the council with the past and those who emphasize its discontinuity can and have found support for their views in *Nostra aetate.* Given the interpretative difficulties presented by the declaration, it is especially important to read it in light of John XXIII's *Pacem in terris* (1963) and Paul VI's *Ecclesiam suam* (1964) and alongside other relevant conciliar decrees. The complex background of these documents need not detain us, but their results matter for understanding *Nostra aetate* and its reception.

Published during the council, both encyclicals bespeak the Holy See's attempts to nudge the work of the bishops in a particular direction. For John XXIII, that direction was the promotion of peace and the assumption of a global view of humanity. As is widely noted, *Pacem in terris* ("On Establishing Universal Peace") was the first papal encyclical not addressed to Catholics alone but to all "people of good will"—a phrase adopted in several conciliar decrees and in the postconciliar magisterium. Written after the Cuban missile crisis to address the proliferation of nuclear weapons in the Cold War, the encyclical pricked the conscience of the world for the causes of human dignity, solidarity, and peaceful coexistence. It asserted that Catholics should work cooperatively with non-Catholics to promote a just society: "The putting of these principles [of social justice] into effect frequently involves extensive co-operation between Catholics and those Christians who are separated from this Apostolic See. It even involves the cooperation of Catholics with men who may not be Christians but who nevertheless are reasonable men, and men of natural moral integrity."[137] In other words, it encouraged interfaith work on the basis of action in pursuit of just causes.

This message struck a chord. "*Pacem in terris* was more than an encyclical—it was an event," Harvard's Mary Ann Glendon once recalled.[138] Written and published just before John XXIII's death, it was reprinted in its entirety by several major newspapers. It helped create the conditions of possibility for the Pontifical Council for Justice and Peace, established in 1967. In 1969 the United Nations devoted a conference to it. West Germany even made its title, with a picture of the aged pope, into a postage stamp. And years earlier, the encyclical hovered over the council after 1963, suggesting the temper it should take, the ethos it should strive for.

Paul VI's first encyclical *Ecclesiam suam* relates even more directly to *Nostra aetate;* the encyclical has been called the "Magna Charta of dialogue."[139] Written by the pope himself—a rarity as these things go—the encyclical appeared on 6 August 1964 in anticipation of the council's third session, its most fractious. At a time when the schema on the Jews had not yet branched out fully to include other faiths, the new pope assayed: "We . . . recognize and respect the moral and spiritual values of the *various non-Christian religions*, and We desire to join with them in promoting and defending common ideals of religious liberty, human brotherhood, good culture, social welfare and civil order." Expressing the likely influence of the Jewish theologian Martin Buber, Paul gave unprecedented prominence to the word *dialogue* (*colloquium*), which appeared no fewer than seventy-seven times in the encyclical, as for example: "But it seems . . . that the sort of relationship for the Church to establish with the world should be more in the nature of a *dialogue*, though theoretically other methods are not excluded. We do not mean unrealistic *dialogue.* It must be adapted to the intelligences of those to whom it is addressed. . . . *Dialogue* with children is not the same as *dialogue* with adults, nor is *dialogue* with Christians the same as *dialogue* with non-believers."[140] Paul identified three concentric circles of dialogue with those outside the Catholic Church: with the world at large, with the monotheistic religions, and with non-Catholic Christian communities. This encyclical "infused the word [dialogue] into the Council's vocabulary," as O'Malley has noted, showing up in *Nostra aetate* and *Gaudium et spes* in particular—as well as informing the "Decree on Ecumenism" (*Unitatis redintegratio*).[141] A writer in *La civiltà cattolica* summed up the encyclical shortly after its release as encouraging "a courteous dialogue [of the church] with contemporary humankind."[142]

Paul VI led by example. With *Nostra aetate* poised for approval, he traveled to India to attend the Eucharistic Congress in Bombay

(Mumbai) in December 1964. There he had the opportunity to address adherents of various Asian faiths, noting that "yours is a land of ancient culture, the cradle of great religions, the home of a nation that has sought God with a relentless desire . . . and in hymns of fervent prayer."[143] Not unlike his prior trip to the Holy Land, the significance of this trip (the first ever of a pope to South Asia) was not lost on the council fathers. "The journey to India," according to Giuseppe Alberigo, "strengthened the connection between the teaching of Pope Montani [Paul VI] and the activity of the Council fathers for a dialogue with believers of all religions and the building of a peaceful world."[144]

This "spirit of dialogue," we might call it, is felt particularly in the conciliar documents *Lumen gentium*, *Ad gentes*, and *Gaudium et spes*. All help foster a proper understanding of *Nostra aetate*.[145] But before discussing these texts, permit a brief word about *Sacrosanctum concilium*, promulgated on 4 December 1964, for it has implications for interreligious dialogue. This might seem unlikely, because its focus was almost exclusively on liturgical matters. But the church tries to think and believe on the basis of its liturgy, its prayers (*lex orandi, lex credendi*), and therefore it is of high significance that this document orients itself not to the Catholic Church alone but to "the whole of mankind," as the first paragraph puts it. Throughout, it evokes the image of Christ as the universal Choirmaster, summoning all peoples to participate in the Divine Office of the Church. Put differently, *Sacrosanctum concilium*, which was the first document approved by the council fathers, exhibits in a manner similar to *Pacem in terris* the new global awareness of the church and a universal message to match this awareness.[146]

Lumen gentium, or "Dogmatic Constitution on the Church," is crucial not only for understanding *Nostra aetate* but for grasping the council as a whole and the thin line it sought to walk between tradition and innovation. The outcome of a tumultuous history at the council, the document underwent nine drafts before its final promulgation on 21 November 1964—a year before *Nostra aetate*.[147] It began as a schema on the church (*De Ecclesia*), produced by conservative curial theologians under the watchful eye of Cardinal Ottaviani, head of the Theological Commission. Its first draft, however, received such impassioned opposition from the bishops that it came to be completely recast.[148] In the process, and through nimble papal pressure, theologians such as Karl Rahner, Gérard Philips, and Yves Congar were brought in to assist with revisions. The final version worked against the highly juridical, Tridentine conception of the church manifest in its first iteration and in much previous ecclesiology. Emphasis shifted instead to understanding the church as a holy mystery, the Kingdom of God, the People of God, a sacrament, a light to the nations—hence its title *Lumen gentium.* It also possesses strong ecumenical and interreligious overtures and accents. The church was to be "the sign and instrument of intimate communion with God and of unity *among the whole human race.*"[149] Most controversially in the eyes of conservatives, the document ceased to identify "the holy Church" founded by Christ exclusively with the Roman Catholic Church. The fullness of the former "subsists in" (*subsistit in*) the latter, to be sure, but without being exhaustively identifiable with it; for, indeed, "many elements of sanctification and of truth are *found outside its visible confines*"—even if these "gifts" properly belong to Christ and are "impelling toward Catholic unity."[150] The shift in language was subtle but significant.[151] Some of the ecumenical implications of the shift were worked out in *Unitatis redintegratio,* the "Decree on Ecumenism" (21 November 1964), which shares a conciliar patrimony with *Nostra aetate.*

The interreligious implications, in addition to appearing in *Nostra aetate,* are indicated in *Lumen gentium* itself, particularly in articles 16 and 17 of chapter 2, "The People of God," labored over especially by Yves Congar, arguably the leading theologian at the council.[152] Chapter 17 anticipates the language of *Nostra aetate* in its recognition that, while called to mission, the church aims to recognize and preserve all that is good in other faith traditions.[153]

Jews and Muslims are explicitly recognized in chapter 16, preceding passages that extend salvation—or at least the hope of salvation—significantly outside the boundaries of the visible church. This chapter merits quoting generously:

> Finally, those who have not yet received the Gospel are related in various ways to the people of God. In the first place we must recall the people [that is, Jews] to whom the testament and the promises were given and from whom Christ

> was born according to the flesh. On account of their fathers this people remain most dear to God, for God does not repent of the gifts He makes nor of the calls He issues. But the plan of salvation also includes those who acknowledge the Creator. In the first place amongst these there are the Muslims, who, professing to hold the faith of Abraham, along with us adore the one and merciful God, who on the last day will judge mankind. Nor is God far distant from those who in shadows and images seek the unknown God, for it is He who gives to all men life and breath and all things, and as Savior wills that all men be saved. Those also can attain to salvation who through no fault of their own do not know the Gospel of Christ or His Church, yet sincerely seek God and moved by grace strive by their deeds to do His will as it is known to them through the dictates of conscience. Nor does Divine Providence deny the helps necessary for salvation to those who, without blame on their part, have not yet arrived at an explicit knowledge of God and with His grace strive to live a good life. Whatever good or truth is found amongst them is looked upon by the Church as a preparation for the Gospel [*praeparatio evangelica*]. She knows that it is given by Him who enlightens all men so that they may finally have life.[154]

This passage represents a remarkable effort of drawing from tradition (*ressourcement*) to engage present concerns (*aggiornamento*), leitmotifs of the council.

But what about other faiths and Christian mission? This task was spelled out extensively in *Ad gentes*, which dealt with the question of the church's missionary activity. Although it did not water down the church's obligation "to strive to preach the Gospel to all men," it bound this obligation with an unusually high regard for positive elements found in the world's religious traditions. Missionary activity should not run roughshod over other faiths and cultures, but instead seek to preserve and redeem whatever is best in them for Christ. Furthermore, *Ad gentes* encouraged missionaries to learn about other religious practices and beliefs and enter into dialogue with them: "[They] should know and converse [*conversentur*] with those among whom they live, that through sincere and patient dialogue they themselves might learn of the riches which a generous God distributed among the nations." Missionaries, in other words, should not only be teachers of the Gospel but inquiring, receptive students of world religions and cultures, uncovering with "gladness and respect those seeds of the Word [*semina Verbi*] which lie hidden among them."[155] This phrase "seeds of the Word" is especially important, here and in other conciliar documents, for it sought to recognize that God's spirit was already afoot and working in other faith traditions, even apart from their explicit acknowledgment of the Gospel.[156] One of these "seeds" lay in monastic practices, especially as cultivated in South Asia. Missionaries were enjoined to "carefully consider how traditions of asceticism and contemplation, the seeds of which were sown by God in certain ancient cultures before the preaching of the Gospel, might be incorporated into the Christian religious life."[157] In summary, Catholic missionaries should go about their work attentively, attempting to discern how God might already be working in cultures and civilizations apart from Christian revelation.

Finally, we come to *Gaudium et spes*, or "Pastoral Constitution on the Church in the Modern World," arguably the most sweeping of the conciliar documents, promulgated on the last day of the council. Addressed to "the whole human family," it developed themes that we have seen in other documents, but it added its own emphases and elaborations. Like *Nostra aetate*, it indicated that all people in the depths of their being ask ultimate questions about the meaning and mystery of life. Echoing *Pacem in terris*, it recognized the dignity of all people—created in the image of God and equipped with reason and conscience—and called for peaceful coexistence, the alleviation of human misery, and a shared search for the true, the good, and the beautiful. Like *Ad gentes*, *Gaudium et spes* esteemed different faiths and civilizations for carrying in their bosom endowments from God. Additionally, it asserted the universal presence of Christ through the Holy Spirit in the hearts of all human beings—a point that Pope John Paul II would later amplify. All good deeds, all promptings of conscience, all feeble attempts to fathom divinity at some level reflect "Christ . . . at work in the hearts of men by the power of his Spirit."[158]

Perhaps most relevant to *Nostra aetate*, *Gaudium et spes* called for the church to enter into dialogue with the modern world as such—and not simply as a doctor addressing a patient, but in a way that involved reciprocal communication and mutual learning.[159] Attempting to exorcize the defensive, retreatist mentality of preconciliar Catholicism, the church was enjoined to engage in "sincere dialogue" that excluded nobody. Further: "Our thoughts . . . go out to all who acknowledge God and preserve precious religious and human elements in their traditions; it is our hope that frank dialogue will spur us all on to receive the impulses of the Spirit with fidelity and act upon them with alacrity."[160] Finally, the document extols the importance of religious freedom as a vital precondition for engagement with others; in this, it echoed *Dignitatis humanae*, "Declaration on Religious Liberty," which was promulgated on the same day and which since Vatican II has been seen as the political sine qua non for enabling peaceable dialogue.[161]

With the completion and promulgation of these documents, the council concluded its business. On 8 December 1965, roughly three hundred thousand people gathered in and around St. Peter's Square for the final ceremony, which was globally televised. Shortly after 10 a.m., the council fathers processed out of St. Peter's to assume their places on the piazza. A Mass was held with a homily followed by short farewell from the pope. The ceremony concluded with the curial Cardinal Felici reading an exhortation from the pope, enjoining that "everything the council decreed be religiously and devoutly observed by all the faithful."[162] Then the pope told the crowd, "*Ite in pace*—Go in peace."[163] With that, the Second Vatican Council finished its work. "It was over," Congar recorded laconically in his journal.[164]

After the Council

But every ending is also a beginning. Vatican II inaugurated for the Catholic Church a different, more open engagement with modernity and with the non-Western world than had been the case beforehand. It also initiated debates within the church over the very meaning of the council and the proper means for implementing it. In the half century since the closing of the council, high-stakes acrimonious arguments have taken place over whether the council represents a rupture with the past or only a reform of it.[165] Should the council be understood through a "hermeneutic of discontinuity" or a "hermeneutic of reform," to use influential, if contested, terms given by Pope Benedict XVI?[166] Yet from either perspective, *Nostra aetate* signaled at least some novelty or "development" concretely manifesting itself in the church's more frequent and friendly engagement with other faiths. What follows, then, will explore aspects of the "reception" or "implementation" of *Nostra aetate*.[167] We shall first look at institutional arrangements within the Vatican bureaucracy or Curia that enabled this implementation. Thereafter, we shall turn to the epochal papacy of John Paul II for interreligious dialogue, focusing in particular on the origins, significance, and legacy of the World Day of Prayer for Peace, a major international interfaith gathering that took place under his papacy in Assisi in October of 1986—and has since become a tradition.

Before the council completed its work, several bishops began to feel that the church would need a new administrative organ to actualize interreligious activity. Bishop Antoine Hubert Thijssen, a Dutchman serving in Indonesia, suggested at a press conference that great value would come from "the formation of a special secretariat for the major non-Christian religions." He was seconded by Cardinal Thomas Tien Ken-sin of China (residing in Taipei), who sent a proposal to the pope in July 1963.[168] Given the likelihood of *Nostra aetate*'s passage, Paul VI voiced approval, and after various twists and turns the Secretariat for Non-Christians was launched in May 1964 as a new Vatican administrative unit, or dicastery.[169] Cardinal Paolo Marella (Italy) was appointed as its first president, Pierre Humbertclaude (France) its secretary, and Pietro Rossano (Italy) its undersecretary. It also had various members and consultors drawn from church leaders throughout the world. In an apostolic letter, Paul VI announced its rationale: "While Vatican Council II is in progress, we thought it useful to institute a special council or secretariat with the task of turning its wholesome attention to those who are without the Christian religion." The purpose of such a work, he continued, is to "stimulate the Church" toward dialogue and engagement "in these times when numerous relationships are being developed between men of every race, language, and religion."[170] The new secretariat was intended to handle relations with all non-Christian religions, but from its inception it had a special section on Islam, headed by Joseph Cuoq of the Society for Missionaries for Africa who helped draft the paragraph in *Nostra aetate* on Islam and previously served with the Congregation of Oriental Churches.[171] Significantly, however, relations with the Jews were kept with Cardinal Bea and the Secretariat for Promoting Christian Unity (1960), later renamed the Pontifical Council for the Promotion of Christian Unity (PCPCU).[172] These relations are cultivated under a special Commission for Religious Relations with the Jews set up in 1974. This arrangement—which recognizes the sui generis status of Judaism vis-à-vis Christianity—has been maintained to the present day.[173]

The aims and structure of the Secretariat for Non-Christians was spelled out further in *Regimini Ecclesiae universae* (15 August 1967), in which Paul VI noted that this secretariat "left intact" the competence and work of the Congregation for the Evangelization of the People.[174] The fact that he felt the need to note this suggests the difficulty of balancing the goals of dialogue and mission. This constitution noted, further, that the goal of the secretariat "is to promote studies [and] . . . foster with great charity the kinds of relations with non-Christians that will increase mutual esteem." Exactly how this ought to be done was largely left in the hands of the secretariat's leaders.[175]

Progress proceeded rapidly. The secretariat played a role in welcoming and hosting guests in Rome who represented various faith traditions and nationalities, including in 1970 a delegation from the Supreme Council of Islamic Affairs in Cairo. Delegates from the secretariat were also often sent to international conferences, and its consultants staged their own conferences. In 1966 a publication was founded, *Bulletin, Secretariatus pro non Christianis*, later renamed *Pro dialogo*. Several additional specific guideline booklets were issued, bearing titles such as *Religions: Fundamental Themes for a Dialogistic Understanding* (1970), *Towards the Meeting with Buddhism* (1970), and *Guidelines for Dialogue between Muslims and Christians* (1969). In 1967, for the first time, a message of good wishes was sent out to Muslims at the end of Ramadan and broadcast on Vatican Radio; later, this tradition was extended to other faiths' holy days. In 1971, two subsections were created for the secretariat: one for Asian religious traditions and another for indigenous African faiths. This decade also witnessed the first of many meetings and collaborations between the secretariat and the recently established Office of Interreligious Dialogue of the World Council of Churches.[176] Finally, considerable time and energy went into training dioceses and parishes for the work of dialogue and interreligious understanding; by the mid-1970s, twenty-five Commissions for Dialogue (often combined with Christian ecumenism) had arisen in Episcopal Conferences throughout the world.[177] Nonetheless, the American Jewish Committee could not unreasonably complain in 1970 that "despite a great many advances" in interreligious work, it remained a preoccupation of elites and thus "the impression remains that the Catholic-Jewish relations do not constitute a major priority for the Church."[178]

Activities of interreligious outreach continued under the secretariat's second president, Cardinal Sergio Pignedoli (Italy), who served from 1973 to 1980. A confidant of Paul VI, he elevated the section on Islam in 1974 to a special Commission for Religious Relations with Islam, paralleling the Commission on the Jews set up in the same year.[179] This paved the way, inter alia, for a high-profile, Vatican-endorsed Islam-Christian dialogue, held in Tripoli, Libya, in 1976.[180] A year earlier, the secretariat welcomed a major delegation of Muslim ulama from Saudi Arabia who enjoyed an audience with the pope.[181] These efforts of outreach to Muslims allowed Pignedoli to play a delicate diplomatic role in the Vatican's initial efforts to establish diplomatic ties with the state of Israel—a major worry during the council, as we have seen, but something that in fact became a reality in 1993.[182] In 1979, during the fledgling papacy of John Paul II, the secretariat organized its first Plenary Assembly to take stock of its work and plan for the future. "You are aware that your work is a delicate one," the new pope reminded the audience, but it must be pursued "with the luminous conviction that dialogue is, in the words of Paul VI, 'a method of accomplishing the apostolic mission; it is an example of the art of spiritual communication.'"[183]

After his unexpected death in 1980, Pignedoli was followed by the Belgian Jean Jadot, whose short tenure witnessed the establishment of a desk for new religious movements such as Wicca, Neo-Paganism, and New Age spiritualities.[184] Jadot was in turn succeeded in 1984 by Francis Arinze from Nigeria, the first non-European appointed to this post. Both men continued the secretariat's busy schedule of activities, publications, and engagements. Of particular significance was Arinze's participation at the fourth Assembly of the World Conference on Religion and Peace in Nairobi, 23–30 August 1984. Established in the 1970s, the hosting body of this conference, Religions for Peace, had emerged by this time as a significant global player in bringing different religious bodies together to denounce warfare, violence, and poverty. Arinze's participation, therefore, represented the coming together of two major streams of twentieth-century interfaith engagement.[185]

In 1988, as part of an overhaul of the Roman Curia, through the constitution *Pastor bonum*, the secretariat was renamed the Pontifical Council for Interreligious Dialogue (PCID), its current title. The negative word "non-Christian" had long displeased many, and the new title was seen to capture better the aims of the body. The key article from this constitution reads that "the Council fosters suitable dialogue with the followers of other religions and encourages various kinds of relations with them. It promotes appropriate studies and conferences to develop mutual information and esteem, so that human dignity and the spiritual and moral riches of people may ever grow. The Council sees to the formation of those who engage in this kind of dialogue."[186] It also maintains a directory of organizations committed to interreligious dialogue.[187]

In 1984, on the occasion of another Plenary Assembly, the dicastery released its first official magisterial document (papally approved and included in the *Acta apostolicae sedis*) with the cumbersome title "The Attitude of the Church towards the Followers of Other Religions. Reflections and Orientations on Dialogue and Mission." Generally referred to simply as "Dialogue and Mission," the title reflects the ongoing tension, left unresolved by the council, between the call for missionary work and the task of dialogue, and the complexity of spelling out the relationship between the two. In it, dialogue is placed in the larger context of the Great Commission, the realization of which was tasked to the Congregation for the Evangelization of Peoples. The two dicasteries were charged to labor together even if they have "distinct" goals. Both mission and dialogue, moreover, must respect the inviolability of an individual's conscience, eschew all forms of coercion, and focus on the shared pursuit of truth with other human beings. This last point is particularly important. Dialogue should not be seen as an end in itself, but as a means of seeking truth. If truth as a regulative ideal of dialogue is forsaken, the task of dialogue is warped. Furthermore, mission should never be undertaken without dialogue: "Any sense of mission not permeated by . . . a dialogical spirit would go against the demands of true humanity and the teachings of the Gospel." "Dialogue and Mission" goes on to identify four types of dialogue, broadening the concept to entail (1) the dialogue of daily life, the side-by-side coexistence of those with different beliefs; (2) the dialogue of action or deeds, working together with non-Christians on "goals of a humanitarian, social, economic, or political nature"; (3) a dialogue of the learned, a form of "particular interest," since it brings together individuals with considerable knowledge of their respective faith traditions; and finally, (4) a dialogue of religious experience, which allows for the devout of different traditions to "share their experiences of prayer, contemplation, faith, and duty, as well as their expressions and ways of searching for the Absolute." Finally, the document makes clear that while the possibility of conversion might be the fruit of Christian witness, this should never be hurried or forced.[188] Not surprisingly, the question of conversion remains a delicate topic—not least with Jews.

In 1991, just after the twenty-fifth anniversary of *Nostra aetate*, a companion publication was released, "Dialogue and Proclamation," which sought to clarify and restate many points in the 1984 document, but to update them to reflect the post–Cold War historical context. Significantly, "Dialogue and Proclamation" noted in its opening paragraphs the international significance of the World Day of Prayer for Peace in Assisi (27 October 1986) and the "encouragement of John Paul II."[189]

John Paul II and the Road to Assisi

The papacy of Karol Wojtyla as John Paul II (r. 1978–2005) and the World Day of Prayer for Peace in Assisi represent key legacies for contemporary interreligious dialogue. "No pope," Michael Fitzgerald has written, "has done as much to foster dialogue . . . with people of all religions."[190] Admittedly, Paul VI had set a precedent with visits to Christian-minority lands such as Jordan, India, Israel, and Turkey, but John Paul II far outpaced him as the most traveled pope ever, meeting with and speaking to thousands of non-Christian peoples in the process.[191] His Polish background and familiarity with the Holocaust informed his sense of responsibility to the Jews, whom he famously referred to as Christians' "elder brother in the faith." He had known one Polish Jew in particular, Jerzy Kluger, from childhood, and the two maintained close ties during his papacy.[192] But John Paul II's interfaith legacy extends far beyond relations with Jews alone. As he said himself in 1992: "I have always considered a very important part of my ministry: the fostering of more friendly relations with the followers of other religious traditions."[193] This was borne out not only in his encyclicals and many addresses (often given during foreign travels), but in bold public symbolic gestures and in intimate meetings with leaders of various faith traditions. In all of this, he sought to balance—not always adequately, in the eyes of his critics—the theological imperative of Christian mission with the conciliar directive toward dialogue. Since the council, in which Wojtyla participated as a theological consultor, defining the relationship between the two—mission and dialogue—had not been a simple task. Still, the pope was "pleased that my ministry in the See of Saint Peter has taken place during the period following the Second Vatican Council, when the insights which inspired . . . *Nostra aetate* are finding concrete expression in various ways."[194]

John Paul II's interreligious concerns manifested themselves in his first encyclical, *Redemptor hominis* (1979), which sought to work out theologically what Vatican II had taught about ecumenism and engagement with other faiths. He often invoked *Nostra aetate*, writing that the council "gave a fundamental impulse to forming the Church's self-awareness by so adequately and competently presenting to us a view of the terrestrial globe as a map of various religions. . . . With regard to religion, what is dealt with is in the first place religion as a universal phenomenon linked with man's history from the beginning, then the various non-Christian religions, and finally Christianity itself. . . . [*Nostra aetate*], in particular, is filled with deep esteem for the great spiritual values, indeed for the primacy of the spiritual, which in the life of mankind finds expression in religion and then in morality, with direct effects on the whole of culture."[195] The pope spotlights Judaism and Islam, as had *Nostra aetate*, because of their "Abrahamic" nearness to Christianity. But the encyclical also strikes a new note: the universal presence of God's Spirit working steadily in the hearts of all people. No human being exists outside the powerful presence of God working through the Holy Spirit. The Spirit is the ubiquitous, mysterious presence and companion in the life of every human being, regardless of one's religious views.[196]

On several occasions, John Paul II addressed the Pontifical Council for Interreligious Dialogue during its plenary and other assemblies. In 1979, shortly after the publication of *Redemptor hominis*, he praised the foresight of Paul VI for setting up the office, which serves as "the symbol and expression of the Church's will to enter into communication with . . . those who seek in the non-Christian religions meaning and guidance for their lives." While the church still had the duty to bear witness to Christ, the pope reminded his audience, it must do so in great humility and simplicity of heart, sensitive to the background of others. For this, and for the task of dialogue in general, more education was needed.[197] At the council's plenary session in 1992, the pope repeated his message, emphasizing the soteriological dimension of dialogue, which "at its deepest level is always a dialogue of salvation, because it seeks to discover, clarify and understand better the sign of the age-long dialogue which God maintains with mankind."[198] In 1999, he addressed the Assembly of World Religions, which had been organized by the council. Among other things, he called for dialogue to result in interreligious humanitarian action.[199]

In a subsequent encyclical, *Redemptoris missio* (1990), John Paul II focused on the connection between dialogue and the task of evangelization—against a rising chorus of voices, Christian and not, who felt that they were simply incommensurate goals. "Interreligious dialogue is a part of the Church's evangelizing mission," he shot back. "The Church sees no conflict between proclaiming Christ and engaging in interreligious dialogue. . . . These two elements must maintain both their intimate connection and their distinctiveness; therefore they should not be confused, manipulated or regarded as the same, as if they were interchangeable." For the pope, dialogue cannot be merely an instrument for evangelization: "Dialogue does not originate from tactical concerns or self-interest, but is an activity with its own guiding principles, requirements, and dignity." Those engaged in dialogue, according to the pope, should be "consistent with their own religious tradition and convictions" but open to learning from others "without pretense or close-mindedness but with truth, humility, frankness, knowing that dialogue can enrich each side." Finally, the encyclical enjoins dialogue for its peacemaking potential.[200]

John Paul II practiced what he preached, interacting with and addressing numerous representatives of other faiths during his long pontificate. Listing these addresses would be a fool's errand, but a sampler offers some sense of the breadth of his interreligious engagements.

- "To Representatives of the Shinto Religion" (Rome, 28 February 1979)
- "To the Muslim Leaders of Kenya" (Nairobi, 7 May 1980)
- "To the People of Pakistan" (Karachi, 6 February 1981)
- "A Message to the People of Asia" (Manila, 21 February 1981)
- "To the Leaders of the Various Religions of Korea" (Seoul, 6 May 1984)
- "To the People of Thailand" (Bangkok, 11 May 1985)
- "To Followers of Various Religions of Togo" (Togoville, 9 August 1985)
- "To the Religious Authorities of India" (Calcutta, 3 February 1986)[201]

In these addresses, certain themes reoccur: the importance of dialogue in general, the need for different faiths to work together for justice, the universal working of God's Spirit in all people, dialogue's role in fostering peace, the importance of following one's conscience, and the beauty of different civilizations. Where John Paul II broke new ground, going beyond Vatican II, was not only in emphasizing the universal presence of the Holy Spirit, but in the significance that he accorded to prayer, from whatever religious tradition it was offered. As he put it in 1981: "What seems to bring together and unite, in a particular way, Christians and the believers of other religions is an acknowledgement of the *need for prayer* as an expression of man's spirituality directed toward the Absolute."[202] This conviction proved foundational for justifying the day of prayer at Assisi in 1986.

The Polish pope regularly exhorted bishops to take seriously the teachings of *Nostra aetate* and related teachings in Vatican II documents. To the bishops of India, for example, he commended to them dialogue as "a serious part of your apostolic ministry. The Lord calls you . . . to do everything possible to promote dialogue according to the commitment of the Church."[203] Frequently, he spoke to bishops on the importance of "inculturation," by which he meant seeing that Christianity operated in generous harmony with, not negation of, particular cultures, esteeming, preserving, and redeeming whatever was true and holy in them.[204] "A genuine inculturation of faith," he told bishops in Zimbabwe, "cannot be reduced to merely adopting the externals of a given culture. True inculturation is from within: it consists, ultimately, in a renewal of life under the influence of grace."[205] Both ecumenical and interreligious dialogue must be pursued even in frustrating circumstances, he told Catholic bishops of the Middle East: "I know that you sometimes experience a negative response to your efforts. The Church nonetheless . . . is irrevocably committed to Christian unity and for a dialogue of truth and peace with all men and women of good will."[206]

But actions often spoke louder than words. John Paul II was a master of symbolic gestures that captured global media attention. His desire to improve Jewish-Catholic relations led him in 1979 to become the first pope to visit the Auschwitz concentration camp, as part of his remarkable trip to his home country, widely credited with loosening the Soviet grip on eastern Europe.[207] In 1986 he became the first pope to visit Rome's synagogue. In 2000, following the example of Paul VI, he traveled to Israel, visiting the Holocaust memorial Yad Vashem and praying at the Western Wall of Jerusalem.[208] Two years prior to this visit, the Holy See had published "We Remember: A Reflection on the Shoah," in which an introductory letter by the pope acknowledged the "unspeakable iniquity" of the Holocaust.

John Paul II's outreach to Muslims was also ambitious. Beginning with a trip to Turkey in 1979, he made several trips to Muslim-majority countries, notably one in 1985 to Morocco: an unprecedented affair—the first time that a pope had ever formally addressed a largely Muslim audience at the invitation of a Muslim leader, King Hassan II (r. 1961–99). Speaking to around eighty thousand Muslims at a stadium in Casablanca, the pope praised what Muslims and Christians had in common and pled for humility and respect concerning matters where they differed. Both should labor for a more "fraternal world," tearing down barriers that are sometimes "caused by pride, [but] more often by weakness and fear." He also highlighted the importance of prayer for both communities.[209] Besides Morocco, the pope made trips, inter alia, to Bangladesh, Egypt, Indonesia, Jordan, Lebanon, Pakistan, Turkey, Sudan, Mozambique, and Syria, in addition to initiating many interactions with European Muslims.[210]

In Syria on 6 May 2001, in another papal first, John Paul II visited one of the oldest and most important mosques in the Islamic world, the famous Umayyad Mosque in Damascus, cherished by both Christians and Muslims for its tomb dedicated to John the Baptist (known as the prophet Yahya to Muslims).[211] There, the pope stressed the importance of Muslims and Christians "explor[ing] philosophical and theological questions together, in order to come to a more objective and comprehensive knowledge of each other's beliefs." He praised Muslims and Christians in Syria for living "side by side for centuries" and for the "rich dialogue of life" that had developed from this. He also emphasized the necessity to educate the young into the path of "respectful dialogue" and again, he upheld the importance of prayer "for the nourishment of our souls."[212]

John Paul II's interfaith engagements extended beyond Jews and Muslims to many other faith communities, even if these two faiths loom the largest in his legacy. He and the Dalai Lama, for example, met no fewer than eight times and developed a remarkable, photogenic friendship as arguably the two most widely recognized religious leaders on the planet.[213] The pope also met with Buddhists in Japan, Sri Lanka, Korea, and elsewhere, and on several occasions received Buddhist visitors in Rome. In 1979 he met with a delegation of lay Buddhist monks from Japan—another papal first—in what he called "an epoch-making event in the history of interreligious dialogue."[214]

Two trips to India during his pontificate allowed him to speak movingly about interfaith matters in a land of extraordinary religious complexity. Strategically visiting India in September 1986, just before the Day of Prayer in Assisi, he made his first public appearance at the memorial to Gandhi in New Delhi. Expressing to the crowd there his desire to experience "the very soul of your country," he praised Gandhi for his message of nonviolence, simplicity, and human equality.[215] The next day, before a religiously mixed crowd in New Delhi, he spoke of the "need for all religions to collaborate in the cause of humanity, and do this from a viewpoint of the spiritual nature of man. Today, as Hindus, Muslims, Sikhs, Buddhists, Jains, Parsees, and Christians, we gather in fraternal love to assert this by our presence [together]."[216] In Calcutta, where he observed firsthand the work of Mother Teresa, he expressed esteem for Swami Vivekananda as "one of the renowned figures connected with this city." Vivekananda's intuition that "service of men is service of God" resonated strongly with Christian ethics, according to the pope, even as he regarded it "also [as] deeply Indian." On several occasions during both trips to India—the second one took place in 1999—he referenced *Nostra aetate* directly, observing that "in the Catholic Church you [Indians] will find a willing partner in the dialogue of truth and in the service of man."[217] Recognizing the fragility of India's young democracy, he enjoined interreligious dialogue to help overcome "barriers and difficulties in the task of nation building." Finally, he praised India, "the cradle of ancient religious traditions," for serving as an enduring rebuke to a worldview more prevalent in the West based exclusively on "the material and biological."[218]

The promise of interreligious dialogue for peacemaking made the pope especially sensitive to areas of the world rent by ethnic conflict. War-torn Lebanon in the 1980s provides one example. In an address from Rome in 1984, he exhorted all Lebanese to remember that they inhabited a "crossroad of religions," a place of "cultural dialogue between East and West." The Catholic Church in Lebanon, he pled, "must ensure in a prophetic way the ministry of dialogue and reconciliation" even amid a society torn apart by the "horrors of war."[219] The collapsed state of Yugoslavia in the 1990s—if we may briefly leap ahead of the Assisi gathering—provides another example, one in which dreadful violence was perpetuated among Orthodox, Catholic, and Muslim factions. In 1993 the pope wrote an open letter to the secretary-general of the United Nations, deploring the "appalling" situation in Bosnia-Herzegovina and calling for intervention on behalf of the international community.[220] "Death, torture, rape and expulsion are the many faces of hatred setting one people against another having different cultural, ethnic and religious roots, but who are geographically and historically close."[221] At his prodding, another interreligious gathering took place in 1993 in Assisi, but this time with just Jews, Christians, and Muslims, who came together to focus attention on the crisis in the Balkans.[222] Wartime conditions prevented the pope from traveling to Sarajevo during the conflict, but he did make two trips afterward, one in 1997 and another in 2003.[223] On both trips he called for mutual forgiveness and prayed that a culture of cooperation and dialogue would supplant one of destruction. On 13 April 1997, he led by example, meeting with leaders from Bosnia's Muslim community and expressing esteem for Islam, using language drawn verbatim from *Nostra aetate*.[224]

Like no pope before him (or since), John Paul II was a champion of interreligious dialogue. By and large, he continued the inclusivist vision set out in *Nostra aetate* and other documents of Vatican II and attempted to apply them to particular situations. For this, he not infrequently received criticism from both pluralists and exclusivists—if for different reasons. In the eyes of exclusivists, some of his interreligious gestures veered too close to syncretism, a dilution of the singularity of the Christian message. As we shall see, this criticism came in spades after the 1986 gathering in Assisi. But just as often he was taken to task by pluralists for not being generous enough toward other faiths and for continuing to link dialogue with mission. He rarely uttered criticisms of other religions in large interfaith gatherings, where goodwill and irenicism generally prevailed. But they did come in other addresses, writings, and in interviews. In an interview with the Italian journalist Vittorio Messori, for example (later published in *Crossing the Threshold of Hope*), the pope candidly admitted his misgivings about Buddhism and Islam. Buddhism, he felt, possessed an essentially "negative soteriology," in which the goal of life is to extinguish the self completely, not restore it to holiness and join it everlastingly with God through love. Because of this, he summed up, "the doctrines of salvation in Buddhism and Christianity are opposed."[225] Although he had great respect for Islam, he felt that its conception of God was too remote from the world of human beings. "Some of the most beautiful names in the human language are given to the God of the Koran," he noted, "but he is ultimately a God outside of the world, a God who is *only Majesty, never Emmanuel*, God with us. *Islam is not a religion of redemption.*"[226] The pope sometimes admonished those engaged in dialogue with Islam, moreover, to be faithful to the fundamentally Trinitarian nature of Christian monotheism—an age-old sticking point between the two faiths.

Finally, not all the pope's interreligious efforts went smoothly. During his visit to the Great Mosque in Damascus, for example, several Muslim clerics stridently took issue with the fact that he did not remove his crucifix nor use the opportunity to repent of past Christian violence against Muslims, notably during the Crusades. His concern for Bosnia in the 1990s was welcomed by all sides, but some criticized him for not being hard enough on Catholic Croat nationalism. What is more, during the conflict, while he did not travel to Sarajevo, he did travel to Zagreb and presided over the beatification of Cardinal Aloysius Stepinic (1898–1960), who during World War II had remained largely silent concerning the Croatian Ustache atrocities and the complicity of many Catholic priests.[227] Other examples of John Paul II's missteps could be adduced. Nonetheless, the rigor, sincerity, and scope of his interreligious efforts remain unrivaled in modern Catholicism.

Assisi, 1986, and Beyond

But we have only discussed aspects of the road to Assisi, not Assisi itself. The most high-profile and innovative of John Paul II's interreligious endeavors, the World Day of Prayer for Peace in Assisi, took place on 27 October 1986. Since then, the Catholic Church has orchestrated several follow-up gatherings there—in 1993, 1999, 2002, 2011, and 2016—undertaken under three papacies, those of John Paul II, Benedict XVI, and Francis. While not without controversy, these meetings have visibly demonstrated to the world, in the words of John L. Allen Jr., "a sea change in Catholic attitudes towards other religions, and an historic addition to the conception of what it means to be pope."[228] How, specifically, did the first event come about?

In 1981, based on a unanimous resolution, the United Nations began observing 21 September as the International Day of Peace, or World Peace Day. Around the same time, the proposal emerged to recognize an entire year, 1986, as one dedicated to peace. In the interim, various religious bodies and international humanitarian organizations signed on, giving the effort momentum and legitimacy. Dispirited by the perdurance of the Cold War and numerous smaller conflicts throughout the world, John Paul II decided that the Catholic Church should participate as well. During this time, the idea that prayer was an underappreciated point of contact among faiths had become a fixture of the pope's thought. He determined, therefore, to invite major religious leaders from around the world to Assisi for the World Day of Prayer for Peace. This city, which calls itself "the city of peace," was selected due to its association with the irenic interfaith legacy of Francis of Assisi.[229] A grand symbolic gesture was in the making.

The event was first announced on 25 January 1986 at St. Paul's Outside the Walls in Rome—deliberately on the same date and in the same place that John XXIII had announced Vatican II. The date settled on was 26 October. Invitations were sent out soon thereafter with the request of a response by 6 April (Easter). The Secretariat for Promoting Christian Unity handled invitations to Christian bodies, while the Secretariat for Non-Christians took care of all others. Experts in Rome and elsewhere—as well as local bishops in foreign countries—were sought out to determine knotty questions about who exactly ought to be invited. As a rule, history and geography played a strong role: where a faith had been born and developed guided decisions. Buddhists were invited from Asia, for example, not from Los Angeles.[230]

Because of the unprecedented nature of the event, the pope and various curial representatives sought to convey in speech and print what was going on and why. "The purpose of this meeting," the pope announced on 6 April 1986, "is to create a point of convergence for the vast movement of reflection and prayer in which the followers of all religious faiths have been engaged up to this time."[231]

Several months later, he explained that "no one should be surprised if the members of the different Christian Churches and of the various religions come together to pray. Men and women who have a religious spirit can in fact be the leaven of a new awareness of the whole of humanity in regard to the common responsibility for peace."[232] In addition, several press conferences were held by curial officials, and Radio Vatican broadcast the rationale for the coming event.

The day was to be at once ecumenical and interreligious, a gathering of diverse Christians and representatives of other faiths—around sixty in all, although many came with small delegations. The roster of luminaries attending included leaders from most major Christian confessions (Catholic, Orthodox, Oriental Orthodox, and Protestant). Other guests included Jews, Buddhists, Hindus, Muslims, Jains, Sikhs, and Zoroastrians as well as representatives of Shinto and various "traditional religions," mainly from Africa and the Americas. Distinguished guests included the Dalai Lama, the chief rabbi of Rome (Elio Toaff), the archbishop of Canterbury (Robert Runcie), the patriarchs of various autocephalous Orthodox churches, the president of the World Conference on Religion and Peace (Inamullah Khan), the leader of India's Zoroastrians (Homi Dhalla), and the head of the Muslim World League (Sheikh Mohammad Nasir Al-Aboudi), among others.[233] Mother Teresa, who had recently won the Nobel Peace Prize, was on hand as a conspicuous onlooker. Numerous governmental figureheads, from Italy and abroad, festooned the medieval city.

But before the big day arrived, many traditionalists wondered if the Catholic Church was headed toward illicit syncretism. The pope and his allies countered with more elaborate theological defenses of their aim. After citing *Nostra aetate*, the pope explained in one address that "what will take place at Assisi will certainly not be religious syncretism but a sincere attitude of prayer to God in an atmosphere of mutual respect." "We know what we believe to be the limits of these [non-Christian] religions," he added, "but that does not at all take away from the fact that they possess . . . outstanding religious values and qualities." Furthermore, the pope insisted that the religious leaders intended "to be together in order to pray" but they were *not* "praying together." This distinction was often cited, although its subtlety remained lost on many.[234]

Several supporters of Assisi made their ideas known in *L'osservatore romano.* Jorge Mejía, the vice president of the Pontifical Commission on Justice and Peace, affirmed the pope's distinction, making clear that Christian prayer was necessarily Trinitarian and thus distinct from prayers in other religious traditions. But it did not follow, he argued, that representatives of various faiths should not be allowed to pray in the presence of one another. They should, in fact. Doing so promised at least three important results. First, it would benefit all present by allowing them to realize just how little they actually knew about one another's traditions. Second, it would amount to a common spiritual witness in an increasingly materialistic world. Finally, it would serve as a major step for the church in realizing what the council had asked of it: to serve as "a universal sacrament of salvation" and "as a sign and instrument of the intimate unity with God and with the whole human race."[235] On similar grounds, the president of the Secretariat for Non-Christians, Francis Arinze of Nigeria, defended the "unprecedented" and "prophetic" step taken by the pope in calling for the Assisi meeting. Citing the pope's own words, conciliar texts, Gandhi, and Buddhist scriptures, Arinze pointed out that major religious traditions shared a "common concern" for promoting justice and peace.[236]

Planning involved four major parts of the Roman Curia—the Secretariat of State and the pontifical councils for Christian unity, for relations with non-Christians, and for peace and justice—in addition to local diocesan authorities. Planners met at the Palazzo San Calisto in Rome a year beforehand to hammer out the details.[237] Two Catholic renewal groups, the Sant'Egidio and the Focolare movements, also took on considerable responsibility for making arrangements and providing hospitality to the guests, as did the Franciscan Order.[238] As planning was under way, sixty governments sent messages to the Vatican supporting the project. Guerrilla fighters and warring parties in eleven countries, at the pope's personal request, agreed to lay down weapons—at least for one day.[239]

And the day finally came. According to the planners' decision, the day was broken into three "moments." It began with a welcoming ceremony at the Portiuncula Chapel of the Basilica of Santa Maria degli Angeli, at which John Paul II greeted and thanked each participant personally. At the request of the Buddhist delegation, all participants had agreed to fast during the day. In a welcoming speech, the pope emphasized the centrality of prayer for their endeavor and stressed that peace had a necessary spiritual component: "The coming together of so many religious leaders to pray is in itself an invitation today to the world to become aware that there exists another dimension of peace and another way of promoting it which is not a result of negotiation, political compromises, or economic bargainings." He also sought, once again, to deflect criticism by emphasizing what the event was not: "The fact that we have come here does not imply any intention of seeking a religious consensus among ourselves . . . [n]or is it a concession to relativism in religious beliefs, because every human being must sincerely follow his or her upright conscience with the intention of seeking and obeying the truth."[240]

After the ceremony, the second moment arrived: those gathered dispersed to various preassigned locations—churches, palazzos, and public buildings—to pray with their co-religionists. The Christians headed to San Ruffino for an ecumenical worship service. Muslims went to the Convent of San Antonio for Franciscan tertiaries to perform their ritual prayer, or *salat*. Keenly aware of the unprecedented nature of the event, onlookers and journalists followed guests around, often focusing on the most exotic, such as John Pretty-On-Top from the Crow American Indian tribe in Montana, who wore an elaborately feathered headdress, or a Zoroastrian from India, who lit a ceremonial fire to accompany his prayers. Buddhist beat drums during devotions, Japanese representatives of Shinto played bamboo instruments, while Sikhs chanted in a smoke-filled room. For the most part, the day proceeded without a hitch. But not entirely. A scantily dressed animist from Africa took ill and was put to bed in a convent. More scandalously, Buddhists placed a statue of the Buddha on the altar at the Church of San Pietro, converting it into a Buddhist shrine—fueling charges of syncretism and even desecration of a holy site from some quarters. A journalist described the overall scene: "Orange-clad Buddhists with shaved heads, kimono-clad Shintos, black-robed patriarchs and bearded Sikhs turn[ed] . . .

the city's altars to the native saint into their own places of worship for a day in their ritual prayers for world peace."[241]

After several hours of prayer apart, members of each delegation gathered for the third movement in the piazza by the eight-hundred-year-old Basilica of St. Francis, which houses keepsakes from the saint's meeting with the sultan, as recounted in chapter 1. There, in a moving climax to the day's events, each group offered public prayers for peace. In a touching gesture, olive branches had been distributed beforehand and participants prayed in front of a frieze of the word *peace* in multiple languages. Most of the prayers followed a predictable script, with each supplicant emphasizing aspects of their tradition that enjoined peace, justice, cooperation.

John Paul II then addressed the crowd in a closing speech. In it, he was unabashedly Christian, on the one hand, expressing his "conviction, shared by all Christians, that in Jesus Christ, as Savior of all, true peace is to be found." On the other hand, he contended that all faiths shared "a common respect of and obedience to conscience, which teaches us all to seek the truth, to love and serve all individuals and people, and therefore to make peace among nations." He apologized that Catholics had "not always been faithful" to their pacific principles before underscoring the novelty (at least with respect to the papal aegis of the event) of their joint undertaking: "For the first time in history, we have come together from everywhere, Christian Churches and Ecclesial Communities, and World Religions, in this sacred place dedicated to Saint Francis, to witness before the world, each according to his own conviction, about the transcendent quality of peace. The form and content of our prayers are very different, as we have seen, and there can be no question of reducing them to a kind of common denominator. [Yet] in this very difference we have perhaps discovered anew that, regarding the problem of peace and its relations to religious commitment, there is something which binds us together." Finally, he idealistically suggested that the prayers offered would "release energies for a new language of peace, for new gestures of peace, gestures which will shatter the fatal chains inherited from history or spawned by modern ideologies."[242]

The day concluded with a simple meal in the refectory at the monastery adjacent to the basilica. William F. Murphy, a planner and participant, movingly described the scene: "We broke the fast and adjourned to the refectory . . . for a simple buffet. Byzantine bishops, the Dalai Lama, . . . Jains, Muslims, Christians, Jews, Zoroastrians—all mingled together to share this meal with John Paul II."[243] Too busy greeting people, the pope hardly had a chance to eat.

The "spirit of Assisi" left a lingering aftertaste in the mouth of the church. Many savored it, but some attempted to spit it out. Among the latter were those who sympathized—if in different degrees—with the criticisms of Assisi made by the (schismatic) Archbishop Marcel Lefebvre of France. During the buildup to Assisi and afterward, Lefebvre condemned the church's course as "apostasy," an unwarranted, syncretistic mingling with other faiths, a relativizing of the Gospel's singularity: "The Congress of Assisi consummates the rupture of the Roman authorities with the Catholic Church" that in his eyes had begun with the Second Vatican Council.[244] Few critics made such a sweeping indictment. Still, John Paul II knew that he needed to respond to more moderate critics, who included Cardinal Joseph Ratzinger, prefect of the Congregation of the Doctrine of the Faith, the highest curial position in doctrinal matters, and the future Pope Benedict XVI.[245] He also knew that he should respond to liberal theologians who felt that Assisi had effectively moved the church away from the inclusivist vision of Vatican II to one of pluralism and hence to "relativism," in the pope's understanding. The pope pursued a twofold strategy.

First, in the months following Assisi, he gave numerous addresses attempting to controvert what he believed were erroneous interpretations of the meeting. None were more significant than a talk given to the Curia on 22 December 1986. While he recognized that Assisi was "somewhat novel," done "in a manner hitherto unknown," it was nonetheless theologically permissible, a legitimate expression of Vatican II and in keeping with the deeper traditions of the church. It should, therefore, be interpreted "without the least shadow of confusion or syncretism." Or, more fully: "The day of prayer at Assisi, showing the Catholic Church holding the hands of brother Christians, and showing us all joining hands with the brothers of other religions, was a visible expression of the Second Vatican Council. With this day, and by means of it, we have succeeded, by the grace of God, in realizing this conviction of ours, inculcated by the Council, about the unity of the origin and goal of the human family, and about the meaning and the value of non-Christian religions." He insisted further that the meeting did not compromise the church's age-old message about the unique salvific mediation of Christ. It did, however, in an audacious manner, bear witness to the church acting as a sacrament for all of humanity, not just a select subset. This the council clearly taught, he argued, referring to *Lumen gentium*'s lines that the church serves "as a sacrament, . . . a sign and instrument of the intimate union with God and of the unity of the human race."[246] Finally, he doubled down on *Nostra aetate*'s message that other faiths possess "rays" of truth from which others can learn, and that Christians and non-Christians share in common "the great questions of the human heart."[247]

Second, the pope authorized the Congregation of the Doctrine of the Faith to work on a document restating the soteriological significance of Christ—and the singularity of Christ's bride, the Catholic Church—for a postconciliar, post-Assisi world. The congregation worked on this document in the 1990s; it was published, with the pope's blessing, in 2000 under the title *Dominus Iesus*. "In contemporary theological reflection," the document reads, "there often emerges an approach to Jesus of Nazareth that considers him a particular, finite, historical figure, who reveals the divine not in an exclusivist way, but in a way complementary with other revelatory and salvific figures." Furthermore: "to justify the universality of Christian salvation as well as the fact of religious pluralism, it has been proposed that there is an economy of the eternal Word that is valid outside the Church and is unrelated to her, in addition to an economy of the incarnate Word." Both points of view, the document thunders, "are in profound conflict with the Christian faith." From this point, *Dominus Iesus* proceeds to defend the "unicity and universality of the salvific mystery of Jesus Christ" and the "unicity and unity of the Church."[248]

While many theologians and onlookers from other traditions were disappointed with *Dominus Iesus*, believing that it was out of step with prior, more generous Catholic teachings on interfaith activity, John Paul II defended it as a laudable effort to keep together the conciliar directive of interreligious dialogue and the church's age-old task of evangelization. "Dialogue certainly does not replace, but rather accompanies *missio ad gentes,*" as *Dominus Iesus* puts it.[249]

To say the least, the postconciliar tension between dialogue and mission was then and remains now a thorny issue.[250] And finally, *Dominus Iesus,* seen in light of what occasioned it and ex post facto interpretations of it, bears witness, once again, to the persistent irony of interfaith engagement precipitating Christian internecine rifts.

Assisi proved to be no one-off event. It has become a minor tradition in contemporary Roman Catholicism—and it has inspired similar events elsewhere, such as a day of prayer "in the spirit of Assisi" first held in 1987 on Mount Hiei, home of Japan's first Tendai Buddhist temple, and now a tradition.[251]

What is more, even while the Congregation of the Doctrine of the Faith worked on *Dominus Iesus,* John Paul II's papacy witnessed additional gatherings at Assisi. As mentioned, in 1993, Jews, Christians, and Muslims met in Assisi to pray for peace, especially in Bosnia. In 1999 the Pontifical Council for Interreligious Dialogue held a three-day conference in Rome involving 230 representatives of twenty different traditions. Those gathered assessed past efforts of dialogue and sought new ways of conversation and cooperation, producing a "joint declaration," a hallmark of many interfaith gatherings.[252] Since 1986, the Sant'Egidio community has held an annual interfaith event and promoted interfaith engagement more generally, frequently appealing to the "spirit of Assisi."[253] In 2002—after 9/11, after *Dominus Iesus,* and after the pope had visited the Western Wall in Jerusalem and the Great Mosque of Damascus—another major gathering was held in Assisi, involving more than two hundred religious leaders. This event culminated with some Franciscan brothers bringing a lighted lamp to the pope, after which ten representatives of different faiths read parts of their jointly produced text on a commitment to peace. This included a rejection of terrorism and a pledge to advocate for the poor and promote intercultural friendship. A papal spokesman, Joaquin Navarro-Valls, made clear, however, that "this is not an act of interreligious prayer. Thus there is no danger of religious indifferentism or syncretism."[254] Significantly, Cardinal Ratzinger was present at this event, even if by this point he had been on record as saying that the 1986 gathering "cannot be the model" for such events.[255]

After Cardinal Ratzinger became Pope Benedict XVI in 2005, he surprised many by continuing the Assisi gathering at its twenty-fifth anniversary, but he effected an important tweak. In 2011 religious leaders met in Assisi, at his request, but among them another voice appeared: that of a secular humanist, the Bulgarian-French philosopher Julia Kristeva. The pope desired to bring Kristeva's secular humanism into dialogue with the church's Christocentric humanism and with the religious humanism(s) of other traditions. In his address, the pope reflected on changes in the world since 1986. Praising the collapse of Communism, he nonetheless indicated that all was not well in the world. On one hand, love of Mammon and power had rendered modern society often rudderless with respect to faith and morals. But on the other, religion itself—or false religion, in his view—had given birth to violence and terrorism. "The Post-Enlightenment critique of religion has repeatedly maintained that religion is a cause of violence and in this way it has fueled hostility toward religions. The fact that, in the case we are considering here [terrorism], religion really does motivate violence should be profoundly disturbing to us as religious persons." While he claimed that acts of violence could never reflect true religion, he recognized the validity of some difficult questions for religious people: "How do you know what the true nature of religion is? Does your assertion not derive from the fact [that] your religion has become a spent force? . . . [and] is there [even] such a thing as a common nature of religion that finds expression in all religions and is therefore applicable to them all?" "We must ask ourselves these questions," he implored, "if we wish to argue realistically and credibly against religiously motivated violence. Herein lies the fundamental task for interreligious dialogue—an exercise which is to receive new emphasis through this meeting."[256] Permit me to note, however, that while the pope raised many important questions, he largely left uncriticized the general Western view of religion—as a genus with global species and as something readily isolatable from other domains of human experience—that had informed previous gatherings. Nonetheless, by inviting Kristeva to the event, he provocatively widened the definition of what might be considered a "religion" and lengthened the list of those who might be asked to participate.

Pope Francis, who canonized both John XXIII and John Paul II (with the retired Pope Benedict at his side), continued the Assisi tradition in 2016 at the thirtieth anniversary of the first event. "Continuing the journey which began thirty years ago, men and women of various religions," he exclaimed to the crowd, "we gather [again] as pilgrims in the city of Saint Francis."[257]

Conclusion

> Religion is a vast and often bewildering field.
>
> —*A Guide to Interreligious Dialogue* (booklet of the American Jewish Committee, 1966)

> A compound being . . . made up of heterogeneous parts.
>
> —SAMUEL PUFENDORF on the Holy Roman Empire

THE CATHOLIC CHURCH'S PIVOT to interreligious dialogue at the Second Vatican Council can be seen as both symbol and catalyst for a broad range of similar developments. *Nostra aetate*, Katherine Marshall has written, seemed to "set in motion a chain reaction whereby religious communities developed and institutionalized approaches to the religious 'other' that have had profound structural impacts on the development of interfaith work and institutions."[1] Since the council, the word *dialogue* has acquired an almost talismanic property in various religious circles and beyond.

In recent decades, the global contemporary interfaith scene might be likened to the former Holy Roman Empire: a vast, decentralized, polymorphic patchwork of large organizations, religious and political actors, NGOs, smaller academic "fiefdoms," and individual efforts—all jockeying for achievement and recognition in a world lamentably rent by ideological, ethnic, and religious conflicts at a time when the academy is abuzz about the "post-secular" tenor of our age.[2] Not without justification, some scholars speak of a global "interfaith movement" currently afoot.[3] This might well be the case, but if so, the movement is marked by highly scattered development and diffusive energies. Achingly idealistic and well intentioned in its aims, it is also a movement confronted by fundamental challenges and potent criticisms. Permit me, in conclusion, to sketch aspects of the contemporary scene before calling attention to several criticisms as well as highlighting various promising ideas and initiatives.[4]

The Contemporary Scene

Vatican II truly marks a watershed, a cultural tipping point that since has witnessed a torrent of interreligious endeavors.[5] Since its official inception in 1948 and especially in the 1960s, the World Council of Churches (WCC), too, had wrestled with how to engage members of other religious traditions.[6] In 1970 at Ajaltoun, Lebanon, the WCC held a major Consultation between Men of Living Faiths, involving Hindus, Buddhists, Christians, and Muslims.[7] The following year, it formally established a "sub-unit," Dialogue with People of Living Faiths and Ideologies. Its task was to "promote dialogue with people of living faiths and ideologies, to encourage theological reflection on the issues that arise, and to help churches to discuss the implications of dialogue for their life and for understanding communication of the Gospel in different situations." Since the 1970s, this body, frequently partnering with others, has fostered numerous bilateral and multilateral interreligious conversations and other activities in a wide range of geographical locations.[8] A landmark moment arrived in 1979 when the WCC adopted "Guidelines on Dialogue with People of Living Faiths and Ideologies," at once promoting and directing greater interfaith involvement while attempting to assuage critics.[9] Since this time, numerous national, regional, or local church bodies have followed suit, setting up offices dedicated to interfaith (often combined with ecumenical) engagement.

Both the Catholic Church and the World Council of Churches—and smaller Christian ecclesial bodies—have continued to struggle with balancing the aims of mission and dialogue. This dilemma—how to be faithful to the missionary impetus of the Christian Gospel while engaging and theologizing about non-Christian faiths—has exhausted much ink in the postconciliar era. Despite the tiredness of the terms, scholars and practitioners of dialogue still roughly fall into the three theological camps of pluralism, exclusivism, and inclusivism. And although this certainly simplifies matters too neatly, it generally holds true that "mainline" or liberal Protestants have gravitated toward theological pluralism, evangelical and Pentecostal Christians toward exclusivism (even if greater openness to dialogue, as I suggest below), and Catholics toward the inclusivist vision—and variations thereof—articulated at the council.[10] The words of "Dialogue in Truth and Charity," a statement from the Pontifical Council for Interreligious Dialogue in 2014, would now seem to apply to all Christians: "Considering the recent proliferation of interreligious initiatives, discernment is necessary."[11] The specific goals of discernment, of course, will vary based on one's theological commitments and, crucially, on the specific historical and geographical context of interreligious interactions.

Since the 1960s, not just Christian bodies but those of other faith traditions have begun—some enthusiastically, others more tepidly—to experiment with interreligious dialogue. In the late 1960s, for example, the International Jewish Committee on Inter-religious Consultations, building on several prior Jewish-Christian joint efforts, was formed to engage the new climate of dialogue.[12] In 1966, the American Jewish Committee released a booklet, *A Guide to Interreligious Dialogue*, extolling dialogue as the "fastest-growing development" in religious life and offering practical advice for going about it.[13] "The time has come," Abraham Joshua Heschel pled to his co-religionists in 1967, to recognize the "ecumenical revolution" taking place and join other faiths "in an honest search for mutual understanding and for ways to lead us out of the moral and spiritual predicament affecting all humanity."[14] Not all Jews have followed Heschel, and Judaism has witnessed the same irony that has affected Christians: dialogue itself precipitating internecine feuds. Still, the level of Jewish involvement in interfaith activity today bears witness to a novum in modern Jewish history.

The World Muslim Congress (1949), the World Muslim League

Cover of A Guide to Interreligious Dialogue, *a publication of the American Jewish Committee, 1966. (Image courtesy of the American Catholic History Research Center and University Archives. The Catholic University of America, Washington, DC.)*

(1962), and the World Islamic Call Society (1972)—as well as famous centers of learning such as Al-Azhar in Cairo—have participated in and hosted interfaith gatherings.[15] The latter has had since the 1990s a Standing Committee for Dialogue with Monotheistic Religions, the title of which suggests that dialogue has come more readily with those faiths that have Qur'anic recognition as "people of the book."[16] Summarizing Muslim engagement with interfaith activity in the postconciliar period, Turan Kayaoglu notes that at first Muslims "responded with caution to Christian overtures for interfaith dialogue. When they participated, they were guests—but rarely hosts." Yet this has changed in recent decades, especially due to global concerns about Islamist extremism, as Muslim leaders have sought to show that terrorism is not the true face of Islam.[17] A landmark moment came in 2007 when 138 Muslim scholars from most major strands of Qur'anic interpretation endorsed "Common Word," a joint statement tethering Islam firmly to peace building, calling for interfaith dialogue and improved Christian-Muslim relations.[18] A new readiness among Muslims for dialogue was on stark display when Pope Francis made a historic visit to the United Arab Emirates in 2019.[19]

Numerous Hindu, Buddhist, and other religious organizations and individuals have enthusiastically embraced interfaith dialogue. In recent decades, India and Japan in particular have witnessed many conferences and events.[20] The combined legacies of Swami Vivekananda and Gandhi have served as powerful interfaith rallying points on the Asian subcontinent and beyond. Delhi alone boasts dozens of interfaith organizations.[21] The Dalai Lama has been a globe-trotting champion for the cause. The International Shinto Foundation, an outfit with many global involvements, has brought Japan's ancient spiritual tradition into dialogue with other traditions.[22] And, as we have already glimpsed, modern movements, whether in the East or West—for example, spiritual descendants of the Brahmo Samaj, Baha'is, Unitarians, Theosophists, and more—have been quite active in participating in and hosting interreligious events, both before and especially since the 1960s.

Alongside religious bodies, a wide range of governmental, academic, and grassroots organizations now contribute to the global institutional architecture of interreligious dialogue. Here is not the place for an exhaustive list, and some of these organizations have been mentioned previously, but a selective panorama of the late twentieth-century scene would include the International Council of Christians and Jews (1946), Temple of Understanding (1960), Religions for Peace (1970), the Interfaith Network of the United Kingdom (1987), the North American Interfaith Network (1988), Abraham Initiatives (1989), Harvard University's Pluralism Project (1991), Oxford's International Interfaith Centre (1993), the Interfaith Alliance (1994), Jordan's Royal Institute for Inter-faith Studies (1994), Alliance of Religions and Conservation (1995), the Global Ethic Foundation (1995), Interfaith Worker Justice (1996), Jerusalem's Elijah Interfaith Institute (1997), World Faiths Development Dialogue (1998), the Interfaith Youth Core (1999), the Rumi Forum for Interfaith Dialogue and Intercultural Understanding (1999), the Global Network of Religions for Children (2000), and the United Religions Initiative (UNI) (2000). The last, spearheaded by the American Episcopal bishop William E. Swing (b. 1936), has been especially active in recent years. Maintaining hundreds of "Cooperation Circles" around the world in over eighty countries, the UNI seeks to "end religiously motivated violence and create cultures of peace."[23] The literature that these and other organizations have generated on interfaith work is voluminous and includes periodicals such as the *Journal of Interreligious Studies*, *Current Dialogue*, *Interreligious Insight*, *Journal of Ecumenical Studies*, *Dialogue and Alliance*, *Interreligious Studies and Intercultural Theology*, and *Interfaith Observer*, among many others.[24]

Recently, the United Nations stepped up its involvement in the interfaith world. In September 2010, King Abdullah II of Jordan proposed to the UN an annual observance of a week dedicated to interfaith cooperation. Just under a month later, on 20 October 2010, this proposal was unanimously adopted by the UN and henceforth the first week of February, every year, has been observed as World Interfaith Harmony Week. Earlier, in 2000, the UN hosted its first-ever major summit of the world's religious leaders. And with bitter irony, given the events of 9/11, the UN had designated 2001 as the International Year of Dialogue among Civilizations.[25]

The events of 9/11 themselves triggered a fresh proliferation of interfaith activities and institution building.[26] Organizations sprouted up, such as Israel's Interfaith Encounter Association (2001), Taiwan's

Museum of World Religions (2002), the European Council of Religious Leaders (2002), the World Council for Religious Leaders (2002), the Malaysian Interfaith Network (2003), Interfaith Foundation India (2005), the Interfaith Center for Sustainable Development (2010), the King Abdullah bin Abdulaziz International Centre for Interreligious and Intercultural Dialogue (2012), and Senegal's Group of Religious Leaders for Health and Development (2014), among many others.[27] Beginning with a 2005 meeting in London, religious leaders have frequently met for summits in advance of G7, G8, and G20 meetings. They have also convened in conjunction with meetings of the World Bank and the World Economic Forum.[28]

In addition to larger national and international organizations, thousands of smaller regional, city, or local ones have sprung up, such as the Interfaith Centre of Melbourne, Australia (2000); Hawaii's Interfaith Alliance (2003); Indianapolis's Center for Interfaith Cooperation (2011), which helps "Hoosiers of Many Faiths in Community"; and Berlin's new House of One (2020). Furthermore, countless civic and university-based "centers," "institutes," "councils," "projects," "initiatives," "forums," "groups," and "alliances" have been called into existence to promote interfaith engagement in some form or fashion. College chaplaincy programs, in particular, have emerged as sites of innovative approaches to interfaith engagement.[29] Holding interfaith vigils after tragic acts of violence has become ritualistic in many pluralistic countries.[30] Furthermore, numerous formal dialogues and trialogues and other conferences promoting interfaith discussion, joint activity, and scholarship have taken place.[31] And this is to say nothing of all the "agreements," "joint declarations," "statements," "condemnations of violence," and the like issued by interfaith organizations. A simple Web search will dredge up thousands of such items.

Since 2014, the American Academy of Religion has recognized the Interreligious and Interfaith Studies Unit, and many are speaking of "interfaith studies" as an emerging academic field. "Scholars from a range of fields," writes sociologist and interfaith activist Eboo Patel, "have long taken an interest in how people who orient around religion differently interact with one another. . . . As the activity in this area increases, one crucial role for the academy is to give some definition to what is clearly an emerging field of research, study, and practice."[32] Interfaith concerns and realities also notably figure in the recently established European Academy of Religion (2016).

In recent years, philanthropic foundations—such as the Arthur Vining Davis Foundation, the Teagle Foundation, the Henry Luce Foundation, the Ford Foundation, the Osprey Foundation, the Andrew W. Mellon Foundation, the Lilly Endowment, and the Alavi Foundation—have gotten into the act as well, funding grants under initiatives with titles such as Interfaith Leadership and Religious Literacy or Interfaith Dialogue and Religious Pluralism.[33] "An acute question of our times," as one representative of the Teagle Foundation writes, "is whether religious diversity will be [a] cause for tension and strife or [an] opportunity for human flourishing."[34] "Interfaith philanthropy"—money spent from one religious community to help another—is increasingly practiced, according to the investor and philanthropist Evelyn Davis.[35]

Of particular contemporary interest: in preparation to mark the 1993 centenary of the 1893 World's Parliament of Religions, the Council for a Parliament of the World's Religions was established and incorporated in the late 1980s. Emerging from Chicago's Vedanta Center (a legacy of Swami Vivekananda), it gained traction in informal meetings among Chicago's Hindu, Buddhist, Baha'i, and Muslim communities and was supported by the Council of Religious Leaders of Greater Chicago, another interfaith group. Motivated to revive the memories and meaning of the 1893 meeting, the council planned a high-profile commemorative gathering in Chicago.[36] In significant measure, its planners succeeded. Around eight thousand people registered, even if slightly fewer than this attended. Chicago's mayor Richard Daley served as honorary chairman. Distinguished guests included the Dalai Lama, the Swiss-German theologian Hans Küng, and Chicago's archbishop, Cardinal Joseph Bernardin.[37] The 1993 event was much more pluralistic in orientation than the one in 1893. This added drama to the event. Three Jewish groups withdrew, objecting to participation by the Nation of Islam. A contingent of Eastern Orthodox leaders pulled out as well, refusing to participate with "Wiccans" and "Neo-Pagans," whom they regarded more as "cults" than religions.[38] Nonetheless, the parliament left a vivid impression on those who attended and in the worldwide media coverage that it received.[39] It prominently featured a call for a "global ethic," the brainchild of Hans Küng; this "Declaration towards a Global Ethic," which outlined how faith communities could contribute to global peace, was circulated and signed by numerous participants. Since 1993, the council has hosted parliaments in Cape Town (1999), Barcelona (2004), Melbourne (2009), Salt Lake City (2015), and Toronto (2018), featuring guests such as Nelson Mandela, Jimmy Carter, and Al Gore. These meetings have become, in the words of one observer, "a capstone event for the global interfaith movement."[40] The parliament defines its mission as "cultivat[ing] harmony among the world's religious and spiritual communities and foster[ing] their engagement with the world and its guiding institutions in order to achieve a just, peaceful and sustainable world."[41] As the word *sustainable* suggests, environmental issues have recently become a major priority for many interfaith groups.[42]

The resurrected parliament—yet another "big player" in the "empire" of comparable organizations and initiatives—suggests that Akbar's dream is alive and well in the twenty-first century. Taken as a whole, this complex, fluid, growing, and increasingly global reality bears witness to an extraordinary, if still inchoate, era in modern intellectual and religious history. Abraham Joshua Heschel's line that "no religion is an island" appears truer than ever as the middle decades of the twenty-first century approach.

But Does Interreligious Dialogue Work?

Given the complexity, dynamism, and polymorphic nature of this new reality, assessing it poses acute challenges, in part because generalizations about one sector of the "empire" might not hold true, or hold only partially true, of another. The rationales behind and approaches to interreligious conversation and engagement run a wide gamut. And this is to say nothing about the complex geographical, political, and socio-historical realities that impinge upon particular contemporary interfaith initiatives and activities. Nonetheless, permit me to conclude this book by offering a few general remarks and itemizing several recurrent criticisms directed toward interreligious dialogue before turning to some eye-catching and hopeful developments.

First, the ascendancy of the very concept of "interfaith" initiatives does suggest if not an absolute historical novum at least a relative one—what Wilfred Cantwell Smith once hailed as humankind's religiously divided history becoming "self-conscious." Writing presciently in 1964, Smith argued, "Mankind all over the globe . . . is today in a process of entering a significant new phase in the religious history of the world," one in which "religious isolationism is coming to an end." The tempo of the emergence of interreligious realities and their breadth of scope suggest that Smith's words ring even truer now than they did in the 1960s. "Throughout the world, each of the major religious communities of mankind is beginning to be conscious of itself as within a context . . . of the others."[43] Again, what Smith grasped in 1964 has come of age—or at least is rapidly coming of age—in the early decades of the twenty-first century, hastened by revolutions in transportation and communication technologies. Interreligious dialogue, of course, is not the main cause of this reality, but it is a crucial aspect of the larger causal nexus, even if it is simultaneously a sign and symbol of the exigencies of other causes. At the same time, we should be wary about such phrases as "Copernican Revolution" (John Hick), which suggest that we have little or nothing to learn from earlier "Ptolemaic" ages, for in fact we do, as I argued in chapter 1. To recall one figure: the fifteenth-century thinker Nicholas of Cusa, I would submit, remains an insightful interlocutor for contemporary theorists and practitioners of interfaith activity.[44]

Second, despite its increasingly global scope, the interfaith movement continues to bear witness to its distinctively Western origins. As we have seen, much interfaith activity has rested on a view of religion as a "genus" and as a cultural variable readily distinguishable from other cultural variables, whether they be social, ethnic, linguistic, or political. But to regard, say, Confucianism or Hinduism as discrete, easily definable "religions" of course raises enormous questions about categorization and the transferability of a Western discourse about religion into non-Western discursive domains, as I (with many others) have argued. To be sure, theorists and practitioners of interreligious dialogue have in recent decades become more sensitive to this problem. And this is a healthy thing. But this recognition in turn has produced a crisis of terminology. Should one prefer *interfaith* over *interreligious*, or vice versa or, as some have argued, should one return to the original meaning of *ecumenical* (worldwide or global) and not confine that term to intra-Christian discussion? Others have lobbied for terms such *interideological*, *intercivilizational*, *intercultural*, *multifaith*, *interworldview*, *interspiritual*, and *multireligious*, among others. Often at stake in the wrangling over terminology is, again, the problem of the applicability and the transferability of Western terms of art—which themselves are highly dependent on a Lockean reconceptualization of religion in the post-Westphalian West—to much wider historical and geographical terrains.

The theologian John Milbank has written provocatively on this matter. In his essay "The End of Dialogue," he notes that although the "assumption" of understanding religion as a genus "certainly undergirds" contemporary interreligious dialogue, "it would be a mistake to imagine that it arose simultaneously among all the [global] participants as the recognition of an evident truth." On the contrary, he continues, "it is clear that the other religions were taken by Christian thinkers to be a species of the genus 'religion,' because these thinkers systematically subsumed alien cultural phenomena under categories which comprise Western notions of what constitutes religious thought and practice." These "false categorizations," Milbank concludes, "have often been accepted by Western-educated representatives of the other religions themselves, who are unable to resist the politically imbued rhetorical forces of Western discourse."[45] If this is true, or even partly true, then significantly more rigorous inquiries need to made into the intellectual and terminological assumptions that have given birth to and still inform present-day interfaith dialogue and activity.[46]

And this brings up, third, the difficult dilemma of who can credibly and knowledgeably speak on behalf of a particular faith tradition. This has long been acknowledged as an Achilles heel of interreligious dialogue despite good-faith efforts to bring to the dialogue table "native expositors," as they were called at the 1924 Conference on Some Living Religions within the Empire in London. To be sure, in some cases, one might readily identify leaders—say, bishops in Roman Catholicism—who can plausibly speak on behalf of a particular tradition. But for other traditions—say, Taoism or Shinto or

Hinduism—it is not exactly clear how one designates an authoritative speaker who can credibly represent others in the same tradition. In the West and even globally today, the same thing is true of Protestantism. What telephone number do you call to get the front desk of Protestantism? I often ask my students, the suggestion being that no such number can exist for such a vast, fissiparous, and internally divided religious phenomenon. The scholar of religion Kusumita P. Pedersen refers to this dilemma as the "Representativity Problem." Most faiths are "polycentric rather than centralized," she observes, and "it is no simple matter to determine how and when a representative may be 'officially' mandated by his or her community to take part in an interfaith activity on behalf of that institution or community."[47] One might further add: who speaks for plural religious identities given, for example, the way Confucian, Taoist, and Buddhist sensibilities have often merged in individuals and communities in South Asia?[48] Finally, it should be noted, as Peggy Morgan observes, that for "many religious communities interfaith activity is not a central concern and those who are involved may well be on the boundaries of their tradition."[49] A conversation with a theologically progressive Episcopalian in Boston, keen to embrace dialogue, might give one a radically different picture of Christianity than a conversation with a more theologically conservative Ugandan Anglican, who is wary of dialogue, even if the latter might represent the demographic future of global Anglicanism better than the former.

Fourth, dialogue has often fallen prey to elitism. Following in the mold of the 1893 parliament, organizers of many subsequent events have placed a premium on elites, especially academic experts, at the expense of seeking out the perspectives of on-the-ground practitioners. Although I readily recognize, following the Catholic Church's Council of Interreligious Dialogue, that "particular interest" inheres in meetings among experts and specialists because they possess more in-depth knowledge of a tradition, the Indian scholar Muthuraj Swamy nonetheless has a point in his nicely argued book, *The Problem with Interreligious Dialogue*, when he contends that the elite-academic character of much interreligious dialogue obscures how "religion" (a word he uses only hesitantly) is experienced at a more grassroots level. Swamy is particularly incisive in showing how a reified dialogist's understanding of "Hinduism" has played into the hands of Hindu nationalists in India, undermining in the process long-standing indigenous, local patterns of interreligious cooperation and coexistence and the not-infrequent plural religious identities among lower-caste Indians.[50] Women, it is often noted in this context, have been marginal in many major interfaith gatherings, becoming more prominent only in recent years.[51]

Fifth, now that the exhilarating novelty of earlier meetings has worn off, many interfaith events have become predictably anodyne affairs, trafficking in bland bromides about the importance of peace and coexistence and having little actual impact. Yes, religions should come together to foster peace. But how long must one listen to speaker after speaker issuing, in the words of Pedersen, the same "vacuous, nonspecific, and nonbinding statements declaring in general terms that peace is good"?[52] In his memoir *Acts of Faith*, Eboo Patel offers a humorous anecdote from his own experience at one of these parliament-style meetings. "The problem with going to these [interreligious] events," he wrote,

> was that they were excruciatingly boring. They were always dinners or conferences with a lot of old people doing a lot of talking. The big goal seemed to be drafting documents declaring that religious people should be dialoguing with each other and then planning the next conference for the document to be reviewed. It was always the same people saying the same things, and still the events went way too long. I remember one especially torturous interfaith dinner. . . . By the time the ninth speaker of the evening took the podium, the audience was long past being discreet about looking at their watches and had begun to shift noisily in their seats. The evening had proceeded like most interfaith activities: a couple of hundred people . . . picking at plates of dry hotel food and listening to a long list of speakers repeating the same reasons interfaith activities are important.[53]

To his credit, Patel has launched his own organization—the Chicago-based Interfaith Youth Core—that seeks to bring younger, nonelite peoples (particularly students) of various religious backgrounds (and none) together to strengthen civil society, engage in service, and promote causes of well-being in their shared communities—an approach to interreligious interactions sometimes tagged "diapraxis." Perhaps more interfaith work should be carried out in this mold? But Patel's words underscore a biting criticism: precisely how relevant are some interfaith events to the world's religious realities?

Sixth, and related, many dialogues have eschewed candidly discussing religious differences and settled for what the former archbishop of Canterbury Rowan Williams has called conversations of "colorless compromise," which eventuate in "superficial joint declarations."[54] In many respects, this desire for irenicism is an understandable and laudable goal, motivated by a desire to avoid the vitriolic polemics of the past. Fair enough. But perhaps an overcorrection has now occurred. In a desire to arrive at tranquility, peace, not truth, too often has become the overbearing goal of dialogue, and the (often unspoken) rules of dialogue work to reinforce this. But perhaps the time is ripe to retrieve an older Platonic sense of dialogue, in which mutual truth seeking is the primary concern. If the interlocutors in Plato's dialogue settled for tranquility, the dialogues might wrap up quite quickly and be boring affairs: the "eros" of truth seeking sedated by the headlong rush to pacification.[55] As the Catholic theologian Avery Dulles once observed, "If methodological rules [of interreligious dialogue] are laid down that require the parties to renounce or conceal points on which they disagree, dialogue can become inhibitive and impoverishing. The fault lies not with dialogue itself but with the theorists who seek to evade its rigorous demands."[56] Perhaps the next stage of interreligious dialogue should be a willingness to reopen questions of religious truth, as confoundingly difficult as this may seem, rather than bypass it or solve it too quickly or too glibly. At the very least, boosters of dialogue should admit the downsides of producing "statements so diluted and broad that they become functionally meaningless."[57]

Seventh, much contemporary interfaith dialogue continues to rest on the questionable assumption that conflicts among the "world religions" constitute a major impediment to world peace. To quote again Hans Küng's well-known global-ethic mantra: "There will be peace on earth when there is peace among the world religions. No world peace without peace among religions; no peace among religions without dialogue between religions." Of course, conflicts between large religious traditions—say, between Christianity and Islam—have been a source of violence in the past. But as I argued in the introduction, it is often hard to tease out religion as the principal variable, because religion is regularly so bound up with other ethnic, political, linguistic, geographical, and historical issues. As Swamy writes of the situation in India: "It is almost always overlooked that what is claimed as 'religious violence' usually stems from the socio-economic and personal struggles of people, and from the political intervention which plays with religious identities of people in order to boost vote-bank politics."[58] The fact that Muslims and Christians, moreover, might get along in Seattle or Toronto but not in Sarajevo or Cairo suggests that far more than religious difference is at work in putatively religious conflicts.

In recent decades, subtler, arguably more intractable conflicts have developed: those *within* a particular tradition between anti-modern traditionalists and pro-modern reformers. In many respects, we might be witnessing today the globalization of what the sociologist James Davison Hunter, in reference to American society in the 1990s, called a "culture war." In Hunter's analysis, the deepest disagreements in American society were no longer between Catholics, Protestants, and Jews, as had historically been the case, but between conservatives within these traditions (whom Hunter calls "the Orthodox") and their more latitudinarian co-religionists (whom he calls "the Progressives").[59] In other words, the key fault lines have less to do with religious divisions per se than they do with social and political ones interposed into a religious idiom. It is arguably more likely that, say, a Lutheran (of the more progressive Evangelical Lutheran Synod of America) would want to enter into dialogue with a Theravada Buddhist or Sufi mystic than he or she would with another Lutheran of the more conservative Missouri Synod. Something similar could be said, mutatis mutandis, about the Sunni-Shia divide within Islam (let alone, say, a Sunni-Ahmadiyya dialogue).[60] Often more exotic "religious others" hold an attraction and beckon one's sympathy in ways that more proximate (and hence more threatening) religious others do not, even if dialogue with the latter might be more feasible and ameliorative of the actual conflicts within a particular location or community. Furthermore, today our globalized culture wars possess a class dimension, as Hunter has since argued, updating his earlier thesis.[61] The wealthier and more educated tend to live in urban, cosmopolitan spaces where interfaith dialogue more readily makes sense and receives nourishment from a politically liberal environment, while the poorer and less educated often (of course not always) tend to live in more homogenous, often rural settings, where in recent decades religiously tinted, nostalgic nationalisms and other varieties of communalism have gained traction against what is perceived as the deracinating threat of globalization/cosmopolitanism. Understanding and managing these types of divisions—the cosmopolitan versus the non- or anti-cosmopolitan or the progressive versus the orthodox—might be more critical for peace in the future than addressing the divides wrought by traditional religious fault lines.[62] If this is the case, the older "world religions" taxonomy and model of dialogue might be faulted not only for being too Western but for being anachronistic.

Eighth, one of the more ironic results of interreligious dialogue has been, despite the rhetoric about peacemaking surrounding it, that it itself has often been the source of internecine divisions within particular faith communities falling roughly along "orthodox" and "progressive" lines. This is seen clearly in the cases of Christianity and Judaism, whereby progressive voices within these communities have strongly championed interreligious dialogue, whereas more conservative voices have worried that it leads down a slippery slope toward relativism or syncretism or worse—a reaction that we have seen several times in the pages of this book. Interfaith ventures often fail, as the sociologist Robert Wuthnow has noted, "because of opposition from other religious groups in the [same] religious community."[63] Today, the regnant ethos governing interreligious dialogue, especially in the academy, is that of pluralism—an ethos heartily embraced by progressives. But such an outlook leads to what Marion H. Larson and Sara L. H. Shady have called the often-unacknowledged "liberal privilege" within the interfaith movement. This is "particularly problematic" for more traditionalist voices, they argue, who not infrequently find that exclusivist faith positions, even if peaceably held and articulated, are summarily dismissed as "proselytizing" and ruled out of bounds.[64]

This dilemma is not likely to be solved any time soon, but allow me to make the humble suggestion that traditionalists might stop exaggerating fears about interreligious dialogue doing harm, whereas progressives should admit that there is something profoundly disingenuous about calling for dialogue while, intentionally or not, stacking the deck against more exclusivist, and even inclusivist, voices within particular traditions.[65] These voices, in fact, arguably constitute the vast majority of rank-and-file believers in many of the world's faith traditions and are ignored at great peril. Interfaith engagement that self-selects, that attracts only those most open to it in the first place, profoundly misconstrues the rhyme and reason for engagement in the first place. Or, as the Lutheran theologian Carl Braaten has bluntly put it: "Why should the dialogues invite only the modernized [pluralist] versions of religions whose representatives may be merely a minority of enlightened liberals with scarcely any religious constituency to speak of?"[66]

Finally, evaluating and measuring the impact of dialogue has been notoriously elusive. Many people agree that interfaith dialogue is generally a "good thing," but in a way that, say, not kicking little old ladies in the head is a good thing. But developing metrics and reliable data to measure success poses acute challenges. "The lack of clearly defined and tangible aims," John Fahy and Jan-Jonathan Bock have written, "renders [interfaith] initiatives difficult, if not impossible to evaluate."[67] Or, as Katherine Marshall notes, "Evaluation work has generally been rather limited and restricted to limited facets or specific events or measures. There is growing recognition that more rigorous metrics of assessment and, more importantly, clearer goals are needed." Otherwise, one winds up, as is often the case, with "general fuzziness" with respect to "tangible outcomes"—the mere "vapourings of amiable idealists," as one critic said of the 1936 World Congress of Faiths.[68]

One could adduce still other criticisms, but the foregoing should give a general sense of the more forceful objections and misgivings that interfaith dialogue has faced and still faces.

Hopeful Signposts

But highlighting these criticisms should not be mistaken for thoroughgoing skepticism about interfaith dialogue. Some criticisms might be warranted, but again, the sheer scale and diversity of interfaith activity today requires that all generalizations, whether negative or positive, be tempered with caution. And in fact, there is much to commend, as theorists and practitioners of interfaith work have often creatively addressed these criticisms and others, while also exploring altogether new terrain. Herewith some hopeful signposts.

The Scriptural Reasoning project, for instance, spearheaded by the Jewish theologian Peter Ochs and the Anglican theologians David Ford and Daniel Hardy (and nourished in part by the postliberal theology of George Lindbeck), brings adherents of different faith traditions—especially Jews, Christians, and Muslims—together to read and discuss in small groups one another's sacred texts. These efforts have worked against the least-common-denominator approach to dialogue adopted by many big-tent organizations. In fact, a premise of the mutual reading exercises is that the "core identities" of each participant be fully on display. Instead of downplaying differences, scriptural reasoning even invites participants to accentuate them in the process of exegesis—even while being in conversation with those who read one's own sacred texts through very different lenses. Respectful disagreement—even aiming for "better quality disagreement"—and preserving particular religious identities are prized more than seeking the shortest route to concord.[69] Today this approach has its own society (Scriptural Reasoning Society) and its own journal (*Journal of Scriptural Reasoning*).

Additionally, many interfaith organizations, tired of the often contextless "world religions" approach, have recognized the need to pay more attention to the geographical and historical particularities in which dialogue takes place. During work on this project, I had the opportunity to travel to the Balkans, for instance, to talk to people involved in the Sarajevo-based Interreligious Council of Bosnia and Herzegovina. Eschewing discussion of Christianity and Islam in the abstract, the council concentrates on helping religious communities understand and come to terms with the conflicts of the 1990s for the purpose of avoiding violence in the future. It is particularly noteworthy that the council sponsors visits of religious leaders to sites where violence has recently occurred. In the aftermath of vandalism at a mosque, for example, the council might dispatch a Catholic priest to pray for the affected Muslim community. The council, moreover, organizes educational experiences for young people (from diverse backgrounds) and monitors instances of violence throughout the country through a website where attacks can be registered.

Art and music are increasingly being recognized for their power to contribute to understanding across religious traditions. Ruth Illman's *Art and Belief: Artists Engaged in Interreligious Dialogue* (2012), for example, explores many contemporary instances of art being creatively employed to foster interfaith conversations and encounters. With respect to music, the annual Festival of Sacred Music in Fez, Morocco, is a choice example. Begun in 1994, it takes place over several days, bringing sacred music traditions from around the world together to promote "the creation of cultural peace" and "interfaith dialogue through music." A "spirit of Fez" organization has since been established in New York City that organizes and promotes similar events, attended by thousands of people, in various locations.[70] "Art," writes the artist Mary Anderson, "offers to interreligious dialogue a generous template for recognizing truth—in the religious other, in the other religion—that is born in the humble kenosis of self-disclosure."[71]

In recent decades, religious communities and traditions, such as North American evangelicalism and the Church of Jesus Christ of Latter-day Saints, that historically have been skeptical of or on the margins of interfaith dialogue, are becoming active, even conversing with one another. (Remember that Mormons were not invited to the Chicago parliament in 1893 and that evangelical revivalists such as Dwight L. Moody castigated the event.) A series of engagements have been hosted by Brigham Young University and at other sites, beginning in the 1990s, that have led to publications such as Craig L. Blomberg and Stephen E. Robinson's *How Wide the Divide? A Mormon and an Evangelical in Conversation* (1997) and Richard Mouw's *Talking with Mormons: An Invitation to Evangelicals* (2012). "No one has compromised or diluted his or her own theological convictions," writes Robert L. Millet about these meetings, "but everyone has sought to demonstrate the kind of civility that ought to characterize a mature exchange of ideas among a body of believers who have discarded defensiveness."[72] In 2010, the evangelical Fuller Theological Seminary in California launched a quarterly, *Evangelical Inter-*

faith Dialogue. These developments suggest that more traditionalist and exclusivist voices, too, have the desire and capacity to participate respectfully in meaningful and thoughtful dialogue.

The importance of involving young people in interfaith activity has become more widely recognized. Chicago's Interfaith Youth Core (IFYC) is a pioneer in inspiring young people with interfaith's ability to nurture civil society and healthy pluralism. Branches of the IFYC now exist on hundreds of American campuses. "Interfaith," according to the organization's website, "is a process in which people who orient around religion differently come together in ways that respect different identities, build mutually inspiring relationships, and engage in common action around issues of shared concern." "Interfaith cooperation does not depend upon shared political, theological, and spiritual perspectives," IFYC's founder Eboo Patel insists. "People who engage in interfaith cooperation may disagree on such matters. The goal of interfaith leadership is to find ways to bring people together to build relationships, learn about each other, and participate in common action despite such differences." A critic of parliament-style dialogue, as we have seen, Patel desires that members of various faith communities learn to work together to increase "social capital" and sustain the virtues and practices necessary for democratic self-government.[73] An approach such as this, the sociologist Robert Wuthnow has written, allows for participants "to focus on concrete, task-specific objections" instead of on "divisive theological issues." Interfaith work oriented toward common action, according to Wuthnow's research, has a greater chance of success.[74] The global COVID-19 crisis and the issues highlighted by the death of George Floyd have given interfaith organizations ample opportunities to engage in this type of activity.

In addition to common action, perhaps common contemplation has a role to play too. A particularly striking development in recent decades has been the coming together of monks, nuns, and other contemplatives from various religious traditions to converse with one another. This is the goal of Dialogue interreligieux monastique / Monastic Interreligious Dialogue (DIMMID), an international monastic organization that traces its roots to the late 1970s and that "promotes and supports dialogue, especially dialogue at the level of religious experience and practice, between Christian monastic men and women and followers of other religions." An expression of the Benedictine charism of hospitality, the organization is a commission of the Benedictine Order and acts in liaison with the Vatican's Pontifical Council for Interreligious Dialogue, welcoming "collaboration with other organizations that foster interreligious dialogue."[75] "What distinguishes the monastic approach to interreligious dialogue," writes the organization's present-day secretary-general William Skudlarek (OSB), "is an emphasis on hospitality and spiritual experience. Almost all events take place in monasteries, and the schedule is built around the liturgical horarium of the monastic community. In meetings with Buddhists, ample time is provided for common meditation. In meetings with Muslims, their times of prayer are also included in the schedule."[76]

Over and beyond interreligious studies itself as an area of study, interreligious dialogue has played a role in giving shape to another academic field: comparative theology. In contradistinction to dialogue proper and comparative religion (which strives for a more neutral approach to religious phenomena), comparative theology insists that the theologian work from the standpoint of a particular tradition, but develop his or her thoughts in close conversation with one or more other/s. As one of its leading theorists, Francis Clooney (SJ), defines it: comparative theology "marks acts of faith seeking understanding which are rooted in a particular faith tradition but which, from that foundation, venture into learning from one or more other faith traditions." "The learning is sought," he continues, "for the sake of fresh theological insights that are indebted to the newly encountered tradition/s as well as the home tradition."[77] While novel in some respects, such an approach has venerable precedents in figures such as Thomas Aquinas and Maimonides, both of whom drew insights from all three Abrahamic traditions but remained committed to their own.[78]

Furthermore, the plight of persecuted religious minorities—such as the Uighurs in China, the Rohingya in Myanmar, Yazidis in Iraq and Syria, and Christian groups worldwide—has been an especially salient rallying cry for interfaith engagement.[79] Of particular note is the so-called Marrakesh Statement of 2016, signed by over two thousand Muslim leaders, pleading for the rights of religious minorities in Muslim-majority countries. Among other things, it called for Muslim countries "to address . . . [the] selective amnesia that blocks memories of centuries of joint and shared living on the same land; we call upon them to rebuild the past by reviving this tradition of conviviality, and restoring our shared trust that has been eroded by extremists using acts of terror and aggression." It concludes by stating that it "is unconscionable to employ religion for the purpose of aggressing upon the rights of religious minorities in Muslim countries."[80] Other religious traditions stand to learn much from this bold statement.

Finally, interfaith activity today is taking place at a time when specialists in foreign policy and international relations, too often beholden in the past to mostly secular analyses of geopolitics, are newly taking stock of how religious actors and communities affect the maintenance of global peace. Douglas Johnston and Cynthia Sampson's *Religion, the Missing Dimension of State Craft* (1994) is one major work of the recent past that helped effect this shift in scholarly outlook, which now includes a reappraisal of the significance of interfaith work.[81] Along with others, this work, writes Katherine Marshall, has helped point out "blind spots in relation to religion in many diplomatic and international affairs circles. It also highlights a sharpening focus on interreligious and religious peacebuilding, both within individual [religious] traditions and as an interreligious endeavor."[82]

Despite the impact of the foregoing initiatives and development, and those of numerous others not profiled in this book, violence and warfare that enmesh religion in political, ethnic, and other factors have not been exorcized from our world. And there are admittedly many people simply not interested in interfaith activity—of whatever variety. Nonetheless, taken together, these and other interreligious initiatives do in fact suggest that a "movement" is afoot. While not without harbingers in earlier ages, the depth and breadth of interfaith activity today has no precedent in human history. In world-historical terms, it represents a new dimension of human religiosity. Akbar's Ibadat Khana, Chicago's parliament of 1893, the London conference of 1924, and Vatican II's *Nostra aetate* have contributed, each in its own way, to a sprawling, dynamic, heterogenous, and energetic legacy. The jury is still out on its efficacy—not to mention its purpose and its most appropriate format and structure. As a historian, I will leave it to others to pronounce more boldly on these matters. My humbler goal has been to examine the deep roots and several more recent turning points of this movement: where it has come from and where it might be going. The future of "interfaith" of course remains unknown, but perhaps a better grasp of its genealogy will contribute to the thoughtfulness necessary for the road ahead.

"Great responsibility now lies with the world's religious communities," Rabbi Jonathan Sacks has recently written. "Against expectations, they have emerged in the twenty-first century as key forces in a global age." But then, quoting Jonathan Swift, Sacks ruefully wonders if, too often, "we have just enough religion to make us hate one another, but not enough to make us love one another."[83] It is my hope that the ideas, energies, and forces that have given rise to and sustained interreligious dialogue might be wisely considered and prudently ordered in support of love, and that this book might make a modest contribution to this important task.

Abbreviations

Archives and Libraries

AAB Archives of the Archdiocese of Baltimore, Associated Archives of St. Mary's Seminary and University (Baltimore)
ACUA American Catholic History Research Center and University Archives (Washington, DC)
AJCA American Jewish Committee Archives (New York City)
ASV Archivio Segreto Vaticano (Rome)
BL British Library (London)
KUSCA Keele University, Special Collections and Archives (Staffordshire, UK)
LPL Lambeth Palace Library (London)
NA National Archives of Great Britain (London)
NL Newberry Library (Chicago)
RSCL Rauner Special Collections Library, Dartmouth University (Hanover, NH)
SOAS School of Oriental and African Studies Archives (London)
UCL University of Chicago Library (Chicago)
UNDA University of Notre Dame Archives (Notre Dame, IN)
USSC University of Southampton, Special Collections (Southampton, UK)
WCCA World Council of Churches Archives (Geneva)

Reference Works, Collected Works, and Other Books

AAS *Acta Apostolicae Sedis* (Vatican City: Typis Polyglottis Vaticanis, 1909–).
AS *Acta synodalia sacrosancti Concillii Vaticani II*, 32 vols. (Vatican City: Typis Polyglottis Vaticanis, 1970–99).

CDV Herbert Vorgrimler, ed., *Commentary on the Documents of Vatican II*, 5 vols., trans. William Glen-Doepel et al. (New York: Herder and Herder, 1966–68).

DRP Richard Hughes Seager, ed., *Dawn of Religious Pluralism: Voices from the World's Parliament of Religions, 1893* (La Salle, IL: Open Court, 1993).

EI P. Bearman et al., eds., *Encyclopedia of Islam*, 2 vols. (Leiden: Brill, 2005–6).

ER Mircea Eliade, ed., *Encyclopedia of Religion*, 16 vols. (New York: Macmillan, 1987).

ESDD Heinrich Denzinger, ed., *Enchiridion symbolorum definitionum et declartionum de rebus fedei et morum / Compendium of Creeds, Definitions, and Declarations on Matters of Faith and Morals*, 43rd ed., ed. Peter Hünermann (San Francisco: Ignatius, 2012).

HVII Giuseppe Alberigo and Joseph A. Komonchak, eds., *History of Vatican II*, 5 vols. (Maryknoll, NY: Orbis, 1995–2006).

IDOT Francis Gioia, ed., *Interreligious Dialogue: The Official Teaching of the Catholic Church (1963–1995)* (Boston: Pauline Books and Media, 1997).

IFJ Katherine Marshall, *Interfaith Journeys: An Exploration of History, Ideas, and Future Directions* (Washington, DC: World Faiths Development Dialogue, 2017).

ODCC F. L. Cross and E. A. Livingstone, eds., *Oxford Dictionary of the Christian Church*, 3rd ed. (Oxford: Oxford University Press, 2005).

OEMIW John L. Episoto, ed., *Oxford Encyclopedia of the Modern Islamic World*, 4 vols. (New York: Oxford University Press, 1995).

RE William Loftus Hare, ed., *Religions of the Empire: A Conference on Some Living Religions within the Empire, Held at the Imperial Institute, London, September 22nd to October 3rd, 1924, under the Auspices of the School of Oriental Studies (University of London) and the Sociological Society* (New York: Macmillan, 1925).

RPP Hans Dieter Betz et al., eds., *Religion Past & Present*, 14 vols., 4th English ed. (Leiden: Brill, 2007–13).

RSV Revised Standard Version Bible.

ST Thomas Aquinas, *Summa theologiae.*

VCII Austin Flannery, OP, ed., *Vatican Council II: The Conciliar and Post-conciliar Documents*, 2 vols., rev. ed. (Northport, NY: Costello, 2004).

WCID Catherine Cornille, ed., *Wiley-Blackwell Companion to Interreligious Dialogue* (Malden, MA: Wiley-Blackwell, 2013).

WPR John Henry Barrows, ed., *World's Parliament of Religions: An Illustrated and Popular Story of the World's First Parliament of Religions, Held in Chicago in Conjunction with the Columbian Exposition of 1893*, 2 vols. (Chicago: Parliament Publishing, 1893).

Journals

AJH	*American Jewish History*
AJT	*Asia Journal of Theology*
BCS	*Buddhist-Christian Studies*
CHR	*Catholic Historical Review*
CSR	*Comparative Social Research*
HJ	*Heythrop Journal*
HR	*History of Religions*
HT	*History and Theory*
HTR	*Harvard Theological Review*
ICMR	*Islam and Christian-Muslim Relations*
IJT	*Indian Journal of Theology*
IS	*Islamic Studies*
ITQ	*Irish Theological Quarterly*
JAAR	*Journal of the American Academy of Religion*
JAC	*Journal of American Culture*
JAOS	*Journal of the American Oriental Society*
JAS	*Journal of Asian Studies*
JCR	*Journal of Contemporary Religion*
JEH	*Journal of Ecclesiastical History*
JES	*Journal of Ecumenical Studies*
JHMT	*Journal of the History of Modern Theology*
JR	*Journal of Religion*
JRH	*Journal of Religious History*
JRS	*Journal of Religion & Society*
LS	*Louvain Studies*
LTP	*Laval théologique et philosophique*
MAS	*Modern Asian Studies*
MT	*Modern Theology*
MW	*Muslim World*
RC	*Religion Compass*
SJT	*Scottish Journal of Theology*
SR	*Studies in Religion / Science religieuses*
TS	*Theological Studies*
TZ	*Theologische Zeitschrift*
ZMR	*Zeitschrift für Missionswissenschaft und Religionswissenschaft*

Notes

Introduction

1. See the Interfaith Center of New York at http://interfaithcenter.org/ (accessed 15 October 2019).
2. See the Interreligious Council of Bosnia and Herzegovina at http://wscf-europe.org/news/history-of-the-interreligious-council-of-bosnia-and-herzegovina/ (accessed 26 December 2017). On its work, see Thomas Albert Howard, "After Genocide: Searching for Reconciliation in the Balkans," *Commonweal* 145 (2018): 19–23.
3. See the website for KAICIID at https://www.kaiciid.org/ (accessed 26 December 2017).
4. Katherine Marshall, *Global Institutions of Religion: Ancient Movers, Modern Shakers* (New York: Routledge, 2013), 129–53. Permit the naming of several other major interreligious organizations founded in the twentieth century: Temple of Understanding (1960), Temple University's Dialogue Institute (1964), Religions for Peace (1970), Interfaith Alliance (1994), Interfaith Center at the Presidio (1995), Muslim-Christian Dialogue Forum (1998), Rumi Forum (1999), and the United Religions Initiative (2000). The Geneva-based World Council of Churches (est. 1948) has been another major promoter of and participant in interfaith activity, especially after it established its "Dialogue Sub-unit" in 1971; see Douglas Pratt, *The Church and Other Faiths: The World Council of Churches, the Vatican, and Interreligious Dialogue* (Bern: Peter Lang, 2010), 63ff. A generous listing of additional interfaith organizations in the United States is found at the website of Harvard's Pluralism Project: http://pluralism.org/interfaith/ (accessed 1 April 2019).
5. See UN resolution 61/222 (2007), "Promotion of Interreligious and Intercultural Dialogue, Understanding and Cooperation for Peace," available at http://www.refworld.org/docid/51e65b0e4.html (accessed 12 February 2018).

6. According to Merriam-Webster's dictionary, *interreligious* was first used in 1847 and *interfaith* in 1932. See also *RPP*, 6:543. Lately, some have turned to terms such as *multifaith*, *interspiritual*, *interbelief*, *interpath*, *interideological*, and *transbelief* (inter alia) in an effort to include atheists, agnostics, and others. Terminology remains a complicated matter; see the World Council of Churches' "Called to Dialogue: Interreligious and Intra-Christian Dialogue in Ecumenical Conversation" at https://www.oikoumene.org/en/resources/documents/wcc-programmes/interreligious-dialogue-and-cooperation/called-to-dialogue (accessed 2 April 2019).
7. Patrice Brodeur, "From the Margins to the Center: The Increasing Relevance of the Global Interfaith Movement," *CrossCurrents* 55 (Spring 2005): 42–53.
8. Leonard Swidler, *After the Absolute: The Dialogical Future of Religious Reflection* (Minneapolis: Fortress, 1990), 5. Of course, one finds instances of conversations (mostly of a polemical nature) here and there between adherents to different faiths. Some of these will be mentioned in chapter 2.
9. On the "mythos" of Akbar in Western literature in the modern era, see Eric J. Ziolkowski, "Waking Up from Akbar's Dream: The Literary Prefigurement of Chicago's World's Parliament of Religions," *JR* 73 (1993): 42–60.
10. On the context of the parliament in the Columbian Exposition, see David F. Burg, *Chicago's White City of 1893* (Lexington: University of Kentucky Press, 1976), 235–85.
11. Richard Hughes Seager, *The World's Parliament of Religions: The East/West Encounter, Chicago, 1893* (Bloomington: Indiana University Press, 1995), 67ff.
12. Friedrich Max Müller, "The Real Significance of the Parliament of Religions," *Arena* 61 (December 1894): 2.
13. I have offered the first major treatment of this conference: see Thomas Albert Howard, "'A Remarkable Gathering': The Conference on Living Religions within the British Empire (1924) and Its Historical Significance," *JAAR* 86 (March 2018): 126–57.
14. See *RE*, 9; and William Loftus Hare, "A Parliament of Living Religions: An Account of the 'Conference on Some Living Religions within the Empire,' Held at the Imperial Institute, London, September 22nd to October 3rd, 1924," *Open Court* 38 (1924): 706–59.
15. A. Douglas Millard, ed., *Faiths and Fellowship; Being the Proceedings of the World Congress of Faiths Held in London, July 3rd–17th, 1936* (London: World Congress of Faiths, 1936).
16. *Acta Leonis XIII Pontificis maximi*, vol. 14 (Graz: Akademische Druck und Verlagsanstalt, 1971), 323–24.
17. See the encyclical at http://w2.vatican.va/content/pius-xi/en/encyclicals/documents/hf_p-xi_enc19280106_mortalium-animos.html (accessed 17

January 2018). See also F. J. Burke, "The Exclusiveness of Truth and the Pope's Encyclical," *Ecclesiastical Review* 80 (February 1929): 143–51.

18. *VCII*, 1:739. On the background to the declaration (and other texts of Vatican II that have implications for interreligious dialogue), see Gerald O'Collins, SJ, *The Second Vatican Council on Other Religions* (Oxford: Oxford University Press, 2013).
19. Risto Jukko, "La prière interreligieuse et l'église catholique," *Nouvelle revue théologique* 130 (2008): 774–91; and Johannes Dörmann, ed., *Die eine Wahrheit und die vielen Religionen: Assisi, Anfang einer neuen Zeit* (Abensberg: Kral, 1988).
20. Since 1986, the Catholic Church has convened religious leaders in Assisi in 1993, 1999, 2002, 2011, and 2016. See John Allen Jr., "Pope's Interfaith Summit in Assisi Belongs to an Ongoing Revolution," *Crux* (14 September 2016). See also Francis X. Clooney, SJ, "Interreligious Learning in a Changing Church: From Paul VI to Francis," *ITQ* 82 (2017): 269–83; and James L. Heft, SM, ed., *Catholicism and Interfaith Dialogue* (Oxford: Oxford University Press, 2012).
21. "Pope Appeals for More Interreligious Dialogue," *New York Times* (22 March 2013).
22. Edward Shils, *The Constitution of Society* (Chicago: University of Chicago Press, 1982), 93.
23. On authority and the construction of plausibility—or what sociologists sometimes call "plausibility structures"—see Peter L. Berger and Thomas Luckmann's classic work, *The Social Construction of Reality: A Treatise in the Sociology of Knowledge* (New York: Penguin, 1966), 174.
24. See Andrew Abbot, "On the Concept of Turning Point," *CSR* 16 (1997): 85–105.
25. As shall be developed more fully later, the prominence of the term owes a significant debt to the twentieth-century Jewish thinker Martin Buber, especially to his 1923 work "I and Thou" (*Ich und Du*) and his 1929 essay "Dialogue" (*Zwiesprache*). See Martin Buber, *Dialogisches Leben: Gesammelte philosophische und pädagogische Schriften* (Zurich: Gregor Müller, 1947), 13–186; and Wolfgang Pauly, *Martin Buber: Ein Leben im Dialog* (Berlin: Hentrich and Hentrich, 2010).
26. Contemporary practitioners of dialogue sometimes make a fourfold distinction: (1) a *dialogue of life*, where people strive to live in a neighborly spirit, sharing their joys and sorrows, their problems and preoccupations; (2) a *dialogue of action*, in which members of different faiths collaborate to achieve various social goods; (3) a *dialogue of theological exchange*, in which learned representatives of religious traditions discuss topics with one another; and (4) a *dialogue of religious or spiritual experience*, where persons, rooted in their own religious traditions, share their spiritual practices and insights. These are drawn from the Vatican's 1991 docu-

ment "Dialogue and Proclamation" at http://www.vatican.va/roman_curia/pontifical_councils/interelg/documents/rc_pc_interelg_doc_19051991_dialogue-and-proclamatio_en.html (accessed 1 April 2019).

27. Jonathan Z. Smith, "Religion, Religions, Religious," in Mark C. Taylor, ed., *Critical Terms for Religious Studies* (Chicago: University of Chicago Press, 1998), 269ff.

28. Ernst Feil, *Religio: Die Geschichte eines neuzeitlichen Grundbegriffs vom Frühchrisentum bis zur Reformation*, vol. 1 (Göttingen: Vandenhoeck and Ruprecht, 1986); and Peter Biller, "Words and the Medieval Notion of 'Religion,'" *JEH* 36 (1985): 351–69. On Roman usage, see Clifford Ando, *Imperial Roman AD 193–284* (Edinburgh: Edinburgh University Press, 2012), 124–45.

29. Wilfred Cantwell Smith, *The Meaning and End of Religion* (1962; repr., Minneapolis: Fortress, 1991), 20–21.

30. In all, the word *religio* appears six times in the Vulgate. William T. Cavanaugh, *The Myth of Religious Violence* (New York: Oxford University Press, 2009), 62.

31. John H. S. Burleigh, ed., *Augustine: Earlier Writings* (London: SCM, 1953), 218–83.

32. One also sees *lex* (law) used, especially when making comparisons among different religious communities and their customs. See Nathan J. Ristuccia, "Eastern Religions in the West: The Making of an Image," *HR* 53 (2013): 170–204.

33. *ST* II-II, q. 81; and Smith, *Meaning and End of Religion*, 32. See also Georges Cottier, "La vertu de religion," *Revue Thomiste* 106 (2006): 335–52.

34. Muthuraj Swamy, *The Problem of Interreligious Dialogue: Plurality and Elitism in Hindu-Christian-Muslim Relations* (London: Bloomsbury, 2016), 72.

35. Guy G. Stroumsa, *A New Science: The Discovery of Religion in the Age of Reason* (Cambridge, MA: Harvard University Press, 2010), 14–38. I should mention here, however, that both Nicholas of Cusa and Marsilio Ficino employ the term *religion* in ways that adumbrate its modern usage. See Cavanaugh, *Myth of Religious Violence*, 70–71. Cusa will be discussed in chapter 1.

36. Görge K. Hasselhoff, "Huldrych Zwinglis Veständnis von '*religio*,'" *Zeitschrift für Religions-und Geistesgeschichte* 67 (2015): 120–41.

37. Frederick Quinn, *The Sum of All Heresies: The Image of Islam in Western Thought* (New York: Oxford University Press, 2008), 17ff.

38. Smith, *Meaning and End of Religion*, 40.

39. Brent Nonngbri, *Before Religion: The History of a Modern Concept* (New Haven: Yale University Press, 2013), 9–10.

40. This quadripartite structure was inherited from the Middle Ages. See Tomoko Masuzawa, *The Invention of World Religions; or, How European*

Universalism Was Preserved in the Language of Pluralism (Chicago: University of Chicago Press, 2005), 47.

41. The definitive study of this topic in this period is Peter Harrison, *"Religion" and the Religions in the English Enlightenment* (Cambridge: Cambridge University Press, 1990). Even so, in his famous dictionary, Samuel Johnson defined *religion* primarily as "virtue, as founded upon reverence of God, and expectation of future awards and punishments." See Johnson's dictionary at https://johnsonsdictionaryonline.com/religion/ (accessed 6 June 2019). The first edition of the *Encyclopedia Britannica*, moreover, practically equates "religion" with "Christian theology." See *Encyclopedia Britannica* (London, 1771), 3:533–46.
42. A publishing "event" in the early eighteenth century that encouraged this development was the appearance of Bernard Picart and Frederic Bernard's *Cérémonies et coutumes religieuses de tous les peuples du monde* (1723–37). In nine sumptuous volumes, it comprised three thousand pages with 250 engravings of religious rites from around the world. Although perhaps overstating matters, Lynn Hunt and others claim that the work "essentially created the category of 'religion.'" See Lynn Hunt et al., eds., *The Book That Changed Europe: Picart and Bernard's Religious Ceremonies of the World* (Cambridge, MA: Belknap Press of Harvard University Press, 2010), 155–57; and Lynn Hunt et al., eds., *Bernard Picart and the First Global Vision of Religion* (Los Angeles: Getty Research Institute, 2010).
43. Smith, *Meaning and End of Religion*, 60.
44. Geoffrey Oddie, *Imagined Hinduism: British Protestant Missionary Constructions of Hinduism* (London: Sage, 2006), 68–72.
45. I follow Smith's dating of these terms. See Smith, *Wilfred Cantwell Smith: A Reader*, ed. Kenneth Cracknell (Oxford: Oneworld, 2001), 161.
46. On Jung's influence, see M. Esther Harding, "Jung's Influence on Contemporary Thought," *Journal of Religion and Health* 1 (1962): 247–59. With over 2 million sold, Huston Smith's *World's Religions* is arguably the main popularizer of these terms. See the fiftieth anniversary edition: Huston Smith, *The World's Religions* (New York: HarperOne, 2009). Smith's work has been the subject of a five-part documentary with Bill Moyers, in which Smith makes the questionable, often-repeated claim (as he does in the book) that all religions, at their core, are the same. *LIFE* magazine's series was subsequently republished and heavily marketed as *The World's Great Religions* (1955). At the academic level, the "world religions" approach to religion has been influenced by the so-called Chicago School of religious study as propagated by Joachim Wach and his successor at the University of Chicago, Mircea Eliade. See Christian K. Wedemeyer and Wendy Doniger, eds., *Hermeneutics, Politics, and the History of Religions: The Contested Legacies of Joachim Wach and Mircea Eliade* (New York: Oxford University Press, 2010). See also Gregory D. Alles,

"Wach, Eliade, and the Critique from Totality," *Numen* 35 (1988): 108–38; and Peden W. Creighton, "The Chicago School: On the Road to Religious Humanism," *Religious Humanism* 26 (1992): 74–84. Finally, it merits noting that Harvard University inaugurated in 1960 the Center for the Study of World Religions. For more on the category of "world religion" and the taxonomy of "world religions," see Masuzawa, *The Invention of World Religions*, 1–36, 107–20, 259ff.; Katherine K. Young, "World Religions: A Category in the Making?" in Michel Despland and Gérard Vallée, eds., *Religion in History: The Word, the Idea, the Reality / La religion dans l'histoirie: Le mot, l'idée, la réalité* (Waterloo, Ontario: Wilfrid Laurier University Press, 1992), 111–30; and Christoph Auffarth, "'Weltreligion' als ein Leitbegriff der Religionswissenschaft im Imperialismus," in Ulrich van der Heyden and Holger Stoecker, eds., *Mission und Macht im Wandel politischer Orientierungen: Europäische Missionsgesellschaften in Afrika und Asien zwischen 1800 und 1945* (Stuttgart: Steiner, 2005), 17–36.

47. Talal Asad, *Genealogies of Religion: Discipline and Reasons of Power in Christianity and Islam* (Baltimore: Johns Hopkins University Press, 1993), 28. On the global export of Western notions of "secularism," see Ashis Nandy, "The Politics of Secularism and the Recovery of Religious Tolerance," *Alternatives* 13 (1988): 177–94.

48. Talal Asad, "Reading a Modern Classic: W. C. Smith's *Meaning and End of Religion*," *HR* 40 (2001): 221; and K. Kollmar-Paulenz, *Zur Ausdifferenzierung eines autonomen Bereichs Religion in asiatischen Gesellschaften des 17. und 18. Jahrhunderts* (Bern: Schweizerische Akademie der Geistes- und Sozialwissenschaften, 2007).

49. Dipesh Chakrabarty, *Provincializing Europe: Postcolonial Thought and Historical Difference* (Princeton: Princeton University Press, 2000), 3–23.

50. Cavanaugh, *Myth of Religious Violence*, 86 (emphasis added). See also John Milbank, "The End of Dialogue," in Gavin d'Costa, ed., *Christian Uniqueness Reconsidered: The Myth of a Pluralistic Theology of Religions* (Maryknoll, NY: Orbis, 1990), 174–91.

51. To be sure, approximations of *religion* have arisen in other languages, but often only under the influence of Western colonialism. Few if any previous words conceived of "religion" as a genus with various species, as I have argued. See, inter alia, Yvonne Yazbeck, "The Concept of *Din* in the Qur'an," *MW* 64 (1974): 114–23; and Lars Kirkhusmo Pharo, "The Concept of 'Religion' in Mesoamerican Languages," *Numen* 54 (2007): 28–70. In Sanskrit, both *dharma* and *bhakti* have sometimes been rendered as "religion," but generally Sanskrit lacks the concept. See Pierre-Sylvain Filliozat, *The Sanskrit Language: An Overview: History and Structure, Linguistic and Philosophical Representations*, trans. T. K. Gopalan (Varanasi: Indica, 2000). On the constructed nature of "religion" (*zongjiao*) in modern Chinese, see Ian Johnson, *The Souls of China: The Return*

of Religion after Mao (New York: Pantheon, 2017), 20–23; Hsi-yuan Chen, "Confucianism Encounters Religion: The Formation of Religious Discourse and the Confucian Movement in Modern China" (PhD diss., Harvard University, 1999); and Bram Colijn, "The Concept of Religion in Modern China: A Grassroots Perspective," *Exchange* 47 (2018): 53–70. Ian Johnson perceptively notes: "In fact, the concept of thinking of oneself as part of a discrete and clearly definable religious system was so foreign to Chinese that when modernizers wanted to reorganize society using Western norms one hundred years ago they had to import the vocabulary of the West" (20). For Japanese, see Hajime Nakamura, "The Japanese Equivalent of the Western Word 'Religion,'" *Transactions of the Japanese Academy* 46 (1992): 39–146. See also Hajime Nakamura, "The Meaning of the Terms 'Philosophy' and 'Religion' in Various Traditions," in Gerald J. Larson and Eliot Deutsch, eds., *Interpreting across Boundaries: New Essays in Comparative Philosophy* (Princeton: Princeton University Press, 1988), 137–45; M. Despland, *La religion en occident: Évolution des idees et du vécu* (Montreal: Fides, 1988); and Robert Ford, "On the Very Idea of Religions (in the Modern West and in Early Medieval China)," *HR* 42 (2003): 288–319.

52. For a restatement of the secularization thesis, see Steve Bruce, *Secularization: In Defense of an Unfashionable Theory* (Oxford: Oxford University Press, 2015).
53. David Hollinger makes a cogent case for the secularizing influence of Western higher education, particularly with reference to natural science and historical inquiry; see his "Christianity and Its American Fate: Where History Interrogates Secularization Theory," in Martin Halliwell, ed., *William James and Religion* (Oxford: Oxford University Press, 2016), 280–303.
54. See Peter Berger, ed., *The Desecularization of the World: Resurgent Religion and World Politics* (Grand Rapids, MI: Eerdmans, 1999). For a more popular-audience articulation of Berger's view, see John Mickelthwait and Adrian Woolridge, *God Is Back: How the Global Revival of Faith Is Changing the World* (New York: Penguin, 2009).
55. Peter Berger, *The Many Altars of Modernity: Toward a Paradigm for Religion in a Pluralist Age* (Berlin: De Gruyter, 2014), 5.
56. Berger, *Many Altars of Modernity*, 15.
57. S. N. Eisenstadt, "Multiple Modernities," *Daedalus* 129 (January 2000): 1–29.
58. Atif Khalil, "Jewish-Muslim Relations, Globalization, and the Judeo-Christian Legacy," *JRS* 17 (2015): 2.
59. Melissa May Borja, "Migrations and Modern American Religious Pluralism," in Paul Harvey and Kathryn Gin, eds., *Oxford Handbook of Religion and Race in American History* (New York: Oxford University Press, 2018). See also Robert Wuthnow, *America and the Challenges of Religious*

Diversity (Princeton: Princeton University Press, 2005), 37–74. Of course, recent decades have witnessed considerable reaction to immigration taking the form of nativism and nationalism. See, e.g., Jean-Yves and Nicolas Lebourg, *Far-Right Politics in Europe*, trans. Jane Marie Todd (Cambridge, MA: Belknap Press of Harvard University Press, 2017); and Timothy Snyder, *The Road to Unfreedom: Russia, Europe, America* (New York: Tim Duggan, 2018).

60. Diana L. Eck, *A New Religious America: How a "Christian Country" Has Become the World's Most Religiously Diverse Nation* (New York: HarperOne, 2001), 1, 384.

61. In fact, I would argue that it is only from our local commitments that we can develop the capacity for enlarging the scope of our understanding and compassion for others. On this point, see Leon Kass, *Leading a Worthy Life: Finding Meaning in Modern Times* (New York: Encounter, 2017), 3–33.

62. Sean Fox, "Urbanization as a Global Historical Process," *Population and Development Review* 38 (2012): 285–310.

63. Kwame Anthony Appiah, *Cosmopolitanism: Ethics in a World of Strangers* (New York: Norton, 2006), xxi. In addition to Appiah, permit me to note the stimulating work of Martha C. Nussbaum, particularly her *Cultivating Humanity: A Classical Defense of Reform in Liberal Education* (Cambridge, MA: Harvard University Press, 1997), 50–84, and *The Cosmopolitan Tradition: A Noble but Flawed Ideal* (Cambridge, MA: Belknap Press of Harvard University Press, 2019).

64. Richard Wayne Lee, "Christianity and Other Religions: Interreligious Relations in a Shrinking World," *Sociological Analysis* 53 (1992): 125–39.

65. See Garrett Wallace Brown and David Held, eds., *The Cosmopolitanism Reader* (Cambridge: Polity, 2010).

66. For a thoughtful criticism of secularist visions of cosmopolitanism from an explicitly Christian theological perspective, see Angela Russell Christman, "The Cosmopolitan Church: Voices from the Tradition," *Cresset* 73 (Easter 2010): 6–17. Christman doubts that a cosmopolitan ethic can be sufficiently "grounded" absent some transcendent/teleological understanding of the human person and of human dignity. See also Jacques Maritain, *The Person and the Common Good*, trans. John J. Fitzgerald (Notre Dame: University of Notre Dame Press, 1966).

67. Jonathan Sacks, *Not in God's Name: Confronting Religious Violence* (New York: Schocken, 2015), 18. See also his *The Dignity of Difference: How to Avoid the Clash of Civilizations* (London: Continuum, 2002).

68. On overcoming "secularist parochialism," see David Brooks's witty "Kicking the Secularist Habit: A Six-Step Program," *Atlantic* (March 2003). For a cogent argument on how universities often promote an intellectually constricting "secularist confessionalism," see Brad S. Gregory, "The

Other Confessional History: On Secular Bias in the Study of Religion," *HT* 45 (2006): 132–49.

69. See Hans Küng, *Global Responsibility: In Search of a New World Order* (London: SCM, 1991); and Hans Küng and Karl-Josef Kuschel, eds., *A Global Ethic: The Declaration of the Parliament of the World's Religions* (London: SCM, 1993).
70. Cavanaugh, *Myth of Religious Violence*, 6. Understanding modern political ideologies, such as nationalism and socialism, as religious or quasi-religious phenomena (or as ersatz religions) has been extensively theorized with great sophistication and nuance in recent decades. See Emilio Gentile, *Politics as Religion*, trans. George Staunton (Princeton: Princeton University Press, 2001).
71. Wilfred Cantwell Smith, *The Faith of Other Men* (New York: Harper, 1963), 101.
72. Jonathan Glover, *Humanity: A Moral History of the Twentieth Century*, 2nd ed. (New Haven: Yale University Press, 2012), 239.
73. Samuel P. Huntington, *The Clash of Civilizations and the Remaking of the World Order* (New York: Simon and Schuster, 1996), 43.
74. Michael A. Sells, *The Bridge Betrayed: Religion and Genocide in Bosnia* (Berkeley: University of California Press, 1996).
75. It is important to distinguish *secularism*, here meant as a category of politics or jurisprudence, from *secularization* as a sociological category.
76. Saba Mahmood, *Religious Difference in a Secular Age: A Minority Report* (Princeton: Princeton University Press, 2016), 3–4.
77. On the often-recognized problem of elitism in interreligious dialogue, see Joseph Victor Edwin, SJ, ed., *Seeking Communion: A Collection of Conversations* (New Delhi: ISPCK, 2018), 101–3. I am grateful to Father Edwin, a longtime practitioner of Muslim-Christian dialogue in India, for conversations about these and other matters.
78. On this point, see Jeremy Salt, "Global Disorder and the Limits of 'Dialogue,'" *Third World Quarterly* 29 (2008): 691–70. On Niebuhrian realism, see Andrew Bacevich's engaging introduction to Reinhold Niebuhr, *The Irony of American History* (Chicago: University of Chicago Press, 2008).
79. For a grim global, contemporary report of the fate of religious minorities in putatively secular states, see Jonathan Fox's instructive *The Unfree Exercise of Religion: A World Survey of Discrimination against Religious Minorities* (New York: Cambridge University Press, 2016).
80. Edward W. Said, *Orientalism* (New York: Vintage, 1979), 3, 14.
81. For an entry point into some of the issues at stake, see *RPP*, 9:371; and Said and Bernard Lewis's well-known exchange in the *New York Review of Books* (24 June and 12 August 1982).
82. On the (tight) relationship between nineteenth-century liberalism's pro-

gressive view of history and the justification of empire, see Uday Singh Mehta, *Liberalism and Empire: A Study in Nineteenth-Century British Liberal Thought* (Chicago: University of Chicago Press, 1999).

83. Irfan Habib, "In Defense of Orientalism: Critical Notes on Edward Said," *Social Scientist* 33 (2005): 44.
84. On the secularist dimensions of Said's work, see Khaled Furani, "Said and the Religious Other," *Comparative Studies in Society and History* 52 (2010): 604–25.
85. On this theme and for her evenhanded critique of Said, see Suzanne Marchand, *German Orientalism in the Age of Empire: Religion, Race, and Scholarship* (New York: Cambridge University Press, 2009). Said also failed to treat early modern "Orientalists" working prior to the extensive development of French and English colonialism. On these few and fascinating individuals, see Alexander Bevilacqua, *The Republic of Arabic Letters: Islam and the European Enlightenment* (Cambridge, MA: Belknap Press of Harvard University Press, 2018).
86. I am told by Mohammad Ali of Jamia Millia Islamia in New Delhi, India, that Said's thesis has sometimes produced the view among conservative Muslim clerics and scholars that scholarship on Islam written in Western languages simply need not be consulted at all because it is inherently tainted by Orientalist assumptions (personal conversation, New Delhi, 12 March 2018).
87. Rita Felski, *Limits of Critique* (Chicago: University of Chicago Press, 2015), 9.
88. See also the critique of Said presented in Jürgen Osterhammel, *Unfabling the East: The Enlightenment's Encounter with Asia*, trans. Robert Savage (Princeton: Princeton University Press, 2018), 5–10, 12, 52.
89. Pluralism here should be regarded as a theological category; previously I used the term as a sociological one.
90. This typology is generally attributed to Alan Race, *Christians and Pluralism: Patterns in the Christian Theology of Religions* (Maryknoll, NY: Orbis, 1982). Treatments of approaches to interreligious dialogue from other religious standpoints can be found in *WCID*. Of course, these categories have considerable effect on Christian missiological questions; see Wesley Ariarajah, *Strangers or Co-Pilgrims: The Impact of Interfaith Dialogue on Christian Faith and Practice* (Minneapolis: Fortress, 2017); and Lamin Sanneh, *Translating the Message: The Missionary Impact on Culture*, rev. ed. (Maryknoll, NY: Orbis, 2009).
91. See Hendrik Kraemer, *The Christian Message in a Non-Christian World* (Grand Rapids, MI: Krugel, 1956). See also Kraemer's *Religion and the Christian Faith* (London: Lutterwirth, 1956); and Wesley Ariarajah, "Interreligious Dialogue and Protestant Mission," *Modern Believing* 51 (2010): 38–47.
92. Kraemer, *Christian Message in a Non-Christian World*, 122.

93. Karl Barth, *Church Dogmatics* I. 2, trans. G. T. Thomson and Harold Knight (New York: Charles Scribner's Sons, 1956), 302. Although Barth himself is often characterized as an exclusivist, he leaned more in the direction of salvific universalism, albeit in starkly Christocentric terms. See Reinhold Bernhardt, "Karl Barths Beitrag zu einer gegenwärtigen Theologie der Religionen," *TZ* 71 (2015): 97–113.
94. Eberhard Bethge, "Bonhoeffer's Christology and His 'Religionless Christianity,'" *Union Seminary Quarterly Review* 23 (1967): 61–77.
95. For a well-articulated example, see Stanley J. Grenz, "Toward an Evangelical Theology of the Religions," *JES* 31 (1994): 49–65. Historically, this perspective has relied heavily on viewing other faiths as species of idolatry. See Pavel Horak, "The Image of Paganism in the Age of Reason: From Idolatry towards a Secular Concept of Polytheism," *Pomegranate* 18 (2016): 125–49.
96. Race, *Christians and Pluralism*, 10.
97. For an especially egregious case of exclusivist reasoning, see Frank Dobbins et al., *False Gods; or, The Idol Worship of the World. A Complete History of Idolatrous Worship throughout the World, Ancient and Modern. Describing the Strange Beliefs, Practices, and Superstitions, Temples, Idols, Shrines, Sacrifices, Domestic Peculiarities, etc., etc., Connected Herewith* (Philadelphia: Hubbord Brothers, 1881).
98. Jean Daniélou, *Les saints "païens" de l'Ancien Testament* (Paris: Editions du Seuil, 1956).
99. Many of these Protestants had extensive experience overseas, either working as missionaries themselves or as the children of missionaries. The knowledge they acquired abroad was brought back to Western countries—often with unpredictable results. This is the story told in David Hollinger's *Protestants Abroad: How Missionaries Tried to Change the World but Changed America* (Princeton: Princeton University Press, 2017).
100. Franceso Iannoe, *Una chiesa per gli altri: Il Concilio Vaticano II e le religione non christiane* (Assisi: Cittadella Editrice, 2014); Giacomo Canobbio, *Chiesa, religioni, salvezze: Il Vaticano II e la sua recezione* (Brescia: Morcelliana, 2007); and Leonard Swidler, "Vatican II: The Catholic Revolution from Damnation to Dialogue," *JES* 50 (2015): 511–24. While it has earlier roots, the teaching *extra Ecclesiam nulla salus* was formally promulgated at the Council of Florence (1438–45). On this, see Gavin D'Costa, *Theology and Religious Pluralism: The Challenge of Other Religions* (Oxford: Basil Blackwell, 1986), 9–10.
101. On Protestant fulfillment theology, see Eric J. Sharpe, *Not to Destroy but to Fulfil: The Contribution of J. N. Farquhar to Protestant Missionary Thought in India prior to 1914* (Uppsala: Gleerup, 1965); and Brian Stanley, *World Missionary Conference, Edinburgh 1910* (Grand Rapids, MI: Eerdmans, 2009), 205–47.
102. *ESDD*, 915–16 (translation modified).

103. Rahner also exercised influence on *Nostra aetate.* See ACUA, Papers of Thomas Stransky, box 22, folder 6. See also Karl Rahner, "Christianity and the Non-Christian Religions," in *Theological Investigations* (Baltimore: Helicon, 1966), 5:113–24; O'Collins, *The Second Vatican Council on Other Religions,* 18; and Jacques Dupuis, *Toward a Christian Theology of Religious Pluralism* (Maryknoll, NY: Orbis, 2005).

104. Jacques Dupuis, "The Cosmic Christ in the Early Fathers," *IJT* 15 (1966): 106–20. Additionally, inclusivism more readily permits the hope that the entire human family will be reconciled with God. See Hans Urs von Balthasar, *Dare We Hope That "All Men Will Be Saved"?* trans. David Kipp and Lothar Krauth (San Francisco: Ignatius, 2014).

105. See especially John Hick and Paul Knitter, eds., *The Myth of Christian Uniqueness: Toward a Pluralistic Theology of Religions* (Maryknoll, NY: Orbis, 1987); and Hick, *God Has Many Faces* (Philadelphia: Westminster, 1982). Hick draws significantly from the later writings of the German scholar Ernst Troeltsch. See especially Troeltsch's essay "The Place of Christianity among the World Religions" (1923), in *Christian Thought and Its Applications* (London: Wipf and Stock, 1999). For criticism of Hick, see G. G. D'Costa, "A Critical Evaluation of John Hick's Copernican Revolution in the Christian Theology of Religions" (PhD diss., Cambridge University, 1986).

106. Paul Griffiths, *An Apology for Apologetics* (Maryknoll, NY: Orbis, 1991), xi.

107. Pluralism is often linked with soteriological universalism, but it is conceptually distinct from it.

108. Race, *Christians and Pluralism,* 70–105. For a criticism of this viewpoint from a "post-liberal" theological perspective, see George Lindbeck's classic work *The Nature of Doctrine: Religion and Theology in a Postliberal Age* (Philadelphia: Westminster, 1984). Lindbeck is especially critical of the notion that all religions are simply expressions of some common core of human experience. Those who begin with this premise, he feels, are forced into the dilemma of having to evaluate which religions are superior and which are inferior expressions of this common experience. By contrast, dialogue partners who assume that religions are "simply different can proceed to explore their agreements and disagreements without necessarily engaging in the invidious comparisons that the assumption of a common experiential core makes so tempting" (55).

109. Carl Braaten, *No Other Gospel: Christianity among the World's Religions* (Minneapolis: Fortress, 1992), 10.

110. Catherine Cornille, *The Im-Possibility of Interreligious Dialogue* (New York: Crossroad, 2008), 6.

111. Thomas Albert Howard, "Seeing with All Three Eyes: The Virtue of Prudence and Undergraduate Education," in David S. Cunningham,

ed., *At This Time and in This Place: Vocation and Undergraduate Education* (New York: Oxford University Press, 2016), 216–34.

112. Charles Taylor, *A Secular Age* (Cambridge, MA: Belknap Press of Harvard University Press, 2007), 29.
113. Jacob Burckhardt, *Judgments on History and Historians*, trans. Harry Zohn (Indianapolis: Liberty Fund, 1999), 1.
114. Raymond Aron, *Introduction to the Philosophy of History: An Essay on the Limits of Objectivity*, trans. George J. Irwin (Boston: Beacon, 1961), 118.

Chapter One. Harbingers

1. For another premodern Eastern example of dialogue, see Friedericke Assandri, "Inter-religious Debate at the Court of the Early Tang," in Friedericke Assandri and Dora Martins, eds., *From Early Tang Court Debates to China's Peaceful Rise* (Amsterdam: University of Amsterdam Press, 2009), 15–32.
2. On this point, see Richard C. Foltz, *Religions of the Silk Road*, 2nd ed. (New York: Palgrave Macmillan, 2010); Jamsheed K. Choksy, "Hagiography and Monotheism in History: Doctrinal Encounters between Zoroastrianism, Judaism, and Christianity," *ICMR* 14 (2003): 407–21; Jiahe Liu, "Early Buddhism and Taoism in China," *BCS* 12 (1992): 35–41; Fabio Mora, "Religionswissenschaftliches Denken in der Antike," *Zeitschrift für Religions- und Geistesgeschichte* 51 (1999): 17–29; Hans-J. Klimkeit, "Christians, Buddhists, and Manichaeans in Medieval Central Europe," *BCS* 1 (1981): 46–50; S. M. Yusuf, "The Early Contacts between Islam and Judaism," *University of Ceylon Review* 13 (January 1995): 1–28; and James Muldoon, ed., *Travelers, Intellectuals, and the World beyond the Medieval World* (Burlington, VT: Ashgate, 2010), among many other sources.
3. Peter Henrici, "The Concept of Religion from Cicero to Schleiermacher," in Karl J. Becker and Ilaria Morali, eds., *Catholic Engagement with World Religions* (Maryknoll, NY: Orbis, 2010), 3. See also Robert Wilken, *Remembering the Christian Past* (Grand Rapids, MI: Eerdmans, 1995), 25–46; and Christian Marek, *In the Land of a Thousand Gods: A History of Asia Minor in the Ancient World* (Princeton: Princeton University Press, 2016), 309ff.
4. Acts 17:22–32 (RSV).
5. On Marcion, see Henry Chadwick, *The Church in Ancient Society: From Galilee to Gregory the Great* (Oxford: Oxford University Press, 2001), 89–92.
6. Jaroslav Pelikan, *Whose Bible Is It? A Short History of Scriptures* (New York: Penguin, 2005), 89–98.
7. Galatians 2:11–21 (RSV).

8. Origen, however, is an outlier among church fathers, for his doctrine of universal salvation included the Jews. Joseph Carola, "Non-Christians in Patristic Theology," in Becker and Morali, *Catholic Engagement with World Religions*, 24–27.
9. Robert L. Wilken, *Judaism and the Early Christian Mind: A Study of Cyril of Alexandria's Exegesis and Theology* (New Haven: Yale University Press, 1971), 229.
10. On these ground-level interactions, see Louis H. Feldman, *Jew and Gentile in the Ancient World: Attitude and Interactions from Alexander to Justinian* (Princeton: Princeton University Press, 1993).
11. Larry W. Hurtado, *Destroyer of the Gods: Early Christian Distinctiveness in the Roman World* (Waco, TX: Baylor University Press, 2016), 76. Evidence of Jewish discussions with Christians and Jewish polemical literature against Christians is surprisingly scant in early rabbinic literature. See "Jewish-Christian Relations in the Roman Empire," in Wilken, *Judaism and the Early Christian Mind*, 31ff.
12. The principal Christian reproach of other deities was that they were "idols," from the Greek *eidolen*, meaning mere "images" or "phantoms." Hurtado, *Destroyer of the Gods*, 49.
13. Gregory the Great, *Life of Saint Benedict*, trans. and ed. Terrence G. Kardong (Collegeville, MN: Liturgical Press, 2009), 49.
14. Gregory I, "Letter to Abbot Mellitus," *Patrologia latina*, vol. 76 (1857), 1215–16.
15. Henry Chadwick, *Early Christian Thought and the Classical Tradition* (Oxford: Oxford University Press, 1966), 1–31.
16. Pierre Ndoumai, "Justin Martyr et le dialogue interreligieux," *LTP* 66 (2010): 547–64.
17. Augustine, *Confessions*, trans. R. S. Pine-Coffin (New York: Penguin, 1961), 58–59, 144–45.
18. Clement, as quoted in Carola, "Non-Christians in Patristic Theology," 38.
19. Richard Fletcher, *The Conversion of Europe: From Paganism to Christianity, 371–1386* (London: HarperCollins, 1997), 369ff.
20. Admittedly, this knowledge was rather scant and came to be eclipsed after the rise of Islam, but figures such as Jerome, Clement of Alexandria, Ambrose, and Augustine make mention of what today we call Buddhism, Jainism, and Hinduism. In Clement's *Stromata* 1.15, for instance, he speaks of the "Indians [who] obey the precepts of the Boutta [Buddha], whom on account of his extraordinary sanctity they have raised to divine honors." Quoted in David Scott, "Christian Responses to Buddhism in Pre-Medieval Times," *Numen* 32 (1985): 89. See also Thomas Hahn, "The Indian Tradition in Western Intellectual History," *Viator: Medieval and Renaissance Studies* 9 (1978): 213–34. On transmission of Alexander the Great's dialogue with Jain monks, see Alexandra Szalc, "Alexander's

Dialogue with Indian Philosophers: Riddle in Greek and Indian Traditions," *Eos* 98 (2011): 7–25. Finally, mention should be made of the fascinating legendary Christian martyrs and saints Barlaam and Josaphat, likely based on the story of the Buddha, transmitted to the West via the Middle East by a Manichaean version of a Sanskrit Mahayana Buddhist text. See Guil de Cambrai and Peggy McCracken, eds., *Barlaam and Josaphat: A Christian Tale of the Buddha* (New York: Penguin, 2014).

21. R. Wittkower, "Marvels of the East," *Journal of the Warburg and Courtauld Institutes* 5 (1942): 159–97.
22. Philip C. Almond, "The Medieval West and Buddhism," *Eastern Buddhist* 19 (1986): 95. Polo gives the most complete account of Buddhism. See A. C. Moule and P. Pelliot, *Marco Polo: The Description of the World* (London: Routledge and Kegan Paul, 1908), 170ff.
23. Manichaeans often engaged in public debates with representatives from other faiths. See Richard Lim, "Manichaeans and Public Disputation in Late Antiquity," in Averil Cameron and Robert Hoyland, eds., *Doctrine and Debate in the East Christian World, 300–1500* (Burlington, VT: Ashgate, 2011), 9–48.
24. George Every, "The Monophysite Question, Ancient and Modern," *Eastern Churches Review* 3 (1971): 405–11.
25. Quoted in Wilken, *Judaism and the Early Christian Mind*, 22.
26. Foltz, *Religions of the Silk Road*, 60–87; and Philip Jenkins, *The Lost History of Christianity* (New York: HarperCollins, 2008), 20–21.
27. John Elverskog, *Buddhism and Islam on the Silk Road* (Philadelphia: University of Pennsylvania Press, 2010). See also Richard C. Foltz, *Spirituality in the Land of the Noble: How Iran Shaped the World's Religions* (Oxford: Oneworld, 2008).
28. Peter Crawford, *The War of the Three Gods: Romans, Persia, and the Rise of Islam* (New York: Skyhorse, 2014).
29. Jonathan Porter Berkey, *The Formation of Islam: Religion and Society in the Near East, 600–1800* (Cambridge: Cambridge University Press, 2003), 76.
30. See, e.g., Marietta Stepaniants, "The Encounter of Zoroastrianism with Islam," *Philosophy East and West* 52 (2005): 159–72.
31. John Meyendorff, "Byzantine Views of Islam," *Dumbarton Oaks Papers* 18 (1964): 115; and Jaroslav Pelikan, *The Spirit of Eastern Christendom, 600–1700*, vol. 2 of *The Christian Tradition* (Chicago: University of Chicago Press, 1974), 227ff.
32. Naiam Iftikur Haider, *The Origins of the Shia: Identity, Ritual, and Sacred Space in Eighth-Century Kufa* (New York: Cambridge University Press, 2011). On the Karaite movement, see Meira Pollack, ed., *Karaite Judaism: A Guide to Its History and Literary Sources* (Leiden: Brill, 2003).
33. Matthew J. Kuiper, *Da'wa and Other Religions: Indian Muslims and the Modern Resurgence of Global Islamic Activism* (New York: Routledge, 2018), 23.

34. Sidney H. Griffith, *The Church in the Shadow of the Mosque: Christians and Muslims in the World of Islam* (Princeton: Princeton University Press, 2008), 7. See also Jacques Waardenburg, ed., *Muslim Perceptions of Other Religions: A Historical Survey* (New York: Oxford University Press, 1999).
35. Kuiper, *Da'wa and Other Religions*, 60. See also E. Wagner, "*Munazara*," in *EI*, 1:565–68.
36. Avril Powell, *Muslims and Missionaries in Pre-mutiny India* (London: Curzon, 1993), 16–18.
37. In what follows, I list only several examples of Eastern Christian engagement with Islam. Fairly exhaustive accounts of these engagements are found in Wolfgang Eichner, "Byzantine Accounts of Islam," and Sidney H. Griffith, "Disputes with Muslims in Syriac Christian Texts: From Patriarch John (d. 648) to Bar Hebraeus (d. 1286)," in Cameron and Hoyland, *Doctrine and Debate in the East Christian World*, 109–96.
38. John of Damascus, *Writings*, trans. Frederic H. Chase (Washington, DC: Catholic University of America Press, 1958), 153. On still earlier Christian encounters with Islam, see Michael Phillip Penn, ed., *When Christians First Met Muslims: A Sourcebook* (Oakland: University of California Press, 2015); and Robert Hoyland, *Seeing Islam as Others Saw It: A Survey of Christian, Jewish, and Zoroastrian Writings on Early Islam* (Princeton, NJ: Darwin, 1997).
39. John V. Tolan, *Saracens: Islam in the Medieval European Imagination* (New York: Columbia University Press, 2002), 127–28; and Griffith, *Church in the Shadow of the Mosque*, 24 n.6.
40. Penn, *When Christians First Met Muslims*, 200–208, 231–32.
41. A. Jeffery, "Ghevond's Text of the Correspondence between Umar II and Leo III," *HTR* 37 (1944): 269–332.
42. Hugh Goddard, *A History of Christian-Muslim Relations* (Chicago: Ivan R. Dee, 2000), 58–59.
43. Griffith, *Church in the Shadow of the Mosque*, 60–63.
44. Meyendorff, "Byzantine Views of Islam," 120–21. The Greek treatises that Abu-Qurrah wrote are published in J. P. Migne, ed., *Patrologia graeca*, vol. 97 (Paris, 1865), 1402–610.
45. Quoted material is taken from Georg Graf, ed., *Des Theodor Abu Kurra Traktat über den Schöpfer und die wahre Religion*, Beiträge zur Geschichte der Philosophie des Mittelaltars, vol. 14 (Munster, 1913).
46. Avery Dulles, *A History of Christian Apologetics* (San Francisco: Ignatius, 2005), 94.
47. The aforementioned treatise is derived from actual debates. On the circumstances of these debates, see Alfred Guillaume, "A Debate between a Christian and Muslim Doctors," centenary supplement to the *Journal of the Royal Asiatic Society* (London, 1924): 233–44; and David Bertaina, "An Arabic Account of Theodore Abu Qurra in Debate at the Court of

the Caliph Ma'mun: A Study in Early Christian and Muslim Literary Dialogues" (PhD diss., Catholic University of America, 2007).

48. Hava Lazarus-Yafeh et al., eds., *The Majlis: Interreligious Encounters in Medieval Islam* (Wiesbaden: Harrowitz Verlag, 1999).

49. Mark R. Cohen and Sasson Somekh, "Interreligious Majalis in Early Fatamid Egypt," in Lazarus-Yafeh et al., *Majlis*, 136.

50. Mun'im A. Sirry, "Early Muslim-Christian Dialogue: A Closer Look at Major Themes of the Theological Encounter," *ICMR* 16 (October 2005): 365. Timothy's account of the debate in Syriac, with an English translation, may be found in Alphonse Mingana, ed. and trans., *Woosbrooke Studies: Christian Documents in Syriac, Arabic, and Garshuni* (Cambridge: Heffer, 1928), 2:1–162.

51. Jonathan Lyons, *The House of Wisdom: How Arabs Transformed Western Civilization* (New York: Bloomsbury, 2009), 55ff.

52. Goddard, *History of Christian-Muslim Relations*, 52.

53. Quoted in Goddard, *History of Christian-Muslim Relations*, 53.

54. Quoted without attribution in Louise Malow, "Interfaith Relations," in *Medieval Islamic Civilization: An Encyclopedia* (New York: Routledge, 2006), 1:393.

55. Ibn Kammuna, *Examination of the Three Faiths*, trans. Moshe Perlmann (Berkeley: University of California Press, 1971); and Barbara Roggema, "Jewish-Christian Debate in a Muslim Context: Ibn Al-Mahruma's Notes to Ibn Kammuna's *Examination of the Inquiries into Three Faiths*," in Han J. W. Drijvers et al., eds., *All Those Nations: Cultural Encounters within and with the Near East* (Groningen: STYX, 1999), 131–39; and Moshe Perlmann, "The Medieval Polemics between Islam and Judaism," in S. D. Goitein, ed., *Religion in a Religious Age* (Cambridge, MA: Association for Jewish Studies, 1974), 122–23.

56. Mark R. Cohen and Sasson Somekh, "Interreligious Majalis in Early Fatamid Egypt," in Lazarus-Yafeh et al., *Majlis*, 136ff.

57. Tolan, *Saracens*, 60.

58. George C. Papademetriou, *Two Traditions, One Space: Orthodox Christians and Muslims in Dialogue* (Boston: Somerset Hall, 2011), 150ff.

59. Manolis Ulbricht, *Die Fragmente einer grieschischen Koranübersetzung überliefert im polemischen Werk des Niketas von Byzanz* (Berlin, 2010).

60. Quoted material is from Meyendorff, "Byzantine Views of Islam," 121–22.

61. John Meyendorff, *Introduction à l'étude de Grégoire Palamas* (Paris: Seuil, 1959), 157–62; and Daniel Sahas, "Gregory Palamas on Islam," *MW* 73 (1983): 1–21.

62. Quoted in Anastasios Yannoulatos, "Byzantine and Contemporary Greek Orthodox Approaches to Islam," *JES* 33 (1996): 513–14.

63. Steven W. Reinert, *Late Byzantine Studies* (Burlington, VT: Ashgate, 2014), 125–50.

64. The address at Regensburg can be found in Benedict XVI, *A Reason Open to God: On Universities, Education, and Culture* (Washington, DC: Catholic University of America Press, 2013), 7–44.
65. Yannoulatos, "Byzantine and Contemporary Greek Orthodox Approaches to Islam," 512.
66. George C. Papademetriou, "Judaism and Greek Orthodoxy in Historical Perspective," *Greek Orthodox Theological Review* 21 (1976): 96ff.
67. Vivian B. Mann, ed., *Jews, Muslims, and Christians in Medieval Spain* (New York: G. Brazillier, 1992); and Kenneth Baxter Wolf, "Convivencia in Medieval Spain: A Brief History of the Idea," *RC* 3 (2008): 72–85.
68. See, e.g., Joseph G. Trabbic, "Maimonides, Aquinas, and Interreligious Dialogue," *Proceedings of the American Catholic Philosophical Association* 77 (2003): 221–33.
69. Thomas E. Burman, "Tafsir and Translation: Traditional Arabic Qur'an Exegesis and the Latin Qur'ans of Robert of Ketton and Mark of Toledo," *Speculum* 73 (1998): 703–32.
70. Quoted in Goddard, *History of Christian-Muslim Relations*, 94–95.
71. Lyons, *House of Wisdom*, 152–53.
72. See *Paradiso*, canto 11; and Bonaventure, *Life of St. Francis*, trans. Ewert Cousins (San Francisco: HarperCollins, 1978), 89–102.
73. Paul Moses, *The Saint and the Sultan: The Crusades, Islam, and Francis of Assisi's Mission of Peace* (New York: Doubleday, 2009), 3.
74. Quoted in Tolan, *Saracens*, 214–18.
75. Odulphus van der Vat, *Die Anfänge der Franziskanermissionen und ihre Weiterentwicklung im nahen Orient und in den mohammedanischen Ländern während des 13.Jahrhunderts* (Werl in Westphalia: Franziskus-Druckerei, 1943), 177–240.
76. On Rubruck generally and his travels in the East, see the entry on him in the *Encyclopaedia Iranica* at http://www.iranicaonline.org/articles/william-of-rubruck (accessed 14 April 2017); and Maria Bonewa-Petrowa, "Rubrucks Reisebeschreibung als soziologische und kulturgeschichtliche Quelle," *Philologus* 115 (1971): 16–31. Rubruck was not the first Latin Christian to show up at the khan's court. For others, see Igor de Rachewiltz, *Papal Envoys to the Great Khans* (Stanford: Stanford University Press, 1971).
77. Benjamin Z. Kedar, "The Multilateral Disputation at the Court of the Gran Qan Möngke, 1254," in Lazarus-Yafeh et al., *Majlis*, 162–83.
78. Tolan, *Saracens*, 223.
79. William of Rubruck, *The Mission of Friar William of Rubruck: His Journey to the Court of the Great Khan Möngke, 1253–1255*, trans. Peter Jackson (London: Hakluyt, 1990), 231. A Latin version—*Itinerarium Willelmi de Rubruc*—is found in Anastasius van den Wyngaert, ed., *Sinica Francisca*, vol. 1, *Itinera et relationes fratrum minorum saeculi xiii et xiv* (Florence: Apud Collegium S. Bonaventure, 1929), 164–297 (hereafter *Itinerarium*).

80. Rubruck, *Mission of Friar William of Rubruck*, 231; *Itinerarium*, 294.
81. Quoted in R. W. Southern, *Western Views of Islam in the Middle Ages* (Cambridge, MA: Harvard University Press, 1962), 49.
82. Rubruck, *Mission of Friar William of Rubruck*, 234–35; *Itinerarium*, 297 (translation modified). The name "tuin" for Buddhists comes from the Chinese *tao-jen*, literally "men of the road" or "men on the way." René Grousset, *The Empire of the Steppes: A History of Central Asia*, trans. Naomi Walford (New Brunswick, NJ: Rutgers University Press, 1970), 597 n.78.
83. Klimkeit, "Christians, Buddhists, and Manichaeans in Medieval Central Asia," 47. In Karakorum, different faiths had their own houses of worship, and Mongol policy toward them was generally mild.
84. Joseph Thiel, "Der Streit der Buddhisten und Taoisten zur Mongolzeit," *Monumenta Serica* 20 (1961): 32–46; and Sechin Jagchid, "The Mongol Khans and Chinese Buddhism and Taoism," *Journal of the International Association of Buddhist Studies* 2 (1979): 7–28.
85. Kwand Amir, *Habib al-siyar*, as quoted in Richard C. Foltz, *Religions of the Silk Road* (New York: St. Martin's Griffin, 2000), 124. Marco Polo quotes Khublai Khan as saying: "There are four prophets who are worshipped and to whom all the world does reverence. The Christians say their God was Jesus Christ; the Saracens Mahomet; the Jews Moses; and the idolaters Sakyamuni Burkhan [the Buddha], who was the first to be represented as God in the form of an idol; and I do honour and reverence to all four, so that I may be sure of doing it to him who is greatest in heaven and truest, and to him I pray for aid." See Marco Polo, *The Travels*, trans. Ronald Latham (London: Penguin, 2004), 124.
86. On Mongol religious policy generally, see J. Melver Weatherford, *Genghis Khan and the Quest for God: How the World's Greatest Conqueror Gave Us Religious Freedom* (New York: Viking, 2016). See also Grousset, *Empire of the Steppes*, 281.
87. Rubruck, *Mission of Friar William of Rubruck*, 236; *Itinerarium*, 298.
88. Quoted in Tolan, *Saracens*, 227.
89. Southern, *Western Views of Islam in the Middle Ages*, 52ff.; and Tolan, *Saracens*, 225–29.
90. Simon Tugwell, ed., *Early Dominicans: Selected Writings* (New York: Paulist, 1982), 25–27.
91. Thomas Aquinas, *De rationibus fidei contra Saracenos, Graecos et Armenos ad Cantorem Antiochenum* (Reasons for the Faith against . . .), trans. Joseph Kennedy, *Islamochristiana* 22 (1996): 33. On the background to the *Summa contra gentiles*, see Thomas J. Murphy, "The Date and the Purpose of the *Contra Gentiles*," *HJ* 10 (1969): 405–15.
92. Tolan, *Saracens*, 234. For Aquinas on unbelief generally, see also *ST* II-II, q. 10.
93. G. A. Wiegers, "The Polemical Works of Muhammad al-Qaysî and

Their Circulation in Arabic and Aljmiado among the Mudejars in the Fourteenth Century," *Al-Qantara: Revista de estudios árabes* 15 (1994): 163–99.

94. Tolan, *Saracens*, 234–55.
95. Alex J. Novikoff, *The Medieval Culture of Disputation: Pedagogy, Practice, and Performance* (Philadelphia: University of Pennsylvania Press, 2013), 172–80.
96. Louis IX did not attend the disputation; it was presided over by the Queen Mother, Blanch of Castille. See Hyam Maccoby, ed., *Judaism on Trial: Jewish-Christian Disputation in the Middle Ages* (East Brunswick, NJ: Associated University Presses, 1982), 22.
97. Maccoby, *Judaism on Trial*, 19–38; and Isidore Loeb, "La controverse religieuse entre les Chrétiens et les Juifs au moyen âge en France et en Espagne," *Revue de l'historie de religions* 17 (1888): 313–37.
98. Robert Chazon, "The Barcelona 'Disputation' of 1263: Christian Missionizing and Jewish Response," *Speculum* 52 (1977): 824–42.
99. On Nahmanides in general, see Nina Caputo, *Nahmanides in Medieval Catalonia: History, Community and Messianism* (Notre Dame: University of Notre Dame Press, 2008); and David Novak, *The Theology of Nahmanides* (Atlanta: Scholars, 1992).
100. Maccoby, *Judaism on Trial*, 102, 133ff.
101. Maccoby, *Judaism on Trial*, 119.
102. Caputo, *Nahmanides in Medieval Catalonia*, 91ff. See also Robert Chazon, *Barcelona and Beyond: The Disputation of 1263 and Its Aftermath* (Berkeley: University of California Press, 1992), 178.
103. Tolan, *Saracens*, 235.
104. Maccoby, *Judaism on Trial*, 12.
105. Dulles, *History of Apologetics*, 98, 104–6.
106. Judah Halevi, *The Kuzari (Kitab al Khazari): An Argument for the Faith of Israel*, trans. Hartwig Hirschfeld (1905; repr., New York: Schocken, 1964), 35.
107. Thomas F. Michel, ed., *A Muslim Theologian's Response to Christianity: Ibn Taymiyya's Al-Jawab al Sahiah* (Delmar, NY: Caravan, 1984), 198ff.
108. Rita George-Tvrtkovic, "After the Fall: Riccoldo da Montecroce and Nicholas of Cusa on Religious Diversity," *TS* 73 (2012): 649.
109. On Llull's life, see Anthony Bonner, ed., *Doctor Illuminatus: A Ramon Llull Reader* (Princeton: Princeton University Press, 1985), 1–44. On Llull's indebtedness to Jewish thought, see Harvey J. Hames, *The Art of Conversion: Christianity and Kabbalah in the Thirteenth Century* (Leiden: Brill, 2000).
110. For an overview of Llull's system, or "Llullism," see Anthony Bonner, *The Art and Logic of Ramon Llull: A User's Guide* (Leiden: Brill, 2007); and R. D. F. Pring-Mill, "Grundzüge von Llulls *Ars inveniendа veritatem*," *Archiv für Geschichte der Philosophe* 43 (1961): 23–33.

111. Bonner, *Doctor Illuminatus*, 151.
112. Bonner, *Doctor Illuminatus*, 47ff.
113. Llull, as quoted in Tolan, *Saracens*, 259.
114. Goddard, *History of Christian-Muslim Relations*, 115.
115. It should be noted that Llull wrote other dialogues as well, including (in English translation) *Book of the Tatar and Christian* (1286), *Book of the Five Wisemen* (1293), and *Disputation of Ramon the Christian with Hamar the Saracen* (1308). Dulles, *History of Apologetics*, 126; and Muriel Mirak-Weissbach, "Raymond Llull: A Great Voice in the Dialogue of Religions," *Dialogue of Civilizations* 28 (2001): 52.
116. Bonner, *Doctor Illuminatus*, 86.
117. Bonner, *Doctor Illuminatus*, 90. See also Tolan, *Saracens*, 264–65.
118. Bonner, *Doctor Illuminatus*, 97–98.
119. Tolan, *Saracens*, 266.
120. Bonner, *Doctor Illuminatus*, 167–69.
121. Tolan, *Saracens*, 273–74.
122. On Cusa's debt to Llull, see Ermenegildo Bidese et al., eds., *Ramon Llull und Nikolaus von Kues: Eine Zeichen der Toleranz: Akten des internationalen Kongresses zu Ramon Llull und Nikolaus von Kues* (Turnhout: Brepolis, 2005); and Eusebio Colomer, *Nikolaus von Kues und Ramond Llull aus Handschriften der Kueser Bibliothek* (Berlin: De Gruyter, 1961).
123. Roger A. Johnson, *Peacemaking and Religious Violence from Thomas Aquinas to Thomas Jefferson* (Eugene, OR: Pickwick, 2009), 115–21.
124. Christopher M. Bellitto et al., eds., *Introducing Nicholas of Cusa: A Guide to a Renaissance Man* (New York: Paulist, 2004), 270ff.; and Georges C. Anawati, "Nicholas de Cues et le problème de l'Islam," in *Niccolò Cusano agli inizi del mondo moderno* (Florence: G. C. Sansoni, 1970), 141–73. On Cusa's interactions with Segovia, see Rudolf Haubst, "Johannes von Segovia im Gespräch mit Nikolaus von Kues und Jean Germain über die göttliche Dreieinigkeit und ihre Verkündigung von den Mohammedanern," *Münchener Theologische Zeitschrift* 2 (1951): 115–29. On his debt to Montecroce, see Nicholas Rescher, "Nicholas of Cusa: A Fifteenth-Century Encounter with Islam," *MW* 55 (1965): 197.
125. Noted in Rescher, "Nicholas of Cusa," 200. On Segovia generally, see Anne Marie Wolf, *Juan de Segovia and the Fight for Peace: Christians and Muslims in the Fifteenth Century* (Notre Dame: University of Notre Dame Press, 2014). Deeming the Crusades to be a failure, Segovia advocated for a meeting (*contraferentia*) as the best means of engaging Muslims. See Claudia Märtl, "Experts, Border-Crossers and Cultural Brokers: The Knowledge of Islam and Contacts to Islamic Cultures at the Curia in the Fifteenth Century," in Mar von der Höh et al., eds., *Cultural Brokers at Mediterranean Courts in the Middle Ages* (Paderborn: Schöningh, 2013), 151. See also Ian Christopher Levy et al., *Nicholas of Cusa and Islam: Polemic and Dialogue in the Late Middle Ages* (Leiden: Brill, 2014).

126. *ODCC*, 1149–50.
127. On this point in Cusa's thought, see James Heft et al., eds., *Learned Ignorance: Intellectual Humility among Jews, Christians, and Muslims* (New York: Oxford University Press, 2011), 1–19.
128. Agostino Pertusi, ed., *La caduta di Costantinopoli. Le testimonianze dei contemporanei*, vol. 1 (Rome: Fondazione L. Valla, 1976).
129. Robert Schwoebel, *The Shadow of the Crescent: The Renaissance Image of the Turk (1453–1517)* (New York: St. Martin's, 1969).
130. Cusa, *On the Peace of Faith*, in William F. Wetz, ed., *Toward a New Council of Florence: "On the Peace of Faith" and Other Works by Nicolaus of Cusa* (Washington, DC: Schiller Institute, 1993), 232.
131. Nicholas of Cusa, *Nicolai de Cusa: Opera omnia* (Hamburg: F. Meiner, 1959), 7:6–7; Cusa, *On the Peace of Faith*, 233 (translation modified).
132. Cusa, *Opera omnia*, 7:9–10; Cusa, *On the Peace of Faith*, 235.
133. Cusa, *Opera omnia*, 7:9–10; Cusa, *On the Peace of Faith*, 231, 235.
134. James E. Biechler, "Interreligious Dialogue," in Bellitto et al., *Introducing Nicholas of Cusa*, 273.
135. Johnson, *Peacemaking and Religious Violence*, 141. See Cicero, *On the Nature of the Gods*, trans. Horace C. P. McGregor (New York: Penguin, 1972), 69–72.
136. Cusa, *Opera omnia*, 7:6.
137. Cusa, *Opera omnia*, 7:3, 11.
138. Cusa, *Opera omnia*, 7:17.
139. "Diversitas enim parit divisionem et inimicitias, odia et bella." Cusa, *Opera omnia*, 7:51.
140. "Quo admisso non turbabant varietates illae rituum." Cusa, *Opera omnia*, 7:51–52.
141. Cusa, *Opera omnia*, 7:62.
142. Cusa, *Opera omnia*, 7:62–63.
143. Pius II, as quoted in Southern, *Western Views of Islam in the Middle Ages*, 100.
144. On Cusa's legacy generally, see Simon J. G. Burton et al., eds., *Nicholas Cusa and the Making of the Early Modern World* (Leiden: Brill, 2019).
145. Biechler, "Interreligious Dialogue," 274.
146. Cusa, *Opera omnia*, 7:4.
147. Maurice Boutin, "Anonymous Christianity: A Paradigm for Interreligious Encounter?" *JES* 20 (1983): 602.
148. B. Pesala, ed., *The Debate of King Milinda: An Abridgement of the Milinda Panha* (Delhi: Motlial Banasidass, 1991).
149. James W. Laine, *Meta-Religion: Religion and Power in World History* (Oakland: University of California Press, 2014), 15–104. One could argue that Ashoka left a legacy similar to Akbar's. The evidence, however, is much scantier, and Ashoka appears to have been more interested in conversions to Buddhism and religious tranquility than in anything resem-

bling open-ended interreligious dialogue. See Charles Allen, *Ashoka: The Search for India's Lost Emperor* (London: Little, Brown, 2012).

150. Abu'l-Fazl, *Akbarnama*, 3 vols., trans. D. C. Phillott (Delhi: D. K. Fine Art, 1927–49); and Abu'l-Fazl, *Akbarnama*, trans. E. Mackenzie (1875; repr., Lahore: Sheikh Mubarak Ali, 1975).

151. Abdul al-Qadir Bada'uni, *Muntakhab al-Tawarikh*, 3 vols., trans. George S. A. Ranking and W. H. Lowe (Delhi: Idarah-i-Adabiyat, 1973).

152. Nizamuddin Ahmad, *Tabaqati-i-Akbari* (A History of India from the Early Musalman Invasions to the Thirty-Sixth Year of the Reign of Akbar), 3 vols., trans. Brajendranath De (Delhi: LP, 1992).

153. *The Dabistan or School of Manners*, 3 vols., trans. David Shea and Anthony Troyer (Paris: Oriental Translation Fund of Great Britain and Ireland, 1843). On the *Dabistan* in historical context, see Aditya Behl, "Pages from the Book of Religions: Encountering Religious Difference in Mughal India," in Sheldon Pollock, ed., *Forms of Knowledge in Early Modern Asia: Explorations in the Intellectual History of India and Tibet, 1500–1800* (Durham: Duke University Press, 2011), 210–39; and M. Arhar Ali, "Muslims' Perceptions of Judaism and Christianity in Medieval India," *MAS* 33 (1999): 243–55.

154. See, inter alia, Pierre du Jarric, *Akbar and the Jesuits: An Account of the Jesuit Missions at the Court of Akbar*, trans. C. H. Payne (New York: Harper and Brothers, 1926).

155. Abraham Eraly, *Emperors of the Peacock Throne: The Saga of the Great Mughals* (New Delhi: Penguin, 1997), 14ff.

156. Giorgio Milanetti, "Religion and Religions at Akbar's Court," in Gian Carlso Calazi, ed., *Akbar: The Great Emperor of India* (Turin: Skiria, 2012), 57.

157. Sri Ram Sharma, *The Religious Policy of the Mughal Emperors*, 3rd ed. (London: Asia Publishing House, 1972), 32–33.

158. The "Peacock throne" is shorthand to refer to the ruling seat of the Mughal kingdom. It takes its name from an actual jewel-encrusted throne with imagery of a peacock that was built in the time of Shah Jahan (r. 1628–58).

159. Jamal Malik, *Islam in South Asia* (Leiden: Brill, 2008), 163.

160. S. Inayet and A. Zaidi, "Akbar's Relations with Rajput Chiefs and Their Role in the Expansion of Empire," *Social Scientist* 22 (1994): 79.

161. S. C. Welch, *Imperial Mughal Painting* (New York: George Braziller, 1978), 15–23.

162. Abu'l-Fazl, as quoted in Annemarie Schimmel, *The Empire of the Great Mughals: History, Art, and Culture*, trans. Corinne Attwood (London: Reaktion, 2004), 13.

163. On the saint and the shrine, see P. M. Currie, *The Shrine and Cult of Muin al-Din Chishti of Ajmer* (Delhi: Oxford University Press, 1989). On Chishti Sufism in Asia more generally, see C. W. Ernst and Bruce B.

Lawrence, *Sufi Martyrs of Love: The Chishti Order in South Asia and Beyond* (New York: Palgrave Macmillan, 2002).

164. Ernst and Lawrence, *Sufi Martyrs of Love*, 3, 8, 65, passim.
165. Arnold Hottinger, *Akbar der Grosse: Herrscher über Indien durch Versöhnung der Religionen* (Munich: Wihelm Fink, 1998), 80–82.
166. Vincent A. Smith, *Akbar: The Great Mogul, 1542–1605* (Oxford: Clarendon, 1917), 104.
167. Excavations from the late twentieth century have established the likely location. See Syed Ali Nadeem Resavi, "Religious Disputations and Imperial Ideology: The Purpose and Location of Akbar's Ibadatkhana," *Studies in History* 24 (2008): 195–209.
168. Quoted in Eraly, *Emperors of the Peacock Throne*, 189.
169. Hottinger, *Akbar der Grosse*, 111.
170. Bada'uni, *Muntakhab al-Tawarikh*, 2:261.
171. M. Athar Ali, *Mughal India: Studies in Polity, Ideas, Society, and Culture* (New Delhi: Oxford University Press, 2006), 159.
172. See "Mahdi," in *EI*, 2:446–47.
173. Religion at Akbar's Court at http://www.columbia.edu/itc/mealac/pritchett/00islamlinks/ikram/part2_12.html (accessed 22 February 2017).
174. Makhan Lal Roy Choudhurty, *The Din-i-Ilahi or the Religion of Akbar* (New Delhi: Mushiram Manoharal, 1952), xxii.
175. Fazl, *Akbarnama*, 3:366.
176. Choudhurty, *Din-i-Ilahi*, 89.
177. B. P. Ambashthya, *Contributions on Akbar and the Parsees* (Patna: Janaki Prakashan, 1976).
178. Choudhurty, *Din-i-Ilahi*, 96–97. See also Shalin Jain, "Interaction with the 'Lords': The Jain Community and the Mughal Royalty under Akbar," *Social Scientist* 40 (2012): 33–57.
179. *Dabistan or School of Manners*, 3:362–63.
180. Quoted in Walter J. Fischel, "Jews and Judaism at the Courts of the Moghul Emperors of Medieval India," *Proceedings of the American Academy for Jewish Research* 18 (1948–49): 10.
181. *The Commentary of Father Monserrate, SJ, on His Journey to the Court of Akbar*, trans. J. S. Hoyland (London: Oxford University Press, 1922), 37, 132–33, 136–38.
182. Quoted from the *Dabistan* in Fischel, "Jews and Judaism," 10.
183. Emily Wellesz, *Akbar's Religious Thought Reflected in Mogul Paintings* (London: Allen and Unwin, 1952), 23.
184. Choudhury, *Din-i-Ilahi*, 99–102.
185. Agnieszka Kuczkiewicz-Fras, "Akbar the Great (1542–1605) and Christianity: Between Religion and Politics," *Orientalia Christiana Cracoviensa* 3 (2011): 79.
186. The letter is cited in full in Choudhury, *Din-i-Ilahi*, 113. On the Jesuit

mission in Goa, see Ines G. Zupanov, *Missionary Tropics: The Catholic Frontier in India, 16th and 17th Centuries* (Ann Arbor: University of Michigan Press, 2005).

187. Eraly, *Emperors of the Peacock Throne*, 198–99.

188. Acquaviva to Rui Vicente (24 July 1582), in John Correia-Afonso, SJ, ed., *Letters from the Mughal Court: The First Jesuit Mission to Akbar (1580–1583)* (St. Louis: Institute of Jesuit Sources, 1981), 110.

189. Correia-Afonso, *Letters from the Mughal Court*, 28, 110; and Choudhury, *Din-i-Ilahi*, 115.

190. *Commentary of Father Monserrate*, 182 (translation modified). For the Latin edition of this work, see Monserrate, *Mongolicae legationis commentarius*, ed. H. Hosten, *Memoirs of the Asiatic Society of Bengal* (Calcutta [Kolkata], 1914), 3:633.

191. The letter in English translation and commentary on it can be found in E. Rehatsek, "A Letter of the Emperor Akbar Asking for the Christian Scriptures," *Indian Antiquary: A Journal of Oriental Research* (April 1887): 135–39.

192. Choudhury, *Din-i-Ilahi*, 115.

193. Choudhury, *Din-i-Ilahi*, 120–21.

194. Besides other motivations, it should be known that Akbar had in fact requested both the second and third mission. Kuczkiewicz-Fras, "Akbar the Great," *Orientalia Christiana Cracoviensa* 3 (2011): 86.

195. Schimmel, *Empire of the Great Mughals*, 121.

196. Ali, *Mughal India*, 162.

197. Laine, *Meta-Religion*, 150–51.

198. Quoted in Jawad Syed, "Akbar's Multiculturalism," *Canadian Journal of Administrative Sciences / Revue canadienne des sciences de l'administration* 28 (2011): 406.

199. See Muzaffar Alam and Sanjay Subrahmanyam, "Frank Disputations: Catholics and Muslims in the Court of Jahangir," *Indian Economic and Social History Review* 46 (2009): 457–511; and F. Guerreiro, *Jahangir and the Jesuits* (1930; repr., London: Routledge, 2014). More generally, see V. Dalmia and M. D. Faruqui, eds., *Religious Interactions in Mughal India* (New Delhi: Oxford University Press, 2014).

200. Laine, *Meta-Religion*, 151; and Amartya Sen, *The Argumentative Indian: Writings on Indian History, Culture, and Identity* (New York: Farrar, Straus and Giroux, 2005), 16, 273, 287. See also Ashis Nandy, "The Politics of Secularism and the Recovery of Religious Tolerance," in Rajeev Bhargava, ed., *Secularism and Its Critics* (Delhi: Oxford University Press, 1998), 321–44.

201. For references to Akbar in Western literature from this time, see Balachandra Rajan, *Under Western Eyes: India from Milton to Macaulay* (Durham: Duke University Press, 1999), 38–39, 68, 80–81.

202. On this topic, see the essays gathered in Linda Gregerson and Susan Juster, eds., *Empires of God: Religious Encounters in the Early Modern Atlantic* (Philadelphia: University of Pennsylvania Press, 2011).
203. Urs App, *The Birth of Orientalism* (Philadelphia: University of Pennsylvania Press, 2010), 20ff.
204. David Chidester, *Empire of Religion: Imperialism and Comparative Religion* (Chicago: University of Chicago Press, 2014), 1–2; and James Lawrence, *Raj: The Making and Unmaking of British India* (New York: St. Martin's, 1998), 3.
205. Quoted in Thomas Metcalf, *Ideologies of the Raj* (Cambridge: Cambridge University Press, 1994), 3:62.
206. Paul Stevens and Rahul Sapra, "Akbar's Dream: Moghul Toleration and English/British Orientalism," *Modern Philology* 104 (2007): 379–411. British Orientalists, as Stevens and Sapra write, often paid "deference to Indian culture [to remind] the Raj of its progressive obligations; [still, this] remains an act of self-serving appropriation, seeking to suggest the authenticity of the English as Indians and the legitimacy of their rule as the means by which India will fulfill the promise of its [own] past" (391).
207. Alfred Lord Tennyson, *The Death of Oeone, Akbar's Dream, and Other Poems* (New York: Macmillan, 1892), 23–47. Scholar Benjamin Jowett appears to have first suggested that Tennyson write the poem. Books on Akbar and India—including Henry Elliot's *History of India* (1866–77, vol. 6) and M. Elphinstone's *History of India* (1874)—were supplied to Tennyson from Balliol College, Oxford, by the Orientalist Sir William Hunter. See Hallam Tennyson, *Alfred, Lord Tennyson: A Memoir* (Cambridge: Cambridge University Press, 2012), 2:372ff.
208. Gail Minault Graham, "Akbar and Aurangzeb: Syncretism and Separation in Mughal India, A Re-examination," *MW* 59 (1969): 106–26.

Chapter Two. Chicago

1. E. L. Rexford, "The Religious Intent," in *WPR*, 1:509.
2. Friedrich Max Müller, "The Real Significance of the Parliament of Religions," *Arena* 11 (1894): 1–11.
3. *WPR*, 1:11.
4. See, e.g., Judith Snodgrass, *Presenting Japanese Buddhism to the West: Orientalism, Occidentalism, and the Columbian Exposition* (Chapel Hill: University of North Carolina Press, 2003), 50ff.; and Dorothea Lüddeckens, *Das Weltparlament der Religionen von 1893: Strukturen interreligiöser Begegnung im 19.Jahrhundert* (Berlin: Walter de Gruyter, 2020).
5. Scattered in the historical landscape are, of course, many small-scale exceptions to this rule, even if most of these are better described as debates or polemics rather than dialogues. See, for instance, Vera B.

Moreen, "A Shi'i-Jewish Debate (*munazara*) in the Eighteenth Century," *JAOS* 119 (1999): 570–89; and Sherali Tareen, "The Polemic of Shahjahanpur: Religion, Miracles, and History," *IS* 51 (2012): 49–67. Organized by British authorities, the Polemic of Shahjahanpur was a three-way debate among Christians, Muslims, and Hindus outside Delhi in 1875–76. This event merits further research. Permit me also to mention a noteworthy literary debate in the spirit of Cusa: Jean Bodin's *Colloquium heptaplomeres de rerum sublimium arcanis abditis* (Colloquium of the Seven about Secrets of the Sublime). Written in dialogue form, this fictional work brought Christian, Jewish, Muslim, and skeptical voices together to discuss matters of religious truth and political tranquility. Written in Latin, it was not published until 1847 and it remains little known. For an English translation and critical edition, see Jean Bodin, *Colloquium of the Seven about Secrets of the Sublime*, trans. Marion Leathers Kuntz (University Park: Pennsylvania State University Press, 2008). Mention should be made, too, of Matteo Ricci's well-known interreligious engagements with Chinese civilization; a very large literature exists on this, but see George Minamiki, *The Chinese Rites Controversy from Its Beginnings to Modern Times* (Chicago: Loyola University Press, 1985). Finally, permit me to mention the fascinating story of the Jesuit missionary Ippolito Desideri (1684–1733), who traveled to Tibet and engaged Buddhists there, becoming the first European to learn Tibetan. See Trent Pomplun, *Jesuit on the Roof of the World: Ippolito Desideri's Mission to Eighteenth-Century Tibet* (New York: Oxford University Press, 2010). Still other examples could be adduced.

6. Jonathan Israel highlights this element of the Enlightenment; see his *Radical Enlightenment: Philosophy and the Making of Modernity, 1650–1750* (Oxford: Oxford University Press, 2001).
7. On this aspect of the Enlightenment, see David Sorken, *The Religious Enlightenment: Protestants, Jews, and Catholics from London to Vienna* (Princeton: Princeton University Press, 2008).
8. On the "ring parable" and its history, see Achim Aurnhammer et al., eds., *Die drei Ringe: Entstehung und Wandel und Wirkung der Ringparabel in der europäische Literatur und Kultur* (Berlin: De Gruyter, 2016). See also Gerhard Kaiser, "Aufklärung und Christentum in Lessings 'Nathan der Weisse,'" *TZ* 63 (2008): 358–80.
9. Perez Zagorin, *How the Idea of Religious Toleration Came to the West* (Princeton: Princeton University Press, 2003), 240ff.
10. *DRP*, 68–70, 198–99, passim.
11. See Nicholas Adams, ed., *The Impact of Idealism: Religion*, vol. 4 (Cambridge: Cambridge University Press, 2013).
12. On Schleiermacher's theological program in general and its historical context, see Claude Welch, *Protestant Thought in the Nineteenth Century* (New Haven: Yale University Press, 1972), 59–85.

13. Sydney Ahlstrom, *The American Protestant Encounter with World Religions* (Beloit, WI: Beloit College, 1962), 7.
14. Friedrich Schleiermacher, *On Religion: Speeches to Its Cultured Despisers*, trans. John Oman (New York: Harper, 1958), 11–12.
15. Ahlstrom, *American Protestant Encounter with World Religions*, 9.
16. On Schleiermacher's general influence on American elite opinion, see Jeffrey A. Wilcox, Terrence N. Tice, and Catherine L. Kelysey, eds., *Schleiermacher's Influences on American Thought and Religious Life*, 3 vols. (Eugene, OR: Pickwick, 2013–14).
17. Comparative religion can boast a longer prehistory, especially among Arabic and Persian scholars, even if their work exercised little influence in the modern West. Still, mention should be made of the *Dabistan-i Mazaheb*, touched upon in the previous chapter, and the writings of the tenth-century scholar Al-Biruni as well as those of Ibn Hazm al-Andalusi, Ali bin Rabn al-Tabari, and Mohammad al-Shahrastani. The Baghdad-based Jewish scholar Ibn Kammuna's *Examination of the Three Faiths* (1280) also merits mentioning again. On these and other works, see Eric J. Sharpe, *Comparative Religion: A History*, 2nd ed. (London: Duckworth, 1986), 11–12.
18. Guy Stroumsa, *A New Science: The Discovery of Religion in the Age of Reason* (Cambridge, MA: Harvard University Press, 2010), 14–38.
19. Sharpe, *Comparative Religion*, 17–19.
20. See Lynn Hunt et al., eds., *The Book That Changed Europe: Picart and Bernard's Religious Ceremonies of the World* (Cambridge, MA: Belknap Press of Harvard University Press, 2010); and Lynn Hunt et al., eds., *Bernard Picart and the First Global Vision of Religion* (Los Angeles: Getty Research Institute, 2010). At 3,000 pages and with 250 pages of engraved images, the work powerfully shaped how Europeans sized up the various faith traditions across the globe. Also see the excellent study by Paola von Wyss-Giacosa, *Religionsbilder der frühen Aufklärung: Bernard Picarts Tafeln für die Cérémonies et coutumes religieuses de tous les peuples du monde* (Bern: Benteli Verlag, 2006). Much content was drawn from Jesuits' encounters with global religious diversity. See Michael Pomedli, "Beyond Unbelief: Early Jesuit Interpretations of Native Religions," *SR* 16 (1987): 275–87.
21. Hans G. Kippenberg, *Die Entdeckung der Religionsgeschichte: Religionswissenschaft und Moderne* (Munich: C. H. Beck, 1997), 18ff.
22. Sir William Jones, "On the Gods of Greece, Italy, and India," *Asiatic Researches* 1 (1788): 221–75.
23. On Jones, see S. N. Mukherjee, *Sir William Jones: A Study in Eighteenth-Century British Attitudes to India* (Cambridge: Cambridge University Press, 1968).
24. Eugène Burnouf, *Introduction à l'historie du buddhisme indien* (Paris: Imprimerie Royale, 1844). On the history of how Western scholarship de-

veloped on the Buddha and Buddhism, see David S. Lopez's engaging *From Stone to Flesh: A Short History of the Buddha* (Chicago: University of Chicago Press, 2013).

25. Carl T. Jackson, *The Oriental Religions and American Thought: Nineteenth-Century Explorations* (Westport, CT: Greenwood, 1981), 45ff.
26. On Schlegel, see Tomoko Masuzawa, *The Invention of World Religions* (Chicago: University of Chicago Press, 2005), 154; and James Turner, *Philology: The Forgotten Origins of the Modern Humanities* (Princeton: Princeton University Press, 2014), 130–31.
27. Michael J. Altman, *Heathen, Hindoo, Hindu: American Representations of India* (New York: Oxford University Press, 2017). See also Arthur Christy, *The Orient in American Transcendentalism: A Study of Emerson, Thoreau, and Alcott* (New York: Octagon, 1963).
28. James Freeman Clarke, *Ten Great Religions: An Essay in Comparative Theology*, 2 vols. (Boston: J. R. Good, 1871); and Masuzawa, *Invention of World Religions*, 74–78.
29. Ahlstrom, *American Protestant Encounter with World Religions*, 10.
30. Friedrich Max Müller, *Introduction to the Science of Religion* (1873; repr., New York: Arno, 1978).
31. Proceedings of these congresses may be found at https://catalog.hathitrust.org/Record/100807046 (accessed 13 June 2017).
32. N. J. Giradot, "Müller's *Sacred Books* and the Nineteenth-Century Production of the Comparative Science of Religion," *HR* 41 (2002): 213–50.
33. *Upanishads*, trans. Friedrich Max Müller (Oxford: Clarendon, 1979), xx.
34. Müller, as quoted in Eric J. Ziolkowski, ed., *A Museum of Faiths: Histories and Legacies of the 1893 World's Parliament of Religions* (Atlanta: Scholars, 1993), 149.
35. Mention should also be made of the German "history of religions school" (*Religionsgeschichtliche Schule*), the representatives of which sought to apply historical-critical methods of inquiry to the religious diversity of the ancient Middle East. See Gerd Lüdemann, ed., *Die "Religionsgeschichtliche Schule": Facetten eines theologischen Umbruches* (Frankfurt am Main: Peter Lang, 1996); and Thomas Albert Howard, *Protestant Theology and the Making of the Modern German University* (Oxford: Oxford University Press, 2006), 390.
36. Louis Henry Jordon, *Comparative Religion: Its Genesis and Growth* (Edinburgh: T. and T. Clark, 1905), 579–91; Sharpe, *Comparative Religion*, 120–21; and Arie Molendiijk, *The Emergence of the Science of Religion in the Netherlands* (Leiden: Brill, 2005), 71ff.
37. Masuzawa, *Invention of World Religions*, 107–10.
38. Richard Hughes Seager, *The World's Parliament of Religions: The East/West Encounter, Chicago, 1893* (Bloomington: Indiana University Press, 1995), xxxix; and Claude Welch, *Protestant Thought in the Nineteenth Century, 1870–1914* (New Haven: Yale University Press, 1985), 2:107–8.

39. Stephen Neill, *A History of Christian Missions*, 2nd ed. (London: Penguin, 1990), 222. See also Oliver Wendell Elsbree, *The Rise of the Missionary Spirit in America, 1790–1815* (Philadelphia: Porcupine, 1980); and Clifton Jackson Phillips, *Protestant America and the Pagan World: The First Half Century of the American Board of Commissioners for Foreign Missions, 1810–1860* (Cambridge, MA: East Asia Research Center, Harvard University, 1969).
40. Altman, *Heathen, Hindoo, Hindu*, 27–47.
41. On this topic, see David A. Hollinger's engaging *Protestants Abroad: How Missionaries Tried to Change the World but Changed America* (Princeton: Princeton University Press, 2017).
42. Mitch Numark, "Translating *Dharma:* Scottish Missionary-Orientalists and the Politics of Religious Understanding in Nineteenth-Century Bombay," *JAS* 70 (2011): 473. To my knowledge, there has been precious little work done on the history of religious cartography, that is, mapping global religious affiliation.
43. Geoffrey A. Oddie, *Imagined Hinduism: British Protestant Missionary Constructions of Hinduism, 1793–1900* (New Delhi: Sage, 2006), 14.
44. Masuzawa, *Invention of World Religions*, xi, 146.
45. Frederick Denison Maurice, *The Religions of the World and Their Relations to Christianity* (London: Macmillan, 1881), 252.
46. Kenneth Cracknell, *Justice, Courtesy and Love: Theologians and Missionaries Encountering World Religions, 1846–1914* (London: Epworth, 1995), 35. After the parliament, the "fulfillment" view came to consummate expression in J. N. Farquhar's *The Crown of Hinduism* (London: H. Milford, 1913), the "crown" being Christ, for whom Hinduism had unwittingly longed.
47. These movements played an outsized influence in early efforts of modern interreligious dialogue, both in North America and in Europe. See Antoine Faivre, *Theosophy, Imagination, Tradition: Studies in Western Esotericism*, trans. Christine Rhone (Albany: State University of New York Press, 2000); and Mary Ann Meyers, *A New World Jerusalem: The Swedenborgian Experiment in Community Construction* (Westport, CT: Greenwood, 1983).
48. Allen, quoted in Cracknell, *Justice, Courtesy, and Love*, 81.
49. Jürgen Osterhammel, *The Transformation of the World: A Global History of the Nineteenth Century*, trans. Patrick Camiller (Princeton: Princeton University Press, 2014), 74.
50. Farquhar, *Crown of Hinduism*, 11.
51. Rossiter Johnson, ed., *A History of the World's Columbian Exposition Held in Chicago in 1893* (New York: D. Appleton, 1897), 10.
52. On the tradition of world's fairs in the nineteenth century, see Paul Greenhalgh, *Ephemeral Vistas: The Expositions Universelles, Great Exhibitions, and World's Fairs, 1851–1939* (Manchester: Manchester University

Press, 1988). The official guide of the 1893 fair can be found at World's Columbian Exposition, 1893, Records (box 1, folder 4), UCL, Special Collections Research Center.

53. *World's Fair Album Atlas and Family Souvenir*, World's Columbian Exposition, 1893, Records (box 1, folder 6), UCL, Special Collections Research Center.

54. Quoted in David F. Burg, *Chicago's White City of 1893* (Lexington: University of Kentucky Press, 1976), 112.

55. Eric J. Ziolkowski, "Heavenly Visions and Worldly Intentions: Chicago's Columbian Exposition and the World's Parliament of Religions (1893)," *JAC* 13 (1990): 10.

56. On the fair in general and visitors' responses, see William Cronon, *Nature's Metropolis: Chicago and the Great West* (New York: Norton, 1991), 341–69; and Joseph Alan Gustaitis, *Chicago's Greatest Year, 1893: The White City and the Birth of the Modern Metropolis* (Carbondale: Southern Illinois University Press, 2013).

57. Henry Adams, *The Education of Henry Adams* (New York: Penguin, 1990), 320.

58. Charles C. Bonney, "The Genesis of the World's Religious Congress," *New Church Review* 1 (1894): 74.

59. Quoted in Bonney, "Genesis of the World's Religious Congress," 79 (emphasis added).

60. The World's Congress Auxiliary encouraged and held lectures and sessions on a vast array of topics, from history to women's rights to medicine to art, and much more. These opened on 15 May 1893 and closed on 30 October 1893. See Charles C. Bonney, ed., *World's Congress Addresses* (Chicago: Open Court, 1900).

61. Walter R. Houghton, ed., *Neely's History of the Parliament of Religions and Religious Congresses at the World Columbian Exposition* (Chicago: Frank Tennyson Neely, 1893), 16.

62. Mary Eleanor Barrows, *John Henry Barrows: A Memoir* (London: Fleming H. Revell, 1904), 253–54; and Philo Adams Otis, *The First Presbyterian Church: A History of the Oldest Institution in Chicago* (Chicago: Clayton F. Summy, 1900), 79.

63. On the denominational affiliation of all sixteen members, see Charles C. Bonney, "The World's Parliament of Religions," *Monist* 5 (1895): 327. Relations between Protestants and Jews, especially between those of a liberal persuasion, had been improving steadily in the late nineteenth century. See Lawrence G. Charap, "'Accept the Truth from Whomsoever Gives It': Jewish-Protestant Dialogue, Interfaith Alliances, and Pluralism, 1880–1910," *AJH* 89 (2001): 261–77.

64. John Henry Barrows referred to Jones as a "helper who means business." See Barrows to Jones (1 January 1892), Jenkin Lloyd Jones Papers (box 1, folder 11), UCL, Special Collections Research Center. See also

Marcus Braybrooke, *Pilgrimage of Hope: One Hundred Years of Global Interfaith Dialogue* (London: SCM, 1992), 17–18.

65. Kenton Druyvesteyn, as quoted in Braybrooke, *Pilgrimage of Hope*, 14.
66. See the communiqué from March 1893, sent from Barrows to John Keane, rector of the Catholic University of America, in ACUA, Presidents' Records, box 1, folder 144.
67. Quoted in Bonney, "Genesis of the World's Religious Congress," 82.
68. The broader work of the committee—of which the Parliament of World Religions was only one part, albeit the most conspicuous—can be seen in J. W. Hanson, ed., *The World's Congress of Religions: The Addresses and Papers Delivered before the Parliament and an Abstract of the Congresses Held in the Art Institute . . . August 25 to October 15, 1893* (Chicago: International Publishing, 1894), 995ff. In all, forty-one religious congresses took place. See also *World's Religious Congresses of 1893, General Programme* (Chicago, 1893), UCL, Special Collections Research Center.
69. Barrows, *John Henry Barrows: A Memoir*, 253, 258.
70. Sadly, most of this correspondence and other materials related to the parliament were destroyed when a fire consumed Barrows's home.
71. *WPR*, 1:10.
72. Bonney, "Genesis of the World's Religious Congress," 87–88.
73. Bonney, "The World's Parliament of Religions," 333.
74. *WPR*, 1:18.
75. Wise was at the forefront of thinking about Jewish-Christian relations. See his *Judaism and Christianity: Their Agreements and Disagreements* (Cincinnati: Bloch, 1883).
76. Burg, *Chicago's White City*, 267.
77. John H. Barrows, "The Religious Possibilities of the World's Fair," *Our Day* 10 (August 1892): 564.
78. Keane, quoted in Barrows, *John Henry Barrows: A Memoir*, 259–60.
79. Burg, *Chicago's White City*, 266.
80. On Webb generally, see Umar F. Abd-Allah, *A Muslim in Victorian America: The Life of Alexander Russell Webb* (Oxford: Oxford University Press, 2006).
81. Barrows, *John Henry Barrows: A Memoir*, 258–59.
82. The parliament took place only three years after Mormons had condemned polygamy. Even though they were excluded from the parliament, Mormons did participate in the exposition in other ways. The exposition witnessed, for instance, the first national performance of the Mormon Tabernacle Choir. See Reid L. Neilson, *Exhibiting Mormonism: The Latter-Day Saints and the 1893 Chicago's World Fair* (New York: Oxford University Press, 2010).
83. Douglass criticized the exposition for excluding African Americans. See Frederick Douglass and Ida Wells, *The Reason Why the Colored American Is Not in the World's Columbian Exposition* (Urbana: University of Illinois

Press, 1999). See also John P. Burris, *Exhibiting Religion: Colonialism and Spectacle at International Expositions* (Charlottesville: University of Virginia Press, 2001), 193; and D. Keith Naylor, "The Black Presence at the World's Fair, 1893," *Religion* 26 (1996): 249–59. There was one lecture given on indigenous American religiosity: "The Religion of the North American Indians," by Alice Fletcher, a Harvard anthropologist. See Burris, *Exhibiting Religion*, 159.

84. See the pope's apostolic letter (8 September 1895) to Archbishop Francis Satolli, apostolic delegate to the United States, printed in *Ecclesiastical Review* 13 (1895): 395.

85. Noted in *WPR*, 1:21–22. Barrows insistently sought the blessing of both the British monarchy and the archbishop of Canterbury, but to no avail. The former deferred to the latter. Barrows wrote Lambeth Palace on three separate occasions in the months leading up to the parliament: on 15 December 1892, 18 January 1893, and 22 July 1893. A fellow bishop thanked Archbishop Benson for taking a stand "against that preposterous gathering in Chicago." See LPL, E. W. Benson Papers, vol. 126, 156–57, 188–95, 198–207, 210–11, and 217–19.

86. Martin Marty, *Modern American Religion: The Irony of It All, 1893–1919* (Chicago: University of Chicago Press, 1986), 1:22–23. Barrows's daughter quoted her father's humorous response to the opposition he received: "I had to toil for an unprecedented achievement with the General Assembly of my own church, forty infallible religious editors, the Sultan of Turkey, and the Archbishop of Canterbury pulling hard on my unclerical coat tails." Quoted in Barrows, *John Henry Barrows: A Memoir*, 256.

87. Barrows expressed delight to Jenkin Lloyd Jones about how enthusiastic the religious press seemed to be concerning the parliament. See Barrows to Jones (19 August 1893), Jenkin Lloyd Jones Papers (box 1, folder 11), UCL, Special Collections Research Center.

88. William Pipe, "The Parliament of Religions," *Outlook* (26 August 1893): 385.

89. "Study of Comparative Religions," *Chicago Tribune* (11 September 1893).

90. John H. Barrows, "The Religious Possibilities of the World's Fair," *Our Day* 10 (August 1892): 560.

91. Barrows, "The Religious Possibilities of the World's Fair," 567.

92. A list of those gathered on the stage for the opening day can be found in *WPR*, 1:64–66.

93. Dubbed for the occasion the "Universal Prayer," the Lord's Prayer along with a moment of silence began each day of the parliament.

94. "Opening of the Great Parliament," *Chicago Tribune* (12 September 1893).

95. *WPR*, 1:62.

96. *WPR*, 1:67, 71–72.

97. *WPR*, 1:71–75.

98. *WPR*, 1:101.

99. "Opening of the Great Parliament."
100. Houghton, *Neely's History of the Parliament of Religions*, 34.
101. "Creeds in Council" [newspaper name not provided], Clippings of the World's Parliament of Religions, UCL, 1; and Braybrooke, *Pilgrimage of Hope*, 23.
102. The entire schedule can be seen in *World's Religious Congresses of 1893, General Programme* (Chicago, 1893), 22–33, UCL, Special Collections Research Center. Put together by Barrows and others, this document was regarded by Bonney as "one of the most remarkable publications of the century." *WPR*, 1:70.
103. Quoted in Braybrooke, *Pilgrimage of Hope*, 23.
104. "Say a Fond Farewell," [Name of newspaper not provided], Clippings of the World's Parliament of Religions, UCL, 216.
105. See *World's Religious Congresses of 1893, General Programme* (Chicago, 1893), UCL, Special Collections Research Center; and *WPR*, 1:117–20, 152.
106. *WPR*, 1:155–56.
107. Charles Andrews Heath, a Chicago businessman, kept a diary recording his visits to the parliament and the larger fair. See Charles Andrews Heath Papers, 1880–1949, diary from 1893 (box 3, folder 40), NL, Modern Manuscripts Collection.
108. Braybrooke, *Pilgrimage of Hope*, 27. A list of major participants may be found in Lüddeckens, *Das Weltparlament der Religionen*, 291–315.
109. *WPR*, 1:158, 162, 167, 172.
110. Quoted anonymously in *WPR*, 1:158.
111. Anagarika Dharmapala to Jenkin Lloyd Jones (4 April 1897), Jenkin Lloyd Jones Papers (box 1, folder 24), UCL, Special Collections Research Center; and WPR, 1:177.
112. *WPR*, 1:160.
113. *WPR*, 1:183–87.
114. *DRP*, 244, 346–47.
115. *DRP*, 221, 348.
116. Quoted in Ziolkowski, *Museum of Faiths*, 89 (emphasis added). For a plea for universal religion from an Asian perspective, see *WPR*, 1:440–43.
117. *DRP*, 319, 321.
118. Ruth Rouse and Stephen Charles Neill, eds., *A History of the Ecumenical Movement*, 2nd ed. (Philadelphia: Westminster, 1967), 353ff.
119. On Schaff generally, see Thomas Albert Howard, *God and the Atlantic: America, Europe, and the Religious Divide* (Oxford: Oxford University Press, 2011), 138–58; and Thomas Albert Howard, "Deutsche Universitätstheologie in den USA: Edward Robinson und Philip Schaff," in Philip Loeser and Christoph Strupp, eds., *Universität der Gelehrten—Universität der Experten: Adaptionen deutscher Wissenschaft in den USA des 19.Jahrhunderts* (Stuttgart: Franz Steiner Verlag, 2005), 31–52.
120. *DRP*, 102, 115.

121. Will Herberg, *Protestant, Catholic, Jew: An Essay in American Religious Sociology* (Garden City, NY: Doubleday, 1955).
122. For Catholic participation in general, see James F. Cleary, "Catholic Participation in the World's Parliament of Religions, Chicago, 1893," *CHR* 55 (1970): 585–608.
123. Keane to the American Board of Archbishops (12 November 1892). Permit a lengthier quote from this letter: "I beg leave to venture the opinion [about the parliament] that, while the objections against the proposal [for participating] are obvious, the reasons in favor of it seem paramount. The obvious objection is, that it will encourage religious indifferentism, will favor an eclectic or synthetic religion superior to all denominations. It is true that to all forms of partial Christianity this objection is fatal;—but the Catholic Church, embodying all that is true and good in all the others, is the only really synthetic religion, the only one that not only can stand such a test but must desire that she should be subjected to it by all serious thinkers. Here she has an unparalleled opportunity of showing to all the religions of the world that whatever they possess for man's enlightenment and improvement she has in superior degree besides. Such an exposition will be the best refutation of the error that one religion is as good as a another. . . . [Therefore] *can the Catholic Church afford not to be there?*" Emphasis in original, 90P6, AAB. The decision for the Catholic hierarchy to participate was made at a meeting of archbishops in New York that took place on 16–18 November 1892. The minutes of this meeting are available at AAB; see "Minutes of the Third Annual Conference of the Most Rev. Archbishops of the United States in New York Nov. 16, 17, 18 A.D. 1892" (90Q3).
124. Braybrooke, *Pilgrimage of Hope*, 28.
125. *DRP*, 172–74; *WPR*, 2:1338.
126. Dennis B. Downey, "Tradition and Acceptance: American Catholics and the Columbian Exposition," *Mid-America: An Historical Review* 63 (1981): 80.
127. In addition to the parliament, there was also a Jewish Religious Congress and a Jewish Women's Congress.
128. For broader historical context about American Jews at this time, see Marc Lee Raphael, *Judaism in America* (New York: Columbia University Press, 2005), 39ff.
129. *DRP*, 242–43.
130. Seager, *World's Parliament of Religions*, 44–45, 56–57; and Yaakov Ariel, "American Judaism and Interfaith Dialogue," in Dana Evan Kaplan, ed., *Cambridge Companion to American Judaism* (Cambridge: Cambridge University Press, 2005), 327–29.
131. *DRP*, 266–67.
132. *DRP*, 278–79; and Charles Little, "The Chicago Parliament of Religions," *Methodist Review* 76 (1894): 209.

133. *DRP*, 272; *WPR*, 1:127.
134. The image is reproduced in *DRP* in a section of pictures after page 270. On American Christians' attitudes toward Islam around this time, see Thomas S. Kidd, *American Christians and Islam: Evangelical Culture and Muslims from the Colonial Period to the Age of Terrorism* (Princeton: Princeton University Press, 2009), 37ff.
135. "Discourses on the Religion of Islam," *Chicago Daily Tribune* (21 September 1893). See also Kambiz Ghanea Bassiri, *A History of Islam in America* (Cambridge: Cambridge University Press, 2010), 115–26. Webb felt that he was treated unfairly by the press, as he later wrote to Jenkin Lloyd Jones (28 September 1893), Jenkin Lloyd Jones Papers (box 4, folder 5), UCL, Special Collections Research Center.
136. Richard Hughes Seager, *Buddhism in America* (New York: Columbia University Press, 1999), 36–37. Not all views of Asian religions were negative. See, e.g., Frederick J. Masters's depiction of Chinese temples in San Francisco in the *Californian* 2 (November 1892): 727–41, partially reprinted in Thomas Tweed and Stephen Prothero, eds., *Asian Religions in America: A Documentary History* (New York: Oxford University Press, 1999), 75–78.
137. On Brahmo Samaj, see David Kopf, *The Brahmo Samaj and the Shaping of the Modern Indian Mind* (Princeton: Princeton University Press, 1979).
138. *DRP*, 357.
139. *DRP*, 358.
140. Joseph M. Kitagawa, *The 1893 World's Parliament of Religions and Its Legacy* (Chicago: University of Chicago Divinity School, 1984), 5. These four, of course, do not exhaust Asians' contributions to the parliament, but, then and now, they have been generally viewed as the most significant speakers there on behalf of Asian religious ideas.
141. See Stephanie Syman, *The Subtle Body: The Story of Yoga in America* (New York: Farrar, Straus and Giroux, 2010), 62–72.
142. On Rinzai Zen Buddhism in general, see Jørn Borup, *Japanese Rinzai Zen Buddhism: Myōshinji, a Living Religion* (Leiden: Brill, 2008).
143. *DRP*, 409.
144. *WPR*, 2:831, 1285.
145. Seager, *Buddhism in America*, 36–38, passim. See also Snodgrass, *Presenting Japanese Buddhism to the West.*
146. Seager, *World's Parliament of Religions*, 158–59. On Suzuki's American career, see Joseph Kitagawa, "Buddhism in America (with Special Reference to Zen)," *Japanese Religions* 5 (1967): 32–57. On Carus, see Kayoko Nagao, "Paul Carus' Involvement in the Modernization of Japanese Education and Buddhism," *Japanese Religions* 34 (2009): 171–85.
147. Seager, *Buddhism in America*, 37–39.
148. *DRP*, 412, 415; *WPR*, 2:1093.
149. Noted in Seager, *World's Parliament of Religions*, 158.

150. P. C. Mojumdar, *The Oriental Christ* (Boston: George Ellis, 1883).
151. On his life, see Churesh Chunder Bose, *The Life of Protap Chunder Mozoomdar*, 2 vols. (Calcutta: Nababidhan Trust, 1940).
152. *DRP*, 448–49.
153. Charles Little, "The Parliament of Religions," *Methodist Review* 76 (March 1894): 211.
154. *DRP*, 449.
155. Sunrit Mullick, *The First Hindu Mission to America: The Pioneering Visits of Protap Chunder Mozoomdar* (New Delhi: Northern Book Centre, 2010), 89ff.
156. This is from Merwin Marie-Snell, the secretary for Bishop John Keane. Quoted in Marie Louise Burke, *Swami Vivekananda in the West: New Discoveries*, 3rd ed. (Calcutta: Advaita Ashrama, 1983), 85.
157. Narasingha P. Sil, *Swami Vivekananda: A Reassessment* (London: Associated University Presses, 1997), 21–33.
158. Christopher Isherwood, *Ramakrishna and His Disciples* (New York: Simon and Schuster, 1959), 186–217.
159. On this topic, see Shamita Basu, *Religious Revivalism as Nationalist Discourse: Swami Vivekananda and the New Hinduism in Nineteenth-Century Bengal* (New Delhi: Oxford University Press, 2002).
160. Braybrooke, *Pilgrimage of Hope*, 32.
161. *WPR*, 1:101.
162. *WPR*, 1:102; *DRP*, 430.
163. *DRP*, 430.
164. *WPR*, 1:102, 170–71.
165. *WPR*, 1:102, 170.
166. Michael J. Altman, "The Construction of Hinduism in America," *RC* 10 (2016): 212–13.
167. Gwilym Beckerlegge, "The Early Spread of Vedanta Societies: An Example of 'Imported Localism,'" *Numen* 51 (2004): 296–320.
168. Philip Goldberg, *American Veda: From Emerson and the Beatles to Yoga and Meditation—How Indian Spirituality Changed the West* (New York: Three Rivers, 2010), 78.
169. See Norris Frederick, "William James and Swami Vivekananda: Religious Experience and Vedanta/Yoga in America," *William James Studies* 9 (2012): 37–55.
170. For his role in shaping contemporary Hindu senses of identity, see Sharma Jyotirmaya, *Restatement of Religion: Swami Vivekananda and the Making of Hindu Nationalism* (New Haven: Yale University Press, 2013).
171. Sil, *Swami Vivekananda*, 155.
172. *WPR*, 1:583–90, 605–38.
173. Seager, *World's Parliament of Religions*, 90.
174. *DRP*, 77; *WPR*, 1:xx–xxiv.
175. Burg, *Chicago's White City*, 239.

176. *WPR*, 2:977–98, 1268–69.
177. George S. Goodspeed, ed., *The World's First Parliament of Religions: Its Christian Spirit, Historic Greatness and Manifold Results: A Brief Summary of the Testimonies Gathered from Many Lands, Indicating What the World Has Said of This Memorable Congress . . . and Its Organizer and Chairman John Henry Barrows* (Chicago: Hill and Shuman, 1895), 5.
178. Arie L. Molendijk, "To Unite All Religions against Irreligion: The 1893 World Parliament of Religions," *JHMT* 18 (2011): 233–34.
179. Barrows, *John Henry Barrows: A Memoir*, 275.
180. Bonney, "The World's Parliament of Religions," 343–44.
181. Jenkin Lloyd Jones, *A Chorus of Faith as Heard in the Parliament of Religions* (Chicago: Unity, 1893), 16, 20–21.
182. See the exchange between Jones and Dharmapala (4 January 1897), in Jenkin Lloyd Jones Papers (box 1, folder 24), UCL, Special Collections Research Center.
183. Quoted in Barrows, *John Henry Barrows: A Memoir*, 297.
184. Chandlin to Bonney (11 October 1893), printed in *Chinese Recorder* 25 (1894): 35–36.
185. Müller, "The Real Significance of the Parliament of Religions," 1–14.
186. Paul Carus, *The Dawn of a New Religious Era* (Chicago: Open Court, 1899). I quote from a chapter in this book that originally appeared as a freestanding article; see Carus, "The Dawn of a New Religious Era," *Forum* 16 (November 1893): 388–96.
187. Burris, *Exhibiting Religion*, 167.
188. Paul Carus, "The World's Religious Parliament Extension," *Monist* 5 (April 1895): 345.
189. Seager, *World's Parliament of Religion*, 129ff.
190. See *The World's Parliament of Religion and the Religious Parliament Extension* (Chicago: Open Court, 1896).
191. Quoted material taken from Goodspeed, *World's First Parliament of Religions*, 40–41.
192. Quoted in Goodspeed, *World's First Parliament of Religions*, 21.
193. James E. Ketelaar, "Strategic Occidentalism: Meiji Buddhists at the World's Parliament of Religions," *BCS* 11 (1991): 50.
194. Seager, *World's Parliament of Religions*, 158; Ziolkowski, *Museum of Faiths*, 25.
195. L. W. Bacon, *A History of Christianity in America* (New York: Christian Literature, 1897), 418.
196. On Moody's crusade, see James Burkhart Gilbert, *Perfect Cities: Chicago's Utopias of 1893* (Chicago: University of Chicago Press, 1991), 169–207.
197. Johnson, quoted in Grant Wacker, "Second Thoughts on the Great Commission: Liberal Protestants and Foreign Missions, 1890–1940," in Joel Carpenter and Wilbert R. Shenk, eds., *Earthen Vessels: American Evangelicals and Foreign Missions, 1880–1980* (Grand Rapids, MI: Eerdmans, 1990), 283; and Marty, *Modern American Religion*, 22.

198. Arthur T. Pierson, "The Parliament of Religions: A Review," *Missionary Review* 7 (December 1894): 881–89. See also Dana L. Robert, *Occupy until I Come: A. T. Pierson and the Evangelization of the World* (Grand Rapids, MI: Eerdmans, 2003), 226–34.
199. Robert, *Occupy until I Come*, 227ff.
200. Ahlstrom, *American Protestant Encounter with World Religions*, 30. The implications of this split are spelled out in James Alan Patterson, "The Loss of a Protestant Missionary Consensus and the Fundamentalist-Modernist Conflict," in Carpenter and Shenk, *Earthen Vessels*, 73–91.
201. On this topic, see Timothy Yates, *Christian Mission in the Twentieth Century* (Cambridge: Cambridge University Press, 1994), 82ff.
202. On American Protestant nativism and anti-Catholicism, see Katie Oxx, *The Nativist Movement in America: Religious Conflict in the Nineteenth Century* (New York: Routledge, 2013).
203. Seager, *World's Parliament of Religions*, 132.
204. See Gibbons's preface to a papal encyclical from 20 June 1894 in *American Catholic Quarterly Review* 19 (1894): 771–72.
205. A. F. Hewit, "Christian Unity in the Parliament of Religions," *Catholic World* 59 (May 1994): 161.
206. On this topic, see John T. McGreevy, *Catholicism and American Freedom* (New York: Norton, 2003).
207. From a speech in Cologne given by Father William H. Tappert of Kentucky, cited in Colman J. Berry, *The Catholic Church and German Americans* (Milwaukee: Bruce, 1953).
208. Knowledge of the parliament in France came, inter alia, from Gaston Bonet-Muary's *Le Congrès des religions à Chicago en 1893* (Paris: Hachette, 1895). A French Protestant, Bonet-Muary had attended in 1893.
209. See, e.g., "Cronaca contemporaenea: Stati uniti," *La civiltà cattolica* 48 (January 1896): 118.
210. Letter of Leo XIII to Satolli (18 September 1895), *Leonis XIII Acta* 14 (Graz: Akademische Druck und Verlagsanstalt, 1971), 323–24; see Francis J. Connell, "Pope Leo XIII's Message to America," *American Ecclesiastical Review* 109 (1943): 244–56. It merits noting that Leo XIII had familiarity with the parliament through Barrows's publication on it; Barrows mentions a correspondence with the pope in a letter to William Rainey Harper (26 September 1894), in William Rainey Harper Papers (box 2, folder 6), UCL, Special Collections Research Center.
211. On this episode, see Patrick H. Ahern, *The Life of John J. Keane, Educator and Archbishop, 1839–1918* (Washington, DC: Catholic University of America Press, 1953), 147–49.
212. Thomas T. McAvoy, "Americanism, Fact and Fiction," *CHR* 31 (1945): 136, 139–40.
213. *Mortalium animos* (6 January 1928), at http://www.papalencyclicals.net /pius11/p11morta.htm (accessed 31 October 2017).

214. *Mortalium animos*.
215. Seager, *Buddhism in America*, 37.
216. Jordon, *Comparative Religion*, 465.
217. Letter of Caroline Haskell to William Rainey Harper (5 May 1894), William Rainey Harper Papers (box 2, folder 12), UCL, Special Collections Research Center. See also John Henry Barrows, *Christianity, the World Religion: Lectures Delivered in India* (Madras: Christian Literature of Indian Society, 1897), 9–11.
218. See Barrows, *Christianity, the World Religion*, 13ff. He also spoke in Japan and elsewhere. On Barrows's globe-trotting and its influence after the parliament, see Mary Eleanor Barrows, ed., *A World-Pilgrimage by John Henry Barrows* (Chicago: A. C. McClurg, 1899). Haskell also established a similar lectureship at Oberlin College, where Barrows later become president. Inspired by the parliament, a group of scholars on the East Coast established the American Committee for Lectures on the History of Religions. Braybrooke, *Pilgrimage of Hope*, 40.
219. D. G. Hart, *The University Gets Religion: Religious Studies in American Higher Education* (Baltimore: Johns Hopkins University Press, 1999), 62ff.; and Sharpe, *Comparative Religion*, 119ff.
220. See the Religious Education Association at https://religiouseducation.net/mission (accessed 20 September 2017).
221. Sharpe, *Comparative Religion*, 138. See also Jean Réville, ed., *Actes du premier Congrès international d'histoire des religions* (Paris: Ernest Leroux, 1901–2); and Nathaniel Schmidt, "The Paris Congress of Religion," *Biblical World* 16 (1900): 47–50.
222. Ziolkowski, *Museum of Faiths*, 24. See the website of the IAHR at http://www.iahr.dk/index.php (accessed 20 September 2017). Its mission is to promote "the scientific study of religion assisting the international collaboration of all scholars, members and affiliated societies contributing to the historical, social, and comparative study of religion."
223. Ziolkowski, *Museum of Faiths*, 24–25.
224. At first the organization was called the International Council of Unitarian and Other Liberal Religious Thinkers and Workers and it underwent several subsequent name changes before becoming the International Association of Religious Freedom. See Robert Traer, "A Short History of the IARF," online at https://iarf.net/wp-content/uploads/2012/04/A-Short-History-of-the-IARF-Bob-Traer.pdf (accessed 8 February 2018); and Braybrooke, *Pilgrimage of Hope*, 47–51.
225. Braybrooke, *Pilgrimage of Hope*, 49.
226. Quoted from Wikipedia site for National Conference for Community and Justice at https://en.wikipedia.org/wiki/National_Conference_for_Community_and_Justice (accessed 3 April 2019). See also Lance J. Sussman, "'Toward Better Understanding: The Rise of the Interfaith

Movement in America and the Role of Rabbi Isaac Landman," *American Jewish Archives* 34 (1982): 35–51.

227. Brian Stanley, *World Missionary Conference, Edinburgh 1910* (Grand Rapids, MI: Eerdmans, 2009), 5ff., 18ff., 303–24. Particularly noteworthy was Commission IV of the Conference, which produced the document "The Christian Message in Relation to Non-Christian Religions"; it categorizes religions on a scale of "lower" and "higher" in their relations to Christian revelation.

228. On Schaff's "prophetic" role as ecumenist, see John C. Meyer, "Philip Schaff as Ecumenical Prophet," *Ecumenical Review* 47 (1995): 52–59.

229. See Charles Frederick Weller, ed., *World Fellowship: Addresses and Messages by Leading Spokesmen of All Faiths, Races and Countries* (New York: Liveright, 1935); and the *Official Guide Book of the Fair 1933* (Chicago, 1933), 82–84.

230. *World Parliament of Religions Commemorative Volume* (Sivanansdanagar, Rishikesh: Sivanansdanagar Publication League, 1956), 5.

231. Carrol J. W. Fisher, "Interfaith Dialogue at the 1893 and 1993 Parliaments of the World's Religions" (PhD diss., Union Institute, 1993), 37.

232. The founding of the Temple of Understanding (1960) by Judith Hollister is a major exception, however. On the Temple of Understanding, see Braybrooke, *Pilgrimage of Hope*, 93–113.

233. On the origins of the 1993 parliament, see Fisher, "Interfaith Dialogue," 39ff. Another major conference (among a few minor ones) marking 1893 took place in Bangalore. Its proceedings are published in Celia Storey and David Storey, eds., *Visions of an Interfaith Future* (Oxford: International Interfaith Center, 1994). I shall return to the events of 1993 in the conclusion.

234. *ER*, 15:444.

Chapter Three. London

1. David Fromkin, *A Peace to End All Peace: The Fall of the Ottoman Empire and the Creation of the Modern Middle East* (New York: Henry Holt, 1989).

2. The war invigorated many of these movements. See Philip Jenkins, *The Great and Holy War: How World War I Became a Religious Crusade* (New York: HarperOne, 2014); and Jeffrey Cox, *Imperial Fault Lines: Christianity and Colonial Power in India, 1818–1940* (Stanford: Stanford University Press, 2002).

3. David Cannadine, *Ornamentalism: How the British Saw Their Empire* (Oxford: Oxford University Press, 2001), 85–87.

4. Peter J. Yearwood, *Guarantee of Peace: The League of Nations in British Policy, 1914–1925* (Oxford: Oxford University Press, 2009).

5. Niall Ferguson, *Empire: How Britain Made the Modern World* (London: Penguin, 2003), 317.
6. The Sociological Society is now defunct, but the School of Oriental Studies continues today as the School of Oriental and African Studies (SOAS). It recently celebrated its centennial anniversary; a brief history of the SOAS is found at https://www.soas.ac.uk/centenary/ (accessed 21 July 2016). On the Sociological Society, see A. H. Halsey, *A History of Sociology in Britain: Science, Literature, and Society* (Oxford: Oxford University Press, 2004), 9ff.
7. See the articles on the theme of "Religion and Empire" in *JAAR* 71 (March 2003). See also John Gascoigne, "Introduction: Religion and Empire: An Historiographical Perspective," *JRH* 32 (June 2008): 159–78.
8. Edward Said, *Orientalism: Western Conceptions of the Orient*, 25th anniversary ed. (New York: Vintage, 1994), 7.
9. John Darwin, "A Third British Empire? The Dominion Idea in British Politics," in Judith M. Brown and William Roger Louis, eds., *Oxford History of the British Empire:* vol. 9, *The Twentieth Century* (Oxford: Oxford University Press, 1999), 63.
10. David Feldman, "Why the English Like Turbans: Multicultural Politics in British History," in David Feldman and Jon Lawrence, eds., *Structures and Transformations in Modern British History* (Cambridge: Cambridge University Press, 2011), 281–302.
11. Simon J. Potter, *Broadcasting Empire: The BBC and the British World, 1922–1970* (Oxford: Oxford University Press, 2012), 14. This speech was featured in the movie *The King's Speech.*
12. Anne Clendinning, "On the British Empire Exhibition, 1924–25," in Dino Franco Felluga, ed., *BRANCH: Britain, Representation and Nineteenth-Century History*, extension of *Romanticism and Victorianism on the Net*, http://www.branchcollective.org/?ps_articles=anne-clendinning-on-the-british-empire-exhibition-1924-25 (accessed 21 July 2016).
13. *Empire Thanksgiving Service. The Stadium, Wembley. 25 May 1924* (Plaistow: Curwen, 1925), 24.
14. Paul Greenhalgh, *Ephemeral Vistas: The Expositions Universelles, Great Exhibitions, and World's Fairs, 1851–1939* (Manchester: Manchester University Press, 1988), 61.
15. Deborah Hughes, "Contesting Whiteness: Race, Nationalism and British Empire Exhibitions between the Wars" (PhD diss., University of Illinois at Urbana-Champaign, 2008). See also John Darwin, "Imperialism in Decline," *HJ* 23 (1980): 657–79; and Timothy Mitchell, "Orientalism and the Exhibitionary Order," in Nicholas B. Dirks, ed., *Colonialism and Culture* (Ann Arbor: University of Michigan Press, 1992), 289–317.
16. *Pictorial and Descriptive Guide to London and the British Empire Exhibition, 1924* (London, 1924), Y.

17. "Pageant of Empire: Great Spectacle at Wembley," *Scotsman* (26 July 1924).
18. *The Pageant of Empire: Souvenir Volume* (London, 1924).
19. "Circular Letter to Local Education and Governing Bodies, British Empire Exhibition, 1924" (12 January 1924), NA, E. 569/1.
20. On this tour, see Agatha Christie, *The Grand Tour: Letters and Photographs from the British Empire Expedition, 1922*, ed. Matthew Prichard (London: HarperCollins, 2012).
21. "British Empire Exhibition (1923): General Handbook of Information," BL, India Office Record, L/E/1186.
22. Fromkin, *A Peace to End All Peace*, 387–402.
23. *Pictorial and Descriptive Guide to London and the British Empire Exhibition, 1924;* and John H. Mackenzie, "The Popular Culture of the British Empire," in Brown and Louis, *The Twentieth Century*, 213–14.
24. *The British Empire Exhibition, 1924: Official Guide* (London, 1924), 13.
25. *The British Empire*, 12 vols. (London: W. Collins, 1924). The institute is now known as the Royal Commonwealth Society.
26. P. G. Wodehouse, *Selected Stories* (New York: Modern Library, 1958), 121.
27. Mackenzie, "The Popular Culture of the British Empire," 215.
28. *The British Empire Exhibition, 1924: Official Guide*, 73–74, 88; and Lionel Heath, ed., *Examples of Indian Art at the British Empire Exhibition* (London, 1925), 124.
29. "British Empire Exhibition (1924): Incorporated Handbook of General Information," BL, India Office Record L/E/1186.
30. *RE*, 3. On Ross, see Christine Woodhead, "Ross, Sir (Edward) Denison (1871–1940)," in H. C. G. Matthew et al., eds., *Oxford Dictionary of National Biography* (Oxford: Oxford University Press, 2004–), http://www.oxforddnb.com/view/article/35834 (accessed 20 October 2016). Hare previously had sought church support, but he received scant response. See Arthur Peacock, *Fellowship through Religion: The Story of the World Congress of Faiths* (London: World Congress of Faiths, 1956), 9.
31. SOAS Archives, *School of Oriental Studies, London Institution, Governing Body Minutes*, vol. 8 (October 1923–July 1924), 6.
32. *RE*, 1. The School of Oriental Studies formally decided to hold the conference under its auspices on 24 January 1924. SOAS Archives, *Governing Body Minutes*, vol. 8, 5. In some notes for his autobiography, Ross reflected that he "had taken the idea [for the 1924 conference] from the Congress of Religions which had been held in connection with the Great Exhibition in Chicago with the difference that instead of having experts on other peoples' religions, each religion should be expounded by some who professed." SOAS Archives, PP MS 8 Ross Collection, file 90, box 34.

33. William Loftus Hare, "A Parliament of Living Religions: An Account of the 'Conference on Some Living Religions within the Empire,' Held at the Imperial Institute, London, September 22nd to October 3rd, 1924," *Open Court* 38 (1924): 711.
34. Some of the early correspondence of the committee is found in KUSCA, GB 172 LP/11/4/36.
35. *RE*, 4.
36. Hare, "Parliament of Living Religions," 709–11.
37. Marjorie Wheeler-Barclay, *The Science of Religion in Britain, 1860–1915* (Charlottesville: University of Virginia Press, 2010); and Joseph M. Kitagawa and John S. Strong, "Friedrich Max Müller and the Comparative Study of Religion," in Ninian Smart et al., eds., *Nineteenth-Century Religious Thought in the West* (New York: Cambridge University Press, 1985), 3:179–214.
38. *RE*, 8–14; and Hare, "Parliament of Living Religions," 710.
39. An early sketch of the conference can be found in a letter from Victor Branford to Denison Ross (4 January 1924), KUSCA, GB 172 LP/11/4/36; *RE*, 4.
40. On the early history of the Imperial Institute, see John M. Mackenzie, "The Imperial Institute," *Round Table* 76 (1987): 246–53. The buildings of the institute were demolished in 1957.
41. One key figure whom they sought out but who did not come was the Indian poet and intellectual Rabindranath Tagore. See Victor Branford to Denison Ross (4 January 1924), KUSCA, GB 172 LP/11/4/36
42. "The Ahmadia Movement Leader to Speak at Wembley Conference," *Manchester Guardian* (13 August 1924).
43. Shoghi Effendi to Bahá'í American National Spiritual Assembly (4 January 1924), Bahá'í Administration Selected Messages, 1922–1932, http://www.bahai.org/library/authoritative-texts/shoghi-effendi/bahai-administration/bahai-administration.pdf?893331f4 (accessed 7 July 2019).
44. *RE*, 320–25; Hare, "Parliament of Living Religions," 735–37. See also the letter of Bahíyyih Khánum to Raymond C. Simpson, President of the National Spiritual Assembly of England (11 June 1924), in Shoghi Effendi, *Unfolding Destiny of the British Bahá'i Community: The Messages from the Guardian of the Bahá'i Faith to the Bahá'is of the British Isles* (London: Bahá'i Trust, 1981), 490.
45. On these movements, see chapter 2; and Peter B. Clark, ed., *Encyclopedia of New Religious Movements* (New York: Routledge, 2006), 40, 64–65.
46. See "Empire Religions: The Wembley Conference," *Times of India* (30 June 1924).
47. Newspaper clippings about the conference can be found at USSC, Papers of the World Congress of Faiths, MS 222 A826 8/1 9/1 (30, 33).
48. USSC, Papers of the World Congress of Faiths, MS 222 A826 8/1 (30).

49. See, e.g., *Christian Life* (13 September 1924), USSC, Papers of the World Congress of Faiths, MS 222 A826 8/1 (33).
50. "Queer Religions of the Empire," *Evening News* (16 September 2016), USSC, Papers of the World Congress of Faiths, MS 222 A826 8/1 (31).
51. "Oriental Holy Men in London," *Daily Mirror* (8 September 1924), USSC, Papers of the World Congress of Faiths, MS 222 A826 8/1 (31).
52. *Inquirer* (20 September 1924), USSC, Papers of the World Congress of Faiths, MS 222 A826 8/1 (38).
53. *Glasgow Herald* (15 September 1924), USSC, Papers of the World Congress of Faiths, MS 222 A826 8/1 (35). On the British Crown's official policy of "noninterference" or "religious neutrality" (and its limitations), which was proclaimed by Queen Victoria after the Indian Revolt of 1857, see Robert Eric Frykenberg, "Christians and Religious Traditions in the Indian Empire," in *Cambridge History of Christianity*, vol. 8, *World Christianities c. 1815–1914* (Cambridge: Cambridge University Press, 2006).
54. On the Ahmadiyya notion of the Mahdi and its place in Islamic eschatological thought, see Yohanan Friedmann, *Prophecy Continuous: Aspects of Ahmadi Religious Thought and Its Medieval Background* (Oxford: Oxford University Press, 2003). Ahmadiyya remains highly persecuted to this day. See S. R. Valentine, "Prophecy after Prophecy, Albeit Lesser Prophets? The Ahmadiyya Jama'at in Pakistan," *Contemporary Islam* 8 (2014): 99–113.
55. "Prayer on Station Platform," *Evening News* (23 August 1924), USSC, Papers of the World Congress of Faiths, MS 222 A826 8/1 (13).
56. See "London's First Mosque," *Manchester Guardian* (26 November 1925).
57. "Mohammedans in East Dulwich: His Holiness the Khalifatul Massih at Drawing Room Party," *South London Times* (12 September 1924), USSC, Papers of the World Congress of Faiths, MS 222 A826 8/1 (33).
58. "Islam Chief on 'the True Religion,'" *Evening News* (3 September 1924), USSC, Papers of the World Congress of Faiths, MS 222 A826 8/1 (143).
59. Sir Denison Ross, "Empire Religions: This Week's Conference," *Morning Post* (22 September 1924), USSC, Papers of the World Congress of Faiths, MS 222 A826 8/1 (40). A religious skeptic himself, Ross wondered in his private papers about the earliest origins of religion: "Perhaps the consideration of the psychology and sociology of religion . . . will be applicable to all religions. There is the absorbing question, for instance, of the origin of religion. Whence did it spring, and at what stage in the ascent of man from his crude ancestors in the forest was religion born?" See SOAS Archives, PP MS 8 Ross Collection, file 90, box 34.
60. USSC, Papers of the World Congress of Faiths, MS 222 A826 8/1 (33); *RE*, 511.
61. *RE*, 5–6.

62. "Empire Religions: Meeting of Richly Robed Theologians," *Daily Mail* (23 September 1924), USSC, Papers of the World Congress of Faiths, MS 222 A826 8/1 (43).
63. Hare, "Parliament of Living Religions," 713.
64. Patrick French, *Younghusband: The Last Great Imperial Adventurer* (London: Flamingo, 1995).
65. Younghusband once described his contact with Asian religions: "In explorations across the Chinese Empire, in the conduct of political missions on the Indian frontier, and [in] Tibet . . . I had come into close touch with men of all the great religions—Confucians, Hindus, Jews, Sikhs, Muslims—and with priests as well as officials. I was humbled by seeing so much of their finest spirituality in these men of other religions. And I found by mutual experience that they had far too refined a spiritual courtesy to show me any airs of superiority. Indeed, Hindus, Buddhists and Muslims have often invited me to speak at their own religious gatherings and that is how it comes so natural to me to invite them to join with us in a common effort to promote a spirituality of world fellowship." Quoted in Peacock, *Fellowship through Religion*, 16.
66. Francis Younghusband, *A Venture of Faith: Being a Description of the World Congress of Faiths Held in London 1936* (New York: E. P. Dutton, 1937), 15–16. On Tolstoy's religious outlook and its influence on Younghusband, see Daniel Moulin, "Tolstoy, Universalism and World Religions," *JEH* 68 (2017): 583–85.
67. Francis Younghusband, *Vital Religion* (London: John Murray, 1940), 6.
68. On this expedition, during which many Tibetan lives were lost and much looting of religious sites occurred, see Tom Neuhaus, *Bayonets to Lhasa: The British Invasion of Tibet* (London: Tauris, 2012); Gordon T. Stewart, *Journeys to Empire: Enlightenment, Imperialism, and the British Encounter with Tibet, 1774–1904* (Cambridge: Cambridge University Press, 2009); and Michael Carrington, "Officers, Gentlemen and Thieves: The Looting of Monasteries during the 1903/04 Younghusband Mission to Tibet," *MAS* 37 (2003): 81–109. See also Tom Neuhaus, *Tibet in the Western Imagination* (New York: Palgrave Macmillan, 2012), 85ff.
69. A fuller account of his experience goes as follows: "The day after leaving Lhasa I went off alone to the mountainside, and there gave myself up to all the emotions of this eventful time. Every anxiety was over—I was full of good-will as my former foes were converted into stalwart friends. But now there grew up in me something infinitely greater than mere elation and good-will. Elation grew to exultation, exultation to exaltation, which thrilled through me with overwhelming intensity. I was beside myself with untellable joy. The whole world was ablaze with the same ineffable bliss that was burning within me. I felt in touch with the flaming heart of the world. What was glowing in all creation and in every single human being was a joy far beyond mere goodness as the glory of the sun

is beyond the glow of a candle. A mighty joy-giving Power was at work in the world—at work in all about me and at work in every living thing. So it was revealed to me." Younghusband, *Vital Religion*, 3–4. See also French, *Younghusband*, 252.

70. French, *Younghusband*, 279–80.
71. *RE*, 17–18. The original handwritten lecture is found at BL, Younghusband Papers, MSS EUR 197/377.
72. *RE*, 17–19.
73. *RE*, 24–25.
74. "The Empires Living Religions Conference in London," *Times of India* (24 September 1924).
75. "Religions of the Empire Conference: Opening of London Conference," *Manchester Guardian* (23 September 1924).
76. *RE*, 32.
77. *RE*, 59–147. The paper on Shia was read by Sir Thomas Arnold and the one on Sufism was read by Dr. Muhammad Din, a member of the Ahmadiyya delegation.
78. "Religions of the Empire: Islam's Day," *Manchester Guardian* (24 September 1924).
79. *RE*, 151ff.
80. *RE*, 275ff.
81. *RE*, 403.
82. Hare, "Parliament of Living Religions," 759.
83. On the broader historical context, see Susan Pederson, *The Guardians: The League of Nations and the Crisis of Empire* (Oxford: Oxford University Press, 2015), 107ff.
84. *RE*, 87, 156, 316, 322–24.
85. *RE*, 158. On Silva's role in the stirrings of Sri Lankan independence, see K. E. O. Dharmadasa, *Language, Religion, and Ethnic Assertiveness: The Growth of Sinhalese Nationalism in Sri Lanka* (Ann Arbor: University of Michigan Press, 1992), 133–43.
86. *RE*, 172, 249.
87. On the long history of British perception of Islam, see, inter alia, Gerald MacLean, *The Rise of Oriental Travel: English Visitors to the Ottoman Empire, 1580–1720* (New York: Palgrave Macmillan, 2006).
88. *RE*, 84, 118–20.
89. *RE*, 120–21.
90. *RE*, 214, 216, 230, 279.
91. *RE*, 308–9.
92. *RE*, 83, 230.
93. *RE*, 290, 302–3.
94. *RE*, 288.
95. "Meeting of East and West," *Near East* (9 October 1924), USSC, Papers of the World Congress of Faiths, MS 222 A826 8/1 (83).

96. *RE*, 304.
97. Hare, "Parliament of Living Religions," 758.
98. *RE*, 511–14.
99. Victor Branford, *Living Religions: A Plea for the Larger Modernism* (London: Leplay, 1924). Modernism, as he defined it, is the impetus "to renew, in the light of current knowledge, yet also of contemporary aspiration, the eternal verities enshrined in ancient faiths" (vii).
100. *RE*, 516, 518–19.
101. J. Tyssul Davis, *A League of Religions* (London: Lindsey, 1926).
102. "Conference of 'Living Religions,'" *Inquirer* (4 October 1924), USSC, Papers of the World Congress of Faiths, MS 222 A826 8/1 (75).
103. "Conference on Empire Religions," *Morning Post* (4 October 1924), USSC, Papers of the World Congress of Faiths, MS 222 A826 8/1 (80).
104. "A Conference on Non-Christian Religions," *Catholic Times* (4 October 1924), USSC, Papers of the World Congress of Faiths, MS 222 A826 8/1 (80).
105. *Christian* (2 October 1924), USSC, Papers of the World Congress of Faiths, MS 222 A826 8/1 (74).
106. Francis Younghusband, "Living Religions within the Empire: A Notable Conference," *Guardian* (10 October 1924), USSC, Papers of the World Congress of Faiths, MS 222 A826 8/1 (83).
107. "Living Religions within the Empire," *Guardian* (10 October 1924), USSC, Papers of the World Congress of Faiths, MS 222 A826 8/1 (83).
108. BL, MSS EUR F 197/133.
109. Leonard Swidler, *Death or Dialogue: From the Age of Monologue to the Age of Dialogue* (Philadelphia: Trinity Press International, 1990).
110. On these binaries applied to religion, see Richard King, *Orientalism and Religion: Postcolonial Theory, India, and the "Mystic East"* (London: Routledge, 1999); and Nicole Goulet, "Postcolonialism and the Study of Religion: Dissecting Orientalism, Nationalism, and Gender Using Postcolonial Theory," *RC* 5 (2011): 631–37.
111. *RE*, 16.
112. See, e.g., William Gould, *Religion and Conflict in Modern South Asia* (New York: Cambridge University Press, 2012), 119–44; and David Motadel, "Islam and the European Empires," *Historical Journal* 55 (2012): 831–56.
113. W. M. Roger Louis, "The Dissolution of the British Empire," in Brown and Louis, *The Twentieth Century*, 329–56.
114. "Study of Religions: Proposed New Society. Sir Denison Ross on the World's Beliefs," *Observer* (16 February 1930).
115. Marcus Braybrooke, *Widening Vision: The World Congress of Faiths and the Growing Interfaith Movement* (Oxford: OneWorld, 1996), 11.
116. Denison Ross, "Introductory Note," *Religions: Journal of Transactions of the Society for Promoting the Study of Religions* 1 (January 1931): v.
117. Younghusband, *Vital Religion*, 67.

118. On the 1933 fair, see *Official Book of the Fair, Giving Pre-exposition Information, 1932–1933, of a Century of Progress International Exposition, Chicago 1933* (Chicago: A Century of Progress, 1932); and Cheryl Ganz, *The 1933 Chicago World's Fair: Century of Progress* (Urbana: University of Illinois Press, 2008).
119. The initial meeting of the World Fellowship on Peace and Brotherhood as Taught by the World's Living Faiths was held in Chicago in May 1929. See Braybrooke, *Widening Vision*, 13. Weller had previously founded the League of Neighbors in 1918 to help marginalized groups in the United States. Das Gupta, who came to Britain from India in 1908, had established an organization called the Union of East and West which, among other things, staged some thirty plays about life in India. In 1920 he accompanied the Indian writer Rabindranath Tagore to the United States and decided to make his home there. The World Fellowship of Faiths merged many aspects of these prior organizations established by Weller and Das Gupta. On the development of the World Fellowship, see RSCL, Charles F. Weller Papers, box 5, folder 8.
120. "Religion: Fellowship of Faiths," *Time* (11 September 1936); and DePaul Library, Special Collections and University Archives, "A Century of Progress Memorabilia Collection, 1933–1999," box 6. However, there were eight large mural paintings at the entrance of the Hall of Religion portraying the aspirations of major world religions. See *Official Guidebook: World's Fair 1934* (Chicago: A Century of Progress International Exposition, 1934), 53. See also John E. Findling, *Chicago's Great World Fairs* (Manchester: Manchester University Press, 1994), 70.
121. George Seaver, *Francis Younghusband: Explorer and Mystic* (London: Murray, 1953), 339.
122. Braybrooke, *Widening Vision*, 12–13.
123. Charles Frederick Weller, ed., *World Fellowship: Addresses and Messages by Leading Spokesmen of All Faiths, Races and Countries* (New York: Liveright, 1935), 9. This volume contains speeches from the Chicago meeting in 1933 and from additional meetings.
124. Weller, *World Fellowship*, xi–xiii, 12–15.
125. Younghusband, *Venture of Faith*, 32.
126. Some of this correspondence is found in RSCL, Charles F. Weller Papers, box 5, folder 10.
127. He often spoke on "The Value of Joy." BL, Younghusband Papers, MSS EUR F197/119.
128. Younghusband, *Venture of Faith*, 32. Pictures of Younghusband, Weller, and Das Gupta together may be found at BL, MSS EUR f/197/647.
129. Younghusband, *Venture of Faith*, 35.
130. French, *Younghusband*, 367.
131. BL, Younghusband Papers, MSS EUR F197/119.
132. BL, Younghusband Papers, MSS EUR F197/123. Otto's idea had brief

institutional embodiment in the 1920s. See Rudolf Otto, "Religiöser Menschheitsbund," *Deutsche Politik* 6/10 (March 1921): 234–38. Another legacy was a small "museum of religions" that was established at the University of Marburg, where Otto taught. It still exists. Permit me also to note that in 1928, various religious leaders gathered in Geneva to make clear their opposition to war. See *World's Religions against War* (New York, 1928).

133. Younghusband, *Venture of Faith*, 35–37; Younghusband, *Vital Religion*, 92–93.
134. USSC, Papers of the World Congress of Faiths, MS 222 A826 2/1.
135. Peacock, *Fellowship through Religion*, 12,
136. The title World Congress of Faiths was not finally decided upon until the committee meeting of 20 October 1936. See USSC, Papers of the World Congress of Faiths, MS 222 A826 1/12.
137. Younghusband, *Venture of Faith*, 44.
138. Quoted material from Shaw in French, *Younghusband*, 368.
139. The "Supreme Ideal" was presented from six perspectives: Christian, Jewish, Hindu, Buddhist, Muslim, and "independent." See Younghusband, *Venture of Faith*, 205–29.
140. Younghusband, *Venture of Faith*, 39.
141. Noted in Peacock, *Fellowship through Religion*, 15.
142. "A Congress of Faiths," *Tablet* (28 September 1935).
143. The letters from Buckingham Palace are dated 5 May 1936 and 17 June 1936, LPL, Papers of Cosmo Gordon Lang, vol. 147. The archbishop's reply, dated 19 June 1936, can be found at USSC, Papers of the World Congress of Faiths, MS 222 A826 2/1.
144. Younghusband, *Venture of Faith*, 55.
145. USSC, Papers of the World Congress of Faiths, MS 222 A826 2/102; and "World Congress of Faiths—All Great Religions—Basis for New World Order," *Guardian* (27 May 1936).
146. USSC, Papers of the World Congress of Faiths, MS 222 A826 2/1.
147. Younghusband, *Venture of Faith*, 55–57; French, *Younghusband*, 368.
148. "Religion—A Changing Force?" *Nature* (4 July 1936): 3.
149. USSC Papers of the World Congress of Faiths, MS 222 A826 3/99 and 3/102.
150. A. Douglas Millard, ed., *Faiths and Fellowship: Being the Proceedings of the World Congress of Faiths Held in London, July 3rd–17th, 1936* (London: J. M. Watkins, 1936), 5; and USSC, Papers of the World Congress of Faiths, MS 222 A826 2/1.
151. A roster of active participants can be found in Millard, *Faiths and Fellowship*, 481–88.
152. Younghusband, *Venture of Faith*, 92, 136, 152.
153. Millard, *Faiths and Fellowship*, 280.
154. Millard, *Faiths and Fellowship*, 7–8, 104ff.

155. Younghusband, *Venture of Faith*, 5.
156. For a panoramic view of this moment in history, see the section entitled "From War to War" in David Stevenson, "International Relations," in Julian Jackson, ed., *Europe, 1900–1945* (Oxford: Oxford University Press, 2002), 26–35.
157. Millard, *Faiths and Fellowship*, 396.
158. Millard, *Faiths and Fellowship*, 15. On views of the League of Nations in the 1930s, and for insights about growing disillusionment toward it, see Helen McCarthy, *The British People and the League of Nations: Democracy, Citizenship, and Internationalism, 1918–1945* (Manchester: Manchester University Press, 2011). Of immediate concern was Mussolini's decision to invade Ethiopia in 1935 and the inability of the League of Nations to deter his actions.
159. Millard, *Faiths and Fellowship*, 264, 358–59. The Nuremberg Laws were passed in the German Reichstag on 15 September 1935. Magnes was not able to attend personally, but his contribution was read.
160. Younghusband, *Vital Religion*, 81. Orders for these services are found in USSC, Papers of the World Congress of Faiths, MS 222 A826 3/98.
161. These services took place respectively on 5 July and 12 July. USSC, Papers of the World Congress of Faiths, MS 222 A826 3/99.
162. Millard, *Faiths and Fellowship*, 131. Inventor of the first respirator, Haldane was an eminent professor at Oxford University. He himself was not present at the congress to deliver his paper as he had passed away several months before.
163. "World Congress of Faiths," *Inquirer* (11 July 1936).
164. "World Congress of Faiths—London Meetings—Exchanging Points of View," *Guardian* (17 July 1936).
165. "World Congress of Faiths Meets to Seek Unities: Representatives of Many Religions Conferring in London," *Evening Standard* (17 July 1936).
166. "World Congress of Faiths," *Gazette* (1 August 1936). The wording is taken from the congress's "Prospectus and Form of Application for Membership," USSC, Papers of the World Congress of Faiths, MS 222 A826 3/102.
167. Peacock, *Fellowship through Religion*, 17.
168. USSC, Papers of the World Congress of Faiths, MS 222 A826 1/11.
169. Seaver, *Younghusband*, 333.
170. On these meetings, see Braybrooke, *Widening Vision*, 54–57; and Peacock, *Fellowship through Religion*, 19–20.
171. Quoted from Seaver, *Francis Younghusband*, 340.
172. Peacock writes of the broadcast's influence: "The broadcast succeeded in bringing this new religious movement before a wider public and there was a pleasing response. . . . The roll of individual membership [in the congress] began to rise." See Peacock, *Fellowship through Religion*, 17–19.

Younghusband's 1938 BBC address can be found at BL, Younghusband Papers, MSS EUR F197/690.

173. Millard, *Faiths and Fellowship*, 404.
174. "World Congress of Faiths Meet to Seek Unities."
175. Kusumita P. Pedersen, "The Interfaith Movement: An Incomplete Assessment," *JES* 41 (2004): 15–16.
176. It should be noted, however, that several individual Catholics participated in the World Congress of Faith's initial meetings. Especially noteworthy is the lecture "Who Is My Neighbor?" by the Catholic philosopher Jacques Maritain that was given at the 1939 meeting in Paris. Maritain made clear that he was presenting as an individual and not as a representative of the Catholic Church. See USSC, Papers of the World Congress of Faiths, MS 222 A826 3/100. An amended version of this address is found in Jacques Maritain, *Ransoming the Time* (1941; repr., New York: Gordian, 1972).

Chapter Four. Rome

1. Marcus Braybrooke, *Pilgrimage of Hope: One Hundred Years of Global Interfaith Dialogue* (London: SCM, 1992), 71; and Arthur Peacock, *Fellowship through Religion: The Story of the World Congress of Faiths* (London: World Congress of Faiths, 1956), 21–25.
2. Douglas Pratt, *The Church and Other Faiths: The World Council of Churches, the Vatican, and Interreligious Dialogue* (New York: Peter Lang, 2010), 29–112.
3. On the "globalization" of Gandhi and King, see Nico Slate, *Colored Cosmopolitanism: The Shared Struggle for Freedom in the United States and India* (Cambridge, MA: Harvard University Press, 2012); and Ramachandra Guha, *Gandhi: The Years That Changed the World, 1914–48* (New York: Knopf, 2019).
4. Tony Judt, *Postwar: Europe since 1945* (New York: Penguin, 2005), 559ff.
5. Sarah Hacket, *Foreigners, Minorities, and Integration: The Muslim Experience in Britain and Germany* (Manchester: Manchester University Press, 2013).
6. A Google Ngram search shows that citations of Buber's name massively increased in the 1950s and 1960s. The first document in the Vatican Archives that deals with the origins of *Nostra aetate* (under the title "Secretariatus ad christianorum unitatem fovendam—De Judaeis") refers to Buber. See ASV, Conc. Vat. II, box 1452.
7. Asher D. Biemann, ed., *The Martin Buber Reader: Essential Writings* (New York: Palgrave Macmillan, 2002), 191. On the mid-century influence of Buber on Catholic understandings of dialogue, see Felix Körner, "Das Dialogverständnis der katholische Kirche: Eine theologische Grundlegung," *ZMR* 101 (2017): 81.

8. Arleen B. Dallery and Charles E. Scott, *The Question of the Other: Essays in Contemporary Continental Philosophy* (Albany: State University of New York Press, 1989).
9. Giuseppe Alberigo, *A Brief History of Vatican II*, trans. Matthew Sherry (Maryknoll, NY: Orbis, 2006), 1ff.
10. On the ongoing controversy surrounding Pius XII during World War II, see José M. Sánchez, *Pius XII and the Holocaust: Understanding the Controversy* (Washington, DC: Catholic University of America Press, 2002).
11. John W. O'Malley, *What Happened at Vatican II?* (Cambridge, MA: Belknap Press of Harvard University Press, 2008), 7.
12. Allen S. Will, *Life of Cardinal Gibbons, Archbishop of Baltimore* (New York: E. P. Dutton, 1922), 1:550ff.; and John Keane to American Archbishops (4 November 1892), AAB, 90P6, Papers of Cardinal Gibbons.
13. Leo XIII to Archbishop Francis Satolli (18 September 1895), cited in *Ecclesiastical Review* 13 (1895): 395.
14. On the question of "Americanism" in the 1890s, see Thomas Timothy McAvoy, *The Americanist Heresy in Roman Catholicism, 1895–1900* (Notre Dame: Notre Dame University Press, 1963); and Gerald P. Fogarty, SJ, *The Vatican and the American Hierarchy, 1870–1965* (Wilmington, DE: Michael Glazier, 1985).
15. *Mortalium animos* (1928), at http://w2.vatican.va/content/pius-xi/en/encyclicals/documents/hf_p-xi_enc_19280106_mortalium-animos.html (accessed 11 May 2018).
16. *ESDD*, 801; and John Borelli, "The Origins and Early Development of Interreligious Relations during the Century of the Church," *US Catholic Historian* 28 (2010): 88. Despite the dangers seen to inhere within non-Catholic ecumenism, these encyclicals left open the possibility of a distinctively Catholic approach to Christian unity.
17. Loe-Joo Tan, "The Catholic Theology of Religions: A Survey of Pre–Vatican II and Conciliar Attitudes towards Other Religions," *SJT* 67 (2014): 287–89.
18. Tan, "Catholic Theology of Religions," 288.
19. See *ST* III, q. 69, a. 4; Francis A. Sullivan, SJ, *Salvation outside the Church? Tracing the History of the Catholic Response* (New York: Paulist, 1992), 88–94; and Louis Capéran, *Le problème du salut des infidèles: Essai historique* (Toulouse: Grand Séminaire, 1934), 62–66.
20. The term "invincible ignorance" also comes from Aquinas, although he conveyed it from earlier sources. See *ST* I-II, q. 76, a. 4.
21. Gerald O'Collins, SJ, *The Second Vatican Council on Other Religions* (Oxford: Oxford University Press, 2013), 44–47.
22. *Mystici corporis*, as quoted in Sullivan, *Salvation outside the Church?* 132–33.
23. See Holy Office, "Letter to Cardinal Cushing," *American Ecclesiastical Review* 127 (1952): 312–13; and Sullivan, *Salvation outside the Church?*

136–40. For an argument that takes issue with Sullivan's interpretation of the Feeney case, see Geertjan Zuijdwegt, "Salvation and the Church: Feeney, Fenton, and the Making of *Lumen gentium*," *LS* 37 (2013): 147–78.

24. Rahner, quoted in O'Collins, *Second Vatican Council on Other Religions*, 51.
25. Karl Rahner, "Christianity and the Non-Christian Religions," trans. Karl-Heinz Kruger, in *Theological Investigations* (London: Darton, Longman, and Todd, 1966), 5:115–34.
26. Rahner, "Anonymous Christians," trans. Karl-Heinz Kruger, in *Theological Investigations* (London: Darton, Longman, and Todd, 1974), 6:390–98.
27. Jean Daniélou, *Les saints "païens" de l'Ancien Testament* (Paris: Éditions du Seuil, 1956).
28. Jacques Dupuis, SJ, *Christianity and the Religions: From Confrontation to Dialogue*, trans. Phillip Berryman (Maryknoll, NY: Orbis, 2003), 47–59.
29. Greg Tobin, *The Good Pope: John XXIII and Vatican II* (New York: HarperOne, 2012), 55–74.
30. Thomas L. McDonald, "John XXIII and the Jews," *Catholic World Report* (3 April 2014). Permit me also to note that during the interwar years combating anti-Semitism by educating against prejudice brought some Christians, including Catholics, and Jews together. In this regard, mention should be made of the American National Conference for Christian and Jews (1924). On it and other educational (i.e., not primarily dialogical) efforts, see Braybrooke, *Pilgrimage of Hope*, 78–83.
31. Tobin, *Good Pope*, 75–88. From Paris, Roncalli was called in 1953 to serve as patriarch of Venice until becoming pope in 1958.
32. I emphasize French sources of overcoming anti-Semitism, but there were others as well. The key treatment of this subject from which I happily draw is John Connelly, *From Enemy to Brother: The Revolution in Catholic Teaching on the Jews, 1933–1965* (Cambridge, MA: Harvard University Press, 2012). On German sources, and especially on the pioneering efforts of the historian (and convert to Catholicism from Judaism) Karl Thieme (1902–63), see Elias H. Füllenbach, "Freunde des alten und des neuen Gottesvolkes," *Rottenburger Jahrbuch für Kirchengeschichte* 32 (2013): 235–52.
33. On the Dreyfus affair and the tremendous influence that it had on French and European intellectual and political life, see Ruth Harris, *Dreyfus: Politics, Emotion, and the Scandal of the Century* (New York: Metropolitan, 2010).
34. On Maritain and the Jews generally, see Robert Royal, ed., *Jacques Maritain and the Jews* (Notre Dame: University of Notre Dame Press, 1994).
35. Richard Francis Crane and Brenna Moore, "Cracks in the Theology of Contempt: The French Roots of *Nostra Aetate*," *Studies in Christian-Jewish Relations* 8 (2013): 1–28. On "la nouvelle theologie," see Gabriel Flynn, "A Renaissance in Twentieth-Century Catholic Theology," *ITQ*

76 (2011): 323–38. On the attempted Aryanization of Christianity during the Third Reich, see Susannah Heschel, *The Aryan Jesus: Christian Theologians and the Bible in Nazi Germany* (Princeton: Princeton University Press, 2008).

36. Henri de Lubac, *Résistance chrétienne à l'antisémitisme: Souvenirs 1940–1944* (Paris: Fayard, 1988); and Bernard Comte, "Conscience catholique et persécution antisémite: L'engagement de théologiens lyonnais en 1941–1942," *Annales* 48 (1993): 635–54.
37. On Isaac generally, see André Kaspi, *Jules Isaac ou la passion de la vérité* (Paris: Plon, 2002); and Norman C. Tobias, *Jewish Conscience of the Church: Jules Isaac and the Second Vatican Council* (Cham, Switzerland: Palgrave Macmillan, 2017).
38. The ten points are found in Borelli, "Origins and Early Development of Interreligious Relations," 87.
39. Jules Isaac, *Jesus et Israël* (Paris: Fasquelle, 1948).
40. Crane and More, "Cracks in the Theology of Contempt," 15.
41. Jules Isaac, *L'enseignement du mépris: Vérité historique et mythes théologiques* (Paris: Fasquelle, 1962).
42. Some Catholics had advocated for this action since the 1920s; see Connelly, *From Enemy to Brother*, 96–97.
43. J. Oscar Beozzo, "The External Climate," in *HVII*, 1:394–95; and Hans Waldenfelds, SJ, "'Nostra Aetate' Vierzig Jahre danach," *ZMR* 89 (2005): 28.
44. On its foundation, see Mauro Velatio, "La proposta ecumenica del segretariato per l'unità dei cristiani," in Giuseppe Alberigo and Alberto Melloni, eds., *Verso il Concilio Vaticano (1960–62)* (Genoa: Marietti, 1993), 273–75.
45. All were established by the same *motu proprio*, *Superno Dei Nutu*, on 5 June 1960.
46. On Bea generally, see Jerome M. Vereb, *"Because He Was a German": Cardinal Bea and the Origins of Roman Catholic Engagement with the Ecumenical Movement* (Grand Rapids, MI: Eerdmans, 2006).
47. ACUA, Papers of Thomas Stransky, box 1, folder 1, a.
48. O'Malley, *What Happened at Vatican II?* 219–20.
49. Thomas F. Stransky, SJ, "The Foundation of the Secretariat for Promoting Christian Unity," in Alberic Stacpoole, ed., *Vatican II by Those Who Were There* (London: Geoffrey Chapman, 1986), 63–87.
50. "Jules Isaac chez Jean XXIII (13 June 1960)," ASV, Conc. Vat. II, box 1452.
51. O'Malley, *What Happened at Vatican II?* 219; and Paul Berger Marx, *Les relations entre les Juifs et les Catholiques dans la France de l'après-guerre 1945–1965* (Paris: Parole et silence, 2009), 434–37. The memorandum—"Della necessità di una reforma dell'insegnamento cristiano nei riguardi di Israele"—is reprinted in M. Vingiani, "Jules Isaac. Il promotore del

dialogo ebraico-cristiano a venti anni dalla morte," *Ecumeniso anni 80* (Verona, 1984): 323–38.

52. Stjepan Schmidt, *Augustin Bea: Cardinal of Unity*, trans. Leslie Wearne (New Rochelle, NY: New City, 1992), 336–37. It should also be noted that in August 1960, several Catholic scholars met at Apeldoorn in the Netherlands and, inspired by the coming council, hammered out a document calling for improved Jewish-Catholic relations. The works and testimony of Jules Isaac influenced this meeting, and several consultors for the newly formed secretariat participated in it. See Connelly, *From Enemy to Brother*, 241–42.
53. Connelly, *From Enemy to Brother*, 182, 240.
54. On the topic of the Holocaust and postwar remembrance in general, see, inter alia, Geoffrey Hartman, ed., *Holocaust Remembrance: The Shapes of Memory* (Oxford: Blackwell, 1994).
55. John Borelli, "Vatican II: Preparing the Church for Dialogue," *Origins* 42 (2012): 166; and ACUA, Papers of Thomas Stransky, box 1, folder 1, t.v.
56. Despite efforts to maintain secrecy, reports of the council's discussion on the Jews appeared quickly; see "Pope Ready to Talk about Jewry," *Jewish Chronicle* (11 November 1960); and "Il concilio ecumenico parlerà anche agli ebrei," *Gazetta del populo* (12 December 1960), ASV Conc. Vat. II, box 1452.
57. Bea, quoted in Thomas Stransky, "The Genesis of *Nostra Aetate*," *America* (24 October 2005): 5.
58. On Ottaviani at the council, see Pietro Palazzini, *Il prefetto del Sant'Offizio: Le opere e i giorni del cardinale Ottaviani* (Milan: Mursia, 1990).
59. Augustin Bea, SJ, *The Church and the Jewish People: A Commentary on the Second Vatican Council's Declaration on the Relation of the Church to Non-Christian Religions*, trans. Philip Loretz (New York: Harper and Row, 1966), 23.
60. On 17 November 1961 Bea had received a requested memorandum from the American Jewish Committee, "Anti-Jewish Elements in the Catholic Liturgy" (AJCA), and before this one, he had received "The Image of the Jew in Catholic Teaching" (ASV Conc. Vat. II, box 1452). Bea met personally with Heschel on several occasions. See Marc H. Tannenbaum, "Heschel and Vatican II: Jewish and Christian Relations" (lecture on 21 February 1983), AJCA. Before the council opened, Bea received a memorandum from Heschel, "On Improving Catholic-Jewish Relations" (22 May 1962), AJCA. See also Susannah Heschel, "An Interfaith Friendship: Augustin Cardinal Bea and Rabbi Abraham Joshua Heschel," in Clemens Brodkorb and Dominik Burkard, eds., *Der Kardinal der Einheit: Zum 50. Todestag des Jesuiten, Exegeten und Ökumenikers Augustin Bea (1881–1961)* (Regensburg: Schneller and Steiner, 2018), 465–79.

61. See, e.g., the memorandum dated 24 January 1961, ASV Conc. Vat. II, box 1452.
62. The draft is found at https://www.catholicsforisrael.com/articles/israel-and-the-church/229-the-origins-and-development-of-nostra-aetate (accessed 30 April 2018).
63. John M. Oesterreicher, *The New Encounter between Christians and Jews* (New York: Philosophical Library, 1986), 160–61.
64. Augustin Bea, *The Church and the Jewish People*, trans. P. Loretz (New York: Harper and Row, 1966), 23.
65. Bea to John XXIII, "Il concilio e la questione del populo ebraico" (December 1962), ASV Conc. Vat. II, box 1453.
66. "De catholicorum habitudine ad non christianos et maxime ad Iudaeos," ASV Conc. Vat. II, box 1452. See also O'Malley, *What Happened at Vatican II?* 220; and Bea, *Church and the Jewish People*, 24.
67. See note from the pope dated 13 December 1962, ASV Conc. Vat. II, box 1452.
68. In March Bea met with Jewish scholars in New York City under the auspices of the American Jewish Committee. See "Conversation of Cardinal Bea with Jewish Scholars and Theologians (New York 31st of March 1963)," AJCA.
69. On the play and its impact, see Mark Edward Ruff, *The Battle for the Catholic Past in Germany, 1945–1980* (Cambridge: Cambridge University Press, 2017).
70. Letters of complaint from Arab prelates and governmental officials were regularly sent to the Vatican secretary of state, Cardinal Amleto Cicognani, who forwarded them to Bea. See ASV Conc. Vat. II, boxes 1453, 1454, 1455.
71. It should also be noted that in his first speech to the council on 29 September 1963, Paul VI surprised many by encouraging the council fathers to look beyond their "own sphere and observe those other religions that uphold the meaning and the concept of God as one, Creator, provident, most high and transcendent, that worship God with acts of sincere piety and upon whose beliefs and practices the principles of moral and social are life founded." *AAS*, vol. 55 (1963), 857–58.
72. Quoted by Judith Banki, "The Interfaith Story behind Nostra Aetate," https://www.ushmm.org/research/the-center-for-advanced-holocaust-studies/programs-ethics-religion-the-holocaust/programs/the-interfaith-story-behind-nostra-aetate/the-interfaith-story-behind-nostra-aetate (accessed 12 March 2019).
73. O'Malley, *What Happened at Vatican II?* 221ff.
74. On this trip in general, see Rodolfo Rossi, ed., *I viaggi apostolici di Paulo VI* (Rome: Edizioni Studium, 2004), 33ff.; and Peter Hebblewaithe, *Paul VI: The First Modern Pope* (New York: Paulist, 1993), 370–83.

75. The official volume on this trip is *Il pellegrinaggio di Paolo VI in Terra Santa, 4–6 gennaio 1964* (Vatican City, 1964).
76. See "Appendix—Declaratio de non-Christianis," ASV Conc. Vat. II, box 1454.
77. In the spring and summer of 1964, Bea's secretariat received a barrage of correspondence urging that the document not be scuttled. See especially the bitingly eloquent letter of Thomas Merton to Bea (14 July 1964), ASV Conc. Vat. II, box 1454.
78. Quoted in Oesterreicher, *New Encounter*, 221.
79. O'Malley, *What Happened at Vatican II?* 221. It should be noted that there were strong reactions against this course. For instance, Abbot Rudloff, in a letter to Willebrands (28 March 1964), asserted that including other religions would dilute the significance of focus on the Jews, adding: "There are so many other religions that deserve consideration . . . that we are in danger of starting a '*processus in infinitum.*'" ASV Conc. Vat. II, box 1454.
80. Borelli, "Origins and Early Development of Interreligious Relations," 92ff. Anawati had been lecturing at the Angelicum (the Dominican University in Rome) on Islam. See G. C. Anawati, "L'Islam à l'heure du concile: Prolègomènes à un dialogue islamo-chrétien," *Angelicum*, 41 (1964): 145–68. See also ACUA, Papers of Thomas Stransky, box 9, folder 2.
81. See *Freiburger Rundbrief* 16/17 (1965): 13.
82. A huge stash of critical articles and editorials from Arab lands can be found in ASV Conc. Vat. II, box 1455.
83. ACUA, Papers of Thomas Stransky, box 10, folder 5.
84. Quoted in John Oesterreicher, "Declaration on the Relationship of the Church to Non-Christian Religions," in *CDV*, 3:66. See also Abraham Joshua Heschel to Bea (29 January 1964), ASV Conc. Vat. II, box 1454.
85. Heschel felt this was an act of *kiddush hashem*, a solemn duty to God. On this meeting, see Edward Kaplan, *Spiritual Radical: Abraham Joshua Heschel in America, 1940–1972* (New Haven: Yale University Press, 2007), 259–60; Joshua Furnal, "Abraham Joshua Heschel and *Nostra aetate:* Shaping the Catholic Consideration of Judaism during Vatican II," *Religions* (8 June 2016); and Susannah Heschel, "Out of the Mystery Comes the Bond: The Role of Rabbi Abraham Joshua Heschel in Shaping *Nostra Aetate*" (unpublished paper). I am grateful to Susannah Heschel for a correspondence about her father's involvement in the council (personal email, 14 June 2018). Heschel followed his meeting with a letter to Paul VI (dated 30 September 1964), in which he spoke of the "grave hour of history" and the opportunity "to create a new climate of charity" between Jews and Christians": ASV Conc. Vat. II, box 1455. More generally on Heschel, see Harold Kasimow and Byron Sherwin, eds., *No Religion Is*

an Island: Abraham Joshua Heschel and Interreligious Dialogue (Maryknoll, NY: Orbis, 1991).

86. ACUA, Papers of Thomas Stransky, box 10, folder 6.
87. On the initial discussions, see *HVII*, 1:52–66; and Henri de Lubac, *Vatican Council: Notebooks*, trans. Anne Englund Nash (San Francisco: Ignatius, 2016), 2:130ff.
88. Oesterreicher, *New Encounter*, 195; and ACUA, Papers of Thomas Stransky, box 10, folder 5.
89. Tannenbaum, "Heschel and Vatican II," 18.
90. Yves Congar, *My Journal of the Council*, trans. Denis Minns, M. Cecily Boulding, and Mary John Ronayne (Collegeville, MN: Liturgical, 2012), 616.
91. *HVII*, 4:192.
92. Quoted in Joseph Neuner, SJ, *Der indische Joseph: Erinnerungen aus meinen Leben* (Feldkirch: Die Quelle, 2005), 70.
93. See the initial outline (21 October 1964), ASV Conc. Vat. II, box 1455. The working group was made up of Willebrands, Yves Congar, Thomas Stransky, Joseph Neuner, Joseph Pfister, and Charles Moeller.
94. John Borelli, "*Nostra Aetate:* Origin, History, and Vatican II Context," in Charles L. Cohen et al., eds., *The Future of Interreligious Dialogue: A Multireligious Conversation on Nostra Aetate* (Maryknoll, NY: Orbis, 2017), 38–40.
95. "De Ecclesiae habitudine ad religiones non christianas," UNDA, Papers of John F. Deardon, CDRD 6/08.
96. *AS*, vol. 3/8, 650.
97. Oesterreicher, *New Encounter*, 126.
98. O'Malley, *What Happened at Vatican II?* 224.
99. Noted in Gavin D'Costa, "Traditions and Reception: Interpreting Vatican II's 'Declaration on the Church's Relations to Non-Christians,'" *New Blackfriars* 92 (2011): 489.
100. George Armstrong, "Vatican Comfort for the Jews—and Others," *Guardian* (19 November 1964): 11.
101. Borelli, "*Nostra Aetate*," 39–40. See also "Council Votes Exoneration of the Jews," *New York Times* (20 November 1964).
102. ACUA, "News Release (20 Nov. 1964)," Papers of Thomas Stransky, box 27, folder 3.
103. Augustin Bea, SJ, "A proposito della Dichiarazione conciliare circa i non cristiani," *L'osservatore romano* (30 November 1964).
104. Again, their complaints were chiefly addressed to Secretary of State Cicognani; see ASV Conc. Vat. II, boxes 1456, 1457, 1458. On this Coetus internationalis patrum, see *HVII*, 4:66, 113, 117, 157–70, passim. See also François Houang, *Les réalités de Vatican II et les désirs de Monseigneur Lefèbvre* (Paris: Fayard, 1978).

105. The report produced by Willebrands is found in *AS*, vol. 5/3, 313–20. Founded by Cardinal Charles Lavigerie (1825–92) in 1868, the Missionaries of Africa, or "White Fathers" (named because of their white cassocks worn with red fezzes), engaged in missions, education, and outreach to Muslims in North Africa. See Joseph Cuoq, *Lavigerie: Les pères blance et les musulmans maghrebins* (Rome: Société des Missionnaries d'Afrique, 1986); and Aylward Shorter, *The Cross and the Flag in Africa: The "White Fathers" during the Colonial Scramble (1892–1914)* (Maryknoll, NY: Orbis, 2006). See also material on this trip in ASV Conc. Vat. II, box 1458.
106. Of particular note during this time was a meeting of bishops that took place on 12–13 May 1965 and a memorandum ("Notes sur la conjoncture de la Decláration de Vatican II sur les religions non-chrétienne" [8 May 1965]) written by Yves Congar. Minutes of the meeting and the memorandum may be found in ASC Conc. Vat. II, box 1458. For notes on the various meetings, see ACUA, Papers of Thomas Stransky, box 9, folders 4, 5, and 6.
107. ACUA, Papers of Thomas Stransky, box 9, folder 6, and box 10, folders 1 and 2.
108. Not all were happy with these changes. As the American bishop Stephen A. Leven wrote Bea in 1965: "The word 'deicide' was invented by Christians and has been hurled at the Jews for centuries to justify persecutions and pogroms. It seems fitting that the Council should specifically reject it." UNDA, Papers of John F. Deardon, CDRD 6/08.
109. On this trip, see material in ASV Conc. Vat. II, box 1459.
110. ASV Conc. Vat. II, box 1459.
111. Congar, *My Journal of the Council*, 827.
112. Oesterreicher, "Declaration on the Relationship of the Church to Non-Christian Religions," in *CDV*, 3:129.
113. Oesterreicher, *New Encounter*, 277. Bea received letters of gratitude and congratulation from many Jewish organizations. See ASV Conc. Vat. II, boxes 1459 and 1460.
114. George Armstrong, "The 'Renovated Face' of the RC Church," *Guardian* (26 October 1865): 13. Many newspaper clippings may be found in ASV Conc. Vat. II, box 1460.
115. Neuner, *Der indische Joseph*, 73.
116. See J. P. Migne, ed., *Patrologia latina*, vol. 58 (1862), 450–52.
117. I cite *Nostra aetate* (in Latin and English) from *ESDD* and *VCII*, 1:738–42. I, finally, am responsible for the translations provided, but I draw heavily from these two works and from the translations given on the Vatican's webpage for the declaration. See http://www.vatican.va/archive/hist-councils/ii_vatican_council/documents/vat-ii_decl_19651028_nostra-aetate_en.html (accessed 10 June 2020). See also *AAS*, vol. 58 (1966), 740–44.

118. *ESDD*, 916–17 (translation modified).
119. As mentioned, special significance is attributed to Romans, chapters 9–11. On contemporary exegeses of these chapters, see Christof Stenschke, "Das paulinische Evangelium und die Christen jüdischer Herkunft im Römerbrief," *Ephemerides Theologicae Lovanienses* 93 (2017): 230–67.
120. For the most part, the documents of Vatican II use the Latin word *colloquium*, following how Paul VI used it in *Ecclesiam suam* (1964), which shall be discussed below. There are instances of *dialogus*, but this word is an innovation in modern Latin usage. Most English translations use "dialogue" to translate both terms. John O'Malley and others have argued that this word—whether *colloquium* or *dialogus*—is key for understanding the council as a whole. See John O'Malley, "The Style of Vatican II," *America* (February 2003): 12–15; and Ann Michele Nolan, *Privileged Moment: Dialogue in the Language of the Second Vatican Council, 1962–1965* (New York: Peter Lang, 2006).
121. *VCII*, 1:738 (translation modified).
122. O'Collins, *Second Vatican Council on Other Religions*, 88.
123. Arthur Kennedy, "The Declaration of the Relationship of the Church to Non-Christian Religions, *Nostra aetate*," in Matthew L. Lamb and Matthew Levering, eds., *Vatican II: Renewal within the Tradition* (New York: Oxford University Press, 2008), 406.
124. *ESDD*, 915–16. The passages on Hinduism and Buddhism were undertaken respectively by the theological consultors Josef Neuner, SJ, and Paul Pfister, SJ. Neuner was *peritus* for the bishop of Pune, Andrew Alexis D'Souza; Pfister for Cardinal Peter Tatsuo Doi, archbishop of Japan. Reflections on their work on *Nostra Aetate* appears in Neuner's memoir: *Der indische Joseph*, 69–73. Neuner would have been familiar with the "ashram Shativanam," an early, experimental Catholic engagement with Hindu spirituality in India pioneered by the Benedictine monks Henri Le Saux (1910–73) and Jules Monchanin (1895–1957) and continued by Bede Griffiths (1906–93). On this experiment and its connections to the council, see Peter G. Riddell, "Catholic Engagement with India and Its Theological Implications: Jules Monchanin, Henri Le Saux, and Bede Griffiths," in Anthony O'Mahony, ed., *World Christianity: Politics, Theology, Dialogues* (London: Melisende, 2004); and Mauro Giani, *Un ponte tra cultura europea cultura indiana: L'intinerario di Jules Monchanin (1895–1957)* (Milan: Jaca Book, 2000). Even before the "ashram Shativanam," the Belgian Jesuits Pierre Johanns and George Dandoy, doing missions in India, founded a journal, *The Light of the East* (12 vols., 1922–34), in which they stated that, although proclaiming Christ, they had "no intention to put out the existing lights. Rather we shall try to show that the best thought of the east is a bud that fully expanded blossoms into Christian thought." Quoted in Gavin D'Costa, *Theology and Religious Pluralism: The Challenge of Other Religions* (Oxford: Basil Blackwell, 1986), 10.

125. For more detailed commentary on *Nostra aetate*'s passages on Hinduism and Buddhism, see Cyril B. Papali, "Excursus on Hinduism," and Heinrich Dumoulin, "Excursus on Buddhism," in *CDV*, 3:137–44, 145–50. See also Jacques Scheuer, SJ, "The Dialogue with Traditions of India and the Far East," *Gregorianum* 87 (2006): 797–809.
126. *ESDD*, 916–17. It is widely documented that the more positive appraisal of Islam followed from the work of the French Catholic scholar Louis Massignon (1883–1962). As Georges C. Anawati noted: "Thanks to him [Massignon] and his pupils there appeared in the Church a trend favorable to the 'islamic-christian dialogue.' This explains how a declaration concerning Islam such as that made at the Second Vatican Council was possible and represents an advance in the Church's attitude to Islam." See Anawati, "Excursus on Islam," *CDV*, 3:152. See also Jacques Waardenburg, "Louis Massignon (1883–1952) as a Student of Islam," *Die Welt des Islam* 45 (2005): 312–42. Massignon was a friend of Paul VI; on this, see Gavin D'Costa, "Continuity and Reform in Vatican II's Teaching on Islam," *New Blackfriars* 94 (2013): 212.
127. *ESDD*, 916.
128. Noted in "Gregory X and the Second Council of Lyons," in Jessalynn Bird et al., eds., *Crusade and Christendom: Annotated Documents in Translation from Innocent III to the Fall of Acre* (Philadelphia: University of Pennsylvania Press, 2013), 467.
129. See Daniel A. Madigan, SJ, "Muslim-Christian Dialogue in Difficult Times," in James L. Heft, SM, ed., *Catholicism and Interreligious Dialogue* (New York: Oxford University Press, 2011), 57; and Douglas Pratt, "The Vatican in Dialogue with Islam: Inclusion and Engagement," *ICMR* 21 (2010): 245–62.
130. *VCII*, 1:739, 742.
131. Sullivan, *Salvation outside the Church?* 141ff.
132. *ESDD*, 917; and *VCII*, 1:742.
133. Raymond Cohen, "Nostra Aetate: An Israeli Perspective," in Zion Evrony, ed., *Jewish-Catholic Dialogue, Nostra Aetate, 50 Years On / Il dialogo ebraico-cattolico, A 50 anni dalla Nostra Aetate* (Vatican City: Urbaniana University Press, 2016), 59–68.
134. Again, consult the press coverage: ASV Conc. Vat. II, boxes 1459 and 1460.
135. "Pope, Council Promulgate 5 New Decrees," *Chicago Tribune* (29 October 1965).
136. House of Congress Resolution 260 (7 November 2005), 109th U.S. Congress, at https://www.congress.gov/bill/109th-congress/house-concurrent-resolution/260 (accessed 26 May 2018).
137. *ESDD*, 844 (translation modified).
138. Noted in J. J. Ziegler, "*Pacem in terris* at 50," *Catholic World Report* (14 June 2003).

139. Francesco Gioa, "The Catholic Church and Other Religions," in George Cairns and Wayne Teasdale, eds., *The Community of Religions: Voices and Images of the Parliament of World Religions* (New York: Continuum, 1996), 86.
140. *AAS*, vol. 56 (1964), 609–59; and http://w2.vatican.va/content/paul-vi/en/encyclicals/documents/hf_p-vi_enc_06081964_ecclesiam.html (accessed 16 May 2018; emphasis added). See also Nolan, *Privileged Moment.*
141. O'Malley, *What Happened at Vatican II?* 203–4.
142. *HVII*, 1:451 n. 354, 451.
143. Address given on 3 December 1964, *AAS*, vol. 57 (1965), 132; and Sullivan, *Salvation outside the Church?* 184.
144. *HVII*, 1:482. On this trip in general, see Rossi, *I viaggi apostolici di Paulo VI*, 154–59.
145. In what follows, I cite from either *VCII*, vol. 1, or *ESDD*. In some cases, I indicate the official Latin drawn from *ESDD*, *AAS*, or from relevant Vatican websites.
146. *ESDD*, 847; and O'Collins, *Second Vatican Council and Other Religions*, 61–68.
147. Jan Grootaers has called the ecclesiological question "the greatest agitation at Vatican II." See *HVII*, 2:391.
148. On the criticism, see Congar, *Journal of the Council*, 224ff.; and O'Malley, *What Happened at Vatican II?* 156–59.
149. *ESDD*, 860 (emphasis added).
150. *VCII*, 1:357 (emphasis added).
151. See Francis A. Sullivan, "*Quaestio Disputata:* Further Thoughts on the Meaning of *Subsistit in*," *TS* 71 (2010): 133–47.
152. O'Collins, *Second Vatican Council on Other Religions*, 69. On Congar generally, see Gabriel Flynn, *Yves Congar: Theologian of the Church* (Grand Rapids, MI: Eerdmans, 2005).
153. *VCII*, 1:368–69.
154. *VCII*, 1:367–68.
155. *VCII*, 1:813, 823, 825.
156. The reference is to the second-century church father Justin Martyr, who used the term *logos spermatikos* as a means for engaging classical thought. See Pierre Ndoumai, "Justin Martyr et le dialogue interreligieux contemporain," *LTP* 66 (2010): 547–64.
157. *VCII*, 1:844.
158. *VCII*, 1:936, 961, 996. For further commentary on *Ad gentes*, see Cardinal Francis George, OMI, "The Decree on the Church's Missionary Activity, *Ad gentes*," in Lamb and Levering, *Vatican II*, 287–310.
159. On this point, see Yves Congar's commentary on *Gaudium et spes* in *CDV*, 5:220.
160. *VCII*, 1:1000.

161. *Dignitatis humanae* had its own tumultuous history at the council. See O'Malley, *What Happened at Vatican II?* 7, 9, 126, 211–18, passim.
162. Quoted in O'Malley, *What Happened at Vatican II?* 288–89.
163. Xavier Rynne, *Vatican Council II* (New York: Farrar, Straus, and Giroux, 1968), 572.
164. Congar, *Journal of the Council*, 875.
165. On postconciliar debates on the meaning of the council, see Massimo Faggioli, *Vatican II: The Battle for Meaning* (New York: Paulist, 2012); and Matthew Levering, *An Introduction to Vatican II as an Ongoing Theological Event* (Washington, DC: Catholic University of America Press, 2017).
166. Pope Benedict XVI, "A Proper Hermeneutic for the Second Vatican Council," *AAS* (6 January 2006), 40–53. See also *The Ratzinger Report: An Exclusive Report on the State of the Church* (San Francisco: Ignatius, 1985), 35ff. For a criticism of these categories, see Joseph A. Komonchak, "Interpreting the Second Vatican Council," *Landas Journal of Theology of Loyola School of Theology* 1 (1987): 81–90.
167. For an overview of this reception, see Gavin D'Costa, "Nostra Aetate," in Matthew L. Lamb and Matthew Levering, eds., *The Reception of Vatican II* (New York: Oxford University Press, 2017), 425–58.
168. Ralph M. Wiltgen, *The Rhine Flows into the Tiber: The Unknown Council* (New York: Hawthorn, 1967), 73–78.
169. In 1965 another dicastery, known as the Secretariat for Non-believers, was set up. Its name was changed in 1988 to the Pontifical Council for Dialogue with Non-believers and then it was merged with the Pontifical Council for Culture in 1993. On the latter, see http://www.cultura.va/content/cultura/en.html (accessed on 10 December 2020).
170. Paul VI, "Progrediente Concilio" (19 May 1964), in *IDOT*, 63–64. A confidential memorandum prepared by the new secretariat was sent to bishops on 26 September 1964 noting that the purpose of the new body was to "create between Christians and followers of other religions a climate of great cordiality and understanding, with sincerity and charity." See UNDA, John F. Deardon Papers, CDRD 6/08.
171. M. L. Fitzgerald, "The Secretariat for Non-Christians Is Ten Years Old," *Islamochristiana* 1 (1975): 87.
172. In 1971, a special Catholic-Jewish Liaison Committee came into existence, comprised of five Jews and five Catholics. It held its first meeting in Paris in September 1971. See Charlotte Klein, "Catholics and Jews—Ten Years after Vatican II," *JES* 12 (1975): 474.
173. This commission produced an important document in 1974: "Guidelines and Suggestions for Implementing the Conciliar Declaration 'Nostra Aetate.'" While mainly concerned with Catholic-Jewish relations, the document has applicability to relations with other faiths as well. For reflections on Catholic-Jewish relations since Vatican II, see the essays in Evrony, *Jewish-Catholic Dialogue;* and Philip A. Cunningham, "The

Road Behind and the Road Ahead: Catholicism and Judaism," in Heft, *Catholicism and Interreligious Dialogue*, 23–42.

174. Founded in 1622 by Pope Gregory, this office, formerly known as the Sacred Congregation for the Propagation of the Faith (*Sacra congregatio de propaganda fide*) was dedicated to the missionary work of the church. See John Patrick Donnelly, "Sacred Congregation *Propaganda Fide:* Its Foundation and Historical Antecedents," in J. S. Cummins, ed., *Christianity and Missions, 1450–1800* (Brookfield, VT: Variorum, 1997), 37–56.
175. Paul VI, *Regimini Ecclesia universae*, in *IDOT*, 80–81.
176. On these meetings, see Pratt, *The Church and Other Faiths*, 63ff., 190ff.
177. Fitzgerald, "The Secretariat for Non-Christians Is Ten Years Old," 87–95.
178. American Jewish Committee, *Vatican Council II's Statement on the Jews* (New York: American Jewish Committee, 1970), 29.
179. It should be noted that there was then an extant scholarly Pontifical Institute for Arabic and Islamic Studies. It traced its origins to 1926 and the work of the Missionaries of Africa (White Fathers) in Tunisia as a training center for missionaries preparing to work in Muslim countries. In 1931 this foundation took the name Institut de belles lettres arabes. Later, in accordance with a Decree of the Sacred Congregation for Seminaries and Universities (1960), the institute was raised to the Pontifical Institute for Oriental Studies. In 1964, the institute was transferred to Rome and its name changed to the Pontifical Institute for Arabic Studies, thus avoiding confusion with another already-existing Pontifical Oriental Institute.
180. Alas, this dialogue was marred on the final day by an unfortunate reference to Zionism unacceptable to the Holy See. See Miguel Angel Ayuso Guixot, "50 Years in the Service of Interreligious Dialogue," at http://www.pcinterreligious.org/site.php?id=184 (accessed 21 May 2018). In fact, there were several high-profile meetings between Muslims and Christians in the 1970s, often organized by the WCC with Vatican representatives in attendance, for example, in Ajaltoun (1970); Broumana (1972); Tunis, Accra, and Cordoba (1974); Chambesy (1976); Cordoba again (1977); and Colombo (1982). See Pontifical Council for Interreligious Dialogue, *Recognize the Spiritual Bonds Which Unite Us: 16 Years of Christian-Muslim Dialogue* (Vatican City, 1994), 9.
181. Dialogue with Muslims has sometimes proven challenging because of the charge of *kufr* (apostasy) by Wahhabists and Salafists against those Muslims inclined toward dialogue. See Aziz al-Azmeth, *Islam and Modernities* (London: Verso, 1993), 117.
182. See the "Fundamental Agreement between the Holy See and the State of Israel," at http://www.vatican.va/roman_curia/secretariat_state/archivio/documents/rc_seg-st_19931230_santa-sede-israele_en.html (accessed 22 May 2018).
183. John Paul II references Paul VI's *Ecclesiam suam* (1964) here. See John

Paul II, "To Members of the Secretariat for Non-Christians" (27 April 1979), at http://www.vatican.va/content/john-paul-ii/en/speeches/1979/april/documents/hf_jp-ii_spe_19790427_segret-non-cristiani.html (accessed 21 May 2018). See also L. Fitzgerald, "Twenty-Five Years of Dialogue," *Islamochristiana* 15 (1989): 112–13.

184. John Salbiba, SJ, "Vatican Responds to the New Religious Movements," *TS* 53 (1992): 3–39.

185. Braybrooke, *Pilgrimage of Hope*, 131–54.

186. See the constitution at http://w2.vatican.va/content/john-paul-ii/en/apost_constitutions/documents/hf_jp-ii_apc_19880628_pastor-bonus-roman-curia.html (accessed 21 May 2018).

187. Pontifical Council for Interreligious Dialogue, *Interreligious Dialogue Directory* (Vatican City, 1997).

188. See "Dialogue and Mission," at http://www.pcinterreligious.org/dialogue-and-mission_75.html (accessed 21 May 2018).

189. See "Dialogue and Proclamation," at http://www.vatican.va/roman_curia/pontifical_councils/interelg/documents/rc_pc_interelg_doc_19051991_dialogue-and-proclamatio_en.html (accessed 19 June 2018).

190. Michael Fitzgerald, "Pope John Paul II and Interreligious Dialogue: A Catholic Assessment," in Byron Sherwin and Harold Kaismow, eds., *John Paul II and Interreligious Dialogue* (Maryknoll, NY: Orbis, 1999), 219. A thorough inquiry into John Paul II and non-Christian faiths is found in Aleksander Mazur, *L'insegnamento di Giovanni Paulo II sulle altre religioni* (Rome: Gregorian University Press, 2004).

191. He made 104 foreign trips, logging more than 725,000 miles—arguably more than all previous popes combined. Many trips were to countries where no pope had ever gone before.

192. See Jerzy Kluger, *The Pope and I: How the Lifelong Friendship between a Polish Jew and John Paul II Advanced the Cause of Jewish-Christian Relations*, trans. Matthew Sherry (Maryknoll, NY: Orbis, 2013).

193. John Paul II, "To the Plenary Session of the Pontifical Council for Interreligious Dialogue" (Rome, 13 November 1992), *IDOT*, 501.

194. John Paul II, *Crossing the Threshold of Hope* (New York: Knopf, 1994), 99.

195. *AAS*, vol. 71 (1979), 275–78; John Paul II, *Redemptor hominis* (1979), at http://w2.vatican.va/content/john-paul-ii/en/encyclicals/documents/hf_jp-ii_enc_04031979_redemptor-hominis.html (accessed 1 June 2018).

196. For commentary on this theme in John Paul II's papacy, see Gerald O'Collins, "John Paul II on Christ, the Holy Spirit, and World Religions," *ITQ* 72 (2007): 323–37.

197. John Paul II, "To the Secretariat for Non-Christians, 27 April 1979," *IDOT*, 216–17.

198. John Paul II, "To the Plenary Session of the Pontifical Council for Interreligious Dialogue, 13 November 1992," *IDOT*, 498–501.

199. John Paul II, "Discorso del Santo Padre all'assembla interreligiosa," (Rome, 28 October 1999), at http://w2.vatican.va/content/john-paul-ii/it/speeches/1999/october/documents/hf_jp-ii_spe_28101999_interreligious-assembly.html (accessed 20 June 2018).
200. *AAS*, vol. 83 (1971), 302–5; *Redemptoris missio* (1990), at http://w2.vatican.va/content/john-paul-ii/en/encyclicals/documents/hf_jp-ii_enc_07121990_redemptoris-missio.html (accessed 1 June 2018); translation modified.
201. See *IDOT*, table of contents.
202. John Paul II, "A Message to the People of Asia" (Manila, 21 February 1981), *IDOT*, 239.
203. John Paul II, "To the Bishops of India" (New Delhi, 1 February 1986), *IDOT*, 312–13.
204. The topic of "inculturation" was dealt with in a document produced by the International Theological Commission (a part of the Roman Curia) in 1988. See "Faith and Inculturation" (1988), at http://www.vatican.va/roman_curia/congregations/cfaith/cti_documents/rc_cti_1988_fede-inculturazione_en.html (accessed 20 June 2018). See also Matthew Lamb, "Interculturation and Western Context: The Dialogical Experience between Gospel and Culture," *Communio* 21 (1994): 123–44.
205. John Paul II, "To the Bishops of Zimbabwe on Their *Ad Limina* Visit" (Rome, 2 July 1988), *IDOT*, 390.
206. John Paul II, "To the Latin Bishops of the Arab Region on Their *Ad Limina* Visit" (Rome, 3 February 1989), *IDOT*, 395.
207. On this trip, see George Weigel, *Witness to Hope: The Biography of John Paul II* (New York: HarperCollins, 1999), 300–325.
208. Noted in "Ending Pilgrimage, the Pope Asks God for Brotherhood," *New York Times* (27 March 2000).
209. Weigel, *Witness to Hope*, 498–500.
210. Pontifical Council for Interreligious Dialogue, *Recognize the Spiritual Bonds Which Unite Us*, 28ff.
211. On the mosque in general, see Finbarr Barry Flood, *The Great Mosque of Damascus: Studies on the Makings of an Umayyad Visual Culture* (Leiden: Brill, 2001).
212. "Meeting with Muslim Leaders at Omayyad Great Mosque," Damascus (6 May 2001), at https://w2.vatican.va/content/john-paul-ii/en/speeches/2001/may/documents/hf_jp-ii_spe_20010506_omayyadi.html (accessed 1 June 2018).
213. See "Pope John Paul II and Christian-Buddhist Dialogue: His Holiness the XIVth Dalai Lama: An Interview with Wayne Teasdale," in Sherwin and Kasimow, *John Paul II and Interreligious Dialogue*, 85–94.
214. John Paul II, "To the Lay Monks of Various Buddhist Schools" (Rome, 26 September 1979), *IDOT*, 219.

215. John Paul II, "Tribute to the Monument of Gandhi" (New Delhi, 1 February 1986), *IDOT*, 309.
216. John Paul II, "To the Followers of Various Indian Religions" (New Delhi, 2 February 1986), *IDOT*, 317.
217. John Paul II, "To the Religious Authorities of India" (Calcutta, 3 February 1986), *IDOT*, 321.
218. "John Paul II, "To Representatives of the Various Religions of India" (Madras, 5 February 1986), *IDOT*, 324.
219. John Paul II, "Message to Lebanon" (Rome, 1 June 1984), *IDOT*, 272. Due to its religious complexity, Lebanon holds particular significance for modern interfaith engagement. See Yvonne Yazbeck Haddad and Rahel Fischbach, "Interfaith Dialogue in Lebanon: Between a Power Balancing Act and Theological Encounters," 26 *ICMR* (2015): 423–42.
220. On this and other interventions of the Holy See on behalf of the crisis in Bosnia in the early 1990s, see Holy See, *L'azione della Santa Sede nel conflitto Bosniaco* (Vatican City: Libreria Editrice Vaticana, 1994).
221. John Paul II, "Message to the Secretary General of the United Nations" (Rome, 1 March 1993), *IDOT*, 510–11.
222. On this gathering, see Jason Welle, "The Evolution of the Assisi Gathering: To Humanism and Beyond," *JES* 48 (2013): 379.
223. On the first trip, see *Sarajevo: Giovanni Paulo II nella città del nostro secolo* (Vatican City: Libreria Editrice Vaticana, 1997).
224. John Paul II, "Address of the Holy Father at the Meeting with the Representatives of the Islamic Community" (Sarajevo, 13 April 1997), at https://w2.vatican.va/content/john-paul-ii/en/speeches/1997/april/documents/hf_jp-ii_spe_19970413_mussulmani-bosnia.html (accessed 1 June 2018).
225. John Paul II, *Crossing the Threshold of Hope*, 84–90. For a Buddhist response, see Thich Nhat Hanh, *Living Buddha, Living Christ* (London: Rider, 1995), 193.
226. John Paul II, *Crossing the Threshold of Hope*, 92 (emphasis in text). For a Muslim response, see Mamoud Ayoub, "Pope John Paul II on Islam," in Sherwin and Kasimow, *John Paul II and Interreligious Dialogue*, 171–86.
227. Michael Sells, "Crosses of Blood: Sacred Space, Religion, and Violence in Bosnia-Hercegovina," *Sociology of Religion* 64 (2003): 326; and Michael Burleigh, *Sacred Causes: The Clash of Religion and Politics from the Great War to the War on Terror* (New York: HarperCollins, 2007), 153, 263, 265–68.
228. John L. Allen Jr., "Pope's Inter-faith Summit in Assisi Belongs to an Ongoing Revolution," *Crux* (14 September 2016).
229. For more detail on the genesis of the event, see Claudio Bonizza, *L'icona di Assisi nel magesterio di Giovanni Paulo II* (Rome: Edizioni Porziuncola, 2002), 57ff.

230. Bonizza, *L'icona di Assisi*, 61–62.
231. *Assisi: World Day of Prayer for Peace, 26 October 1986* (Vatican City: Pontifical Commission "Iustitia et Pax," 1987), 15.
232. John Paul II, "Angelus, 21 September 1986," in *Assisi: World Day of Prayer for Peace*, 18.
233. A list of participants may be found in *Assisi: World Day of Prayer for Peace*, 189–202.
234. John Paul II, "General Audience, 22 October 1986," in *Assisi: World Day of Prayer for Peace*, 25–28. He reiterates here the point that the Assisi event must be understood "in light of the Council."
235. Jorge Mejia, "A Theological Reflection on the World Day of Prayer for Peace," *L'osservatore romano* (17 September 1986), in *Assisi: World Day of Prayer for Peace*, 31–38.
236. Cardinal Francis Arinze, "The Contribution of the Various Religions to the Building of Peace," *L'osservatore romano* (27 September 1986), in *Assisi: World Day of Prayer for Peace*, 39–49.
237. William F. Murphy, "Remembering Assisi after 20 Years," *America* (23 October 2006).
238. Weigel, *Witness to Hope*, 513.
239. Bonizzi, *L'icona di Assisi*, 93ff.; and Robert Suro, "12 Faiths Join the Pope to Pray for Peace," *New York Times* (28 October 1986).
240. *Welcoming Ceremony at the Basilica of St. Mary of the Angels* (Amsterdam, NY: Noteworthy, 1986), 1.
241. "Peace Has a Prayer in Assisi," *Chicago Tribune* (28 October 1986).
242. John Paul II, "Address of John Paul II to the Representatives of the Christian Churches and Ecclesial Communities and of the World Religions" (Assisi, 27 October 1986), at http://w2.vatican.va/content/john-paul-ii/en/speeches/1986/october/documents/hf_jp-ii_spe_19861027_prayer-peace-assisi-final.html (accessed 5 June 2017).
243. Murphy, "Remembering Assisi after 20 Years."
244. Archbishop Lefebvre and Bishop de Castro Meyer, "1986 Declaration against Assisi," at http://archives.sspx.org/archbishop_lefebvre/1986_declaration_against_assisi_archbishop_lefebvre-bishop_de_castro_mayer.htm (accessed 6 June 2017).
245. John L. Allen Jr., "Assisi Inter-religious Assembly Marks 20th Anniversary," *National Catholic Reporter* (8 September 2006).
246. *ESDD*, 860.
247. This address is replete with references to *Lumen gentium*, *Nostra aetate*, and *Ad gentes*. See John Paul II, "To the Roman Curia" (22 December 1986), *IDOT*, 359–67.
248. *AAS*, vol. 92 (2000), 742–58; and *ESDD*, 1138–45. *Dominus Iesus* generated a very large literature. For a theological inquiry into the document and criticism of its detractors, see Matthew W. I. Dunn, "The CDF's Declaration *Dominus Iesus* and Pope John Paul II," *LS* 36 (2012): 46–75.

For a more critical view of *Dominus Iesus* itself, see, inter alia, John D'Arcy May, "Catholic Fundamentalism? Some Implications of *Dominus Iesus* for Dialogue and Peacemaking," *Horizons* 28 (2001): 271–93. See also Stephen J. Pope and Charles Hefling, eds., *Sic et Non: Encountering "Dominus Iesus"* (Maryknoll, NY: Orbis, 2020); and Loe-Joo Tan, "'Things Are Not What They Seem': *Dominus Iesus*, Ecumenism, and Interreligious Dialogue," *JES* 48 (2013): 523–34. Around the time of *Dominus Iesus*'s release, the church was particularly concerned with the writings of the Belgian Jesuit Jacques Dupuis (1923–2004). Dupuis was investigated by the Congregation for the Doctrine of the Faith, but never formally disciplined. Similar concerns focused on the Vietnamese American theologian Peter Phan, who was significantly influenced by Dupuis. On these cases, see Ambrose Mong, "Investigating Peter Phan's Theology of Religious Pluralism: Orthodoxy versus Orthopraxis," *AJT* 25 (2011): 187–206.

249. *AAS*, vol. 92 (2000), 743.
250. John Pawlikowski, "Mission and Dialogue in Contemporary Catholicism," *Modern Believing* 51 (2010): 47–55.
251. Stephen Covell, "Interfaith Dialogue and a Lotus Practitioner: Yamada Etai, the Lotus Sutra, and the Religious Summit Meeting on Mt. Hiei," *Japanese Journal of Religious Studies* 41 (2014): 191–217.
252. Welle, "Evolution of the Assisi Gathering," 379.
253. Ambrogio Spreafico, "Der Friedensbeitrag des Religionsdialog nach der Erfahrung der Gemeinschaft Sant'Egidio," *ZMR* 91 (2007): 93–101. See also Robert P. Imbelli, "The Community of Sant'Egidio: Vatican II Made Real," *Commonweal* 121 (1994): 20.
254. Welle, "Evolution of the Assisi Gathering," 380.
255. *Die Presse* (4 April 1998). See also John L. Allen Jr., *Pope Benedict XVI: A Biography of Joseph Ratzinger* (New York: Continuum, 2000), 216–20.
256. Benedict XVI, "Address of His Holiness Benedict XVI at the Meeting for Peace in Assisi" (27 October 2011), at http://w2.vatican.va/content/benedict-xvi/en/speeches/2011/october/documents/hf_ben-xvi_spe_20111027_assisi.html (accessed 28 June 2018). On Ratzinger and interreligious dialogue more generally, see Emil Anton, "Mission Impossible? Pope Benedict XVI and Interreligious Dialogue," *TS* 78 (2017): 879–904.
257. Francis, "Address of the Holy Father" (Assisi, 20 September 2016), at http://w2.vatican.va/content/francesco/en/speeches/2016/september/documents/papa-francesco_20160920_assisi-preghiera-pace.html (accessed 6 June 2018). On Pope Francis and interfaith engagement more generally, see Harold Kasimov and Alan Race, eds., *Pope Francis and Interreligious Dialogue: Religious Thinkers Engage with Papal Initiatives* (Cham, Switzerland: Palgrave Macmillan, 2018).

Conclusion

1. *IFJ*, 15–16.
2. Lori Branch, "Postsecular Studies," in Mark Knight, ed., *Routledge Companion to Literature and Religion* (New York: Routledge, 2016), 91–101.
3. Kusumita P. Pedersen, "The Interfaith Movement: An Incomplete Assessment," *JES* 41 (2004): 2.
4. In addition to archival and library work, this conclusion draws on experiences from trips taken to understand interfaith work at various global destinations, including Croatia, Bosnia and Herzegovina, Serbia, Kosovo, Spain, Morocco, Canada, India, Qatar, Egypt, and the United Kingdom.
5. Jacques Dupuis, SJ, *Christianity and the Religions: From Confrontation to Dialogue*, trans. Phillip Berryman (Maryknoll, NY: Orbis, 2001), 59–66.
6. The annual meeting of the WCC in Kandy, Sri Lanka, in 1967 was particularly significant. At this meeting, several theologians strongly contested the more exclusivist line of thinking that had been championed by Hendrik Kraemer (inter alia) since a meeting in Tambaram, India, in 1938. See Klaus Klostermaier, "Christians in Dialogue with Men of Other Faiths," *Clergy Monthly Supplement* 8 (1967): 240–46.
7. This event was preceded by several smaller-scale ones that also witnessed interfaith engagement. On the gathering at Ajaltoun, see S. J. Samartha, "More Than an Encounter of Commitments," *International Review of Mission* 69 (1970): 392–403.
8. For the quoted material and an overview of the WCC's interreligious activities, see Douglas Pratt, *The Church and Other Faiths: The World Council of Churches, the Vatican, and Interreligious Dialogue* (New York: Peter Lang, 2010), 63–65.
9. Pratt, *The Church and Other Faiths*, 79–83. Various materials relevant to this document can be found in WCCA, file box 4612. See especially the text titled "Where Do We Go from Nairobi?" Work on the 1979 document began earnestly in 1977 at the WCC's meeting in Chiang Mai, Thailand. General worries in the 1970s that the WCC had drifted away from mission in embracing dialogue played a role in galvanizing evangelical Protestants to found the Lausanne Congress on World Evangelization (1974) and the resulting "Lausanne Movement," which places a theological premium on the Great Commission. See Robert A. Hunt, "The History of the Lausanne Movement, 1974–2011," *International Bulletin of Missionary Research* 45 (April 2011): 81–84.
10. The relationship of Eastern Orthodoxy to interreligious dialogue in the twentieth century invites further inquiry. In 1998 the Ecumenical Patriarch Bartholomew of Constantinople (Istanbul) convened a major conference on interreligious dialogue. See George C. Papademetriou, "An Orthodox View of Non-Christian Religions," at https://www.goarch.org/-/an-orthodox-christian-view-of-non-christian-religions (accessed

1 October 2018). See also Anastasios Yannoulatos, "Facing People of Other Faiths," *Greek Orthodox Theological Review* 8 (1993): 131–52.

11. See "Dialogue in Truth and Charity," at http://www.pcinterreligious.org/dialogue-in-truth-and-charity_246.html, paragraph 86 (accessed 3 September 2018).
12. Pier Francesco Fumagelli, "Gerhart M. Riegner: Pioneer for Jewish-Catholic Relations in the Contemporary World," in Menachem Z. Rosensaft, ed., *The World Jewish Congress, 1936–2016* (New York: World Jewish Congress, 2017), 82. On earlier Jewish endeavors, see Lance J. Sussman, "'Toward Better Understanding': The Rise of the Interfaith Movement in America and the Role of Rabbi Isaac Landman," *American Jewish Archives* 34 (1982): 35–51. On Judaism and interfaith dialogue generally, see, inter alia, David Novak, *Jewish-Christian Dialogue: A Jewish Justification* (New York: Oxford University Press, 1989).
13. *A Guide to Interreligious Dialogue* (1966), ACUA, Papers of Thomas Stransky, box 10, folder 6, w.
14. Abraham Joshua Heschel, "From Mission to Dialogue," *Conservative Judaism* 21 (1967): 8–11. Heschel insisted that Christians must abandon missions to Jews as a prerequisite for dialogue.
15. See *OEMIW*, 3:203; Douglas Pratt, *Christian Engagement with Islam: Ecumenical Journeys since 1910* (Leiden: Brill, 2017), 60–61, 102, 105, 122, 260; and Muhammad Zia-ul-Haq, "Muslims' Participation in Interfaith Dialogue: Challenges and Prospects," *JES* 49 (2014): 613–46. See also Leonard J. Swidler, ed., *Muslims in Dialogue: The Evolution of a Dialogue* (Lewiston, NY: Edwin Mellen, 1992).
16. I was told, for example, during a visit to the Doha International Centre for Interfaith Dialogue in Qatar that dialogue there focused on Christianity and Judaism, but not on Buddhism and Hinduism, which were considered "man-made philosophies."
17. Turan Kayaoglu, "Explaining Interfaith Dialogue in the Muslim World," *Politics and Religion* 8 (2015): 236–37. See also Mohamed Talbi, "Islam and Dialogue—Some Reflections on a Current Topic," in Paul Griffiths, ed., *Christianity through Non-Christian Eyes* (Maryknoll, NY: Orbis, 1990), 83–101; and Tariq Ramadan, "Interreligious Dialogue from an Islamic Perspective," in C. Timmerman and Barbara Segaert, eds., *How to Conquer the Barriers to Intercultural Dialogue* (Brussels: Peter Lang, 2006), 85–100.
18. Neil MacFacquhar, "In Open Letter, Muslims Seek Cooperation with Christians as a Step toward Peace," *New York Times* (12 October 2007). See also Yvonne Yazbeck Haddad and Jane I. Smith, "The Quest for a 'Common Word': Initial Christian Responses to a Muslim Initiative," *ICMR* 20 (2009): 369–88. Still, one should not underestimate the challenges to interfaith dialogue in the Muslim world. As Charles Kimball writes: "Many Muslims are wary of the entire enterprise owing both to

the long history of enmity [between Muslims and Christians] and the more recent experiences of colonialism. . . . Still other Muslims suspect that dialogue is a new guise for Christian missionary activity." The neuralgic issue of the state of Israel has greatly impeded successful Jewish-Muslim dialogue. See *OEMIW*, 3:205ff. On recent interfaith dialogue generally in the Middle East, see Mohammed Abu-Nimer et al., *Unity in Diversity: Interfaith Dialogue in the Middle East* (Washington: DC: United States Institute of Peace, 2007), especially chapter 7. Also of relevance is Patrice C. Brodeur, "From Postmodernism to 'Glocalism': Toward a Theoretical Understanding of Contemporary Arab Muslim Constructions of Religious Others," in Birgit Schaebler and Leif Stenberg, eds., *Globalization and the Muslim World: Culture, Religion, Modernity* (Syracuse: Syracuse University Press, 2004), 188–205.

19. "Pope Francis Makes 'Historic' Gulf Tour amid Yemen Crisis and Repression of Christians," *New York Times* (3 February 2019); and Gabriel Said Reynolds, "After Abu Dhabi," *Commonweal* (12 April 2019): 10–12.
20. Patrice C. Brodeur, "From the Margins to the Center: The Increasing Relevance of the Global Interfaith Movement," *CrossCurrents* 55 (2005): 44–45.
21. John Fahy and Jan-Jonathan Bock, *Beyond Dialogue? Interfaith Engagement in Delhi, Doha, and London* (Doha: Georgetown University in Qatar and the Woolf Institute, 2018), 25.
22. *IFJ*, 75.
23. *IFJ*, 62. While the UNI's charter dates from 2000, its roots go back to 1993 at a conference hosted by Bishop William Swing. See Swing, *A Bishop's Quest: Founding a United Religions* (Cambier, OH: XOXOX Press, 2015).
24. For a longer list of publications, see the website of the Pluralism Project at http://pluralism.org/research-report/interfaith-publications/ (accessed 7 September 2018).
25. Jonathan Sacks, *The Dignity of Difference: How to Avoid the Clash of Civilizations* (London: Continuum, 2002), 5.
26. Amy Bakalian and Medhi Bozormehr, *Backlash 9/11: Middle Eastern and Muslim Americans Respond* (Berkeley: University of California Press, 2009), 230.
27. For a fairly detailed directory of contemporary interfaith organizations, see the Parliament of Religions Interfaith Directory at https://parliamentofreligions.org /interfaith-directory (accessed 3 September 2018).
28. *IFJ*, 65; and Sacks, *Dignity of Difference*, 13.
29. See the Pluralism Project's "America's Growing Interfaith Infrastructure" at http://pluralism.org/encounter/today's challenges/americas-growing-interfaith-infrastructure/ (accessed 27 March 2019). See also Karin Thornton, "Interfaith Worship on Campus," *CrossCurrents* 40 (1990): 27–33.

30. See, e.g., "Interfaith Vigils Held in the Wake of NZ [New Zealand] Shootings," *World Religion News* (19 March 2019).
31. Julian Sheetz-Willard et al., "Interreligious Dialogue Reconsidered: Learning from and Responding to Critique and Change, *JES* 47 (2012): 266.
32. Eboo Patel, "Toward a New Field of Interfaith Studies," *Liberal Education* 99 (2013): 38. See also Eboo Patel, Jennifer How Peace, and Noah J. Silverman, eds., *Interreligious/Interfaith Studies: Defining a New Field* (Boston: Beacon, 2018); and Hans Gustafson, ed., *Interreligious Studies: Dispatches from the Field* (Waco, TX: Baylor University Press, 2020).
33. Patel, Peace, and Silverman, *Interreligious/Interfaith Studies*, xvi. The titles are respectively from the Arthur Vining Davis Foundation and the Alavi Foundation.
34. Loni M. Bordoloi Pazich, "Philanthropy and the Interfaith Imperative," at https://philanthropynewyork.org/news/philanthropy-and-interfaith-imperative (accessed 6 September 2018).
35. Evelyn Davis, "Interfaith Philanthropy: Giving across Faith in Christianity, Islam and Judaism" (2006), *Capstone Collections* 78, at https://digitalcollections.sit.edu/capstones/758 (accessed 10 September 2018).
36. In 1993 a similar major event was held in Bangalore, India. See Sarva-Dharma Sammelana, ed., *Visions of an Interfaith Future: Proceedings—Religious People Meeting Together, Bangalore, India, 19–22, 1993 August* (Oxford: International Interfaith Centre, 1994).
37. See the program: *1993 Parliament of the World's Religions: August 28–September 5, Chicago, Illinois* (Chicago: Council for a Parliament of the World's Religions, 1993). Archival material concerning the 1993 parliament (some seventy-eight boxes), largely unexplored, is held at DePaul University Special Collections and Archives. See the catalogue for these holdings at https://libguides.depaul.edu/ld.php?content_id=10135897 (accessed 23 March 2020).
38. Pedersen, "The Interfaith Movement," 16.
39. On the 1993 parliament in general, see Richard H. Roberts, "The 'Parliament of the World's Religions' (Chicago 1993) in Theoretical Perspective," *JCR* 10 (1995): 121–37.
40. Josh Borkin, "The Next Generation," in *Building the Interfaith Youth Movement: Beyond Dialogue to Action* (Lanham, MD: Rowman and Littlefield, 2013), 85.
41. See "The Council for a Parliament of the World's Religions," http://www.theinterfaithobserver.org/journal-articles/2011/11/13/the-council-for-a-parliament-of-the-worlds-religions.html (accessed 3 September 2018).
42. Steven C. Rockefeller et al., eds., *Spirit and Nature: Why the Environment Is a Religious Issue: An Interfaith Dialogue* (Boston: Beacon, 1992).
43. Wilfred Cantwell Smith, "Mankind's Religiously Divided History Ap-

proaches Self-Consciousness," *Harvard Divinity Bulletin* 29 (1964): 12–13.

44. For Cusa's relevance in action, see James L. Heft, SM, et al., eds., *Learned Ignorance: Intellectual Humility among Jews, Christians, and Muslims* (New York: Oxford University Press, 2011).
45. John Milbank, "The End of Dialogue," in Gavin D'Costa, ed., *Christian Uniqueness Reconsidered: The Myth of a Pluralistic Theology of Religions* (Maryknoll, NY: Orbis, 1987), 176.
46. Fahy and Bock also write perceptively on the usage of "religion" at interfaith events: "The category of 'religion' is often uncritically mobilised in interfaith circles, where it is assumed to refer to a set of beliefs, or to connote adherence to selective scriptural injunctions. It is often presented through exclusively theological categories that serve to essentialise religious traditions in terms of the ideals they espouse, while paying less attention to 'lived religion,' or how adherents themselves understand, practice or struggle with their faith in their everyday lives. The emphasis on abstractions limits the ability of interfaith initiatives to shape broader conversations about religion and society in the public sphere." Fahy and Bock, *Beyond Dialogue?* 11.
47. Pedersen, "The Interfaith Movement," 15.
48. Wolfgang Pfüller, "Das Problem mehrfacher Religionszugehörigkeit," *ZMR* 93 (2009): 25–36; and Karla Suomla, "Complex Religious Identity in the Context of Interfaith Dialogue," *CrossCurrents* 62 (2012): 360–68.
49. Peggy Morgan, "The Study of Religions and Interfaith Encounter," *Numen* 42 (1995): 162.
50. Muthuraj Swamy, *The Problem with Interreligious Dialogue: Plurality, Conflict, and Elitism in Hindu-Christian-Muslim Relations* (London: Bloomsbury Academic, 2016).
51. *WCID*, 168–83; and Catherine Cornille and Jillian Maxey, eds., *Women and Interreligious Dialogue* (Eugene, OR: Cascade, 2013). See also Melanie Prideaux, "Muslim-Christian Dialogue: The Gap between Theologians and Communities," *International Journal of Public Theology* 3 (2009): 460–79. Prideaux provocatively argues that "the distance between Christians and Muslims is perhaps not as great as the distance between interfaith theology [elites] and religiously diverse communities [nonelites]."
52. Pedersen, "The Interfaith Movement," 15–16.
53. Eboo Patel, *Acts of Faith: The Story of an American Muslim, the Struggle for a Generation* (Boston: Beacon, 2007), 71.
54. Rowan Williams, "Muslim-Christian Dialogue in Britain and Beyond," *ICMR* 19 (2008): 336.
55. Kent F. Moors, "Plato's Use of Dialogue," *Classical World* 72 (1978): 77–93.
56. Avery Dulles, "Travails of Dialogue," *Crisis* (1 February 1997): 7.
57. John P. Bloch, "A Whisper toward Peace: A Theoretical Analysis of the

Council for a Parliament of the World Religions," *Journal of the Scientific Study of Religion* 47 (2008): 616.

58. Swamy, *Problem with Interreligious Dialogue*, 8.
59. James Davison Hunter, *Culture Wars: The Struggle to Define America* (New York: Basic, 1991).
60. Douglas Pratt, *The Challenge of Islam: Encounters in Interfaith Dialogue* (Aldershot, UK: Ashgate, 2005), 51–74.
61. See Jason Willick, "The Man Who Discovered 'Culture War,'" *Wall Street Journal* (25 May 2018).
62. Robert D. Kaplan, *The Return of Marco Polo's World: War, Strategy, and American Interests in the Twenty-First Century* (New York: Random House, 2018), 221.
63. Robert Wuthnow, *America and the Challenges of Religious Diversity* (Princeton: Princeton University Press, 2005), 301.
64. Marion H. Larson and Sara L. H. Shady, "The Possibility of Solidarity: Evangelicals and the Field of Interfaith Studies," in Patel, Peace, and Silverman, *Interreligious/Interfaith Studies*, 154.
65. Philosophical relativism is not a necessary consequence of social or religious pluralism, but this category mistake is made quite often. See Anindita N. Balslev, "Religious Pluralism and Relativism: The Possibility of Inter-religious Communication," *Journal of Indian Council of Philosophical Research* 8 (1991): 57–71.
66. Carl E. Braaten, *No Other Gospel: Christianity among the World's Religions* (Eugene, OR: Wipf and Stock, 1992), 10.
67. Fahy and Bock, *Beyond Dialogue?* 9.
68. Katherine Marshall, *Global Institutions of Religion: Ancient Movers, Modern Shakers* (London: Routledge, 2013), 132.
69. *WCID*, 64–86; and David Ford and C. C. Pecknold, *The Promise of Scriptural Reasoning* (Oxford: Blackwell, 2006). See also Peter Ochs, "Philosophic Warrants for Scriptural Reasoning," *MT* 22 (2006): 465–82; and Jennifer L. Geddes, "Peacemaking among the Abrahamic Faiths: An Interview with Peter Ochs," *Hedgehog Review* (2004): 90–102.
70. See the Fez musical festival at http://fesfestival.com/2017/en/ (accessed 8 September 2018).
71. *WICD*, 107. See also Michael S. Bird, ed., *Art and Interreligious Dialogue: Six Perspectives* (Lanham, MD: University Press of America, 1995); and David Cheetham, "Exploring the Aesthetic 'Space' for Inter-religious Encounter," *Exchange* 39 (2010): 71–86.
72. *WCID*, 468–78. See also Terry C. Muck, "Evangelicals and Interreligious Dialogue," *Journal of the Evangelical Theological Society* 36 (1993): 517–29.
73. See Interfaith Youth Core at https://www.ifyc.org/interfaith (accessed 8 September 2018). See also Eboo Patel, *Interfaith Leadership: A Primer* (Boston: Beacon, 2016). I am pleased to acknowledge a conversation

with Eboo Patel about his work that took place in Chicago on 27 July 2018.

74. Wuthnow, *America and the Challenges of Religious Diversity*, 303.
75. See the website of Monastic Interreligious Dialogue at https://dimmid.org/ (accessed 8 September 2018); and Fabrice Bleé et al., eds., *The Third Desert: The Story of Monastic Interreligious Dialogue* (Collegeville, MN: Liturgical, 2011). The initiative finds its charter in a letter (12 June 1974) from Cardinal Sergio Pignedoli, the second head of the Vatican's Secretariat for Non-Christians, in which he wrote: "The existence of monasticism at the heart of the Catholic Church is, in itself, a bridge connecting all religions." It also owes its origins to a prior organization from the 1960s: Aide a l'implementation monastique, which sought to provide support for Catholic monks located in countries (mostly in Asia) where Christians were in the minority. See UNDA, CMID.4.4. f. 190, "History of Monastic Interreligious Dialogue."
76. From an email exchange with Father Skudlarek (16 September 2018).
77. Francis X. Clooney, SJ, *Comparative Theology: Deep Learning across Religious Borders* (Malden, MA: Wiley-Blackwell, 2010), 10.
78. *ER*, 3:578, 14:446–55; David Burrell, *Towards a Jewish-Christian-Muslim Theology* (Chichester, UK: Wiley-Blackwell, 2014); Michael Barnes, SJ, *Theology and the Dialogue of Religions* (Cambridge: Cambridge University Press, 2002); and Betül Avci, "Comparative Theology: An Alternative to Religious Studies or Theology of Religions?" *Religions* 9 (2018): 1–9.
79. On the severity of Christian persecution in global perspective, see Daniel Philpott and Timothy Samuel Shah, eds., *Under Caesar's Sword: How Christians Respond to Persecution* (Cambridge: Cambridge University Press, 2018).
80. See the Marrakesh Declaration at http://www.marrakeshdeclaration.org/ (accessed 8 September 2018). On the general topic of Islam, religious minorities, and religious freedom, see Daniel Philpott, *Religious Freedom in Islam: The Fate of a Universal Human Right in the Muslim World Today* (New York: Oxford University Press, 2019).
81. See also Daniel Philpott, "The Challenge of September 11 to Secularism in International Relations," *World Politics* 55 (2002): 65–95.
82. *IFJ*, 18. Global health concerns also stand to benefit from interfaith perspectives; see, e.g., Susan R. Holman, *Beholden: Religion, Global Health, and Human Rights* (New York: Oxford University Press, 2015).
83. Sacks, *Dignity of Difference*, 4.

Index